The Cambridge Companion to Jewish Music

The term "Jewish music" has conveyed complex and diverse
meanings for people around the world across hundreds of years.
This accessible and comprehensive *Companion* is a key resource for
students, scholars, and everyone with an interest in the global history
of Jewish music. Leading international experts introduce the broad
range of genres found in Jewish music from the biblical era to today,
including classical, religious, folk, popular, and dance music.
Presenting a range of fresh perspectives on the field, the chapters
explore Jewish liturgy, klezmer, music in Israel, the music of
Yiddish theater and cinema, and classical music from the Jewish
Enlightenment through the postmodern era. Additional
contributions set Jewish music in context and offer an overview of the
broader issues that arise in its study, such as questions of diaspora,
ontology, economics, and the history of sound technologies.

JOSHUA S. WALDEN is a member of the Faculty of Musicology at the
Peabody Institute of the Johns Hopkins University. He is the author
of *Sounding Authentic: The Rural Miniature and Musical Modernism*
(2014), and editor of *Representation in Western Music* (Cambridge,
2013). He has published articles on subjects including Jewish music,
film music, eighteenth-century music, and intersections between
music and the visual arts in journals including the *Journal of the
American Musicological Society*, *Journal of the Royal Musical
Association*, *Journal of the Society for American Music*, and *Musical
Quarterly*.

The Cambridge Companion to

JEWISH MUSIC

. . . .

EDITED BY
Joshua S. Walden
Peabody Institute of the Johns Hopkins University

CAMBRIDGE
UNIVERSITY PRESS

CAMBRIDGE
UNIVERSITY PRESS

University Printing House, Cambridge CB2 8BS, United Kingdom

Cambridge University Press is part of the University of Cambridge.

It furthers the University's mission by disseminating knowledge in the pursuit of education, learning and research at the highest international levels of excellence.

www.cambridge.org
Information on this title: www.cambridge.org/9781107623750

© Cambridge University Press 2015

First published 2015

Printed in the United Kingdom by TJ International Ltd. Padstow Cornwall

A catalogue record for this publication is available from the British Library

ISBN 978-1-107-02345-1 Hardback
ISBN 978-1-107-62375-0 Paperback

Cambridge University Press has no responsibility for the persistence or accuracy of URLs for external or third-party internet websites referred to in this publication, and does not guarantee that any content on such websites is, or will remain, accurate or appropriate.

To my parents and brother

Contents

Music examples and figure

Contributors

Philip V. Bohlman is Mary Werkman Distinguished Service Professor of Music and Humanities at the University of Chicago and Honorarprofessor at the Hochschule für Musik, Theater und Medien Hannover. Among his recent books are *Revival and Reconciliation: Sacred Music in the Making of European Modernity* (2013) and *Wie sängen wir Seinen Gesang auf dem Boden der Fremde! Jüdische Musik zwischen Aschkenas und Moderne* (2016). He is Artistic Director of the New Budapest Orpheum Society, with whom he received the AMS Noah Greenberg Award for the CD *As Dreams Fall Apart: The Golden Age of Jewish Stage and Film Music, 1925–1955* (2014).

Theodore W. Burgh is Associate Professor at the University of North Carolina Wilmington, in the Department of Philosophy and Religion. He completed his graduate work at the University of Arizona. Burgh is an archaeologist who works in Jordan and Israel. His sub-specialty is archaeomusicology, and he examines the use of music in ancient Israel. He explores music, depictions of musical activity, and musical instruments to study various aspects of past cultures. He has contributed a number of articles and chapters on archaeology and ancient music culture. He is also a professional musician and composer.

Judah M. Cohen is the Lou and Sybil Mervis Professor of Jewish Culture and Associate Professor of Musicology at the Indiana University Jacobs School of Music. He is the author of *The Making of a Reform Jewish Cantor: Musical Authority, Cultural Investment* (2009), and *Sounding Jewish Tradition: The Music of Central Synagogue* (2011). Recent articles include the "Jewish Music" article in the second edition of the *Grove Dictionary of American Music*, and the "Music" entry for Oxford Bibliographies in Jewish Studies. He has also published extensively on Caribbean Jewish history and HIV/AIDS and the arts in Africa.

David Conway is an Honorary Research Fellow at the Department of Hebrew and Jewish Studies of University College London. He is the author of *Jewry in Music* (Cambridge, 2012) and has published articles in *The Wagner Journal, Jewish Renaissance*, and *Hubodný život*. He is a committee member of the British Alkan Society and of the International Centre for Suppressed Music. Conway is the founder and musical director of the annual music festival "Indian Summer in Levoča" (Slovakia), which regularly features music by Jewish composers of the past two centuries. He also works for the European Commission as a senior expert on development aid programs in the countries of the former Soviet Union.

Tina Frühauf teaches at Columbia University and is editor at Répertoire International de Littérature Musicale in New York. She has received multiple fellowships and grants, most recently from the American Musicological Society, the Leo Baeck Institute, and the Memorial Foundation for Jewish Culture. She has published articles in *Musical Quarterly, Musica Judaica*, and *TDR: The Drama Review*, and contributed numerous book chapters on German Jewish music culture. She is the author of *The Organ and Its Music in German-Jewish Culture* (2009/2012), and editor of *An Anthology of German-Jewish Organ Music* (2013), *Hans Samuel:*

Selected Piano Works (2013), and *Dislocated Memories: Jews, Music, and Postwar German Culture* (2014). Frühauf is currently completing a monograph on music in the Jewish communities of Germany after 1945.

Lily E. Hirsch is a Visiting Scholar at California State University, Bakersfield. She has published the books *A Jewish Orchestra in Nazi Germany: Musical Politics and the Berlin Jewish Culture League* (2010) and *Music in American Crime Prevention and Punishment* (2012), and is co-editor of *Dislocated Memories: Jews, Music, and Postwar German Culture* (2014). Her research has also appeared in *Rethinking Schumann, Sound Studies, Musical Quarterly, Philomusica,* the *Journal of Popular Music Studies, American Music, Music & Politics, Popular Music, Popular Music and Society, The Guardian,* and the journal *Law, Culture, and the Humanities,* among other publications.

Jehoash Hirshberg is a Professor Emeritus in the Musicology Department, Hebrew University, Jerusalem. He holds a Ph.D. from the University of Pennsylvania (1971). His diverse fields of research include the music of the fourteenth century, the Italian violin concerto at the time of Vivaldi (with Simon McVeigh of Goldsmiths, University of London), and Italian opera in the decade of unification, 1860–70. He has primarily concentrated on music in the Jewish society of Palestine during the years of the British mandate and in the early years of Israel, having published a historical study (1996) and monographs on the composers Paul Ben Haim, Alexander U. Boskovich, and Yehezkel Braun (forthcoming), as well as numerous articles on that subject.

Joshua R. Jacobson is Professor of Music and Director of Choral Activities at Northeastern University and Visiting Professor in the School of Jewish Music at Hebrew College. He is founder and artistic director of the Zamir Chorale of Boston. Over one hundred of his choral works have been published and are performed by choirs around the world. He is the author of *Chanting the Hebrew Bible,* a finalist for the National Jewish Book Award, and co-author of *Translations and Annotations of Choral Repertoire, Volume IV: Hebrew Texts.* He holds degrees from Harvard College, the New England Conservatory, and the University of Cincinnati.

Mark Kligman is the inaugural holder of the Mickey Katz Endowed Chair in Jewish Music and Professor of Ethnomusicology and Musicology at the University of California, Los Angeles, in the Herb Alpert School of Music. From 1994–2014 he was on the faculty of Hebrew Union College – Jewish Institute of Religion, where he taught in the Debbie Friedman School of Sacred Music. He specializes in the liturgical traditions of Middle Eastern Jewish communities and various areas of popular Jewish music. He is the Academic Chair of the Jewish Music Forum and co-editor of the journal *Musica Judaica.* Mark is also a board member of the Association for Jewish Studies.

James Loeffler is Associate Professor of History at the University of Virginia. He also serves as Scholar-in-Residence at the Pro Musica Hebraica Foundation, Academic Vice Co-Chair of the Jewish Music Forum of the American Society for Jewish Music, and Research Affiliate of the Jewish Music Research Centre at the Hebrew University of Jerusalem. His first book, *The Most Musical Nation: Jews and Culture in the Late Russian Empire,* was published by Yale University Press in 2010. He has also written on the Holocaust in Soviet music, the history of klezmer music, and Polish-Jewish musical relations.

Joel Rubin is Associate Professor (Music/Jewish Studies) and Director of Music Performance in the McIntire Department of Music at the University of Virginia. He holds a Ph.D. in ethnomusicology from City University of London (2001). Prior to UVA, he taught at Cornell University, Syracuse University, Ithaca College, and Humboldt Universität Berlin. Rubin is co-author of the books *Klezmer-Musik* (1999) and *Jüdische Musiktraditionen* (2001), and author of *Mazltov! Jewish-American Wedding Music for Clarinet* (1998). His most recent work on klezmer in Germany has appeared in the anthology *Dislocated Memories: Jews, Music, and Postwar German Culture* (2014) and in *Ethnomusicology Forum* (2015). Rubin is an internationally acclaimed performer of klezmer music and has recorded seven CDs. His most recent, *Azoy Tsu Tsveyt*, with acclaimed pianist and composer Uri Caine, was chosen by exclaim.ca as one of the ten favorites in the category Improv & Avant-Garde for 2011, and *Midnight Prayer* was ranked one of the most important recordings of 2007 by *Jewish Week*.

Edwin Seroussi is the Emanuel Alexandre Professor of Musicology and Director of the Jewish Music Research Centre at Hebrew University of Jerusalem. Born in Montevideo, Uruguay, he immigrated to Israel in 1971, where he received undergraduate and graduate degrees in musicology at Hebrew University, continuing on to earn his Ph.D. from UCLA in 1987. He taught at Bar Ilan and Tel Aviv Universities in Israel, and was visiting professor at universities in Europe and in North and South America. He has published on North African and Eastern Mediterranean Jewish music, Judeo-Islamic relations in music, and Israeli popular music. He founded the Yuval Music Series, and is editor of the acclaimed CD series Anthology of Music Traditions in Israel.

Mark Slobin is the Winslow-Kaplan Professor of Music at Wesleyan University and the author or editor of many books, on Afghanistan and Central Asia, eastern European Jewish music, and ethnomusicology theory, two of which have received the ASCAP-Deems Taylor Award: *Fiddler on the Move: Exploring the Klezmer World* (2000) and *Tenement Songs: Popular Music of the Jewish Immigrants* (1982). He has been President of the Society for Ethnomusicology and the Society for Asian Music.

Joshua S. Walden is a member of the Faculty of Musicology at the Peabody Institute of the Johns Hopkins University. He is the author of *Sounding Authentic: The Rural Miniature and Musical Modernism* (2014) and editor of *Representation in Western Music* (Cambridge, 2013). His articles on subjects including the music of Ernest Bloch, the folk and popular music arrangements of Jascha Heifetz, and music in Yiddish theater and cinema appear in periodicals including the *Journal of the American Musicological Society*, *Journal of the Royal Musical Association*, and *Journal of the Society for American Music*.

Susana Weich-Shahak was born in Argentina, and has lived in Israel since 1958. She earned her MA at the Israel Academy of Music and her PhD at Tel Aviv University. She is a researcher of Sephardic musical tradition at the Jewish Music Research Centre of the Hebrew University, Jerusalem. Her fieldwork recordings are catalogued at the National Sound Archive of the National Library. She has conducted interdisciplinary projects with grants from the Spanish Ministry of Culture and Sciences for research at the Consejo Superior de Investigaciones Científicas. Her publications include "Judeo-Spanish Moroccan

Songs for the Life Cycle," *Romancero Sefardí de Marruecos: Antología de tradición oral*, *Romancero Sefardí de Oriente*, *Repertorio Tradicional Infantil Sefardí: Retahilas, juegos, canciones y romances de tradición oral*, and others. Her numerous recordings include "Traditional Sephardic Songs and Ballads from Morocco" and "Traditional Sephardic Songs and Ballads from the Balkan Countries."

Amy Lynn Wlodarski is Associate Professor of Music at Dickinson College. Her research centers on the postwar phenomenon of musical Holocaust representation, with specific attention to its traumatic and expressive potentials, and has been published in leading musicological journals including the *Journal of the American Musicological Society* and *Journal of Musicology*. She is the author of *Musical Witness and Holocaust Representation* (Cambridge, 2015) and co-editor (with Elaine Kelly) of *Art Outside the Lines: New Perspectives on GDR Art Culture* (2011). She earned her Ph.D. in musicology from the Eastman School of Music.

Acknowledgments

I wish to offer my thanks first and foremost to the many authors who participated in the creation of this book by contributing their thoughtful chapters. I am grateful to Philip V. Bohlman for his help early in the conception of the project, and to Walter Frisch, Gabrielle Spiegel, and my colleagues at the Peabody Institute for offering support and advice. I owe particular gratitude to Victoria Cooper for her enthusiasm about this project when we first discussed it several years ago and her attentive and thoughtful advice throughout the process of assembling the book. I am thankful also to Sara Barnes, Kate Brett, Rebecca Coe, Emma Collison, Fleur Jones, and Rebecca Taylor at Cambridge University Press for their help in bringing the volume to fruition.

As always, my deepest gratitude is due to my family. My parents Judith Schelly and Michael Walden and brother Daniel are my most valuable editors and interlocutors, at all times sharing sage advice and warm support.

Introduction

JOSHUA S. WALDEN

The cover of this essay collection displays an illuminated initial-word panel that opens the book of Ecclesiastes in a Hebrew Bible created in Germany during the early fourteenth century. The gilt Hebrew letters, surrounded by medallions containing a menagerie of animals, spell *divrei*, meaning "words of." In the upper portion of the illumination, set within a Gothic-style architectural space, is the image of a robed King David playing the harp, flanked by a lion and stag, a pairing of animals common in Jewish iconography.[1] The story of David's harp playing is one of the earliest recorded accounts of music in Jewish history. According to the biblical description, David was so skilled a musician on the harp that the sound of his instrument was able to soothe and refresh his father-in-law and predecessor King Saul when he was troubled by an evil spirit sent by God. When this cover image, with its representation of Jewish music making and gold-leaf text, is read in the manner of a simple rebus (which is not the way it was meant to be interpreted, but is tempting, nonetheless), it offers an apt description of this volume: words about Jewish music. The book you are reading features a set of essays contributed by sixteen leading scholars of music in Jewish history and culture. In addition to comprising words about Jewish music, this collection is also a study about the *words* "Jewish music," which, as the following chapters will show, have conveyed multiple disparate meanings for different people across hundreds of years and around the globe.

The inherent ambiguity of the term "Jewish music," which so many authors of the essays collected here address in their studies of music in various times and places of Jewish religious and secular history, becomes evident when we begin to look more closely even at specific pieces that might seem at face value to be clear and unassailable instances of Jewish music. An example is provided by "Hatikvah" (The Hope), which has been the official national anthem of the State of Israel since 2004, but which served as an important Zionist anthem since the late nineteenth century and then as the de facto, if disputed, national anthem since Israel's founding in 1948.[2] The two stanzas of "Hatikvah" stem from what was originally a nine-stanza poem called "Tikvatenu" (Our Hope) from 1878, written in Hebrew by the Galician poet Naftali Hertz Imber (1856–1909) in the city of Iaşi, Romania. The lyrics describe a "Jewish spirit [that] yearns deep in the heart" and expresses the "hope of two millennia/ To be a free people in our land,/ The land of Zion and Jerusalem." These unambiguously Jewish and nationalistic lyrics are set to a mournful melody – with a rising gesture in the second half that seems to reach upward toward hope amid sadness. It is a tune that in itself, for many listeners, might seem immediately identifiable as "Jewish."

But in fact this melody traveled a surprisingly circuitous route to this Jewish and national context. The music was arranged in Palestine in the 1880s by a Zionist immigrant pioneer, Samuel Cohen, who based the tune on a Moldavian folk song called "Carul cu Boi" (Cart and Oxen). In the previous decade, the same melody had been a source of quotation for the Czech composer Bedřich Smetana, who incorporated it into his set of symphonic poems in the form of a Czech national epic, *Má Vlast* (My Life), in a section called *Die Moldau* (1874) that represented the Vltava river. Reaching still further back in the history of this melody, musicologists have linked its contour to a typical pattern of tones at the core of numerous folk songs found outside of the Jewish tradition across Europe, from Sweden to Italy, including the French song "Ah! vous dirai-je, maman," the model for "Twinkle, Twinkle, Little Star." Ultimately, then, the seeming Jewishness of this anthem's music first arose only partway through the melody's history, in its pairing with Imber's Hebrew text and its association at various points across the twentieth and twenty-first centuries with Zionist, anti-fascist, and Israeli national politics. This sort of inquiry does not challenge the Jewish meanings the melody communicates for many listeners, or the important role it has played in Zionist history and identity; but it does begin to illuminate the fascinating ambiguities that emerge in the study of Jewish music's long and varied history.

The first four chapters of this Cambridge Companion explore various ways "Jewish music" has been defined and conceived, and the historical, social, cultural, and technological influences that have helped shape these often conflicting understandings. In Chapter 1, Philip V. Bohlman considers Jewish music from the perspective of ontology, the area of thought that treats questions relating to the nature of being and existence. He views multiple ways and reasons that people have proposed varying definitions of "Jewish music" at particular moments in history, examining these in relation to a set of five frequently converging conditions: religion, language, embodiment, geography, and identity. Recognizing that Jewish communities have frequently responded to the surrounding world through musical means, Bohlman argues that Jewish music's various ontologies and definitions have played a vital role throughout the course of Jewish history.

Among his case studies, Bohlman considers issues relating to diaspora, a subject that commonly arises in studies of Jewish music, and that serves as the focus of Edwin Seroussi's chapter that follows. Seroussi considers how the term "diaspora" has been used inside and outside the academy in discussions of Jewish music. His essay asks whether diaspora remains a useful term in this context, outlining the values and shortcomings of the concept in the mapping of historical and contemporary Jewish musical cultures. The third chapter, by Judah M. Cohen, continues to survey the ways people have conceived of "Jewish music," by examining the roles of institutions in the development of the concept. Cohen describes how organizations and educational bodies devoted to varying religious, educational, philanthropic, and other concerns have supported the study and creation of genres, styles, and canons of Jewish music in order to promote particular claims about Jewish culture and identity. Through his study, Cohen shows multiple impacts of socioeconomic concerns and financial support on the very ways Jewish music has been defined.

Chapter 4 addresses another key source of influence on concepts and practices of Jewish music in the twentieth century: sound reproduction technologies. From the wax cylinder phonograph to the MP3 player, devices for sound recording and playback have been used for ethnographic research in Jewish communities, for the development of performers' and composers' careers, and for the creation of new musical genres and styles. Sound recording devices have also permitted listeners access to a growing body of music that could be heard in radio broadcasts, purchased as discs, downloaded as digital files, or streamed on electronic devices. This chapter shows that, far from being neutral modes of sound reproduction incorporated into existing structures of musical performance, composition, and listening, these technologies have triggered substantial changes in the ways Jewish music has been created, consumed, and defined.

The four chapters that follow explore music in selected Jewish religious, folk, and popular traditions, focusing in particular on music in the Bible, liturgy, Judeo-Spanish song, and klezmer music. In Chapter 5, Theodore W. Burgh introduces the music of biblical Palestine during the Iron Age. He presents evidence of musical practices that survive in the form of instruments and iconography, as well as in descriptions of musicians and music making in the Hebrew Bible. Although most details about the sounds and the purposes of music during this period remain lost to history, archaeomusicologists continue to uncover details of the kinds of instruments used and the settings and contexts in which people sang and played these instruments. In Chapter 6, Mark Kligman addresses the long history of music in Jewish religious, liturgical, and paraliturgical contexts. This chapter describes the various sources that provide details about the early Jewish musical traditions, and presents an overview of music in the Tanakh, or Hebrew Bible, and the Temple service. Discussions of biblical cantillation, *nusaḥ* (psalmody), and liturgical chant are followed by detailed and comparative studies of Ashkenazic and Sephardic liturgical practices. Finally, the chapter concludes with an exploration of new music written for synagogue worship, particularly in American Reform, Conservative, and Orthodox synagogues.

The following chapter explores the performance tradition associated with Judeo-Spanish song, both in its historical settings and in the present day. Introducing examples of three major generic categories, the *romance*, *copla*, and *cantiga*, Susana Weich-Shahak discusses the traditional social context of these songs, considering questions of who sang them – men or women, solo performers or groups, with or without instrumental accompaniment – and where and when they were performed. Having introduced historical performance practices from various regions occupied by the Sephardic diaspora, Weich-Shahak then turns to the question of contemporary performance of the repertoire, addressing where it often fails to reproduce traditional modes of singing as well as the ways some musicians have incorporated ethnographic research into their more successfully imitative performance techniques.

Chapter 8 provides a history of klezmer music and musicians. Joel Rubin explores the various repertoires and styles associated with klezmer and overlapping genres across several centuries and up to the present day. His chapter examines the history of this instrumental repertoire, beginning with its centuries-old European roots, continuing through its performance by immigrant musicians in the United States in the early twentieth century, and finally viewing the popularity it has achieved in recent decades, since the start of what is known as the "klezmer revival" in the 1970s.

The subsequent chapters in this volume chart a generally chronological course through the history of a variety of genres, places, languages, and styles of Jewish music. In Chapter 9, Joshua R. Jacobson takes us to Renaissance Italy, to introduce Salamone Rossi, an important and innovative figure, as one of the few Jewish musicians to compose music for Jewish worship before the Jewish Enlightenment – the *Haskalah* – beginning in the late eighteenth century. Little is known about this Mantuan, who lived at the turn of the seventeenth century, and whose collection of polyphonic motets in Hebrew was a landmark accomplishment in the history of Jewish music. Jacobson examines Rossi's career and his compositions to view the role music played in his navigation of a complex dual identity, as an employee of the Catholic Mantuan court and a resident of the Jewish ghetto. In Chapter 10, we move forward to the mid-eighteenth century to view the rise of Jewish participation in European classical music. David Conway explores the social contexts in which Jews entered the mainstream of the musical profession during this period, and the role of the Jewish Enlightenment in supporting this rise in participation, as well as the anti-Semitic judgments and accusations such composers faced. The chapter views this history up to 1850, the year of the publication of Richard Wagner's influential essay "Das Judentum in der Musik" (Jewry in Music) in the periodical *Neue Zeitschrift für Musik*, in which Wagner proposed his own derisive definition of the term "Jewish music."

The following chapter, by James Loeffler, describes how the story of Jewish involvement in art music continued in the period after Wagner's screed, between 1850 and 1925. During this era, increasing numbers of Jewish musicians studied in European conservatories, and many composers began to pursue novel methods of representing Jewish identities in their music. Such musicians and their listeners and critics continued to engage in efforts to define the notion of modern Jewish art music, debating how it should reflect particular geographic and historical roots and religious and cultural values. In his chapter, Loeffler views the principal figures and debates in the field of Jewish music in this period, and considers how conceptions of Jewish music differed from place to place and over time.

Chapter 12, by Tina Frühauf, focuses on the synagogue music of the Jewish Reform movement. The chapter begins by examining the origins of Reform in the early nineteenth century, and describes the role and music of the cantor, a figure who in this context succeeded the traditional *ḥazzan*. Frühauf also describes the way the organ was introduced into the Reform liturgy, as part of the influence of church music on the music of Reform, as well as the controversies inspired by this new practice. The chapter introduces major cantors and composers involved in the movement, and the new religious musical repertoires they produced.

In Chapter 13, Lily E. Hirsch examines Jewish musical activities and the various ways Jewish musicians and listeners conceived of Jewish music between 1925 and 1945. This was an era in which conditions of war, internment, exile, and immigration influenced notions of Jewish music and its role in Jewish culture in a variety of ways, while Jewish musicians were forced to respond to increasingly restrictive Nazi and Soviet policies about Jewish participation in the arts and the content of their works. Hirsch's chapter examines such issues during this period in three particular contexts: immediately before the Nazi era, in the work of the Jewish Culture League during the Third Reich, and during the Holocaust, among composers living in captivity and in exile.

Mark Slobin writes in Chapter 14 about another genre that developed during the periods explored in the previous several chapters: the music of Yiddish theater and cinema of the late nineteenth to mid-twentieth centuries. Yiddish theater and cinema were highly musical multi-media cultural forms that quickly reached audiences on multiple continents, and that frequently addressed, in scenarios, scores, and song lyrics, the subjects of Jewish displacement, assimilation, cultural maintenance, and the meeting of tradition and modernity. Many of the Yiddish songs popularly known as folk songs today originated in the works of musical theater and cinema. Slobin views this repertoire in relation to theatrical and musical precedents in Jewish culture of prior eras, as well as in the context of other contemporary modes of cultural expression in Europe and America, and discusses Yiddish theater and film scores' regional character and transnational circulation.

In Chapter 15, Jehoash Hirshberg directs our attention to the music of the Yishuv – the Jewish community in Palestine under the British mandate – and the state of Israel. This chapter describes a rare scenario in the history of music, in which a national musical culture was created almost entirely by immigrant musicians, in many cases refugees. Hirshberg shows the important role of amateur choirs in the establishment of Hebrew as the dominant language, and describes the establishment of music academies on the central European model. Considering a range of compositions by Israeli composers from across the decades since the nation was founded, he explores the development of musical idioms that, through various means and for different audiences, evoke a sense of locality and cultural belonging in the region. In the final chapter, Amy Lynn Wlodarski treats the representation of Jewish subject matter in art music after 1945. The arts of this period are often said to exhibit a character of postmodernism, a term that can be difficult to define, but that Wlodarski shows to be helpful in discussions of what "Jewish art music" has meant since the end of World War II. To explore this topic, Wlodarski focuses on a series of case studies, three musical works that take on the difficult task of responding to and memorializing the Holocaust, by the composers Arnold Schoenberg, George Rochberg, and Steve Reich.

The *Cambridge Companion to Jewish Music* is intended as a collection of detailed studies, a useful reference resource, and a research starting point for readers interested in the history of the music of Jewish cultures and traditions around the world. As the chapters in this book demonstrate, the term "Jewish music" is a deceptively simple way to describe a subject that is in fact extremely diverse, comprising, among other genres, folk songs in multiple languages, dance music played by ensembles of instrumentalists, forms of religious music developed in the synagogue and the home in far-flung communities, methods of chanting the text of the Hebrew Bible, classical music written for the concert hall, and commercial popular music disseminated in sound recordings, on the radio, and in venues from Borscht Belt clubs to vast performance arenas. Like a friendly, knowledgeable companion, this book, as it accompanies you along your journey through the study of Jewish music, will tell stories about people and places, answer multiple questions while raising others, and offer new points of view for future discussion.

Notes

1 In Jewish folk art, the image of the lion referred to the words "Judah is a lion's whelp," from Genesis 49:9. The stag might refer to the line "Naphtali is a hind let loose," in Genesis 49:21. Naphtali is indirectly associated with music, as Deborah, a member of Naphtali's tribe, is called upon to "awake, awake, utter a song," in Judges 5:12. See Klára Móricz, *Jewish Identities: Nationalism, Racism, and Utopianism in Twentieth-Century Music* (Berkeley and Los Angeles: University of California Press, 2008), 27.

2 On "Hatikvah," see Philip V. Bohlman, "Before Hebrew Song," in Michael Berkowitz (ed.), *Nationalism, Zionism and Ethnic Mobilization of the Jews in 1900 and Beyond* (Leiden: Brill, 2004), 25–59 (37–42); James Loeffler, "Hatikvah: The Colorful History of the Israeli National Anthem," *My Jewish Learning*, http://www.myjewishlearning.com/culture/2/ Music/Israeli_Music/Folk_Music/hatikvah .shtml?p=1 (accessed February 20, 2015).

PART ONE

Conceptions of Jewish music

1 Ontologies of Jewish music

PHILIP V. BOHLMAN

The song that opens this chapter on ontologies and definitions of Jewish music is as unlikely as it is uncommon (Example 1.1). Hanns Eisler's "Der Mensch" is unlikely because Eisler (1868–1962) rarely appears in the catalogues of twentieth-century composers contributing to a modern repertory of Jewish music. It is uncommon because the song actually does bear profound witness to a Jewish life shaped by modern history.[1] It is unlikely because the song appears in a collection of songs composed by Eisler while in American exile, during the years 1942–3, when he hoped to make a career in Los Angeles composing for Hollywood films. "Der Mensch" is uncommon because it conforms to none of the genres and styles that might reflect the conventions of popular song, which, indeed, he knew well and incorporated into his music for stage and film with great skill.

"Der Mensch" announces itself as Jewish, and this, too, was uncommon for Hanns Eisler, whose attitude toward his own Jewishness, religious or cultural, was largely ambivalent. There is little ambivalence, however, in "Der Mensch." Eisler attributes the text to "words from the Bible," unique among the songs of the *Hollywood Songbook*, which draw heavily on the poetry of his most frequent collaborator, Bertolt Brecht, but freely set poetry by Goethe, Eichendorff, Hölderlin, Pascal, and others, situating the *Hollywood Songbook* in a historical and stylistic moment between the Romantic song cycle and the Great American Songbook.[2]

An unlikely moment for the enunciation of Jewishness, but it is for this reason that this moment of Jewish music is even more arresting. There is no equivocation in Eisler's deliberate evocation of sacred song. The song text, written by Eisler himself in 1943,[3] combines passages from the Hebrew Bible, recognizing liturgical and exegetical practice common to many Jewish communities:[4]

> Line 1 – Job 14:1 – The human is born of woman and lives for only a brief time, full of troubles.
> Line 2 – Exodus 12:7 – Take the blood of the lamb and spread it on the sides and the upper threshold of the doorframes.
> Line 3 – Exodus 12:12 and 12:23 – In order that the angel passes over our house for many years to come.

> (translation adapted from Eisler's German)

Example 1.1 Hanns Eisler, "Der Mensch" (1943), from the *Hollywooder Liederbuch*, © by Deutscher Verlag für Musik.

Melodically, Eisler enhances his biblical setting by using stepwise motion with declamatory rhythm, transforming what might initially seem tonal, dominant-tonic movement between G and C, through chromatic tension in the individual movement of the sparsely layered voices of the piano accompaniment. This song of suffering and exile, of the beginning and ending of human existence, belies the simplicity of resolution, textually and musically. The G# with which the voice seeks to find comfort on its final note, on "home," turns dissonant with the piano's fortissimo move to G natural. How do we come to believe the song has reached its end?

The question that "Der Mensch" raises is both ontological and definitional: Does it define, or is it defined by, Jewish music? Does Eisler's intent to articulate an ontological moment biblically and musically suffice to enunciate Jewishness, because of or despite the song's unlikely uncommonness? Such are the questions I pose in the course of this chapter. They are questions that ultimately transform the unlikely and the uncommon into conditions that we experience as familiar when, in fact, we enter the ontological moments of Jewish music. Hanns Eisler's "Der Mensch," too, becomes familiar as Jewish music when we place it in the five conditions that define moments of ontology in the section that follows: religion, language, body, geography, identity – they are all there. They converge musically to expand the field of definitions through which we have come to sound and experience Jewish music.

The problem and paradox of definition

The ontology of Jewish music is tied to the critical need to define and delimit. At many moments in Jewish intellectual history that critical need becomes virtually obsessive. The musicality of sacred texts and worship has been crucial to biblical exegesis and traditions of commentary, in other words, to the tradition and transmission of Torah and Talmud. Extending the boundaries of sacred song to secular song proved fundamental to creating national music during the early decades of modern Israeli statehood. Anti-Semites and philo-Semites alike sought ways to make Jewish music identifiable and to calculate its impact on cultural identity.[5] Ontological questions were as pressing for those who asserted that virtually no music was truly Jewish as for those who believed virtually every music had the potential to be Jewish. The questions seem never to abate, with debates that seek resolution or even consensus still raging across the Internet of the twenty-first century.

The ontological search to identify and define Jewish music, moreover, took the form of action and agency, transforming the abstract to the material. At various moments in Jewish liturgical history, when sacred-music specialists sought repertories that would lead them toward professionalism, they discovered and invented, collected and created anew practices of Jewish music that would allow them to become cantors and composers. Religious and musical specialists in communities at the greatest extremes from the Ashkenazic and Sephardic diasporas, for example, the Falashim in eastern Africa and the Bene Yisrael in South Asia, consolidated musical practices that distinguished them as Jewish. The ideological challenge of generating "Jewish folk music" or "Jewish popular music" in eras of shifting political boundaries sent collectors to the field and performers to street and stage alike.[6] Moments of anxiety about the absence of Jewish music – the loss of Judeo-Spanish *romancero* after the *reconquista* or klezmer after the Shoah – inspired the agency that led to their revival.

The concerted efforts to make Jewish music material, hence, to afford it with the meaning necessary for religious, social, and political action, accrue to what I call "ontological moments" in this chapter. At these ontological moments Jewish music becomes identifiable because of what it can do by contributing to the definition of self, other, or both at moments of historical change and, often, political exigency. At such moments, Jewish music is not simply passed along as definable identities with authenticity and authority from the past, rather it responds to the need to define identities that respond to the present. The old and the new converge at the ontological moments in which Jewish music acquires its identities, shaping the ways in which Jewish history itself unfolds. The historical conditions and musical subjectivities that yield the ontological moments I consider here combine ontologies and definitions of Jewish music in different and distinctive ways. I should like to outline these conditions and subjectivities briefly before turning to the series of ontological moments I further explore in this chapter. The five conditions and subjectivities are neither definitive nor exhaustive, but they are meant to be comprehensive, thereby opening the historiographical field of this chapter and the volume in which it appears below.

Ontological moments of Jewish music – conditions and subjectivities

1) Sacred ontologies / religious definitions: Revelation of sacred voice
2) Textual ontologies / linguistic definitions: Jewishness conveyed by Jewish language (Hebrew, Yiddish, Ladino, Judeo-Arabic, etc.)
3) Embodied ontologies / contextual definitions: Genealogical descent and identity
4) Spatial ontologies / geographical definitions: Jewish music in the synagogue or ritual practices
5) Cultural ontologies / political definitions: Music and survival in a world of otherness

At the core of the paradox of defining Jewish music is the frequent belief in authenticity, chosenness, and uniqueness. No definition of Jewish music has more currency in the past half-century than that of Curt Sachs (1881–1959), an immigrant German-Jewish comparative musicologist and organologist, who is reputed to have established at the 1957 International Conference on Jewish Music in Jerusalem that Jewish music is "by Jews, for Jews, as Jews." Sachs's own distinguished career – the classification system for musical instruments that he developed with his Jewish Berlin colleague Erich M. von Hornbostel (1877–1935) remains the standard worldwide almost a century after it was formulated – would hardly confirm that he placed much currency in such an essentialist definition.

The frequency with which we encounter the definition, nonetheless, suggests it reveals a belief in the selfness of music that many wish to will into existence. It represents a class of definitions that accepts that, whatever else Jewishness is, it is self-contained, biologically determined, and borne with other attributes of chosenness. Historically, we witness the ways in which such definitions express a concern for pollution and chosenness, as well as anxieties for the boundaries and borders with the non-Jewish. The continuum of definitions from exclusive to inclusive represents the persistent tendency to define Jewish music by what it *is not* and *should not* be: secular, hybrid, mixed gender, too beautiful, too noisy or dissonant. There is a sharp critical awareness that is turned toward music that does not fulfill the definitions of Jewish music, even when – or even especially when – those definitions are not stated.

A more expansive history of music in Jewish thought and experience, however, reveals that exclusive definitions form along a continuum that also accepts inclusiveness and the accompanying contradictions. Music "by Jews" may not be compatible with performance "as Jews." Subjectivities of exclusivity may create boundaries within self even more than with other. Such is the case, for example, with injunctions against hearing *kol isha* (woman's voice) in orthodox Jewish sacred music, which has historically justified gender separation in the synagogue no less than the refusal to allow women to worship and sing at many of the most sacred of all Jewish sites in Israel, notably the Western Wall. In contrast, the revival of the repertory and practice of popular music regarded as most Jewish of all in post-Shoah Europe, klezmer, has attracted far more non-Jewish performers and audiences than Jewish. Complicating the definitional paradox even more are the traditions in which Jewish musical professionals dominated the performance of music that was not "theirs," for example, the art music of Muslim courts in the Middle East and Central Asia. Under other historical circumstances, say, in the history of the modern musical and film music, the creation of music that was not exclusively "theirs" was crucial to a process of musical translation and social transformation.

In the section that follows I explore the historically changing meanings of Jewish music by examining multiple ontological moments. Jewish intellectual history accrues to these moments as a set of responses to changing historical landscapes and conditions, particularly the relations of individual Jewish communities and their social practices to the world about them. Historically, music provided one of the most powerful means and voices for response, and it is for these reasons that the ontologies and definitions of Jewish music are so critically important to understanding the larger forces that shaped Jewish history.[7]

Ontological moments of Jewish music

Be-reshit – ontological moments of musical translation
The ontological moments of Jewish music begin as acts of translation. Jewish music comes into being when an original text or ritual process undergoes transformation that expands upon its meanings, enhancing them within the

multiplying contexts of Jewish culture and history. The enhancement of biblical text or prayer through cantillation and chant is possible because of the
musical attributes of *targum*, a translation that functions also as interpretation. The ontological moment from which sacred Jewish music emerges,
thus, retains the essential elements of its original forms, but it allows them
to serve in new ways, responding to changing texts and contexts. The forms
of translation that create Jewish music are themselves strikingly evident
in the intellectual history of Jewish thought. Biblical translation begins at
the beginning, with the Torah, and continues unabated as the tradition of
interpretation that historically unifies and transforms the metaphysics of
Judaism to the present. Torah recitation relies on the translatability that
sustains the changing sameness of interpretation over the historical *longue
durée*, as well as under the immediate constraints of the present. Biblical translation also expands the field of difference. Accordingly, every act
of translation is political, whether by establishing contemporary linguistic
meaning from related languages or establishing the limits of interpretation for the different religions, especially those constituting the Abrahamic
faiths of Judaism, Christianity, and Islam that draw upon biblical texts and
narratives.[8]

An intellectual history of Jewish music, therefore, accrues to the ontological moments as acts of translation and interpretation come into being.
Such moments are fully evident *be-reshit*, in Genesis, the first book of Moses
in the Torah. Accounts of the origins of music appear in both the fourth and
twenty-second chapters of Genesis. In the first account, we encounter different narratives about the human attributes of music (Yuval as the inventor
of music generated by the body) and those that describe attributes forged
through artifice (Tubal Cain as the inventor of instruments from bronze
and iron). In the second account, the *Akeda*, or "Binding of Isaac," it is the
shofar, the ram's horn left after the burnt sacrifice that replaces the sacrifice
Abraham was prepared to make of his own son, that enters Jewish ritual
history as the horn blown during the High Holidays.

From the beginnings in Genesis, musical instruments enter the Bible in
ever-increasing numbers from sources within and outside the Jewish communities that constitute the historical landscape and polity of the Bible. The
Psalms identify instruments played as components of ritual and community praise. Psalm 150, for example, accounts for a full orchestra, used to
accompany dance no less than prayer and praise in the sanctuary of God.
The Psalms also contain frequent references to genre, for example *shir ha-
ma'alot* (song of degrees), at the beginning of Psalms 120–34, sung during
pilgrimage festivals.

As texts that identify musical attributes, the biblical references to music
were – and are – open to interpretation, and it is for this reason that we
are able to understand the meanings of music that they convey as acts of

translation.[9] Such acts of translation function in different ways and rely on different forms of transformation in the intellectual history of Jewish music, and it is crucial to recognize these differences as we seek meaning and definition for Jewish music. Musical translation, for example, frequently takes the form of mediation. Sacred voice or sacred acts are performed by intermediates, such as Yuval or the angel of God in the passages on the origins of musical instruments in Genesis. Musical translation is necessary because of the several languages spoken and used in Jewish communities throughout history, making polyglossia and intertextuality normative. The exile of Jews in Babylon provided only the first of many historical narratives yielding allegories about musical distinction and interpretation. Musical translation characterizes communities that form around borders of all kinds, where it accommodates movement and migration. As ontology translation ensured the historical processes that could renew music as Jewish.

Shir ḥadash – ontological moments of diaspora

1. By the rivers of Babylon, there we sat down,
   yea, we wept, when we remembered Zion.
2. Upon the willows in the midst thereof we hanged up our harps.
3. For there they that led us captive asked of us words of song,
   and our tormentors asked of us mirth:
   "Sing us one of the songs of Zion."
4. How shall we sing the LORD's song in a foreign land?

Psalm 137, 1–4

Even the biblical narratives of diaspora challenge the ontological status of Jewish music. In Psalm 137, the very possibility of singing a "song of Zion" in a place of otherness is called into question, establishing conditions of otherness that appear repeatedly across the successive diasporas that would define Jewish history. Many forms of encounter have shaped the history of Jewish diaspora – religious, racial, cultural, political, military – each of them accompanied significantly by musical encounter. The crucial questions are already evident in Psalm 137. How does the music of Jewish selfness – the abandoned harp, the song of Zion – enable survival? Is lament the only means of musically representing the past? If music making only brings mirth and celebration to the tormenting others, does it shift the boundaries between self and other? Psalm 137 does contain responses to the questions of its opening lines, troubling as they are, in a call for remembering the loss of Jerusalem also with a music of vengeance and survival. In the sixth line the Psalmist continues: "Let my tongue cleave to the roof of my mouth, if I remember thee not, if I set not Jerusalem above my chiefest joy."

The resolution of self and other remains in question in the countless moments of musical encounter that form the historical *longue durée* of Jewish diaspora. Ontological boundaries form in the ways music defines encounter, even in the earliest communities forming after the destruction of the Second Temple in Jerusalem in 70 CE, historically imagined as the site at which Jewish musical practices were canonized. In exile from Jerusalem, Jews would need to worship locally in the synagogue, yet bear with them the traditions that they could experience through memory alone. Musical practices changed to accommodate the local, with oral and written traditions forming a counterpoint that contributed to the resolution of self and other.

It is hardly surprising that Jewish music enters modern historiography as evidence for the local worship practices resolving the encounter of self and other. Abraham Zvi Idelsohn (1882–1938), for example, regarded the spread of musical practice in diaspora synagogues as critical to Jewish music itself.[10] In his comparative studies, the musical markers of Jewishness were resilient, not because they could be reduced to authenticity, but because they accommodated the possibilities of generating "new song" (*shir ḥadash*), hence the survival of Jewish communities in diaspora.

The ontological moments of diaspora also yield hybridity, religious and cultural subjectivities in which selfness and otherness are interdependent. When rituals and repertories change, they respond to the exchange of music across religious and cultural boundaries. The systems of mode that provide the structural framework for diaspora traditions most often absorb local traditions, even when these signify musical practices that have little to do with Jewish worship. The oldest Jewish communities in India, for example, the Bene Yisrael and the Cochin Jews – the former settled for at least two millennia, the latter for about 1300 years – use *rāga*, the theoretical basis of Indian classical music. The standardized modal system used in the synagogues of Israel today, the "Jerusalem-Sephardi" tradition, is based on *maqām*, or mode, in the Arabic classical music of the Eastern Mediterranean.

Folk- and popular-music traditions, in the Jewish diaspora or from the Jewish diaspora, depend extensively on hybridity. The Israeli popular music known as *musica mizrakhit* (eastern music) often makes use not only of *maqām*, but also of genres from Arabic popular music, such as *layālī*.[11] Jewish folk music in the Ashkenazic traditions of central and eastern Europe often forms repertories around the boundary regions in which intercultural exchange is most intensive and normative.[12] Individual songs in such regions often circulate in Yiddish and German, as well as their many dialects. Similarly, they may combine additional linguistic variants, published in translations to and from Hebrew, or in regional languages. In diasporic music traditions hybridity is fluid and responsive to the changing historical conditions that prescribe the ontological moments of Jewish music.

Vox populi – musical ontologies of collection and community

At each stage in a Jewish intellectual history constituted of ontological moments, there was a renewal and revival of Jewish music as new and modern. The modernity of a repertory was assured by the ways it gathered parts from the past and provided a new context for them in the present. The modernity of early modern Jewish musical practice in the wake of the expulsion of Jews from Spain and Portugal at the end of the fifteenth century was measured in the pace of change from *prima* to *seconda prattica* (first and second practice) in the late Renaissance repertories of sacred music by Jewish composers in northern Italy, notably Salamone Rossi (c. 1570–c. 1628), whom Don Harrán identifies as one of the first historical figures designated as a "Jewish musician."[13] New repertories, no less than repertories of new Jewish music, led to the formation of new categories of musician with responsibility for upholding the presence of the traditional in the modern. The early modern developments in music printing, for example, led to the publication of new works and genres of Jewish music for sacred and secular practice, among them Rossi's *Ha-shirim asher lishlomo* (Songs of Solomon, c. 1622), in which his role as composer is evident in the play between the names of the biblical and modern musicians, Solomon, thus a clear modernization of the usual title, *Shir ha-shirim* (Song of Songs).

Other Jewish repertories formed as a response to modern technologies of musical reproduction. The first printings of European ballads from the fifteenth century consolidated repertories of songs with Hebrew orthography that served to locate narrative genres from medieval Ladino and Yiddish oral traditions in broadsides and folios that circulated in the growing public sphere of early modern Europe.[14] These would attract the attention of the early collector of folk song in the Enlightenment, Johann Gottfried Herder (1744–1803), who first invented the term *Volkslied* (folk song) for his collections of the 1770s, among which Jewish ballads are to be found, for example, "Die Jüdin" (The Jewish Woman), already part of a canon of ballads from the late Middle Ages.

As folk-song collecting became one of the most important media for the expression of nationalism in the nineteenth century, the search for Jewish folk song, too, accelerated. A vocabulary that circumscribed Jewish folk music may have developed later in the nineteenth century, probably in the early 1880s, but within decades thereafter, volume upon volume appeared, containing modern editions of Jewish folk music that needed to be protected against loss.[15] The songs now called Jewish in these modern collections resulted from considerable acts of collection, translation, and dissemination. German-language collections contained parallel song texts, in modern Yiddish and High German, enhancing their literary value.

Collections of urban popular music included texts that spoke to the social conditions of the day. Instrumental collections documented the paths of ensembles from East to West, representing the earliest histories of klezmer musicians.

Collecting Jewish music contributed substantially to the rise of a modern class of Jewish professionals primarily engaged with music. That rise is spectacularly evident in the transformation of the *ḥazzan* and the *ḥazzanut* to the cantor and the cantorate in the nineteenth century. Cantors came to fulfill many different roles in the European urban synagogue – teacher, composer, choral director, sometimes even star performer in the community – many of which served as an index to growing professionalism. The repertories used by cantors increasingly appeared in print, frequently with new compositions, which reveal the shifting of borders that connected them to an ontological moment. In Salomon Sulzer's *Schir Zion* (Song of Zion) of 1840/41, for example, there are compositions by other composers of the day, among them Franz Schubert, who contributed a setting of Psalm 92.[16] Cantorial societies were forming by the mid-nineteenth century, and these published journals that connected cantors worldwide. By the early twentieth century, the modernization of the cantorate had produced inroads into early recordings. Jewish music was becoming very modern indeed, and its modernity was sounded across an expanding public sphere, both Jewish and non-Jewish.

The in-gathering of Jewish music – recorded ontologies

> The prayer following the Passover meal had been recited, the end of the *hagadah* had been reached, and the *seder* had come to its conclusion. Everyone passed into the living room, where a phonograph with Joseph's narrative on a cylinder stood on the table . . . David sat down beside the machine and turned the horn toward the listeners.
>
> Theodor Herzl, *Altneuland*[17]

Recorded sound and song were critical to the histories that paved the return to the Yishuv, the modern settlement of the land of Israel. Phonographs and the sounds they reproduced appear in Zionist narratives in all genres, from the utopian fiction in Theodor Herzl's novel *Altneuland* (1904), from which the above epigraph is taken, to the scientific reports that amateur and professional scholars, such as Idelsohn, brought back to the scientific commissions that sponsored their field research.[18] The early twentieth-century recording excursions in the Yishuv took as their model the first uses of wax-cylinder and wax-disc technology used to gather the sounds of cultural difference and distinction – folk song and folk music, language and dialect – from places far away in order that they could be heard again and organized into the repertories and social hierarchies that gave order to history and culture. The early ontological moments that captured sound and music formed what Mark Katz calls "record events."[19] The proliferation and spread of such record events paralleled the transformations in Jewish history that began in the final decade of the nineteenth century and led to the foundation of Israel in the mid-twentieth century. The record event consolidates and shapes ontological moments. Listening to a recording of a Yemenite Jewish song, for example, is a shared experience. Recordings reach into disparate pasts, but they sound common presents. Spatially defined by their tangibility, they replay the common dimensions of the Jewish music they physically establish.

It would be possible, in fact, to write modern Jewish and Israeli history as a succession of record events that influenced, no less than they were influenced by, social, cultural, political, linguistic, and musical of modernity. Recordings gave Jewish music a new reality, the tangibility and portability Katz claims as the result of record events. With recording machines, themselves portable, it was possible to traverse the diaspora in search of Jewish music, to find it wherever Jewish communities were found, and to gather it, consolidating both commonness and difference as repertory, genre, ritual, and history – as sound and the materials that captured it. Recordings transformed sound to history, and Jewish music on record made history. Recordings located Jewish music in time, and the collectors and scholars of Jewish music reimagined and rewrote Jewish history by connecting past to present to future. Idelsohn's wax-disc recordings in Jerusalem from 1911–13 were foundational to his most influential writings, especially *Jewish Music in Its Historical Development*. Robert Lachmann's wax-cylinder recordings in Jewish communities on the island of Djerba off the coast of Tunisia freed them from temporal isolation and retrieved them, sonically, for Jewish history.[20]

The proliferation of recordings of Jewish music, as well as the materiality of their reproducibility through 78-rpm shellacs, LPs, cassettes, and digital technology, reflects an ontology of in-gathering. It is that in-gathering – from the centers of diaspora communities no less than from the farthest peripheries – that motivated the establishment of archives and Jewish music research in its twentieth- and twenty-first-century forms. The historical path from Idelsohn's wax-disc recordings to their publication in the early volumes of the *Hebräisch-orientalischer Melodienschatz* (The Thesaurus of Hebrew Oriental Melodies),[21] to their accessibility to the first generation of Israeli composers and to their digitization[22] lends Jewish music specifically technological dimensions, which in turn are ever expanding. The intellectual history of Jewish music research that began with Lachmann's archival impulse in Berlin and led to the establishment of the Archives of Oriental Music in Jerusalem, which in turn provided the foundations for the Jewish

Music Research Centre at the Hebrew University, has been critical for the subject formations that afford Jewish music a common set of ontologies for all subdisciplines of modern Jewish music scholarship. It is this field of Jewish music that the contributors to the present volume share.

Film and music – mediating Jewish ontologies

Jewish music was part of sound film from the beginning. The very subject of the first full-length talkie, Alan Crosland's *The Jazz Singer* (1927), based on Samuel Raphaelson's novel *The Day of Atonement*, formed around the decision faced by an immigrant Jewish son, Jakie Rabinowitz/Jack Robin, to remain true to the traditional world of his orthodox family or enter the world of popular American music. Throughout the film the "jazz singer" crossed musical borders, between the ritual practices of home and synagogue, between the stages claimed by great cantors, notably Yossele Rosenblatt (1882–1933), and the clubs and theatrical venues claimed by Al Jolson (1886–1950) playing a leading role both fictional and real. *The Jazz Singer* posed ontological questions and provided answers to them, but ultimately multiplied the ways in which the viewer could understand and define Jewish music.

The first German sound film, Josef von Sternberg's 1930 *Der blaue Engel* (The Blue Angel), similarly placed jazz and Jewish music on the stage representing its center – "The Blue Angel" was the name of a cabaret in the harbor district of a larger German city, where much of the movie is musically enacted – but poses yet other ontological questions about what these musics might signify in modern society. Musical borders and boundaries crisscross throughout the film, undoing the distinctions between the worlds realized musically on and off the cabaret stage. The house band at the Blue Angel, Weintraub's Syncopators, performs diegetically throughout the film, with songs by Friedrich Holländer, leader of the Syncopators, drawn from his signature jazz style for Marlene Dietrich, who played the lead in the film. The Jewishness of the music in *The Blue Angel* is at once obvious and thrown into question. As sound film and film music developed – and both Holländer and Dietrich would follow careers that intersected with the history of film music through the 1930s and then the Shoah – ontological questions would multiply, always at the intersection of modern film and Jewish history.

The mediation of Jewishness in film music shaped vastly different historical processes and cinematically portrayed complex social formations. Among the first experiments with sound film were modernist compositions in the mid-1920s, and among these one of the most influential was Hanns Eisler's *Opus III*, composed as an accompaniment to Walter Ruttmann's 1925 *Berlin, die Sinfonie der Großstadt & Melodie der Welt* (Berlin,

Symphony of the City and Melody of the World). In *Opus III* Eisler concerned himself with the representational borders between shifting, abstract
shapes and musical sound. Throughout his long and influential career as
a film composer Eisler moved in different ways between film and music,
from his earliest collaborations with Bertolt Brecht (*Kuhle Wampe*, 1932),
through those with Fritz Lang (*Hangmen Also Die*, 1943) and Charlie Chaplin (*The Circus*, 1947), to the soundtrack for the first large-scale documentary about Auschwitz, Alain Resnais's 1955 *Nuit et brouillard* (Night and
Fog). The music in these films also expressed Jewishness in vastly different
ways, sometimes not at all, at other times dispassionately, directly, as in
the Auschwitz film. In his extensive theoretical writings on music and film,
especially in the first major book on film music, co-authored with Theodor
W. Adorno, *Composing for the Films* (1947), Eisler provides more questions
than answers.[23] The condition he describes as "dramaturgical counterpoint"
leaves the borders between music and narrative representation in film intact.
The question of Jewish film music remains unresolved.

In the short-lived age of Yiddish film, however, the possibility of resolving
the question is unequivocal. In the 1930s, the decade immediately following
the emergence of sound film, Yiddish film flourished. In less than a decade,
film studios in Poland mustered actors and musicians, screenwriters and
composers, from across the diaspora to produce a series of classic films,
among them Joseph Green's 1936 *Yidl mitn fidl* (Yidl with His Fiddle)
and 1937 *Der purimshpilr* (The Purim Actor; also called The Jester). As in
The Jazz Singer and *The Blue Angel*, Jewish music itself – klezmer and the
theatrical traditions of the Purim season – provide means of exploring the
musical attributes of cinema. The borders between the stage and reality,
traditional music and modern popular music, too, are plied. The worlds
sounded with music are Jewish, but they are fragile, and as history would
prove, endangered. The music that filled these cinematic worlds, too, was
endangered, but for that reason as well, was powerfully and poignantly
Jewish.

Jewish music as Israeli music – national and nationalist ontologies

The exile, displacement, and return that rerouted modern Jewish history in
the early twentieth century were no less dramatic in resituating the ontological questions about the meaning of Jewish music. Rather than being posed
primarily in the lands of the diaspora and the Holocaust, the new questions
began to equate Jewish music and Israeli, and they searched for answers
in the culture and ideology of the State of Israel, even before its founding
in 1948. The early collectors began the process of rerouting Jewish music
history to the Yishuv, for example, when Idelsohn made his wax-cylinder
recordings in the communities formed of immigrants from the diaspora. In

the wake of World War I, with the collapse of nineteenth-century European nations and empires, Jewish settlers returned to mandatory Palestine, where they actively employed music in the processes of nation-building.[24] Ambitious plans were enacted to create recording collections, such as Robert Lachmann's in Berlin and after 1935 in Jerusalem,[25] and to build archives that would provide nothing short of a "World Centre for Jewish Music."[26] Folk songs in modern Hebrew were gathered from the *kibbutzim* (communal settlements) and circulated to Jewish composers throughout the world who might collectively create a national repertory of Israeli art song even prior to statehood.[27] Modern Jewish music, combining the old and the new, should become the music of Israel.

The new music of Israel provided contexts for reconfiguring the ontological moments of Jewish music as national – and as international. Israeli folk music, for example, would differ from Jewish folk music insofar as it resulted from the musical repertories and practices of immigrant and ethnic communities in Israel. Musical scholars turned their attention to the musical cultures of Yemenite-, Iraqi-, or Syrian-Israelis, many of which developed repertories and rituals in languages that were identifiably Jewish, such as the Judeo-Arabic of the Yemenite Jewish *diwan* tradition. The study of liturgical music in Israel spread to Moroccan *baqqashot* and Sephardi *romances* in the South American, Greek, or Turkish community. Israeli music was vast enough to embrace the multitude of differences that had historically distinguished Jewish musics.[28]

Israeli art-music composers, too, confronted the need to accept or reject concepts of Jewish music. Those composers who chose to create a style that would reflect the modern nation, for example Paul Ben-Haim (1897–1984), had the opportunity of drawing from a vast store of sounds, genres, and repertories to shape movements such as Eastern Mediterraneanism. Composers preferring, instead, to reject a strictly nationalist compositional style, for example Josef Tal (1910–2008), still engaged with the historical materials of Jewish music to shape their more personal or cosmopolitan vision of Israeli music.

Popular music in Israel, too, followed a historical course that moved through numerous repertories that contained traditional Jewish practices, or had formed along the borders with non-Jewish neighboring communities.[29] *Musica mizrakhit* (eastern music) provided the basis for popular music in the rapidly growing eastern Jewish ethnic communities at the end of the twentieth century, but it contained a rich store of sounds for other popular musicians to make their musics Israeli. At its most cosmopolitan extremes, popular musics in Israel are notable because they rarely forego sounding Israeli in some way, and this often means not foregoing the identifiably Jewish. Israeli jazz festivals in Europe or the United States, for example, regularly turn to synagogues for concert venues. The mix of global and local that Israel brings to the annual Eurovision Song Contest also insists on a fusion of the Jewish and the Israeli, often to political and ideological ends. The musicians of modern Israel, whether creators of folk, popular, or art music, whether working with traditional materials or forging avant-garde experimentalism, sustain a history of defining and redefining Jewish music and the twenty-first-century ontological moments in which we experience that music.

Jewish music beyond itself

By setting biblical texts in "Der Mensch" (Example 1.1) Hanns Eisler was not trying to compose music that was in some way specifically Jewish, or that would conform to the expectations of those compelled to define music as Jewish. He aspired, instead, to create a moment in which the Jewish elements from which he drew allowed the song to become more than itself. His turn to an ontological moment of Jewish music was for Eisler a search for transcendence. By recognizing its ontology as Jewish music Eisler actually unleashed it from definitions that would limit and isolate Jewish music to no more than itself, a cipher of essentialized identity unable to escape itself. Definitions of Jewish music made evident the permeability of borders and boundaries, the sites of agency. Eisler recognized, indeed believed, that Jewish music had the potential to make history – historiographically and ontologically – in those moments when Jewish music could be more than itself.

The explorations of meaning that I undertake in this chapter illustrate the paradox and counterpoint that determine the many paths of Jewish music history. The counterhistories that we witness at the ontological moments of Jewish music are many rather than few, and they rarely afford us the materials for definitions. Jewish music today bears witness to what we might call the "anti-teleology" of Jewish history. The belief that history converges with an in-gathering after diaspora is countered by the expanded and more complex presence of Jewish music in the world – and Jewish music in world music. When we consider ontologies and definitions historically and situate them in Jewish intellectual history, however, we recognize that they have long been anti-teleological: they are responsive and resistive; they make space for self and other; they may be highly exclusive and broadly inclusive. It is these many processes that we witness in the chapters of this volume that ultimately bring us closer to a field of definitions and ontologies of Jewish music that expands at each ontological moment as Jewish music becomes more than itself.

Notes

1 See Andrea F. Bohlman and Philip V. Bohlman, *Hanns Eisler: In der Musik ist es anders* (Berlin: Hentrich & Hentrich, 2012).

2 Andrea F. Bohlman and Philip V. Bohlman, "(Un)Covering Hanns Eisler's *Hollywood Songbook*," *Danish Yearbook of Musicology*, 35 (2007): 13–29.

3 Hanns Eisler, *Hollywooder Liederbuch* (Leipzig: Deutscher Verlag für Musik, 2008), 96.

4 See, for example, the broad use of these techniques in the biblical songs recorded by Abraham Zvi Idelsohn, in Gerda Lechleitner (ed.), *The Collection of Abraham Zvi Idelsohn (1911–1913)* (Vienna: Verlag der Österreichischen Akademie der Wissenschaften, 2005), three compact discs and booklet.

5 See, for example, Ruth HaCohen, *The Music Libel against the Jews* (New Haven: Yale University Press, 2011).

6 Philip V. Bohlman, *Jüdische Volksmusik – Eine mitteleuropäische Geistesgeschichte* (Vienna: Böhlau, 2005); idem, "Wie die Popularmusik jüdisch wurde," *Transversal*, 7.1 (2006): 61–75.

7 See Philip V. Bohlman, "Music," in Martin Goodman, Jeremy Cohen, and David Sorkin (eds.), *The Oxford Handbook of Jewish Studies* (Oxford University Press, 2002), 852–69.

8 Cf. Heidy Zimmermann, *Tora und Shira: Untersuchungen zur Musikauffassung des rabbinischen Judentums* (Bern: Peter Lang, 2000); Naomi Seidman, *Faithful Renderings: Jewish-Christian Difference and the Politics of Translation* (University of Chicago Press, 2006); Paul Ricoeur, *On Translation*, trans. Eileen Brennan (London and New York: Routledge, 2006), 18–22.

9 Rüdiger Bartelmus, *Theologische Klangrede: Musikalische Resonanzen auf biblische Texte* (Münster: LIT Verlag, 2012).

10 See, for example, Abraham Z. Idelsohn, *Jewish Music in Its Historical Development* (New York: Henry Holt, 1929), 92–128.

11 See Motti Regev and Edwin Seroussi, *Popular Music and National Culture in Israel* (Berkeley and Los Angeles: University of California Press, 2004).

12 Philip V. Bohlman and Otto Holzapfel (eds.), *The Folk Songs of Ashkenaz*, Recent Researches in the Oral Traditions of Music 6 (Middleton, WI: A-R Editions, 2001).

13 Don Harrán, *Salamone Rossi: Jewish Musician in Late Renaissance Mantua* (Oxford University Press, 1999).

14 See, for example, "Graf von Rom" (The Count of Rome), in its printed version with Hebrew letters from 1600, in Bohlman and Holzapfel (eds.), *Folk Songs of Ashkenaz*, 90–102.

15 Bohlman, *Jüdische Volksmusik*.

16 Salomon Sulzer, *Schir Zion: Gesänge für den israelitischen Gottesdienst*, 2nd edn. (Leipzig: M. W. Kaufmann, 1865; orig. publ. 1840–1).

17 Theodor Herzl, *Altneuland* (Berlin: Jüdischer Verlag, 1935; orig. publ. 1904), 214.

18 Abraham Zvi Idelsohn, *Phonographierte Gesänge und Aussprachsproben des Hebräischen der jemenitischen, persischen und syrischen Juden* (Vienna: Alfred Hölder, 1917).

19 Mark Katz, *Capturing Sound: How Technology Has Changed Music*, rev. ed. (Berkeley and Los Angeles: University of California Press, 2010).

20 Robert Lachmann, *Gesänge der Juden auf der Insel Djerba*, Yuval Monograph Series 7 (Jerusalem: Magnes Press of the Hebrew University, 1978; orig. publ. 1940).

21 Abraham Zvi Idelsohn, *Hebräisch-orientalischer Melodienschatz*, 10 vols. (Leipzig: Breitkopf and Härtel, 1914; Jerusalem, Berlin, and Vienna: Benjamin Harz, 1922–9; and Leipzig: Friedrich Hofmeister, 1932).

22 Lechleitner (ed.), *Collection of Abraham Zvi Idelsohn*.

23 Theodor W. Adorno and Hanns Eisler, *Composing for the Films* (Oxford University Press, 1947).

24 Jehoash Hirshberg, *Music in the Jewish Community of Palestine, 1880–1948: A Social History* (Oxford University Press, 1995).

25 Ruth F. Davis (ed.), *The "Oriental Music" Broadcasts 1936–1937: A Musical Ethnography of Mandatory Palestine*, Recent Researches in the Oral Traditions of Music 10 (Middleton, WI: A-R Editions, 2013).

26 Philip V. Bohlman, *The World Centre for Jewish Music in Palestine, 1936–1940: Jewish Musical Life on the Eve of World War II* (Oxford University Press, 1992).

27 Hans Nathan (ed.) *Israeli Folk Music: Songs of the Early Pioneers*, Recent Researches in the Oral Traditions of Music 4 (Madison, WI: A-R Editions, 1994).

28 Philip V. Bohlman and Mark Slobin (eds.), *Music in the Ethnic Communities of Israel*, special ed. of *Asian Music*, 17.2 (1986).

29 Regev and Seroussi, *Popular Music and National Culture*.

2 Jewish music and diaspora

EDWIN SEROUSSI

Diaspora (from Greek διασπορά, "scattering, dispersion") referred in Greek Antiquity to a population of a specific geographical origin that became scattered throughout a wider area. The Israelites, who were substantially dispersed throughout the Middle East and the Mediterranean basin already during the Hellenistic period (roughly the fifth to first centuries BCE), became a paradigm for the application of this concept in a wider sense and hence its modern association with the Jews. In the past half century diaspora was adopted (not only by scholars) to describe every possible physical or imagined, voluntary or forced displacement of individuals or communities from their real or imaginary homeland for multiple reasons (political, economic, racial, religious). Considering its dramatic expansion, it is questionable whether the concept of diaspora can still serve as an effective working tool for the study of the musical cultures of the Jews.[1] If diaspora has become such a precarious concept due to the human propensity to be on the move since the shadows of history, why insist on using it? Or why prefer diaspora to alternative concepts with similar connotations, such as displacement or exile,[2] global ethnoscapes,[3] networks and hubs,[4] etc., brought in periodically to add to the inexhaustible supply of academic jargon? And yet, how can one discuss any aspect of Jewish culture, let alone music, by dispensing with diaspora, at least in the plural? For by saying "musical cultures of the Jews," we imply from the get-go a sonic multiplicity that challenges any monolithic notion of *a* diaspora that modern nationalist Jewish discourses, Zionist or diasporic, constructed as their other/inner self.[5]

Before moving on to a discussion of diaspora in relation to Jewish musical cultures, a brief summary of its use in music studies is due. The short but incisive discussions of diaspora by Slobin are the best point of departure.[6] He stresses that diaspora "is heavily contextual." It can mean a blessing or a threat, an ideal or a curse. It also refuses standardization, as shown by Slobin's critique of the loose uses and abuses of the term in ethnomusicological studies, and "threatens to spiral out of control."[7] He warns us particularly of the overly metaphorical applications of the term that detach it from the actual bodies of the displaced individuals that are the object of research. And he concludes that diaspora is most effective as an explanatory tool when applied, simply, to "the existence of an identified population that feels that it is away from its homeland, however imagined, however distant in time and space," and more subtly, that "it involves more than demographics... some sort of consciousness of separation, a gap, a disjuncture [that] must be present."[8]

Interestingly Slobin finds solace from his critical and rather pessimistic assessment of the (ab)uses of diaspora in ethnomusicology in studies of Jewish musical cultures (including his own work on klezmer). While discussing Kay Kaufman Shelemay's study of the music of the Aleppo (Syrian) Jewish enclave in Brooklyn,[9] a classic case of multilayered Jewish and Arabic diaspora, he poetically draws what appear to be the limits that the concept of diaspora must maintain to remain viable: "Small groups tack with the steering winds to find their way to the communal harbor of their imagination. In so doing they may refuse to take fellow passengers on board."[10] Diaspora is therefore marked by the subjects' act of excluding others. In his final remarks, Slobin brings into the discussion "the [diasporic] scholar [subject] as [a] central agent in the drama of diaspora," for she may either conceal in her research her own diasporic experience or stress too much her own subjective positioning in the field.[11] Slobin also emphasizes the "intersection of diaspora and globalization, not in the commercial, but in the affinity sense of intercultural traffic."[12] In the volatile present, diaspora as a demographic or social fact is hardly sustainable, for it can also denote "anything from a marketing strategy to a state of mind."[13]

In short, these days the concept of diaspora inhabits its own diasporic niche. In this process of recalibration, diaspora rejects its rather restrictive past connotations in favor of much more fluid ones, of explanatory powers that can address the unbound musical reality of the present. From this vantage point no other case study is more worthy of using diaspora as a theoretical tool than "Jewish music" in its uncontrolled contemporary developments. But before addressing the contemporary Jewish music scene, some remarks about the historical backdrop of Jewish diaspora(s) are in order.

Recent scholarship has demolished the two basic binaries that marked any discussion of Jewish diaspora in the past, i.e., Land of Israel/diaspora and homeland/dispersion. Substantial numbers of Israelites lived outside the Promised Land (even in its most generous boundaries) after the destruction of the First Temple (586 BCE). In the heyday of the Jewish Kingdoms during the Second Temple period, substantial contingents of Jews inhabited the Mediterranean rim from Western North Africa and Italy to present-day Turkey and beyond to Babylonia. In short, 70 CE (the date of destruction of the Second Temple by the Roman armies) is only a crucial point in a long history of Israelite dispersion, not its "official" beginning. Doron Mendels and Aryeh Edre'i argue that following the destruction of the Temple, two radically different Judaic diasporas co-existed in late antiquity, a Greek-(and later Latin-) speaking one West of Palestine and an Aramaic/Hebrew-speaking one in the Middle East (Palestine, the Arabian Peninsula, and Babylonia).[14] At the same time, a substantial Jewish population flourished in the Land of Israel under Roman Byzantine rule until the Arab/Muslim conquest (634 CE), thus subverting the basic condition of any diaspora: a physical detachment from the homeland soil. Put differently, diaspora became associated with the loss of national independence and not necessarily with being uprooted from the national territory; Jews experienced (and flourished in) the diaspora in their Promised Land for about half a millennium.

By the early medieval period the diasporic Jewish centers in western Europe (especially the Iberian Peninsula, France, and Germany), North Africa, and the Arab and Persian Near East were well established, and only then did the Land of Israel become a distant object linked to messianic hopes. Forced and voluntary migrations from these medieval centers to central and eastern Europe (from Germany and France) and later on to the Ottoman Empire (from Spain and Portugal) created further displacements. Layers of memories (including musical ones) from more recently lost homelands were added to the remembrance of the supra-temporal Zion, the place to which Jews longed to return as expressed in their daily prayers. The creation of the transnational Sephardic polity after the expulsion of the Jews from Spain and Portugal is a classic example of a second-stage displacement that sometimes generated an overemphasized longing for a lost "homeland" (the Iberian Peninsula, especially around the celebratory quincentenary of 1992[15]), but it is not the only one. Jewish life in the early modern Austro-Hungarian and Russian empires, and later on in the nation-states that emerged from the ashes of these empires, established new boundaries of Jewish diasporism. Transnational, imagined homelands marked by language and liturgical practices such as "Ashkenaz" (the heirs to the entire commonwealth of Eastern European communities) collided with discrete diasporic spaces, such as Prague, which was home to a large, idiosyncratic, and ever-changing Jewish community. Modern political/territorial Zionism and the eventual establishment of a Jewish nation-state in 1948 did not end diaspora as we have already hinted, but rather exacerbated its presence as a permanent reality as well as a working concept in scholarly discourses, musicology included.

Diaspora was supposed to lose its perennial status as the transitional and yet unbounded temporal and physical space inhabited by Jews until messianic redemption, when modern Jewish nationalism framed its limits between two points of ethno-national independence, the Second Temple Kingdom and the modern State of Israel. However, the majority of modern

Jews did not join the territorial project and many opposed it vehemently in the name of diaspora. Diaspora Jewish nationalism became an alternative (or oppositional) practice, as articulated, for example, in the scholarly writings of Daniel and Jonathan Boyarin.[16] Yet, while the Jews who joined the Jewish nation-state project by choice or by lack of alternative may have left the diaspora behind, the diaspora did not leave them. The craving for diasporic pasts became a permanent feature of Jewish sovereign territory and the Israeli culture that developed in it;[17] and the "negation of the diaspora," the constitutive figure of speech of political Zionism, admitted *de facto* the strong theological conception of the Jews as an exiled people upon which modern Jewish territorial nationalism built its foundations (the Hebrew concept of *galut* has a much stronger theological connotation of "exile," as opposed to *golah* or *pezurah*, the watered-down modern Hebrew terms for diaspora in the sense of "dispersion"[18]). As we shall see below, music became the field of cultural expression in which diaspora had one of its strongest showings against its rhetorical negation.[19]

Diaspora was supposed to be eradicated by the restoration of territorial "normality," with the founding of the state of Israel. But there is no "normal" type of human existence, only ever-changing patterns of social adjustment dictated by the prevailing social order of each period and place. The paradigm of "normal" modern existence is citizenship in a secular nation-state, a feeble corporation that is relentlessly challenged by its various cohabiting ethnic, racial, religious, and socioeconomic constituencies and minorities or by other threatening nation-states. Jews succumbed to this paradigm of modern "normality" and thus diverse forms of nationalism became the centerpiece of modern Jewish policies and practices, music included.

To summarize this introduction: the musical cultures of the Jews as they reached us in the modern period (which are the main resource for research since the Jewish musical pasts are hardly documented) consist of multiple strata. They betray numerous musical experiences based on layers of memory of and longing for several past homelands at the individual and community levels. Musicological discourse on Jewish music has attempted to manage this multiplicity along crude ethno-geographical boundaries, such as the common binary set Ashkenazic/Sephardic or subsets such as East/West Ashkenazi. The mapping out of clusters of Jewish musical styles and repertoires along such modern divides obliterated countless nuances based on place and time.

Jewish musical cultures in the diaspora emerged, then, in two fundamental social settings: imperial (in their order of appearance on the stage: Greco-Roman, Byzantine, Persian, Arab/Islamic, Russian/Polish, Ottoman, and Austro-Hungarian) and national, as a result of the dismantling of empires and the birth of modern nation-states in their stead (starting technically with the French Revolution, but with antecedents in early modern nations such as the Netherlands). Yet transimperial and transnational networks are also crucial components in understanding Jewish musical cultures as diasporic. For example, many musicians, especially cantors, crossed great distances (even in the medieval period) and carried musical capital from place to place, homogenizing sometimes-liturgical repertoires across the frontiers of empires and nations.

Another way of mapping out diasporic Jewish musical cultures is by language divides. While the use of Hebrew in the liturgical context helped to maintain a certain sense of a transimperial and transnational Jewish nation, major vernacular Jewish languages such as Judeo-Arabic, Judeo-German, Judeo-Persian, and Judeo-Spanish contributed to a sense of musical commonwealths across political boundaries. Minority Jewish groups living in relatively greater isolation maintained other languages (such as Berber in the Atlas Mountains in Morocco; Neo-Aramaic and Kurmanji throughout the Kurdish areas of Turkey, Iraq, and Iran; Juhuri in the eastern Caucasus; Malayalam in south-west India, and so forth) and therefore discrete musical traditions.

Transimperial and transnational criteria and linguistic areas are not enough to account for the great musical diversity of diasporic Jews. A third module is the various degrees of affinity between the music of the Jews and that of the non-Jewish surrounding cultures, or put differently, to what degree there is a justification in separating the music of the Jews from that of non-Jews sharing the same place. Social interaction and exchanges of musical capital between Jews and non-Jews vary of course according to coordinates of time and place. Modern assumptions about the relative isolation of pre-modern Jews through religious discrimination, physical segregation (Jewish quarters, villages, ghettos, etc.), and, later on, racial intolerance, as well as the continued series of expulsions, led to perceptions of Jewish musical exceptionality. Jews certainly participated in their co-territorial soundscape, but the degrees of their access to or adaptation of the surrounding music varied in time and place.[20]

Let us examine cases of musical interactions across denominations in a space where Jews were usually perceived (from the modern standpoint) as being utterly segregated: medieval Western Europe. A central musical institution in that space, the church, was of course inaccessible to Jews. And yet, one cannot discard *tout court* the exposure of Jews to Christian musical repertoires, for example in shared spaces such as taverns, open-space Christian processions, or regional fairs. Conspicuous contemporary accounts of such interdenominational musical contacts emerge from traditions embedded in the foundational twelfth-century tractate *Sefer Hasidim*, stemming from the pietistic circles of Hasidei Ashkenaz in the Rhein valley. Scenes depicted in this source reveal Jews performing Christian music, for example as a strategy of survival: "One said: 'And when I am among the Gentiles I sing [lit. "say"] songs [*mizmorim*, here perhaps meaning Psalms] in their language to fulfill [the command] wisdom preserves in the lives of its possessors [Ecclesiastes 7:12].'"[21] In other cases it is the Christian side that is after the Jewish musical lore: "If there is a priest who wishes to create a [sacred] song [*piyyut*] for idolatry ['*avodah zarah*] or a gentile [wishes] to sing a [non-religious] song [*zemer*] and he says to a Jew: 'tell me a pleasant tune [*niggun na'im*] that you praise your God with it,' he shall not tell him [the tune], [and is better] not to be next to him [to the Gentile]."[22] Written evidence from the late medieval period shows that Judeo-German songs were set not only to the melodies of shared German folk songs, but also to Christian tunes.[23]

Moving into the realm of instrumental music, the Gentile-Jewish inter-action is even more intense, due to the semantic neutrality of these reper-toires. Making instrumental music is also a craft that allows the Jewish musi-cian to service non-Jewish constituencies without major compromises. This interdenominational flow of instrumental repertoires in eastern Europe, evident in the klezmer repertoires recorded commercially in the early twen-tieth century, was reciprocal. Instrumental tunes not only traversed from the non-Jewish to the Jewish repertoires, but also moved in the opposite direc-tion when *klezmorim* performed, for non-Jewish audiences, tunes from the Jewish sphere that were recognized as Jewish by the gentiles. On the other hand, non-Jewish musicians served Jewish constituencies, infusing internal Jewish spaces with the sounds of the majority. For example, in Tunisia in the seventeenth century, the traveling Rabbi Abraham Ibn Mūsā (Tetuán c. 1680–Tunis 1733) testified: "I witnessed a scandal . . . [Jews from Tunis] bring to their houses on holidays, and sometimes on week days, gentiles who play *kinnor* [Ar. *kamanja*] and *nevel* [Ar. '*ūd*] and *tof* [drum, probably *ṭār*] and *ḥalil* [wind instrument, perhaps the *ghayṭa*] . . . and men intermingle with women."[24] Such destabilizing sonic breaches in the barriers marking discrete denominational spaces are a constant feature of Jewish life under Islam and Christianity from the medieval to the modern period.

Tracing down the musical repertoires on the basis of geo-political units, considering linguistic criteria, and being aware of the shared musical spaces of Jews with non-Jews allow some systematic orientation in the otherwise untidy maze of diasporic musical heritages of the Jews. In light of this diasporic musical diversity, whereas Jews in every place and time constructed their soundscapes on a local basis, the creation of the Zionist-inclined musicological model designed by Abraham Zvi Idelsohn (1882–1938) in the earlier ("Palestinian") period of his career becomes clear. Looking for

exceptional Jewish musical traits in the sonic labyrinth of the Jewish diaspora
on the basis of racial criteria (even if in a concealed language) was a *sine
qua non* of Idelsohn's modern national enterprise of what Ruth Katz has
referred to as "exemplifying Jewish music."[25]

But the vast musical and literary evidence that Idelsohn compiled was
hard to digest, especially when one enters the early modern period. Even
within the confines of the innermost soundscape shared and scrupulously
maintained by Jews everywhere, Biblical cantillation, awareness of distinctions on the basis of diasporic traditions popped up as early as pre-modern
times. Biblical cantillation was discussed in the medieval period by rabbinical scholars such as Yehuda Halevy and Profiat Duran as a music genre;
according to them, this Hebrew *ur-musik* was assumed to be shared by all
Jews and remained untouched by external musical influences. As soon as the
late fifteenth century, however, such a monolithic perception was challenged
and diasporic variety emerged even from this most sacred of sacred musical spaces. A text that Idelsohn also uncritically quotes, the tractate *Sefer
Tuv Ta'am* (Venice, 1539) by the grammarian Eliyahu Bakhur (1469–1549),
provides a vivid example of internal Jewish perceptions of musical self and
other.[26] Bakhur opens his treatise on the *te'amim* (Masoretic accents) saying
"Anochi Ha-Ashkenazi Eliyah" (I, Eliyah the Ashkenazi), immediately situating himself as a member of a Jewish subculture writing for the multiethnic
Jewish audience of early modern Venice. Later he says:

> The reading [of the Torah] of the Sephardim and the *Lo'azim* [the
> autochthonous Italian Jews] [is unique in that] they do not sing
> [*menaggnim*] anything other than the important *malakhim* ["Kings," the
> main stopping accents] and perhaps some others such as *zarqah, pazer,
> gershayim*, and *tlisha* and the like. But they sing almost all the *meshartim*
> ["Serfs," the subsidiary accents that connect between the stops] with one
> [and the same] melody, unlike us the Ashkenazim who do read each accent,
> whether a "King" or a "Serf," with its unique melody. And all the melodies
> of the [Ashkenazi] *te'amim* were already printed by the Gentiles in
> accordance with the science of song [*hokhmat hashir*] that is called *musiqa*
> and whoever knows the science of song is able to sing them as we do,
> without any mistake.[27]

From this passage clear sonic distinctions emerge between three diasporas,
Ashkenazic, Sephardic, and Italian, separated by an internal Jewish ethnic
discourse based on comparative parameters. Such a discourse appears in
Renaissance Italy when Jews of diverse provenances ("diasporas") settled
in very close physical proximity, allowing comparisons to surface. But the
contemporary dialogue between Jewish scholars in Italy and Renaissance
Christian Hebraists also emerges from this document. Bakhur refers in it

to the epoch-making musical transcriptions of the Ashkenazic (German) Biblical cantillation by Johannes Reuchlin (1455–1522), in his treatise *De Accentibus, et orthographia linguae hebraicae* (Haguenau, 1518). For Reuchlin, the (Ashkenazic) performance that he observed (or rather listened to) represented the recitation of the Bible by the entire "Jewish nation" rather than the discrete subculture of his Judeo-German informant. On the other hand, Bakhur readily accepts the power of the new technology, printed musical notation, to represent his tradition and to enable its decoding with remarkable consistency (namely, in a scientific manner that challenges oral transmission). This seminal text by Bakhur shows that diaspora awareness, at least in Italy by the early sixteenth century, was delineated among Jews themselves in terms of musical practices. In a parallel move, Gentile savants interested in Jewish music perceived the music of any Jew, regardless of ethnic origins, as specimens representing the sound of the entire Jewish nation.

We move in a giant leap forward from the early sixteenth century to the mid-nineteenth century, when the concept of "Jewish music" started to emerge among scholars and practitioners in major European urban centers, such as Berlin, Vienna, Paris, and Saint Petersburg. All scholarly practices of modernity, including ethnography, classification, canonization, publication, and institutionalized education, were recruited by cantor-scholars to demarcate "Jewish music." The delineation of music styles, genres, and performance practices by Jewish "ethnic groups" became the main strategy. From this moment on, the self-perceptions of Jewish individuals and small groups as possessing distinct musical capitals was erased, not in practice but in the public discourses about such practices.

The rise of ethnography is particularly pertinent for the present discussion of diaspora. For urban (and generally assimilated) European Jewish ethnographers, "diaspora" becomes the place authentic Jewish culture inhabits, and in which it is in danger of disappearance under the inevitable weight of modernization and urbanization. Those scholars – one can mention the Russian Joel Engel (1868–1927) as the archetypal one – distanced as they were from the folk traditions that they set to freeze through ethnography, conceptualized themselves as living outside of the diaspora, in the "real" world. Ethnography of course also became a resource for the creation of national Jewish music, among both territorialized Zionist as well as diasporic Jewish composers.[28]

The major work of Jewish musical codification of the early twentieth century, Idelsohn's *Thesaurus* (1914–32) was instrumental in the processes of modern musical regeneration more than any other previous publication on Jewish music.[29] Idelsohn's cataloguing of Jewish musical traditions in ten volumes introduced to the public arena categories of diasporic Jewish music that obliterated other more discrete perceptions of place. Of course, his decisions were shaped by technological constraints and the financial considerations of his publishers. And yet, there is a clear sense that Idelsohn attempted to draw a programmatic division of the global Jewish musical map on the basis of variables that we have mentioned above in defining Jewish diasporas, i.e. language, geography, history, liturgical text, and more. Clearly, the providers of musical information for Idelsohn had limited agency in the design of his outline.

To flesh out this process of elaboration by Idelsohn, let us briefly consider the fifth volume of the *Thesaurus*, dedicated to the Moroccan Jews.[30] The volume is based on information provided to Idelsohn by a few members of the Maghrebi (North African) Jewish community residing in Jerusalem (most of whom emigrated in the mid-nineteenth century) that later on was complemented by data from two Jewish singers from Gibraltar. Such musical specimens could hardly encompass the richness of Jewish musical traditions within the Moroccan Sultanate in the early twentieth century. Idelsohn was relatively unaware of the intense Jewish involvement in and performance of Andalusian music, the "classical" music of the Moroccan elites and Sufi sects, in its Hebrew variant. As one learned half a century after Idelsohn's publication (with the massive immigration of Moroccan Jews to Israel), the Andalusian repertoire of which he was incognizant was a crucial component of the urban Moroccan Jewish musical self.

Yet the category "music of the Moroccan Jews" persisted once the vast majority of the multifaceted Moroccan Jewish diaspora moved to Israel during the 1950s. Certain distinctions on the basis of geographical provenance within Morocco (especially between the cities of the shore, the inner valleys, and the mountains) were maintained among the immigrants in Israel. These memories of localized diaspora persisted for a brief period but blurred under the pressure of social mobility and the internal Israeli politics of identity, whereas the artificial construct "music of the Moroccan Jews" could be manipulated to advance political agendas on the basis of ethnic interests. The establishment, in the early 1990s, of the Israeli Andalusian Orchestra, an institution dedicated to the exclusive performance of the "classical" music of urban Moroccan Jews, is the clearest example of such manipulation.[31] The founding repertoire of the orchestra (since then it has diversified) did not represent the entire spectrum of Moroccan Jewish Andalusian traditions, but rather the hegemonic repertoire from the southern cities of Marrakesh and Essaouira. Performers from these cities became dominant in the pre-emigration Jewish hub of Casablanca, the administrative French port to where a large contingent of Moroccan Jews from all parts of the country gravitated towards the end of the colonial period (mid-twentieth century). In sum, the Moroccan case shows how perceptions of diaspora within and about one Jewish group evolved through a short period of time from local to regional to national and post-national. Such perceptions eventually determined the survival of repertoires, performance practices, and power relations in the mass media at the outset of the twenty-first century.

To end this chapter, and in a sharp U-turn from the previous paragraph, I would like to return to the contemporary unrestrained use of diaspora against which Slobin so judiciously warned us. American discourses about Jewish music of recent times abound in glorifications of sonic diasporas, sometimes as a marketing strategy, sometimes as an ideology justifying aesthetic choices. One can just glance at the programming of events invoking diaspora such as "Voices of the Jewish Diaspora" (held in New York City on February 10 and 12, 2009), which featured "songs in many languages celebrating the culturally diverse Jewish communities that flourished as the tribes of Israel spread out across the globe."[32] The program included "Sephardic melodies" arranged by the contemporary American composer of Puerto Rican origin Roberto Sierra; Second Avenue tunes by Irving Berlin and Abraham Ellstein; art songs by Anton Rubinstein, Dmitri Shostakovich, Maurice Ravel, and Gustav Mahler; and music by George Gershwin, Leonard Bernstein, and Harold Rome. The "diasporic" diversity suggested by such a musical selection tells us little about how Jewish voices from discrete times and places related to each other in the past or present. Of course, the strategy of such an awkward musical line-up is merely commercial; tickets, after all, had to sell to an American public that was able to recognize the names of musicians as "Jewish." Yet it is poignant for any individual vaguely informed on music history that for the sake of marketing, "Jewish diaspora" composers such as Rubinstein and Mahler cannot escape, even in their graves, the Jewish genes that inhabited their bodies and from which they wanted to distance themselves just to be able to survive in their (well, diasporic...) hostile environments.

Besides such loose uses of the concept of Jewish diaspora in the American music market, the "condition of Diaspora" also provides the ideology behind, or the source for, the creative impetus of some American musicians of Jewish background. Forging "unexpected connections" between disparate musical styles is one of the benefits attributed to the "power of Diaspora" as much as a compelling explanation for the ideological eclecticism of the recordings in John Zorn's Radical Jewish Culture Series.[33] However, these dynamic and hybrid tendencies are not distinctively American. As Philip V. Bohlman has illustrated, they characterize the political and aesthetic challenges that "Jewish music" faced when encountering modernity in central Europe a century or so before.[34]

We can address now the paradox embedded in the persistent, late modern binary opposition of Israel versus diaspora in the field of music. Ever since the 1980s, the Israeli musical nationalism that reached its peak in the 1960s has been dwindling under the pervasive claims for sound spaces by the various musical diasporas exiled within its "independent" territory and the parallel global impulses motivating Israeli musicians to connect with the outside world. At the same time, American Jewish musical nationalism asserts itself as a confident contestant against what is perceived as Israeli claims of supremacy in setting the path for late modern Jewish culture, an argument that has been articulated by several American Jewish scholars and intellectuals.[35] Such diasporic musical alternative is cast on the (wishful) blurring of the religious/secular divide through common musical denominators, on a last-minute rescue of the vanishing eastern European Jewish soundscape, and on the rhetoric of American multiculturalism and world music. One can just think about Zorn and his Tzadik label, ensembles such as the Klezmatics and Pharaoh's Daughter, or academics such as Josh Kun, who has shown that an autochthonous American Jewish musical entertainment has grown out of and benefited from the complex of blessings and curses that resulted from the particularities of the American diasporic situation.[36]

Scholar and klezmer revivalist Hankus Netsky has recently articulated this self-celebrating "made in USA" secular Jewish musical diasporism, and his statement is worth quoting in its entirety:

> In twenty-first century America, creative Jewish artists and members of their audience are joined together on an inward search where boundaries defined during a previous century have fallen by the wayside. It is a time of new juxtapositions and re-contextualizations, as a generation looks to see what discards it can salvage to create meaning out of contemporary Jewish identity. Their musical mix might, at any moment, include secular songs devoid of the ideology that spawned them, or religious songs separated from the observance that used to give them meaning.
>
> It is hardly surprising that, in such a scene, feathers are occasionally ruffled and the Jewish establishment shakes its collective head wondering what's going on but, at this point, it's hardly for them to decide. Today's Jewish music scene is rich, diverse, confusing, occasionally controversial, sacred, secular, traditional, and innovative, very American – and very much alive.[37]

American Jewish musical diasporism brings back the relentless Jewish quest for a "center" that will alleviate the burden of diaspora. Bismarck's Second Reich and Franz Joseph's Austro-Hungarian Empire were serious (if ephemeral) candidates as final destinations for Jews to end all diasporas.

The rich musical expressions that Jews created in the urban centers of these empires, be it for internal consumption or as a contribution to the society at large, were as harmonious with the contemporary non-Jewish aesthetic sensibilities in all registers of musical creativity (art and popular) as later on would be the music of Sholom Secunda, George Gershwin, Irving Berlin, Moishe Oysher, and Leonard Bernstein in America.

Returning as a coda to the opening remarks of this chapter, it is safe to propose that Jewish musical cultures are contingent on a dialectical tension between a long series of periodical forced displacements of short and long *durée* that exposed Jews to a plethora of musical languages, and the quest for a center, any center (including a musical one), in the present. The assumption that the present demographic spread of the Jewish people, with two strong competing but grudgingly interacting triumphalist centers in (North) America and Israel whose musical cultures are nurtured by memories from other (nowadays mostly Jew-less) places, is here to stay forever cannot find strong support in historical experience. At the same time, an incisive critique of American Jewish diasporic and Israeli exceptionalism has emerged among late modern European Jewish intellectuals who challenge it in the name of diasporic Jewish Europeanism.[38]

The reemergence of a post-(World and Cold)War European Jewry on the wings of the European Union certainly proposes an interesting third stream with its own Jewish musical agendas. But the repatriated diasporic musical repertoires in present-day Europe are more frequently performed by non-Jews in spaces where the Jewish presence, if present at all, consists primarily of roots-seeking tourists.[39] In an interesting twist, non-Jewish Europeans are the carriers, as performers and audiences, of diasporic Jewish musical memories on the very soil of a most meaningful, long, and cataclysmic Jewish diaspora. And this turn of events further reinforces the temptation to dismiss diaspora from the vocabulary of cultural and social, let alone musicological, criticism.

Notes

Research for the writing of this article was supported by the I-CORE Program of the Planning and Budgeting Committee and The Israel Science Foundation (grant No. 1798/12).
1 Rogers Brubaker offers the most complete survey so far of the rather unbounded use of the term "diaspora" in the present-day social sciences and humanities, in "The 'Diaspora' Diaspora," *Ethnic and Racial Studies*, 28.1 (January 2005): 1–19. He was preceded by, among others, James Clifford's influential essay that includes a provocative and yet problematic section on Jewish diaspora, "Diasporas," in *Routes: Travel and Translation in the Late Twentieth Century* (Cambridge, MA: Harvard University Press, 1997), 244–78; and Robin Cohen, *Global Diasporas: An Introduction*, 2nd edn. (London and New York: Routledge, 2008 [1997]). The establishment of the specialized journal *Diaspora* in 1991 was the clearest symptom of the centrality of this concept in the study of culture and society in the post-national period. Brubaker's discussion moves forward by criticizing the tenets established by this journal.

2 Erik Levi and Florian Scheding (eds.), *Music and Displacement: Diasporas, Mobilities, and*

Dislocations in Europe and Beyond (Lanham, MD: Scarecrow Press, 2010).

3 Arjun Appadurai, *Modernity at Large: Cultural Dimensions of Globalization* (Minneapolis: University of Minnesota Press, 1996), ch. 3.

4 For these two last concepts that stress networks of individual musicians rather than discrete communities, see the articles in the online journal *Music and Arts in Motion*, 3.3 (2011), at www.musicandartsinaction.net/index .php/maia/issue/view/Vol%203%2C%20No %203 (accessed February 17, 2015), which emerged from a 2009 conference titled "Diaspora as Social and Cultural Practice: A Study of Transnational Networks across Europe and Africa."

5 For a comprehensive and yet succinct discussion of all shades of modern Zionist and diasporic Jewish nationalism and their interrelations, see Simon Rabinovitch, "Diaspora, Nation, and Messiah," in Simon Rabinovitch (ed.), *Jews and Diaspora Nationalism: Writings on Jewish Peoplehood in Europe and the United States* (Waltham, MA: Brandeis University Press, 2012), xv–xli.

6 Mark Slobin, "The Destiny of 'Diaspora' in Ethnomusicology," in Martin Clayton, Trevor Herbert, and Richard Middleton (eds.), *The Cultural Study of Music: A Critical Introduction* (New York: Routledge, 2003), 284–96. Slobin extensively rewrote his essay for the new 2012 second edition of *The Cultural Study of Music* (96–106), with which I became acquainted when the present chapter was mostly written. The new essay is not only more geographically inclusive but also more incisive than the former one in its lucid critique of "diaspora," suggesting as an option the "sliding away from these sorts of terms" and towards recognizing new forms of transnational citizenship. I am indebted to Professor Slobin for sending me a copy of his new text as well as for reading this article and contributing, as usual, insightful remarks. Slobin pioneered the discussion of the concept of diaspora in ethnomusicology when he edited a special issue of the journal *Diaspora*, 3.3 (Winter 1994), dedicated to music.

7 Slobin, "Destiny of 'Diaspora'" (2003), 295.

8 *Ibid.*, 288.

9 Kay Kaufman Shelemay, *Let Jasmine Rain Down: Song and Remembrance among Syrian Jews* (University of Chicago Press, 1998).

10 Slobin, "Destiny of 'Diaspora'" (2003), 290.

11 *Ibid.*, 291.

12 *Ibid.*, 292.

13 *Ibid.*

14 Doron Mendels and Aryeh Edre'i, *Zweierlei Diaspora zur Spaltung der antiken jüdischen Welt* (Göttingen: Vandenhoeck & Ruprecht, 2010).

15 See, for example, Judith R. Cohen, "'No so komo las de agora' (I'm Not Like Those Modern Girls): Judeo-Spanish Songs Meet the Twenty-First Century," *European Judaism*, 44.1 (2011): 151–64.

16 Daniel Boyarin and Jonathan Boyarin, "Diaspora: Generational Ground of Jewish Identity," *Critical Inquiry*, 19.4 (1993): 693–725.

17 Eli Lederhendler, "The Diaspora Factor in Israeli Life," in Anita Shapira (ed.), *Israeli Identity in Transition* (Westport, CT: Praeger, 2004), 109–36.

18 See Amnon Raz-Krakotzkin, "Exile through Sovereignty: A Critique of the 'Negation of the Exile' in Israeli Culture," *Theory and Criticism*, 4 (Fall 1993): 23–55 (Part 1), and 5 (Fall 1994): 113–32 (Part 2) (in Hebrew); and Anita Shapira (ed.), "Whatever Became of 'Negating Exile'?" in Shapira (ed.), *Israeli Identity*, 69–108.

19 For art music, see Assaf Shelleg, "Israeli Art Music: A Reintroduction," *Israel Studies*, 17.3 (Fall 2012): 119–49.

20 Edwin Seroussi, "Music: The 'Jew' of Jewish Studies," *Jewish Studies*, 46 (2009): 3–84 (5).

21 *Sefer Hasidim*, Bologna 1538, 220. (Translated by Edwin Seroussi.)

22 *Sefer Hasidim*, manuscript Parma 3280H, par. 1348. (Translated by Edwin Seroussi.) My research on music in *Sefer Hasidim* benefits enormously from the Princeton University Sefer Hasidim Database, http://etc.princeton.edu/ sefer_hasidim/index.php (accessed February 17, 2015), and I am deeply thankful to the team that established and maintains this database.

23 Diana Matut, *Dichtung und Musik im früühneuzeitlichen Aschkenas*, Studies in Jewish History and Culture 29, 2 vols. (Leiden and Boston: Brill, 2011).

24 MS Add. 19786, British Library, London, fol. 164v. See George Margoliouth and Jacob Leveen, *Catalogue of the Hebrew and Samaritan Manuscripts in the British Museum* (London: Trustees of the British Museum, 1965), no. 440.

25 Ruth Katz, "Exemplification and the Limits of 'Correctness': The Implicit Methodology of Idelsohn's *Thesaurus*," *The Abraham Zvi Idelsohn Memorial Volume*, Yuval Studies of the Jewish Music Research Center 5 (Jerusalem: Magnes, 1986), 365–71.

26 Abraham Zvi Idelsohn, *Gesänge der babylonischen Juden*, vol. II of *Hebräisch-orientalischer Melodienschatz* (Jerusalem, Berlin, and Vienna: Benjamin Harz, 1922), Introduction.

27 Eliyahu Bakhur, *Sefer Tuv Ta'am* (Venice, 1539), 7. (Translated by Edwin Seroussi.)

28 James Loeffler, *The Most Musical Nation: Jews and Culture in the Late Russian Empire* (New Haven: Yale University Press, 2010), 57–79.

29 Abraham Zvi Idelsohn, *Hebräisch-orientalischer Melodienschatz*, 10 vols (Leipzig: Breitkopf and Härtel, 1914; Jerusalem, Berlin, and Vienna: Benjamin Harz, 1922–9; and Leipzig: Friedrich Hofmeister, 1932).

30 Abraham Zvi Idelsohn, *Gesänge der marokkanischen Juden*, vol. V of *Hebräisch-orientalischer Melodienschatz* (Jerusalem, Berlin, and Vienna: Benjamin Harz, 1929).

31 On the Israel Andalusian orchestra, see Merav Aharon, "Riding the Culture Train: An Ethnography of a Plan for Social Mobility through Music," *Cultural Sociology*, 7 (2013): 447–62.

32 www.broadwayworld.com/article/Kaufman-Center-Presents-VOICES-OF-THE-JEWISH-DIASPORA-20090210 (accessed February 17, 2015).

33 Jeffrey Matthew Janeczko, *"Beyond Klezmer": Redefining Jewish Music for the Twenty-First Century*, Ph.D. dissertation, University of California, Los Angeles (2009).

34 Philip V. Bohlman, *Jewish Music and Modernity* (Oxford University Press, 2008).

35 Jonathan Boyarin and Daniel Boyarin, *The Powers of Diaspora: Two Essays on the Relevance of Jewish Culture* (Minneapolis: University of Minnesota Press, 2002).

36 See, for example, Josh Kun, *Audiotopia: Music, Race, and America* (Berkeley and Los Angeles: University of California Press, 2005), ch. 2.

37 Hankus Netsky, "Secular Jewish Musical Expression – Is Nothing Sacred?" *Journal of Synagogue Music*, 37 (Fall 2012): 173–86.

38 See, for example, Michael Galchinsky, "Concepts of Diaspora and Galut," in Sandra Lustig and Ian Leveson (eds.), *Turning the Kaleidoscope: Perspectives on European Jewry* (New York: Berghahn Books, 2006), 63–78.

39 The presence of Jewish music in late modern European spaces devoid of Jewish populations is an important subject in Ruth Ellen Gruber's groundbreaking book on representations of Jewish culture in contemporary Europe. See Ruth Ellen Gruber, *Virtually Jewish: Reinventing Jewish Culture in Europe* (Berkeley and Los Angeles: University of California Press, 2002).

3 The institutions of Jewish musical meaning

JUDAH M. COHEN

Western aesthetic traditions often present musical encounters as immaterial acts. Presented in a manner that emphasizes the purity of experience, these moments promote sound's ability to raise humanity into unencumbered, transcendent realms. Music, stripped of physical constraints, becomes its own basis for "appreciation" to listeners, critics, and many scholars. What you hear, in other words, serves as a starting point for discussions of musical identity, form, genre, and quality. As a practical consequence, we tend to prioritize the abstract concept of sound – massless pulses traveling through space – over the social, economic, and physical conditions that make such sounds possible.

The sounds and performances variously interpreted as "Jewish" music face similar criteria: religious services and concerts, combined with a well-maintained canon of melodies, styles, and compositions, parlay the immediacy of "the music itself" into more general claims about Judaism, tradition, and communal identity. Such claims stand as a founding premise for the scholarly study of Jewish music. Abraham Zvi Idelsohn (1882–1938), credited as a father of the modern field, saw his work as a means of recreating the original music of the Jews, thereby offering a new/ancient soundtrack for revitalizing Jewish life in Palestine, Europe, and America. Cantors similarly used academic rigor to establish their ability to present Jewish sound to the lay public. Alongside composers, conductors, and others who linked Jewishness to specific sounds, these figures saw value in the idea that the Jew who hears "Jewish music" should resonate with it, and reconnect with an internal sense of Jewish heritage, while those who did not resonate immediately could be taught to do so.

Yet this approach presents only a part of the picture. Just as important as the moment of sonic encounter is the institutional framework that makes such encounters possible. As collective entities created to define, transmit, and/or conserve values and identities through the collection and distribution of resources – such as synagogues, schools, Jewish community organizations (such as Federations), and "Jewish identity organizations" funded by private philanthropies – institutions typically devote resources to self-interested agendas. At the same time, these groups in aggregate create an ecosystem that supports artists and exposes their work to targeted populations. The forces that make the concert, the religious service, or the wedding dance possible, therefore, also tend to direct listeners in how to interpret music in the first place. Viewed from this perspective, music's qualities become quite different: paradoxically, institutions must devote substantial material resources in order to manifest music's immaterial status. Training and support, as well as appropriate instruments and venues, become *prerequisites* for musical activity. Performance sites, moreover, impose cultural expectations on the music presented therein; and the criteria for access to those sites, such as ticket purchases, help to define both the audience and the values of music listening. Advertisements, sheet music, and recordings require the services of skilled individuals as well as meaningful distribution outlets, all of whom need funding to operate. As with other performance-based modes of expression, music exists in large part because someone *pays* for it to exist.

Some streams of scholarship view the financial and artistic dimensions of music as incompatible or even antithetical, particularly if institutional concerns are seen to compromise romanticized notions of music's cultural integrity. Yet recent, and expanding, literature on musical genres and the music industry show significant advantages to exploring the two in tandem, revealing that creativity rarely takes place in a true vacuum.[1] The multivalent category of "Jewish music" provides a particularly salient example, since institutions have been heavily involved in constructing, disseminating, and mediating ideas about Jewish musical tradition for at least the last two centuries, even as they have excelled at erasing their efforts from the historical record.[2] By reintroducing them into the discussion, we open a world of negotiated expectations that complicates the way we think of aural tradition. Rather than just accepting "Jewish music" as an artistic conceit, in other words, we can see how changing socioeconomic conditions, combined with communal needs, have shaped the ways that people define and encounter it.

A discussion of the brief but ubiquitous melody to the prayer known as the *Shema* (Hear O Israel, Deuteronomy 6:4) serves as a useful way into this mode of thinking. Illustrated in Example 3.1, the tune emerged from several triple-time variants between the 1830s and 1920s; but the exact melody used today appears to have gained popularity on or around 1932, when the American Reform Jewish movement published its new edition of *The Union Hymnal*.[3] This new hymnal, the movement's first since 1914, reflected renewed attempts to find a musical style that would attract Jews to religious services by appealing to ancient Jewish tradition. Seemingly consistent with this mission, editor Abraham W. Binder (1895–1966) added the tune to the book more than once, calling it "Traditional" or leaving out attribution altogether.

Example 3.1 The "Sulzer" *Shema*, harmonized according to the 1932 *Union Hymnal* (New York: Central Conference of American Rabbis), 433.

After the founding of the Hebrew Union College School of Sacred Music in 1948, the *Shema* tune's fortunes changed somewhat. Cantors, seeking partly to model their training after music conservatories, sought to reestablish a culture of authorial and compositional attribution in the Western art music tradition. Consequently, when Gershon Ephros (1890–1978), a cantor and instructor at the School of Sacred Music, included the tune in the fifth volume of his *Cantorial Anthology* (1957), he gave it a stylistic attribution to renowned Vienna cantor/composer Salomon Sulzer (1804–90). Because of the book's centrality to a renewed cantorial education, the tune's new attribution spread. By the end of the twentieth century, cantors made Sulzer's authorship of the *Shema* a major teaching point for congregants. By linking it to Europe's best-known synagogue music reformer, they reinforced a strong sense of Reform Jewish heritage, while tying themselves to the figure they credited with founding the modern cantorate.

Although this shift had an organic appearance, institutions in fact made it possible: they necessitated and funded the creation of new reference materials (*The Union Hymnal, The Cantorial Anthology*), centralized their use (through new cantorial schools), and established communal distribution networks. The result, even on this small scale, shows the power that financial and institutional support has to direct conversations about "Jewish" music. While scholarship has typically dealt with this phenomenon glancingly, it is impossible to overstate its importance. So much of the literature has been connected with these institutions, moreover, that it has become, in many cases, an inextricable yet unstated part of the conversation.

This example also reveals the fundamentally fragile nature of the term "Jewish music" itself. Rather than accepting the term at face value, we must assume that the decision to designate sound as Jewish ultimately resides somewhere between the efforts of the individual and the collective. Yet concerns for the collective tend to set the agenda, determining through the allocation of resources and institutional support the identity of sounds, note patterns, and "Jewish" qualities. While it might be too strong to claim that financial support *makes* "Jewish music," in other words, it remains important to incorporate into the conversation the considerable, deep, and invested relationship such support has had in shaping the field's history, trajectory, and contemporary concerns. Exploring who supports Jewish music, and why, opens us up to an alternate Jewish music "tradition" that exists in counterpoint with more standard sound-based and practitioner-based studies.

Studying the physical products that have come out of this support – known among scholars as "material culture" – offers one important window into this phenomenon, as Philip V. Bohlman and others have shown in central Germany, or as James Loeffler has discussed in relation to the "An-sky Expeditions" (funded by Vladimir Gintsburg in memory of his father Baron Horace Gintsburg) of 1912–14.[4] In a number of cases, these objects, from songbooks to monographs, were created for a specific purpose, and then resignified over time into touchstones of Jewish music history. Education, the institution-based drive to establish a sense of tradition through communal, centralized pedagogical methods, provides a second angle for understanding the development of different Jewish music paradigms. Communal Jewish music training programs such as cantorial schools typically set agendas for the groups those schools represent, while setting the parameters of knowledge and authority for their graduates. The relationship between music and community-based Jewish outreach, a third area, has had particular relevance in the wake of warily received Jewish population studies in the late twentieth century. Often borne from the anxiety of Jewish institutions and their funders to ensure relevance in future generations, these initiatives have given us such phenomena as Matisyahu (b. 1979) and the Jewish hip-hop scene. All these areas ostensibly rely on each other. Students in a "school" of Jewish music, for example, typically use printed and recorded materials as part of their education; those materials in turn change their meaning over time as a result of their usage; and the institution itself becomes a center for airing anxieties about the Jewish future and remedies for its amelioration. Ultimately, they together highlight a communal process by which the sonic conferral of identity (in this case, a Jewish identity) is highly contingent, complementing music-centered models that emphasize the intergenerational transmission of musical figures and qualities.

The remnants of music

We construct both history and heritage around what remains, using artifacts to create narratives of the past. An inexact science to begin with, history finds particular challenges when facing matters of Jews and music. On one level, we can attribute these challenges to questions of institutional support. Our existing history of "Western" music, for example, relies on centuries of Catholic church-related groups' efforts to develop systems of adopting, notating, reproducing, and storing the music accompanying their regular rituals. In contrast, we currently know of only one Jewish equivalent before the sixteenth century: the work of the Masoretes, a relatively mysterious group of people dedicated to preserving the text and sound of the Hebrew Bible. Their efforts led to the creation of the tenth-century Aleppo Codex, which codified the system of cantillation symbols ("trop/trope") still in use today (for more discussion, see Chapter 6 in this volume). Yet in contrast with medieval neume notation with which they are strenuously compared, the cantillation symbols do not indicate specific pitch levels, thus limiting our ability to parse the sound of the past. The other musical notation we have dates from a twelfth-century convert to Judaism named Obadiah the Proselyte who, by his own account, learned musical notation during his monastic education.[5] Obadiah's music, discarded, survived only because it resided in a genizah – a storage place for discarded documents – whose rediscovery in the late nineteenth century transformed it into a treasure. Both of these efforts relied on communal support networks: the first to preserve a key document for Jews, and the second from the Catholic institutional system. Their stories, conversely, highlight the long-term absence of Jewish institutional support for written musical preservation and dissemination. Music undoubtedly played a significant role in Jewish worship and leisure activities, but, like so much of the world's music, it has not been preserved. We tell history from what survives.

When we view the publications that emerged later through a similar lens, we gain a different understanding of music's place in the local culture. The creation of Salamone Rossi's 1622/3 compilation *Ha-shirim asher lishlomo* (Songs of Solomon) – one of a few Jewish liturgical works printed in seventeenth-century Venice, though the only one to survive in full – happened because of patrons. Rossi's employment in the Gonzaga court in Mantua brought him to prominence; Venetian rabbi Leon Modena (1571–1648) issued a religious opinion that made Rossi's use of polyphony in synagogue singing communally acceptable; and Rossi likely composed his music for the private synagogue of patron Moses Sullam. The collection's introductory material includes Modena's opinion, as well as Rossi's dedications to his patrons. But it also includes Rossi's explicit mention of the cost of such an undertaking, and his hope that his patrons might pick up the tab. No wonder, then, that the front matter radically redefined "Jewish music" to include Rossi's work, advertising his mastery of the "science" of melody and music, and (via a different introduction by Modena) spiritually tracing his technique to Biblical times. More than just a neutral outcropping of Jewish music tradition, *Ha-shirim asher lishlomo*, like other published works both Jewish and non-Jewish, represented a pooling of resources that reflected the institutional configuration in which Rossi worked.

The completion of the eighteenth century and the start of the nineteenth saw a sharp increase in Jewish communal interest in musical programs. Across Italy, Europe, and the United States (and probably elsewhere), a renewed effort to create bridges between Jews and their host populations flowered. In addition to theological efforts facilitated by a new generation of seminaries and spiritual leaders, Jewish communal groups increasingly supported the creation of original compositions and musical styles in both public worship and private leisure. Musicians and composers achieved significance through their training in mainstream conservatories; and in a number of cases, synagogues started to hire dedicated musical personnel. Vienna's Reform Jewish community, for example, accompanied the building of their new sanctuary in the 1820s with a stepped-up music-commissioning program and the hiring of Salomon Sulzer (1804–90) as their new musical leader. Sulzer, in turn, refined the musical performances, raising the status of the synagogue; and he commodified his efforts by mid-century, having the new repertoire compiled, printed, and distributed as both a testament to his leadership and an exemplar to other congregations – not to mention a teaching tool for Jewish leadership academies arising in central and western Europe. It can be assumed that the budgets for supporting such elaborate Jewish musical programs ballooned in Vienna, as well as in Berlin, Paris, London, Königsberg, New York, and elsewhere where music became highly valued as a public face for Judaism. Communal initiative thus made the music possible, ensuring an outlay to hire singers and music specialists. In doing so, moreover, the communities had the opportunity to extend their philosophical spheres of influence. Their music became a surrogate for their theological agendas; and, through circular logic, the definition of Jewish music changed accordingly.

Similar movements can be followed through the rest of the twentieth century, with pooled resources both creating and defining the nature of "Jewish music" on large and small scales. The infrastructure of eastern European Jewish life supported both a traveling network of prayer leaders (*hazzanim*) and a class of wedding musicians (*klezmorim*) that extended into the United States from the 1880s onward, while the emerging recording and sheet music industries helped to preserve their sounds across time and space – even if they were literally forgotten to history. Chabad Lubavitch, after World War II, initiated a centralized project to collect and preserve their holy melodies, resulting in the three-volume *Sefer HaNigunim* (The Book of Melodies), and numerous recorded music albums; yet their preservation project could also be viewed as a redefinition of the Hasidic dynasty's sound in the United States. Musical "revivals," in turn, relied on existing materials to help musicians recreate the world of the past in ways that spoke to the resources and funding patterns of the present.

The organized collective, in other words, often set the agenda in which the individual could operate within the world of Jewish music. Musicians and scholars who adopted that agenda gained access to communal resources, an interested population, and a platform for amplifying their messages. In return, supporting institutions produced musical materials that complemented and shaped their own communal missions.

Jewish music and education

Education, a process that speaks to core concepts of Jewish continuity, serves a complementary role to institutions in determining the nature and use of music in Jewish life. "Classical" visions of music education emphasized one-to-one transmission from teacher to student, focusing on personal care and individual artistry. Since at least the early nineteenth century, however, this model has coexisted in Jewish life with a communal "extended conservatory" model that emphasizes curriculum and a uniformity of knowledge. And this second system has arguably been the more influential of the two: not only in producing Jewish musical figures in significant numbers, and in publishing and collecting musical materials, but (paradoxically) also in preserving the moral value of the one-to-one model in modern society.

At the same time, Jewish music-based educational initiatives have allowed institutions to reinforce what David Roskies has called a "usable past": a connection with select historical events that justify an institution's mission and promotes a common set of identity tools.[6] Music, in its immateriality, has played an important public role in expressing these philosophies efficiently; and music curricula, crafted jointly by musical and non-musical authorities alike, helped disseminate those messages.

We do not know if Jewish music "schools" existed before the late eighteenth century. As Jews became increasingly accepted in modern society, however, they sought mechanisms for balancing their Jewish identities with their civic and national identities. Geoffrey Goldberg has written extensively on the *Lehrerseminar* (teaching academy) model that arose as a result. More prevalent in central and western Europe than in eastern Europe, the *Lehrerseminar* conformed to governmental requirements for teacher certification, under which rabbis and cantors qualified. Just as they did with rabbis in a parallel track, authorities determined to integrate Jews into general society complied by creating specific courses and requirements for achieving mastery of cantorial skills. To assist in their education, some of the instructors created, published, and distributed curricular materials (*Hilfs-mittel*, or learning aids), making the process more uniform. Students who enrolled in these multi-year programs consequently gained state recognition for their expertise, participated in a communal musical experience, and earned membership in a growing professional role. Several of these institutions continued to operate into the mid-twentieth century, when the Nazi era obliterated most of them and erased their memory.

The United States became the center of this practice after World War II, even though they did not openly acknowledge their European predecessors at the time. Between 1948 and 1954, the three major American Jewish seminaries, representing the Reform, Conservative, and Modern Orthodox movements, created their own schools of Jewish music. Overseen by rabbis, scholars, and cantors, the schools reissued some of the *Lehrerseminar* materials, while creating new ones at the hands of their own respected cantorial authorities. Significantly, each cantorial school used music to reinforce its supporting institution's theology; and each, while claiming to prepare cantors for any religious setting, overwhelmingly directed its graduates to its movement's congregations. Graduating hundreds of cantors since the 1950s, these schools have regularized the cantor as a presence in liberal (and some orthodox) synagogues, and created networks of practice and communication that tie closely to broad scholarly discussion. Just as importantly, however, the spread of cantors to congregations across the country has helped each movement coordinate national music-based identity-building initiatives, from music commissioning programs, to the announcement of special musical Sabbaths (such as the events surrounding Shabbat Shirah, the Sabbath associated with the biblical reading of Exodus 15 in January/February), to the central development of lay education campaigns for scriptural chanting. Cantors, moreover, have substantially expanded the market for music scholarship, both as readers and contributors, thereby giving the field a particular shape.

Music also plays an important role in religious education curricula. A. Irma Cohon, for example, created the first American Jewish music textbook in the 1920s as a synagogue-focused adult education course distributed by the National Council of Jewish Women.[7] Young people, however, received particular emphasis as Jewish musical vessels. Viewed as a separate demographic category from adults, particularly after the turn of the twentieth century, youth came to embody a test of institutional success. Throughout Europe, the Middle East, and the Americas, and across the religious and political spectrum, the adult leadership of Jewish youth groups crafted songbooks for their members, on the premise that participation in singing equaled ideological commitment. Similar institution-sponsored efforts aimed to create music for youth-oriented religious services ("Junior Congregation"), Day Schools, and forms of supplementary Jewish education including after-school Hebrew schools and summer camps. The songs young people sang in these contexts often became a soundtrack for inclusion in Jewish life, inspiring many to continue their engagement with the sponsoring institutions, and fulfilling institutional hopes of renewed leadership.

The songleading phenomenon in Reform Judaism, for example, began in 1939 at the first camping experience of the National Federation of Temple Youth (NFTY, now the North American Federation of Temple Youth). Students were initially unfamiliar with group singing, but eventually the leadership pieced together a repertoire that reflected Reform Jewish "values" – combining songs from the folk revival and German Jewish youth movements with Palestinian/Israeli pioneer songs, Reform hymns, and songs written specifically for Reform Jewish youth. Over the years, campers took up the mantle and began to write their own liturgical and paraliturgical songs, extending the repertoire through movement-sponsored songwriting contests, recordings, publications, regional and national youth gatherings, and songleader training courses. Songleading, as a result, shifted from an educational initiative to a normative sound of the movement as a whole. Similar stories can be told of other movements – both religious and cultural – involving locally appropriate sets of musical strategies.

Education has, in essence, served as an important vessel for the discussion, normalization, and dissemination of Jewish music. Whether for professionals or the laity, it offers a way for religious communities to connect with their constituents while reinforcing their own theological boundaries.

Music and the philanthropy of outreach

Beyond education, music has played a role in culturally-based communal efforts to stave off a perceived sense of Jewish attenuation. Based in long-held perceptions of the arts as vessels for spawning social and emotional attachment, these efforts, while promoted as "new" or "radical," address deep, internally fueled, institutional anxieties.

Jewish groups have periodically turned to the arts as ways of mediating between Jewish communal needs and the attractions of the "outside world," affecting everything from synagogue architecture, to the creation of Jewish museums, to the marketing of Judaica objects. Chabad Lubavitch advocated creativity among some of its members as a form of ministry building after

World War II; Reform Judaism brought prominent artists to annual retreats at the Kutz Camp Institute in Warwick, New York, during the mid-1960s; and in the 1970s–80s, Yiddishists built a linguistic revival on the performing arts, including the establishment of a retreat later known as KlezKamp. All developed their "artistic turns" as a way to engage a broader variety of people in their respective movements, thus ensuring survival during moments of self-described existential peril.

Another major turn to the arts took place beginning in 1991, when the Council of Jewish Federations publicized the results of its 1990 National Jewish Population Survey – revealing in particular an exogamy ("intermarriage") rate of between 40 and 60 percent, depending upon interpretation. Alarm at the potential of Jewish self-extinction spread among Jewish federations and other institutions, leading to broad-based efforts to "engage" young people in Jewish communal activities – the better to ensure Jewish-Jewish marriages, and, subsequently, Jewish babies. Jewish institutions joined with philanthropists, using the arts as one of several social engineering strategies.

To understand how music factored into this funding cycle, which lasted from the late 1990s through about 2010, we can turn to the career of Matisyahu, a figure initially connected with both the Hasidic Chabad Lubavitch community and "new" Jewish culture initiatives. Raised in a liberal Jewish household as Matthew Miller, Matisyahu turned to Chabad during college, where he began to develop his career as a performer.

Appearing in "standard" Hasidic dress during his concerts – black hat, coat, and pants, white shirt and fringed undershirt, beard, and sidelocks – Matisyahu inspired a broad landscape of American, and American Jewish, discourse. Yet an analysis of Matisyahu himself addresses only a part of this performer's complex cultural topography. Just as important is the "back end" of that topography: the producers who noticed, mediated, and marketed Matisyahu as part of a broader artistic and philanthropic effort to engage young American Jews in discussions about Jewish identity and authenticity.

Like almost every other commercially successful musical artist, Matisyahu did not become a figure of public interest on his own. Rather, he was the first major promoted artist for the JDub record label, which was created to "push forth a new understanding of how one can connect to Judaism."[8] Co-founded in December 2002 by NYU Music Business program graduates Aaron Bisman and Benjamin Hesse, JDub received its seed funding from the Joshua Venture, one of the earlier Jewish venture philanthropy organizations to arise at the turn of the twenty-first century. The Joshua Venture's "primary goal [was] to strengthen a new generation of leaders who are launching innovative projects and organizations that contribute to a vibrant, just, and inclusive Jewish community."[9]

Bisman's selection as a 2003–5 fellow after a competitive application process ensured that the label – provocatively named after a derogatory Syrian Jewish term for Ashkenazic Jews – would follow a similar agenda. Along with other recipients, including Amichai Lau-Lavie (who founded Storahtelling, a theater troupe devoted to dramatic and sometimes radical reenactments of Jewish scripture) and Idit Klein (Keshet, an LGBT organization for Jews in greater Boston), the label took on an explicit agenda of Jewish cultural transformation by actively seeking alternate, generation-specific modes of Jewish belonging.

Like other Jewish media-based organizations coming up at the time (such as Jennifer Bleyer's *Heeb Magazine* and Roger Bennett's *Reboot*), JDub had to figure out how to serve a miniscule and largely unsustainable market (i.e., young Jews) while appearing to maintain a broad presence that would have relevance to a widespread audience. *Reboot*'s record label, Reboot Stereophonic (later renamed the Idelsohn Society for Jewish Music), accomplished this task by engaging in a full-bore, professional media campaign while making a small amount of actual product. Bisman and Hesse, meanwhile, carefully built Matisyahu's career by combining the efforts of a "street team," successful attempts to include Matisyahu in widespread interest stories about the new hipster Jewish cultural agenda, and effectively chosen and marketed events promoting Matisyahu to Jewish young adults and college students as a hip Jewish ambassador. Matisyahu, for his part, also capitalized on resources provided by the media-savvy Chabad Lubavitch, whose leaders pursued a religious outreach agenda for largely the same population with a similarly hip image. Through these actions, Matisyahu often became the literal face of the storied new approach to Jewish identity; and JDub, as a result, became a model for successful Jewish venture philanthropy.

The careful development and marketing of Matisyahu also brought the singer strategically into the reggae scene through creative genre marketing – a flexible matter derived from his jam-band background. Although JDub promoted him from the beginning as a "Hasidic Reggae Superstar," Matisyahu's initial media appearances largely framed him within the much larger hip-hop scene: singing alongside Israeli and Palestinian rap artists in a JDub-sponsored "Unity Sessions" concert in Brooklyn that attracted 3,000 people in summer 2004, emphasizing his beat-boxing skills in 2004 and early 2005 national television interviews on CNN and other national media outlets, and being introduced by Jimmy Kimmel on his first major talk show appearance as "the most popular Jewish rapper since

MC Hammer."[10] Especially in the latter two cases, Matisyahu benefitted from low expectations – Kimmel, according to a conversation I had with Bisman, initially wanted to feature Matisyahu as a novelty act, and eventually gave in when JDub insisted that the show give him a full musical guest treatment; he then proceeded to surprise his host with an "uncharacteristically" effective performance.[11] JDub thus used the flexible boundaries between reggae and rap/hip-hop in the mainstream entertainment world to its advantage in both introducing Matisyahu and shifting the discourse about his abilities from novelty to "for real."

The reggae scene, in turn, pumped up Matisyahu's popularity: JDub's Jewish-themed concerts generally hosted a few hundred people each at the time; appearances at much larger venues, such as Carifest and Bonnaroo, hosted predominantly non-Jewish audiences. Matisyahu's friable Jewish positioning here – as framed by his management and its mandate – thus joined larger discussions about the presentation of Jamaican and mainstream musical authenticity; but his ability to channel both Jewish and Jamaican musical aesthetics in his performance also became an effective vehicle for bringing Matisyahu to larger and larger stages.

When Matisyahu's album sales began to top the reggae charts, however – an observation that to many artificially connotes both commercial and cultural dominance – the critical tide began to turn, with reggae critics in particular going on the offensive. The 119,000 copies Matisyahu's album *Youth* sold in its first week ranked it #4 on the overall *Billboard* albums chart, just below the 137,000 copies of the *High School Musical* soundtrack (which by then had been out for several weeks).[12] But because Matisyahu's album sales also counted in the smaller reggae market, it became the greatest one-week sale of a reggae album of all time. This level of notoriety (preceded by the success of his *Live at Stubbs* album on the same charts) changed the game significantly: as with other top-ten non-Jamaican reggae artists before him (such as Snow and UB40), Matisyahu became both an important figure for the financial wellbeing of the reggae genre, and a controversial representative of its authenticity.

New York Times reviewer Kelefa Sanneh's withering critique of Matisyahu's race and nationality after a Hammerstein Ballroom concert and album launch in March 2006 reflected the consternation his career had generated among reggae purists.[13] Slate writer Jody Rosen, meanwhile, assailed Matisyahu *because* of his popularity, bringing into play a Jewish cultural studies field that had grown tremendously over the past few years alongside Jewish venture philanthropy's focus on "culture" funding; six months later, notably, Rosen would himself capitalize on the "Jewface" discourse he employed in his article through the release of the *Jewface* album on the Bronfman-funded Reboot Stereophonic.[14] Matisyahu, meanwhile, left JDub for more mainstream representation soon after Sanneh's review; and shortly thereafter he left Chabad (and eventually religious Judaism more generally), breaking out of the "Jewish" frames each organization imposed upon him in pursuit of larger markets and a greater (and likely more ambiguous) freedom of self-expression. The Christian music industry was one of these markets (it sold more than 53 million units in 2006, compared with just over half a million units in the reggae industry in 2009).[15] Matisyahu's c. 2006 decision to record with Christian metal group P.O.D. (Payable on Death), a group whose previous two albums had sold more than 6.3 million copies worldwide, became a shrewd career move as well as a "spiritual" collaboration.[16] The authenticity debates surrounding Matisyahu by such scholars as Sarah Imhoff, therefore, did not take place around a static figure.[17] Rather, Sanneh, Rosen, and others engaged with the image of an artist/artiste whose transitioning management was already seeking new identity valences with which to promote him. Matisyahu's rise and subsequent critiques, in other words, derived as much from a reading of the music industry as they did from Matisyahu's own choices.

In essence, then, Matisyahu's early career used discourses of Jewish and black authenticity to construct a self-fulfilling prophecy. On the other side, or "back end," of this period, the conversations Matisyahu engendered in the first phases of his career were ostensibly funded by venture philanthropies, who felt that open questioning of Jewish authenticity and identity would revitalize Jewish life; and the conversations themselves were curated and promoted by a recording company founded on the premise of furthering this transformative Jewish agenda using mainstream discursive techniques. JDub's successful marketing of Matisyahu, in turn, opened a space for the reggae industry to herald the singer's arrival, and, upon his domination of the reggae charts, provided fodder for a backlash. Matisyahu's case thus shows how effectively this back end transparently shaped ideas about Judaism and music, through a judicious and interconnected seeding of the broader entertainment industry, media critics, and – via the conversation sustained in this forum and others – the flows of academic discourse.

Matisyahu existed alongside numerous other musical initiatives supported by philanthropic funds and their related institutions: from the Jewcy festival in Los Angeles to Birthright Israel's sponsorship of mega-concerts and follow-up events. And more recently, initiatives such as the Piyyut Project (sponsored by the Avi Chai Foundation in both Israel and the United States) have used the paraliturgical hymns of Jewish ethnic communities to inject religion into perceived "secular" Jewish populations. Music in this context becomes an instrument that, sponsors often hope, will change statistics of institutional affiliation for the future.

Conclusion

These examples illustrate the significant historical presence of institutions in the development, promotion, and dissemination of "Jewish music" and its scholarly study – a practice that continues openly today. While rarely hidden, their activities tend to fade with time, leaving us to study the musical artifacts that remain in ways that privilege the music over the forces that brought it into existence. Maintaining an awareness of institutional support presents its challenges. But in complicating the field, it also exposes music's relevance to a wide range of people beyond the musicians themselves, opening opportunities for us to engage well beyond the sound with crucial ideas and materials we might otherwise overlook.

Notes

1 For example, Keith Negus, *Music Genres and Corporate Cultures* (New York: Routledge, 1999).

2 Judah M. Cohen, "Modes of Tradition? Negotiating Jewishness and Modernity in the Synagogue Music of Isadore Freed and Frederick Piket," *Jewish History and Culture*, 5.2 (Winter 2002): 25–47; Judah M. Cohen, "Music Institutions and the Transmission of Tradition," *Ethnomusicology*, 53.2 (Spring/Summer 2009): 308–25.

3 Ethan Goldberg has best documented this phenomenon, in "In the Shadow of Sulzer: The Mixed Legacy of Cantor Alois Kaiser," B.A. honors thesis, Brandeis University (2012), 35–7.

4 Philip V. Bohlman, *Jewish Music and Modernity* (Oxford University Press, 2008); James Loeffler, *The Most Musical Nation: Jews and Culture in the Late Russian Empire* (New Haven: Yale University Press, 2010).

5 Norman Golb, "The Music of Obadiah the Proselyte and His Conversion," *Journal of Jewish Studies*, 18.1–4 (1967): 43–63.

6 David G. Roskies, *The Jewish Search for a Usable Past* (Bloomington: Indiana University Press, 1999).

7 A. Irma Cohon, *An Introduction to Jewish Music in Eight Illustrated Lectures* (New York: National Council of Jewish Women, 1923).

8 www.jdubrecords.org, April 19, 2003, http://web.archive.org/web/20030618040339/http://www.jdubrecords.org/ (accessed March 4, 2013).

9 http://web.archive.org/web/20011206000240/www.joshuaventure.org/mainindex.html (archives the site as of November 21, 2001; accessed February 18, 2015).

10 www.dailymotion.com/video/x76v1_matisyahu-live-on-jimmy-kimmel-show_creation (accessed March 2, 2014).

11 I received a similarly surprised "You know, he's actually pretty good!" reaction from hip-hop scholars when I first discussed his career in a paper at the Society for Ethnomusicology's annual meeting in November 2004.

12 Katie Hasty, "Juvenile's 'Reality' Upends Ne-Yo At No. 1," *Billboard*, March 15, 2006.

13 Kelefa Sanneh, "Dancehall with a Different Accent," *New York Times*, March 8, 2006.

14 Jody Rosen, "G-d's Reggae Star: How Matisyahu Became a Pop Phenomenon," *Slate*, March 14, 2006, www.slate.com/articles/arts/music_box/2006/03/gds_reggae_star.html (accessed March 2, 2014).

15 I have been unable to find reggae album sales from before 2009. They were likely somewhat higher in 2006, though not nearly reaching the figures achieved by the Christian music industry (44.9 million units in 2006). "Reggae Sales Struggle," *Dancehallusa.com*, November 13, 2009, http://www.dancehallusa.com/?p=7043 (accessed February 15, 2010); "Christian/Gospel Music Album Sales Rise in 2006," January 4, 2007, www.businesswire.com/news/home/20070104006100/en/Christian-Gospel-Music-Album-Sales-Rise-2006#.UwLG1XljZG4 (accessed February 17, 2014); "Industry Overview 2009," www.cmta.com/GMA_Industry_Overview_2009.pdf (accessed February 16, 2010).

16 P. D.'s 2006 album, however, did not do as well as its predecessors, selling c. 500,000 copies worldwide. Nonetheless, that number was approximately equal to the reggae industry's *total* 2009 sales – which included 57,000 copies of Matisyahu's next album, *Light*.

17 Sarah Imhoff, "The Man in Black: Matisyahu, Identity, and Authenticity," Religion and Culture Web Forum, Martin Marty Center, University of Chicago, February 2010, https://divinity.uchicago.edu/sites/default/files/imce/pdfs/webforum/022010/Matisyahupaginated.pdf (accessed March 2, 2014).

4 Jewish music and media of sound reproduction

JOSHUA S. WALDEN

Writing in 1878 of his hopes for the future of his recent invention, the phonograph, Thomas Edison described a number of the device's groundbreaking "*faits accomplis*," including the following:

1. The captivity of all manner of sound-waves heretofore designated as "fugitive," and their permanent retention.
2. Their reproduction with all their original characteristics at will, without the presence or consent of the original source, and after the lapse of any period of time.
3. The transmission of such captive sounds through the ordinary channels of commercial intercourse and trade in material form, for purposes of communication or as merchantable goods.
4. Indefinite multiplication and preservation of such sounds, without regard to the existence or non-existence of the original source.[1]

In envisioning specific uses for his creation – such as replacing stenography, delivering aural greetings from far-flung friends, and preserving the voices of loved ones before death – Edison did not, unsurprisingly, anticipate its impacts on concepts and practices of music among ethnic and religious communities. But the general accomplishments included in this list were to prove of vital importance to the history of Jewish music beginning around the turn of the twentieth century. For example, it was only after the advent of sound recording technology that Jewish ethnographers could collect the sounds of Jewish folk and religious music, taking advantage of the phonograph's capacity to capture for posterity the "fugitive" strains of the music of far-flung Jewish communities and transport them back home. And as recorded performances of Jewish music in various genres were reproduced and transmitted through "ordinary channels of commercial intercourse and trade," in the form of records and radio broadcasts, composers and performers could develop international reputations, while listeners could choose to hear in their own homes the repertoire that was previously reserved for particular places and functions, such as the synagogue or the wedding ceremony.

Throughout the pages of this volume, technologies of sound reproduction emerge in discussions of multiple repertoires, settings, and contexts. Chapters describe the uses of the phonograph in the ethnographic fieldwork of figures such as Abraham Zvi Idelsohn (1882–1938), Robert Lachmann (1892–1939), and Joel Engel (1868–1927). They explain the ways ethnographic recordings served as guides for folk music transcription, study, and categorization, as models for composers to cite, adapt, and transform in art music compositions, and as physical objects to be collected in academic sound archives. Other chapters discuss the crucial role professional sound recording played in the development of the careers of klezmer musicians, the eastern European performers of music for weddings and other celebrations, many of whom immigrated to the United States early in the twentieth century, and show how these recordings were later recovered and studied by klezmer revivalists of the 1970s. And several essays explore how the commercial market for radios, records, cassette tapes, and compact discs provided a launching pad for the creation of novel musical genres and fusions that invoked Jewish traditions in eclectic ways, by musicians such as Mickey Katz (1909–85), John Zorn (b. 1953), and Matisyahu (b. 1979), and also provided a vehicle for various organizations to promote their religious and political interests.

Although technologies of sound reproduction often arise as part of the story in studies of Jewish music since the turn of the twentieth century, they are rarely addressed in their own right as a central force in the development of definitions and genres of Jewish music, and in initiating modern modes of performing, listening to, and talking about Jewish repertories. In *Understanding Media: The Extensions of Man*, Marshall McLuhan famously writes, "The medium is the message"; though this phrase has been interpreted, adapted, and sometimes misused in countless contexts, McLuhan's original meaning is apt in a discussion of the role of sound reproduction media in the history of Jewish music. He explained of his influential phrase, "This is merely to say that the personal and social consequences of any medium – that is, of any extension of ourselves – result from the new scale that is introduced into our affairs by each extension of ourselves, or by any new technology." Sound media are not mere transparent carriers of content, conduits between the musical performer and the listener's ears. Rather, they operate as mechanisms that expand or elaborate our capabilities of expression and communication, and thus they can play crucial roles in initiating social and cultural change. Content – whatever particular music is recorded on a CD or broadcast over the radio – is, of course, of central importance, and for this reason, throughout this volume, invocations of these media are generally guided by discussions of their content. But it is also helpful to view the roles of media including the wax cylinder phonograph, the record, the radio, the compact disc, and the MP3 in the history of Jewish music during the past century.

This chapter considers multiple ways that technologies for recording and playing back sound have been employed in the creation and transmission of Jewish music. It examines three case studies, focusing on the market for records of cantorial singing early in the century, the rise of Yiddish radio in New York, and the creation of new "radical" genres of Jewish music on John Zorn's Tzadik CD label. It concludes with an overview of the ways our modern technologies of handheld devices for private listening, from the Walkman to the smartphone, have paved the way for the development of new modes of producing, disseminating, and consuming Jewish music. The chapter proposes that technologies of sound reproduction, far from simply being incorporated into existing structures of musical performance and composition in Jewish life around the globe, have been instrumental in the generation of new works and genres of Jewish music, and have initiated fundamental changes in the ways people have listened to, remembered, shared, and even defined Jewish music.[2]

Cantors on record

The phonograph's capacity to fix ephemeral performances that would earlier have been immediately lost outside of listeners' memories suddenly permitted unprecedented scrutiny to be placed on the individual performance. With the sound recording, scholars and musicians could listen to performances repeatedly for the purposes of study and analysis. The phonograph directly altered the career of the professional performer as well, as it opened up new possibilities for musicians who would previously have been known primarily among local listeners to garner national or international attention and earn payment from the production and sale of recordings. Sound recording also introduced a new venue for performance, the recording studio, which brought its own demands, including the need to direct one's performance into the recording trumpet and, later, microphone, as well as to sing or play with a quality and precision worthy of posterity. As technologies became more sophisticated, they also allowed performers to splice together different takes and adjust sound levels and even intonation, to achieve a level of quality that could elude the live performer.

The phonograph additionally initiated considerable changes in the experience of listening to music. One need no longer go to the synagogue or the concert hall to hear music once intended for these venues, but could instead choose to listen to these repertoires on discs in the home. And rather than worshipping in a gathering in the presence of cantorial singing, or dancing along to a klezmer ensemble's rendition of a wedding dance, one could experience the sounds of these musical performances in privacy

and silent contemplation. With multiple genres of Jewish music now transformed into physical commodities – records – and made available in what
Edison called "the ordinary channels of commercial intercourse," one could
choose one's favorite pieces and performers, purchasing discs for a personal
collection and listening to them repeatedly, assigning to memory not only
the music's text or its melodies and harmonies, but the particular musician's
interpretive cadences as well.

The advent of recording technologies also had a formative influence
on the ways music could operate in the construction of identities. The
historian Josh Kun has written that compiling his personal record collection
played an important part in the construction of his personal identity: for
him, purchasing and listening to records "were themselves acts of musical
identity-making, moments when my identity became a geography of crossed
and crossing sounds, a mobile space of musical interaction."[3] He calls the
notional space to which the record transports the listener an "audiotopia," "a
possible utopia for the listener, . . . a space that we can enter into, encounter,
move around in, inhabit, be safe in, learn from."[4] This metaphorical utopian
sonic "space" can replace the traditional spaces of listening to Jewish musical
genres, such as the synagogue, the celebration hall, the theater, the home,
or the town square, and unlike those physical locations, it is easily able to
accommodate all genres of Jewish music together, even those that would
never before have been heard in the same space.

At the start of the twentieth century, recording studios began producing
records of cantors, allowing their music – *ḥazzanut* in Hebrew, *khazones* in
Yiddish – to be purchased and collected for private listening. As cantorial
records proliferated, advertisements suggested the albums would offer a
way of satisfying immigrants' nostalgia for the "old country."[5] Many commentators hoped that these musical commodities would have a positive
effect on the circumstances for growing numbers of Jewish immigrants and
their children, both as a focus of common Jewish listenership that would
heighten solidarity within Jewish communities, and as a positive display
of Jewish culture that would impel non-Jewish listeners to develop a sym-
pathetic view of their Jewish neighbors.[6] For cantors, however, entering
into the commercial world of making and selling sound recordings could
also create friction with their religious values. Jeffrey Shandler writes that
new sound recording technologies "aestheticized cantors' devotional musicianship, . . . transform[ing] the cantor from a spiritual messenger into a
celebrity performer, who has become the center of communal attention as
opposed to a conduit to the divine."[7] As this repertoire became detached
from some of its liturgical meanings, it also took on new cultural associations – for example nostalgia, ethnic solidarity, or the musical demonstration of Jewish identity for non-Jewish listeners – now that it was being

marketed as a commodity for purchase, listened to as a form of domestic entertainment, and considered alongside music of other styles and genres.[8]

The phenomenon of cantorial recordings also had a significant impact on the musical repertoire. The three- to four-minute capacity of each side of a recorded disc, for example, resulted in the division of the repertoire into short repeatable "hits." While in many synagogues instrumental accompaniment to cantorial singing was still banned out of mourning for the destruction of the Second Temple in 70 CE, this music could be accompanied by organ or ensembles of instruments in the secular setting of the recording studio.[9] Along with radio, sound recording also made possible the rise of the female professional cantor, or *khaznte*, a figure forbidden in synagogue worship by rabbinic law.[10] Furthermore, the recording industry contributed to the broadening of cantors' interest in secular repertoire, such as operatic numbers, *Lieder* (art songs), and Yiddish popular songs. Some cantors had already entered these musical arenas during the late nineteenth century, but with the medium of sound recording the practice accelerated.[11] At the same time, certain liturgical "numbers" derived from traditional cantorial repertoire, particularly the *Kol Nidre* (All Vows), entered the repertoire of musicians associated with other musical genres, such as opera and vaudeville stars.

One of the cantors whose rise to celebrity was facilitated by the sound recording industry was Yossele Rosenblatt (1882–1933, born in Biała Cerkiew, Russia). Rosenblatt had already achieved renown in Europe by the time he immigrated in 1912 to New York, where, dubbed the "Yiddish Caruso," he forged a successful career recording primarily for the Victor and Columbia record labels, selling sheet music, and performing cantorial music and Yiddish songs, among other repertoire.[12] Rosenblatt's 1913 Victor recording of *Kol Nidre*, whose well-known and frequently adapted melody appears to date at least from the sixteenth century, was one of dozens of 78-rpm discs of the chant produced during the early twentieth-century explosion of commercial cantorial recordings.[13] *Kol Nidre* is chanted on Yom Kippur (the Day of Atonement), and thus carries associations with the holy day's themes of atonement and forgiveness. In his recording, which is approximately four minutes long, Rosenblatt is accompanied by an organ that plays a bare chordal accompaniment as Rosenblatt chants with a fast vibrato on extended notes.[14] He embellishes some longer-held tones with vocal ornaments, and produces lengthy melismas, strings of changing pitches sung to the same syllable of text. His interpretation is declamatory, following the rhythms of the text without organizing the music into any fixed sense of meter. The track begins poignantly as Rosenblatt drags his voice through a brief and narrow glide up toward the first pitch on the word "kol," the minor tonality emphasized by the organ's accompanying chord, and then moves downward on the sighing half-step descent of the word "nidre." It concludes in a more uplifting tone in the major mode. This early recording of Rosenblatt's celebrated rendition of one of the most widely recognized of Jewish liturgical melodies demonstrates some of the ways sound recording served as a catalyst for developments in cantorial performance and listenership, as well as the musical parameters and cultural uses of the repertoire, in the early decades of the twentieth century.

Yiddish songs on the radio

In the early 1920s, the advent of radio broadcasting and the manufacture of affordable devices for the home meant that individuals and families could tune in and listen to music, dramas, news, and other programming alone or with family, but also in the knowledge that thousands of others were listening at the same time to the same material. The radio thus had the potential to produce in its audiences a sense of collectivity resembling what Benedict Anderson, in writing about nationalism, has called an "imagined community" among far-flung listeners, who shared ideas, interests, and cultural characteristics but might never encounter one another.[15] Thus an article published in *Colliers* magazine in 1922, only two years after the first English-language broadcast reached the airwaves in Pittsburgh, characterized the radio as a significant social force capable of "spreading mutual understanding to all sections of the country, . . . unifying our thoughts, ideals, and purposes, [and] making us a strong and well-knit people."[16]

Jewish-themed programming followed closely behind the first radio broadcast, and regularly incorporated performances of Jewish music from multiple genres. The first radio programs with Jewish content were a pair of shows broadcast in 1923 with the sponsorship of the United Synagogue, an institution promoting the religious values of American Conservative Judaism. These were arranged around the High Holidays – the Jewish New Year's celebration of Rosh Hashanah and the Day of Atonement, Yom Kippur – and featured renditions of the music associated with their synagogue services, sung by a cantor with choral accompaniment.[17] But as working and using electricity are forbidden on the High Holy Days and the Sabbath by Jewish law, these programs were broadcast several days in advance of Rosh Hashanah and Yom Kippur.[18] They did not, therefore, qualify as religious observation of the *yom tov*, or holy day, but were rather, in the phrase coined later by the Yiddish-language paper the *Forward*, "*yom toverdiker*" – holy day-like.[19]

The first radio broadcast in Yiddish was heard in 1926, and over time North American radio dials came to include over fifty stations in cities across the United States and Canada carrying Yiddish programming, aimed principally at Yiddish-speaking immigrants from eastern Europe and their American-born descendants.[20] These stations were multilingual: even the best-known Yiddish radio stations, such as New York's WEVD (named for Eugene V. Debs, the five-time socialist presidential candidate, and originally founded to promote socialist causes) carried programming in English and other languages as well as Yiddish.[21] The first Yiddish radio program was musical in its theme, a concert presented by a rabbi and cantor accompanied by guitar.[22] Over time, Yiddish radio would feature performances by cantors, art music reflecting the influence of Jewish traditional music, folk songs and musical numbers from Yiddish theater and cinema, klezmer, advertising jingles that adapted Jewish songs, and the music that was part of radio plays and talk shows.[23] Much of this music is notable for its hybrid character: reflecting the linguistic and thematic eclecticism found throughout the Yiddish radio, it involved text in Yiddish, English, and Hebrew sometimes also merging the former two into "Yinglish," as well as technical elements adapted from both Jewish traditional music and American popular song. The Yiddish radio in America thus further complicated the changing sense of identity of a Jewish community that already spoke multiple languages and engaged with both the music they brought with them from Europe and the sounds they encountered in their new home.[24] Whether it transformed the religious music of the synagogue into prayer or entertainment for the home or combined characteristics of Jewish folk song with those of American jazz and swing, music was a critical component of the radio's role in relation to the negotiation of modern American Jewish identities.

This sort of musical fusion could be heard before the 1930s in recordings of novelty songs, particularly those of the Russian Jewish immigrant and Tin Pan Alley songwriter Irving Berlin (1888–1989), with titles such as "Yiddle on Your Fiddle Play Some Ragtime" (1909); in Yiddish theater scores; and in the repertoire of many klezmer and club date musicians who played at Jewish wedding and bar mitzvah celebrations and other events.[25] Singers known for a variety of styles, from opera to vaudeville, recorded Yiddish songs from both Europe and America in productions involving genre cross-over. In 1918, for example, Victor Records released a disc of the operatic tenor Naum Coster (né Kostany) singing "Oif'n pripetshok" (*Oyfn pripetshik*, On the Hearth). This song, about a *rebbe* educating young *cheder* (religious school) students in the *alef beys* (alphabet), with its poignant lines about the tears that lie within the letters that make up the language of the Jews in exile, was written in Europe by the Ukrainian Jewish poet and songwriter Mark Warshawski (1848–1907), whose Yiddish works had been "discovered" and published by the popular author Sholem Aleichem (1859–1916). In Coster's recording, it becomes an operatic aria accompanied by a classical chamber orchestra. While songs like "Oyfn pripetshik" were brought to America where they became known through the dissemination of sound recordings, as well as through the oral tradition and sheet music publishing, other Yiddish songs produced on American records were homegrown. A popular example is "My Yiddishe Momme" (in Yiddish, *A yidishe mame*), a 1925 number by Lou Pollack and Jack Yellen, whose yearning lyrics state that nothing in the world is better than a Jewish mother, that the home is light and beautiful in her presence but that all becomes dark when God brings her to heaven. "My Yiddishe Momme" was recorded by multiple artists, including the cantor Yossele Rosenblatt (His Master's Voice, 1926), as well as Sophie Tucker (1884–1966), the popular Jewish singer, actress, and entertainer with a famously husky voice – she was known as "The Last of the Red Hot Mamas" – who released a disc with Decca in 1928 in which she sang the song in English on the A-side and Yiddish on the B-side.

The recording industry suffered during the Depression, however, and as the production of Jewish-themed discs declined, radio helped pick up the slack. With radio technologies improving, devices becoming increasingly affordable, and stations with Jewish programming multiplying, the radio studio became a principal setting for the further development of Jewish musicians' careers and of this hybrid form of music.[26] The program "Yiddish Melodies in Swing," broadcast from 1938 to 1955 on the New York station WHN, became one of the most popular venues for this musical fusion, dubbed in the introduction to the program as constituting "Yiddish songs played both *heymish* [homey] and hot."[27] The goal of these fifteen-minute shows, which incorporated singing and comic banter, was described by the show's announcer as merging the sounds of the old and new worlds: "'Yiddish Swing' takes old Yiddish folk songs and finds the groove for them in merry modern rhythms."[28] Created by Sam Medoff, whose father David had been a star of the Yiddish theater, the show featured the studio performances of his twelve-piece "Swingtet," which included the klezmer clarinetist Dave Tarras (1895–1989). The ensemble accompanied The Barry Sisters, introduced as "the daughters of the downbeat," a duo that sang in close harmonies, in both Yiddish and English.[29] Born in the Bronx to Yiddish-speaking immigrant parents, Clara (b. 1920–2014) and Minnie Bagelman (c. 1923–76) began their careers as The Bagelman Sisters, before they changed their names to Claire and Merna Barry. They viewed their musical fusion as reflecting the hybridity of modern Jewish identity in America: Claire Barry later recalled, "We wanted to be Jewish and American at the same time. That was what our music was always meant to speak to."[30] Medoff's radio program explored this cultural negotiation for nearly two decades through the addition of elements of klezmer to American songs, and of swing to songs in Yiddish and Hebrew.

Over their careers, the Barry Sisters built their reputation with interpretations of a diverse range of songs. These included Yiddish songs such as "Rumenye Rumenye," by Yiddish theater composer and performer Aaron Lebedeff (1873–1960), with its lively music and humorous lyrics about the pleasures of food, wine, and love in the "old country," as well as the poignant and nostalgic Russian Jewish folksong "Tumbalalaika," whose lyrics recite a series of riddles interspersed with the refrain's onomatopoetic imitation of the strumming of the balalaika, and which was later popularized by folk singers including Pete Seeger (1919–2014) and Theodore Bikel (1924–2015). The Barry Sisters also sang Hebrew songs, ranging from the traditional Passover *seder* song "Dayenu" (It Would Have Been Enough for Us) to "Hava Nagila" (Let Us Rejoice), written in 1918 by Idelsohn, who brought together the wordless melody of a nineteenth-century Hasidic *nigun* from Ukraine with a text echoing Psalm 118:24, creating a celebratory number that would soon become one of the best-known Israeli and later American-Jewish Hebrew songs.[31] Meanwhile, the Barry Sisters also transformed works from the American songbook into Yiddish hits, for example with their translated version of Gus Kahn and Walter Donaldson's 1928 "Makin' Whoopee," originally written as a theatrical vehicle for Eddie Cantor.

The encounter between languages and musical idioms enacted in The Barry Sisters' performances on "Yiddish Melodies in Swing" is exemplified by their rendition of "Bei Mir Bist Du Schön." The original version of this song, with a title spelled "Bei Mir Bistu Shein," in a transliteration of the Yiddish phrase meaning "To me you are beautiful," was written in 1932 by Sholom Secunda (1894–1974) with lyricist Jacob Jacobs (1890–1977) for a work of Yiddish theater. Much of the music for Yiddish theater was ephemeral, and Secunda, certain that interest in the song would be should-lived, was persuaded to sell the rights to J & J Kammen, publisher of numerous Yiddish songs, for a mere thirty dollars, which he shared with Jacobs.[32] But the number had a surprising afterlife, entering the repertoire of the African American duo Johnny and George, who performed it in Yiddish at the Apollo Theater in Harlem. Here the Broadway songwriter Sammy Cahn heard it for the first time; recognizing a potential hit, he wrote new lyrics in English and respelled the title – also the main hook of the refrain – as "Bei Mir Bist Du Schon." The song became a tremendous radio success, a fact Secunda learned only by chance when he happened to tune in, in time to hear it performed in its English adaptation. In this version, it was swiftly made famous by the Andrews Sisters in 1938, followed by Benny Goodman, Guy Lombardo, and numerous others. The song, through sound recording, sheet music sales, and radio broadcasts, propelled the careers of the Andrews Sisters, the owners of J & J Kammen, and Sammy

Cahn – nearly everyone involved in its genesis, in fact, except Secunda and Jacobs.[33]

It was reportedly the very day they first heard the rendition of the Andrews Sisters – a popular trio of female singers who were not Jewish – singing "Bei Mir Bist Du Schön" that the Barry Sisters decided to change their names and build careers singing their unique form of musical fusion. In the version of the song they performed on radio and recorded on LP (and titled again in transliterated Yiddish as "Bei Mir Bistu Shain"), the listener can hear from the brief instrumental introduction an ensemble that features the muted trumpet, brass section, and vibraphone common to swing bands.[34] The Barry Sisters sing the first verse and refrain in Yiddish in their signature tight harmonies. They extend individual notes to add a jazzy syncopation, and sing a downward augmented second at the end of the verse that, in this musical context, recalls at once both the blue notes of swing and the recurrence of this particular interval in Yiddish song. In the second stanza, which they sing in English, the Barry Sisters bend their pitches to incorporate more blue notes and they further syncopate the rhythms, but this is followed by the most klezmer-like moment yet, as the clarinet emerges from the band to play a solo riff at a faster tempo in the klezmer style made popular by their frequent collaborator Tarras.[35] This abrupt change in tone is followed just as suddenly by a return to the swing style, as the clarinet's phrase is completed at the original tempo by piano and muted brass. By juxtaposing instruments, language, and melodic and rhythmic elements associated with swing and klezmer, the Barry Sisters' interpretation of this song reflects the linguistic and thematic hybridity of so much of the programming of Yiddish radio. With its musical programming, the Yiddish radio helped to chart a way forward for many of its listeners to negotiate acculturation in America while maintaining aspects of tradition brought from overseas during immigration.

Staging radical Jewish culture on compact discs

At the conclusion of the twentieth century, the recording company Tzadik Records (Tzadik is Hebrew for "righteous one"), founded in 1995 in New York City by the saxophonist and composer John Zorn, played an influential role in the development of a new repertoire embodying both a revival of Jewish genres and their cutting-edge fusion with other musical idioms. Tzadik's Radical Jewish Culture series has featured combinations of such traditional genres as cantorial singing, klezmer, and folk song with music ranging from contemporary classical to free jazz, from punk to Tuvan throat singing. The website of Zorn's company describes the Radical Jewish

Culture series – with reference to the klezmer revival of the 1970s – as "Jewish music beyond klezmer: adventurous recordings bringing Jewish identity and culture into the 21st century."[36] Taking full advantage of the capabilities of sound reproduction technologies and the infrastructure of the recording company, Zorn's series conjures the diversity of American Jewish identities through its eclectic musical juxtapositions. These discs suggest a view of cultural identity as constructed and represented through the combination of elements from present-day and historic modes of expression.[37]

Zorn's Radical Jewish Culture series emerged out of an experimentalist musical scene centered in downtown New York City clubs and performance spaces in the 1990s.[38] This movement's signature musical fusion is exemplified by Zorn's quartet Masada, which borrowed from the modes of the Ashkenazi synagogue and klezmer ensemble in novel combinations, in performances that took on the instrumental and formal structure of free jazz in the style of Ornette Coleman.[39] Through Zorn's recording company and the marketing and distribution networks on which its recordings were sold, this local music scene became available to listeners worldwide, and attracted far-flung musicians to participate in new projects for the label.[40] For example, the first track of the 1998 album "Smash, Clap," recorded for Tzadik by the band Naftule's Dream, opens with nearly a minute of free-form wailing on the trombone, which scratches and bends pitches in a manner that evokes the *krekhts* effect (Yiddish for "sob") typical of klezmer clarinet and fiddle performance, as well as an air-raid siren or shofar blast. What follows in this number, titled "Black Wedding," is a klezmer dance performed as though by a carnival band. The melody conforms to the "Ukrainian Dorian" mode common in klezmer and Yiddish song, in which the third scale degree is lowered and the fourth is raised to produce the interval of an augmented second.[41] But the ensemble includes a modern drum set, an electric guitar, and a piano played in the spirit of jazz improvisation, as well as a heavy, low brass section, and the track is structured as a jazz number, in which the ensemble joins together to repeat the melodic "head," in alternation with improvisatory riffs taken in turn by different instruments.

In 2006 Zorn contributed to the label's website an essay that operates as a sort of manifesto detailing his conception of Jewish music and its future. He writes, "As the jewish [*sic*] people continue to grow into the 21st century, they carry their culture along with them. Tradition, history and the past have always played a strong role in the life of the jews but it is also important to think about the future. As we grow as a people, it seems natural that our culture should grow along with us."[42] Zorn proposes that the discs in the series aim to address several fundamental questions about Jewish music at the turn of the twenty-first century: "What is jewish music? What is its future? If asked to make a contribution to jewish culture, what would you do? Can jewish music exist without a connection to klezmer, cantorial or yiddish theatre?"

If the first two of these questions relate to what might be considered "ontologies" of Jewish music – what Jewish music *is* and *will be* to different people, a subject addressed by Philip V. Bohlman in the opening essay in this volume – the third asks musicians to consider what role they might play in the course of Jewish music's development as a form of cultural expression. The final question deals with a persistent subject of Zorn's work (recall his description of the series as "Jewish music beyond klezmer"), an attempt to move away from the stylistic tropes associated with those genres originating in eastern Europe, whose sounds are most commonly invoked in contemporary American musical expressions of Jewishness.[43] Zorn's aim is to attempt to answer these questions by promoting musical collaborations and stylistic fusions in the discs released by his record label. But the questions underlying Zorn's series do not relate only to the present day and the future: they are important to our consideration of Jewish music's past as well.[44] With his Radical Jewish Culture series, Zorn promotes new contributions to contemporary Jewish music that highlight the hybridity of so many global Jewish musical forms throughout their history.

Listening at the turn of the twenty-first century

With the advent of portable sound technology in the late twentieth and early twenty-first centuries such as the Walkman and the MP3 player, listening has become simultaneously more private and more public: with headphones, one can listen alone in a crowded space. Dubbing this the "Walkman effect," Shuhei Hosokawa writes that listening in the age of portable playback devices becomes "listening *and*," meaning that rather than directing full attention to the music in an exclusive act of listening, people often listen while attending to other activities; piped through headphones, the music becomes the setting for seemingly unrelated daily tasks.[45] The social context for listening has become smaller than the religious congregation, the community of radio listeners, the neighborhood, or the household: it has become individualized. Meanwhile, the range of possible venues for listening has expanded beyond specific places, such as the synagogue, the festival celebration, the town square, the concert hall, or the domestic space, to potentially anywhere one can carry a portable listening device. But Jewish music, often fully wrested from its original functions, now becomes the sonic context for whatever activities we choose to accompany with it: a *freylekhs* (a common genre of fast klezmer dance) by the Klezmatics or a song by the Israeli pop singer Ofra Haza (1957–2000) can become the soundtrack for a shopping trip, a workout on the elliptical machine, or a walk in the park.

Another turn-of-the-century medium that has had a transformative effect on the course of Jewish music is the World Wide Web. Several libraries and musical institutions host websites that serve as portals to access the sounds of Jewish music through digitized archival sound recordings as well as recordings of contemporary performances of historic compositions. For example, the organization Pro Musica Hebraica, which carries out the aim of "Bringing Jewish music to the concert hall," has a website that provides historical background about composers of art music on Jewish themes such as the members of the St. Petersburg Society for Jewish Folk Music, as well as recent recordings of numerous works performed on their concert programs.[46] The Milken Archive of Jewish Music offers biographical essays about composers and performers, oral histories, photographs, videos, and historical documents, as well as new recordings of works by Jewish composers in America. The organization defines its objectives as preserving "music related to the American Jewish experience," encouraging the performance of this repertoire and the composition of new music "that speaks to the American Jewish experience," and serving the curatorial and pedagogical aims of compiling written and visual archives of materials related to this theme.[47] The capabilities of the website medium are crucial to this institution, which began in 1990 by producing compact discs of new recordings but has expanded to found a "virtual museum" that takes advantage of this platform to present "*all* of the Milken Archive's resources... simultaneously, interactively and, most importantly, contextually."[48] Another website, the Judaica Sound Archives, is an online collection based at Florida Atlantic University that hosts discographies and streams recordings of music by singers from the early twentieth century to the present including cantors, stars of Yiddish theater and Tin Pan Alley, klezmer musicians, and performers in multiple other genres.[49] Additional archival discs of klezmer, cantillation, and other music captured on early recording devices are reproduced to illustrate music-related entries in the *YIVO Encyclopedia of Jews in Eastern Europe*.[50]

There is also a growing quantity of electronic applications for smartphones and tablets dedicated to the archiving and dissemination of Jewish music. One such app, The Jewish Radio, offers streaming access to international Jewish-themed radio programming. Another, Jewish Rock Radio, plays Jewish-themed rock music from around the world. Its developers' description of their vision of the app's social contribution reflects early observations about the unifying potential of the newly invented radio: they write, "JRR is a global communication channel for Jewish youth and young adults to communicate with each other about the wealth of opportunities for meaningful engagement and connection in the Jewish world."[51] Sounds associated with Jewish celebration and worship can be played back on multiple apps released by the company Rusty Brick, the creator of The Jewish Radio, replacing traditional tools and instruments as sources of these effects; for example, the Megillas Esther app plays the cacophonous *grager* (noise-maker) heard on the holiday of Purim, and the traditional patterns of blowing on the *shofar* (the traditional instrument made from a ram's horn) can be sounded using the Shofar app. Liturgical cantillation can be heard through multiple apps produced by Cantor Emanuel Perlman under the umbrella label of Pocket Shul, including "A Cantor's Seder," "Blessings of Health," "High Holiday Highlights," and "Torah Blessings." In an echo of early twentieth-century arguments about the use of the phonograph as a medium for preserving music that was feared to be in danger of dying out in the face of modernity, Perlman believes the medium of the app will play a critical role in protecting cantorial music from disappearance in the contemporary age because of its potential to provide listeners with ready access to this repertoire whenever and wherever they might require it. He explains, "In every age, we have to adapt to the way information is transmitted . . . and today that means the app . . . But the message is still the same."[52]

* * *

As we see from the histories recounted in this chapter, however, changes in the medium of transmission ineluctably contribute to changes in the message. The advent of sound recording provoked musicians, record producers, and audiences to alter the ways cantorial music was sung, listened to, and defined, and the ways cantors developed their careers. The multilingual programming and audiences of Yiddish radio were conducive to the development of stylistically mixed music that served as a vehicle for the formation of communities among American Jews in the early twentieth century. And Zorn's Tzadik record label provided the infrastructure for the creation and dissemination of a repertoire of musical stylistic fusions under the rubric of "Jewish music," to represent the hybrid sense of identity shared by many contemporary Jewish listeners at the turn of the twenty-first century. New media of sound reproduction are not simply incorporated into existing structures of musical performance and listening; rather, they offer new ways of making and experiencing music, and in this manner they effect how musical categories are constructed, defined, and viewed in relation to contemporary Jewish identities.

Notes

1 Thomas A. Edison, "The Phonograph and Its Future," *North American Review*, 126 (1878): 530–6 (530).
2 Considering the transformative impacts of new media on American Jewish cultures more generally, Jeffrey Shandler writes, "American Jews' encounters with new media have become a means of continually redefining their notions of religious literacy, propriety, authority, communality, and spirituality." *Jews, God, and Videotape: Religion and Media in America* (New York University Press, 2009), 4–5.
3 Josh Kun, *Audiotopia: Music, Race, and America* (Berkeley and Los Angeles: University of California Press, 2005), 22.
4 *Ibid.*, 3.
5 Shandler, *Jews, God, and Videotape*, 17.
6 *Ibid.*, 18–19.
7 *Ibid.*, 10.
8 *Ibid.*, 24.
9 *Ibid.*
10 *Ibid.*, 21–2.
11 *Ibid.*, 19.
12 *Ibid.*, 26–7.
13 Mark Kligman, "The Music of Kol Nidre," in Lawrence A. Hoffman (ed.), *All These Vows: Kol Nidre* (Woodstock, VT: Jewish Lights Publishing, 2011), 67–70 (67–8).
14 The recording can be heard online at www.yivoencyclopedia.org (accessed February 20, 2015).
15 Benedict Anderson, *Imagined Communities: Reflections on the Origin and Spread of Nationalism* (London: Verso, 1991). See also Michele Hilmes, "Radio and the Imagined Community," in Jonathan Sterne (ed.), *The Sound Studies Reader* (London and New York: Routledge, 2012), 351–62 (351).
16 Quoted in Hilmes, "Radio and the Imagined Community," 352–3.
17 Ari Y. Kelman, *Station Identification: A Cultural History of Yiddish Radio in the United States* (Berkeley and Los Angeles: University of California Press, 2009), 30.
18 *Ibid.* On debates in Israel over radio broadcasting on holidays, see Yoel Cohen, *God, Jews and the Media: Religion and Israel's Media* (London and New York: Routledge, 2012), 66–7.
19 Kelman, *Station Identification*, 50.
20 *Ibid.*, 2.
21 *Ibid.*, 20.
22 *Ibid.*, 41, 95.
23 For an oral history of music on the Yiddish radio with multiple archival sound examples, see Dave Isay, Henry Sapoznik, and Yair Reiner, *Yiddish Radio Project: Stories from the Golden*

Age of Yiddish Radio (Minneapolis: HighBridge, 2002), compact disc.
24 Kelman, *Station Identification*, 25.
25 See Henry Sapoznik, *Klezmer! Jewish Music from Old World to Our World* (New York: Schirmer Books, 1999), 118–25.
26 See Sapoznik, *Klezmer!*, 125–32.
27 *Ibid.*, 143. This followed the practice of "swinging the classics," which can be found in the repertoire of bandleaders including Tommy Dorsey and Benny Goodman. See Charles Hiroshi Garrett, "'Shooting the Keys': Musical Horseplay and High Culture," in Jane F. Fulcher (ed.), *The Oxford Handbook of the New Cultural History of Music* (Oxford University Press, 2011), 245–63 (257–9).
28 Isay, Sapoznik, and Reiner, "Yiddish Radio Project," episode 1.
29 Sapoznik, *Klezmer!*, 143.
30 Josh Kun, liner notes to *The Barry Sisters: Our Way* (Stereophonic, 2008), compact disc.
31 For a history of "Hava Nagila" see James Loeffler, "Hava Nagila's Long, Strange Trip: The Unlikely History of a Hasidic Melody," http://www.myjewishlearning.com/culture/2/Music/Israeli_Music/Folk_Music/Hava_Nagila.shtml (accessed February 20, 2015).
32 Marvin Caplan, "The Curious Case of Bei Mir Bist Du Schön," *Congress Monthly*, 62.1 (Jan/Feb 1995): 13–16.
33 *Ibid.*, 14.
34 This recording can be heard on *The Barry Sisters* (Banner Records, BA-1009), LP.
35 This turn to klezmer in the middle of the track was a common element of their songs, a formal quality heard also in the recordings of the comedian, musician, and radio host Mickey Katz (1909–85), who would typically sandwich an energetic passage of klezmer clarinet playing between jazzy opening and closing sections. See Josh Kun, "The Yiddish Are Coming: Mickey Katz, Antic-Semitism, and the Sound of Jewish Difference," *American Jewish History*, 87.4 (1999): 343–74 (351).
36 http://www.tzadik.com (accessed February 27, 2014).
37 Jonathan Freedman, *Klezmer America: Jewishness, Ethnicity, Modernity* (New York: Columbia University Press, 2008), 91.
38 See Tamar Barzel, *New York Noise: Radical Jewish Music and the Downtown Scene* (Bloomington: Indiana University Press, 2014).
39 See Tamar Barzel, "An Interrogation of Language: 'Radical Jewish Culture' on New York City's Downtown Music Scene," *Journal of the Society for American Music*, 4.2 (2010): 215–50 (210–11); idem, "If Not Klezmer, then What?

Jewish Music and Modalities on New York City's Downtown Music Scene," *Michigan Quarterly Review*, 42.1 (Winter 2003): 79–94 (81).

40 On the origins of this movement, see Jeff Janeczko, "Negotiating Boundaries: Musical Hybridity in Tzadik's Radical Jewish Culture Series," in Lisa Ansell, Josh Kun, and Bruce Zuckerman (eds.), *The Song is Not the Same: Jews and American Popular Music*, The Jewish Role in American Life 8 (West Lafayette, IN: Purdue University Press, 2011), 137–68 (137–9).

41 See Moshe Beregovski, "The Altered Dorian Scale in Jewish Folk Music (1946)," in Mark Slobin (ed. and trans.), *Old Jewish Folk Music: The Collections and Writings of Moshe Beregovski* (Syracuse University Press, 2000), 549–67.

42 Throughout his essay Zorn avoids using capital letters for words such as "jewish" and "yiddish." http://www.tzadik.com.

43 Judah M. Cohen addresses the question of the familiar aural tropes that typically prompt listeners to identify music as "Jewish," and the ways these tropes are used in records in Zorn's series, in "Exploring the Postmodern Landscape of Jewish Music," in Vincent Brook (ed.), *You Should See Yourself: Jewish Identity in Postmodern American Culture* (New Brunswick, NJ: Rutgers University Press 2006), 97–118 (103).

44 See also Freedman, *Klezmer America*, 91.

45 Shuhei Hosokawa, "The Walkman Effect," *Popular Music*, 4 (1984): 165–80 (171).

46 promusicahebraica.org (accessed February 20, 2015).

47 www.milkenarchive.org/about/message/lowell#/about (accessed February 20, 2015).

48 www.milkenarchive.org/about/message/lowell#/about/why_a_virtual_museum (accessed February 20, 2015).

49 faujsa.fau.edu/jsa/home.php (accessed February 20, 2015).

50 www.yivoencyclopedia.org (accessed February 20, 2015).

51 https://itunes.apple.com/us/app/jewish-rock-radio/id393347609?mt=8 (accessed February 20, 2015).

52 Simi Horwitz, "Cantor's Apps Bring Jewish Prayers to the iPhone Crowd," *Jewish Daily Forward*, February 15, 2013.

PART TWO

Jewish music in religious, folk, and popular contexts

5 The music of Israel during the Iron Age

THEODORE W. BURGH

Ancient Israelite culture and music

Music is a ubiquitous means of expression and communication and an indelible part of nearly every ancient and modern culture. It transcends spoken language, ethnicity, and chronology. People craft musical sounds in multiple creative ways, including to match the sounds heard in nature. These organized sounds become features of a culture. Sometimes combined with words or other unique human sounds, music becomes a way of life, and people use music to mark cultural and life cycle events such as birth, death, illness, war, travel, and entertainment. Moreover, the objects used to create music come from nature. They are often organic materials such as various types of wood (e.g., bamboo, acacia), clay, and animal remains (e.g., bone, sinew, teeth), and at times nature itself may be the instrument – for example in stomping or beating on the ground, the slapping of bodies of water, and the manipulation of the air to make tones by twirling overhead instruments like prehistoric bullroarers.[1]

Music sets the mood of an event or activity. For instance, in past cultures and some today, wailing women and men assist in the mourning process and in honoring the dead (Celtic, Africa), celebratory songs uplift soldiers returning from victorious battles, and mnemonic lyrics help to teach valuable school lessons to children, convey clandestine messages, and preserve family lineages and cultural history.

The geographical focus of this chapter is the land of Israel during the Iron Age (1200–586 BCE), a time identified by many as the biblical period. Ancient Israelites used music in many similar ways. Unfortunately the exact sounds and most intricate details regarding early Israelite music are lost and unrecoverable at this point. Ancient texts, however, in particular the Hebrew Bible and archaeological artifacts, give insight regarding performers, the types of instruments used, and possible performance contexts. Scholars continue to discover and research informative aspects of ancient Near Eastern cultures in general and the Israelites in particular. The relatively new field of archaeomusicology contributes to our understanding of the development and use of music in early societies. This chapter employs the discipline to explore the roles of music in Israelite culture, the primary characteristics of the music, the types of instruments used, and the questions of who served as musicians and where these musicians performed.

Types of instruments in early Israel

Ancient and modern instruments are typically classified using the Sachs-Hornbostel system of chordophone, aerophone, membranophone, and idiophone, which is also referred to as the CAMI system. The following is a brief description of each instrument classification, modern equivalents, and early Israelite examples.

I Chordophones

These are stringed instruments. A string or strings are often stretched across a surface, and the player strikes or plucks the string with the hand or object (e.g., pick, plectrum). The player may also rub a bow across the string to produce sound. The vibration of the string creates the sound, and the tautness of the string determines the pitch. In some chordophones, the strings are stretched across a box, gourd, or other hollow body with an opening and connect to pegs usually at the opposite end of the instrument. When the player strikes the strings stretched across the opening, the sound is amplified. Modern examples of chordophones include the acoustic guitar and violin.

Chordophones in Early Israel. The lyre (Hebrew: *kinnor*) and harp (Hebrew: *nevel*) were the primary chordophones in ancient Israel. While these instruments are very close in design, there are important differences. The Israelite lyre has a basic U-shaped body. The arms are parallel, for the most part, and attach to a bar that lies across the top and connects them. Ornamentation or decoration of the wood often appears at the top of each arm (e.g., the head of an animal, a flower), and there are tuning pegs along the top of the cross-bar. The tuning pegs control the tautness and intonation of the strings, which extend down over the body of the instrument and connect the lower portion. The body of the lyre is usually hollow. The harp is angular in shape, resembling a sideways "V" or the letter "L." The strings attach to the upper and lower arms, and like the lyre, there are tuning pegs on the upper arm. Israelite harps do not have a hollow body or sound box.

Archaeological artifacts and the Hebrew Bible show the popularity of these instruments, as they appear frequently in both. Hebrew Bible writers mention the lyre most often (in over twenty-four verses), and there are instances in which the lyre and harp appear together (Psalm 57:8). Likewise, the lyre is most prevalent in artifacts, often included in artists' depictions or displayed with figures in figurines. It is important to note that in all of the examples available to us, no two are exactly alike, which suggests that the instruments were not mass-produced. The lute may have been an instrument played at specific times or in select events in Israelite culture, but many questions remain regarding its consistency among the instruments used and its identification in ancient texts.

II Aerophones

These are wind-blown instruments; Israelite aerophones included the pipe, flute, shofar, and trumpet. Generally speaking, the player blows air directly into the instrument, sometimes with the aid of a mouthpiece. Some aerophones have single and double reeds, which vibrate when air passes over them. Examples of modern aerophones include trumpets, tubas, oboes (double-reed), and saxophones (single-reed).

Aerophones in early Israel. The most popular aerophone in ancient Israel was the pipe (*ḥalil*), sometimes referred to as the flute. Because of the materials used in their construction (typically animal bone or clay), flutes do not survive well in the archaeological record. There are, however, remains of single and double pipes. The single pipe is similar to a whistle. It usually has one or two holes in the body of the instrument. The player blows into one end and covers or opens the holes on the body. The double pipe is the same type of instrument, but there are two pipes side by side or in a "V" shape, joined by string, clay, or other adhesive. The pipes typically have reeds, through which the player blows. One pipe may sound a drone, while melodic lines can be played on the other.

The Israelites also used the trumpet (*hatsotsera*) and the shofar. It appears that the Israelite trumpet was similar to the modern bugle in the way it was played. There were no valves or additional tubes like those found on the modern instrument; the player manipulated the sound with the lips. To date, archaeologists have not discovered any physical remains of the trumpet. The shofar, an aerophone constructed from an animal's horn, usually from a ram or bovine, is played in the same manner as the Israelite trumpet or bugle. While both instruments were a part of musical performance, they were also symbols of Israelite culture and were used as signalers and conveyors of information.

III Membranophones

These are instruments in which a membrane is stretched over an opening and the surface is struck with the hand or a stick or other object. There are many examples of modern membranophones (e.g., snare drum, congas).

Membranophones in early Israel. Membranophones often suffer the natural fate of artifacts made of organic materials, thus most of the examples available to us appear in drawings and figurines. The most popular membranophone in ancient Israel is the frame drum. The frame drum is similar to the tambourine, but the membranophones of ancient Israel did not have the metal jingles around the edges. There are questions regarding whether the drums were struck with the hand, or with a stick or other device. All of these possibilities are plausible and should be considered.

IV Idiophones

These are self-sounding instruments or instruments that sound within themselves. Modern examples include rattles and cymbals.

Idiophones in early Israel. Rattles and cymbals were the primary idiophones in ancient Israel. Rattles were made from clay and have been discovered in anthropomorphic and geometric shapes, as well as representations of vegetables and other objects. Peas, seeds, or hardened clay enclosed inside the rattle hit the walls and create a sound when the player shakes or strikes the instrument. Cymbals are usually played when struck against each other or with a stick. These discs average eight inches in diameter and are typically made of bronze.

V Miscellaneous instruments in early Israel

Some instruments can span more than a single category, but generally are placed in only one of them. Although not yet found in ancient Israel, tambourines, of which Middle Eastern types are known as the *duff* or *daff*, have jingles and a membrane, which place them in the membranophone and idiophone categories. Excavations have revealed that the Israelites used an Egyptian instrument called the *sistrum*. The sistrum is shaped like a paddle. A handle connects to an oval- or ankh-shaped frame. Jingles hang on wire strings that extend to each side of the body. When the player shakes or strikes the instrument, the jingles strike each other to produce sound. The sistrum was a favorite instrument of the Egyptian goddess Bastet.

General music of the Israelites via the Bible and archeology

The Hebrew Bible and archaeological artifacts paint a picture of an Israel in which people wove music into daily life, and because music was an integral part of the culture, everyone participated. The biblical writers describe inclusive musical activities in events such as Moses and the Israelites singing together following their daring escape from Egypt (Exodus 15:1); the celebration of a king once he is anointed (1 Kings 1:39–40; 2 Kings 9:13); and the sound of the shofar to praise an Israelite deity (Psalm 150:3). Music was a useful element that entertained, aided in teaching, and conveyed information.

Israelite musical performers

It is clear that music was essential in Israelite culture and a part of people's lives in numerous ways. Yuval is the first person the biblical writers mention who is connected specifically with musical instruments and musical performance, as well as with the etiology of music: "His brother's name was Yuval; he was the ancestor of all those who play the lyre and the pipe" (Genesis 4:21, *New Revised Standard Version*). The writers also describe cultural events involving music in which large groups of people or "all of Israel" participated (e.g., 1 Kings 1:40; 2 Samuel 6:5). Singing, chanting, clapping, blowing whistles, and shaking rattles are ways that were inclusive, but there were some individuals that had more specialized roles in musical performance.

Portrayals of the temple in Jerusalem present men working in several capacities (e.g., as priests, prophets, and gatekeepers), but in addition to these duties, some were musicians. The Chronicler explains that when David – who served as court musician for King Saul and was a popular psalmist – established a working system of assignments in the temple, he charged Asaph, Heman, and Jeduthun to prophesy with cymbals (1 Chronicles 25:1). They were also leaders in the performance of temple music. A number of singers and musicians were under their direction (1 Chron. 25:6). Music in the temple was elaborate and the relationships between participants were intricate. Musicians played trumpets, cymbals, harps, and lyres. There were choirs. Everyone had a specific location, and activities were carefully choreographed and synched.

In most musical scenes in the Hebrew Bible, it is implied or accepted that men were the primary performers. Women were a major part of ancient Israelite musical performance, however, and archaeology and the biblical text offer valuable information regarding their involvement. One of the first instances concerns Miriam, the sister of Moses and Aaron. Following Moses' singing with the Israelites ("Song of Moses," Ex. 15:1–19), Miriam leads the women of Israel in celebration of their escape from oppression. Miriam begins singing and dancing with a frame drum, and "all the women" follow her (Ex. 15:20–1). It is interesting to note that the writers state that all of the women in this celebration had drums. Women with frame drums dancing and singing together to celebrate victories appear to have been a traditional part of Israelite culture. A similar event takes place when David returns home with Saul and the rest of the Israelite army following his famous encounter with and slaying of the infamous Philistine giant Goliath. Women with frame drums and other instruments gather to meet the young warrior and King Saul as they make their way home following war with the Philistines. As the women play their instruments they sing a song, slightly disparaging to Saul, about the heroic accomplishments of David and the King (1 Sam. 18:6–7).

These women were participants in what Eunice Poethig calls the Victory Song Tradition.[2] Women with instruments such as the frame drum sere-naded victorious soldiers returning from battle. Jephthah's daughter also performs with drums and sings for her father as he returns home from a suc-cessful war. The victory song troupes and this type of performance appear to have been established cultural activities during this period in ancient Israel.

There are numerous female figurines dating to the time identified as the biblical period that display frame drums. For the most part, there are two styles of figurines: figurines in the round and plaque figurines. Figurines in the round are similar to small statues. Parts of them are made from molds and other parts are fashioned by hand. They typically stand on their own, and one can walk around them and view them from all sides. Plaque figurines are made from a mold and are usually leaned against a wall or some other object. Excavations at the coastal sites of Shikmona and Achzib have produced excellent examples of figurines in the round with frame drums and double pipes. Although the archaeological data and a host of figurines indicate that women played the frame drum primarily, men played this instrument as well. Plaque figurines with frame drums have been discovered at Tel Tanaach and Megiddo.

There are questions regarding the involvement of women and musical performance in the Israelite temple. For instance, the Chronicler states after listing the family members of Heman the seer:

> All of these were the sons of Heman the king's seer, according to the promise of God to exalt him; for God had given Heman fourteen sons and three daughters. They were all under the direction of their father for the music in the house of the LORD with cymbals, harps, and lyres for the service of the house of God. Asaph, Jeduthun, and Heman were under the order of the king. (1 Chron. 25: 1–6)

This passage suggests that the daughters of Heman along with the men were involved in temple musical performance. There is also a psalmist's description: "Your solemn processions are seen, O god. The processions of my God, my King, into the sanctuary – the singers in front, the musicians last, between them girls playing frame drums" (Ps. 68:24–5).

Early Israelite culture and musical performance

Music and musical instruments were a part of important decisions and actions in Israelite culture. After the Israelites escape from Egypt, Moses is scheduled to speak with the deity of Israel on Mt. Sinai (Ex. 19:1–19). The deity and Moses converse in the midst of smoke that engulfs the mountain. While they are together, someone sounds a trumpet or shofar or ram's horn, often translated as "trumpet," possibly indicating the god's presence. The writers describe a similar instance with two priests as trumpeters, Benaiah and Jahaziel. David instructs them to blow their trumpets continuously before the Ark of the Covenant, an act that may let the people know the deity was among them.

The Israelites used the trumpet as a signal to act, move, assemble, or disperse. In the destruction of Jericho, the Israelites have the task of taking the major city that is surrounded by a massive wall. Instead of brute force, the people march around the city seven times, and on the seventh they blow trumpets and shout. The wall falls flat, and they are able to take the city and destroy its inhabitants. The people listen the sound of the trumpet as an indicator of battle and act accordingly (Numbers 9:10). The prophet Jeremiah exemplifies this: "for I hear the sound of the trumpet, the alarm for war" (Jeremiah 4:19).

Music was also a means to inquire and comprehend the will of the deity, particularly in prophesy. When King Jehoshaphat requests divine instruction from the deity by way of prophet Elisha, the prophet says, "get me a musician" (2 Kings 3:15). As the musician plays, he makes a connection with the deity to reveal the prophecy. The writers do not indicate what kind of instrument was involved, but the musician plays to aid the prophet. Note that in this instance, the prophet is an active participant, one who seeks the will of the deity, using music to achieve a certain elevated or enhanced state. According to the text, there may have been times when bystanders became passive participants in prophetic activity that involved music. This happens to King Saul. As he and Samuel are speaking, a band of musicians (lyre, harp, frame drum, cymbals, and pipe) are coming down from the high place. The prophets are in a prophetic frenzy from the deity. Samuel tells Saul that he will soon be caught up in the frenzy with them. As the musicians and prophets pass, Saul is pulled to their group, which causes people to ask, "Is Saul also among the prophets?" (1 Sam. 10:5–11).

The Israelites treated illnesses with the sounds of music. At the beginning of his downfall, Saul, Israel's first king, receives an evil spirit from the deity, which torments him with psychotic problems and causes him to act violently. His servants enlist the musical services of David the lyre player. The young musician temporarily relieves Saul's illness with his skillful lyre playing (1 Sam. 19:9).

Music was a part of birth and death in Israel. Specific songs sung at or during the birthing process are not in the text, but a child entering the world would have been welcomed and serenaded at some point by music. It is also clear that music was part of death. Wailing was a part of the grieving process, as specific individuals sang wails and laments for the deceased (Judges 11:40; 2 Chron. 35:25). It is not clear whether instruments other than the voice were used in singing laments, but both men and women sang them in Israelite culture (2 Chron. 35:25).

Ideas about the sound of music in Ancient Israel

The most perplexing enigma regarding music in early Israel is the question: What did the music sound like? An accurate answer to this query would be a priceless discovery, but finding such a thing is highly unlikely. First, there is no concrete reference point regarding how the music of antiquity sounded. Second, how will we know when or if we have achieved it? Unfortunately, there are a host of subtleties that are unrecoverable. This is one of the issues that comes with studying the past. Voices, some colors, tastes, smells, and sounds are essential but fragile parts of life that do not survive in the archaeological record and critical details about them cannot be found in ancient texts. While it is an asset to have artifacts and ancient texts, we have to remember that we were not the intended audience and writers were not writing for posterity. Thus, how these objects are used in the study of the past is crucial and will affect the questions we ask as well as the outcomes of the research.

When it comes to the sounds of the music of early Israel, we can say conclusively that musicians used many types of instruments. Employing our present knowledge, we can explore ideas regarding the sounds created through reconstructions, virtual instruments, and other means. Yet matters such as the different colors a player may have been able to produce on a lyre or harp with different strings or plectrums, or the sounds of instruments made from various woods, the timbres of drums with skins from different animals, and their thickness and other variable attributes, remain elusive. These types of subtleties make music come alive. It tells us about preferences and likes and dislikes within the culture. When we hear singers and musicians today in most genres, we can detect so much information from their voices and their color, depth, vibrato, and strength. These characteristics were present in antiquity, but sadly are now lost to us. Even with all of the technical information we can derive from the text and archaeology, we are limited in our attempts to reproduce such an organic artistry from the past.

Although these obstacles are indelible in the study of how early Israelite music may have sounded, a number of groups have offered unique ideas and interpretations in the ancient Near East in general and Israel in particular. Many of these are well-researched and excellent productions. One of the earliest works is the album entitled *Sounds from Silence*.[3] Anne Kilmer and her team recorded information regarding Babylonian chordophone tunings and a musical interpretation of a Hurrian Cult song. Kilmer sang this hymn with lyre accompaniment. Their musical ideas came from translations of mathematical and musical tablets.

Among the literature on the subject of early Israelite music is *The Music of the Bible Revealed*, by Suzanne Haïk-Vantoura, a world-renown organist and composer.[4] Haïk-Vantoura presents the musical system called the *te'amim*, which allows one who understands the system to sing most of the Masoretic text (for further discussion, see Chapter 6 in this volume). She also completed recordings of the musical ideas she discusses. There are numerous questions and controversies regarding her work, as she was not a trained biblical scholar; however, she was a world-class musician who presents a thorough discussion of the system and very intriguing recordings of her ideas. Ancient texts and artifacts show the importance of music to the Israelites. This pervasive art form provides an insightful perspective about this enigmatic culture.

Notes

1 Joachim Braun, *Music in Ancient Israel/Palestine: Archaeological, Written, and Comparative Sources* (Grand Rapids, MI, and Cambridge: Wm. B. Eerdmans, 2002).

2 Eunice Poethig, *The Victory Song Tradition of Women of Israel*, Ph.D. dissertation, Union Theological Seminary (1985).

3 Anne Draffkorn Kilmer and Richard L. Crocker, *Sounds from Silence: Recent Discoveries in Ancient Near Eastern Music* (Bit Enki Publications, 1976), LP.

4 Suzanne Haïk-Vantoura, *The Music of the Bible Revealed: The Deciphering of a Millenary Notation*, ed. John Wheeler, trans. Dennis Weber, 2nd rev. edn. (Richland Hills, TX: D. and F. Scott Publishing, 1991).

6 Jewish liturgical music

MARK KLIGMAN

Introduction

The study of Jewish music is a challenging endeavor. One typically expects the liturgical music of a cultural group to be homogeneous and definable through melodic or rhythmic characteristics. But Jewish music is neither homogeneous nor definable. Due to the complex history of the Jewish people in the diaspora, Jewish music reflects a variety of contacts with local cultures throughout time. Therefore, the musical traits found in Jewish music are often characterized as adaptations of music from various local cultures, within a Jewish context. This is not to say that Jewish music is only made up of adapting music from other sources. Many genres, such as cantorial recitatives, Hasidic songs, *klezmer* repertories, Ladino songs, and *piyyutim* (the singing of religious poems), are unique to and centrally a part of Jewish culture. The fact that there is no universal feature to Jewish music does not diminish its value or importance. Rather, it is a reflection of the richness and development of Jewish musical culture. Jewish music needs to be considered within the context of the culture in which it is found, and situated within its place in history.

This chapter approaches the use of music in Jewish religious, liturgical, and paraliturgical situations (events for religious enrichment that are not mandated services). Both Ashkenazic and Sephardi/Mizrahi traditions are discussed in several geographic contexts.

Sources and challenges

The history of Jewish music is based upon a variety of sources: written, non-written, and oral. Each source provides a piece of a puzzle that creates an overall picture of Jewish music's past. The written sources include the Jewish textual tradition: Bible, midrash, Mishnah, Talmud, and responsa. These sources provide the primary basis from which to derive an understanding of the role of music during ancient, biblical, temple, and medieval Jewish life. Non-written sources include physical evidence of musical instruments found through archeological explorations. In addition, iconography (pictorial representations) from frescoes, mosaics, pottery decorations, and images on coins make up the many visual representations of music's use during the same early period of the written textual sources (ancient, biblical, and medieval times). Notated musical sources provide the most concrete record. Unfortunately, notation of Jewish music prior to 1700 is minimal, as only a few manuscripts are extant.[1] The oral tradition provides the richest source of melodic materials. Several regional traditions are represented in Abraham Zvi Idelsohn's monumental collection *Thesaurus of Hebrew-Oriental Melodies*, which was published in ten volumes between 1914 and 1932.[2] The regions represented in this collection include Yemen, Iraq, Persia, Syria, the "Jerusalem-Sephardic" tradition,[3] Morocco, eastern Europe, and central Europe. This collection provided the basis for study throughout the twentieth century. Present-day recordings of scholars and private collections from individuals and institutions have added a vast dimension available for examination.

Some scholars have tried to uncover the sound of Jewish music from antiquity. However, any attempt to connect modern practice with historic sources is wrought with dilemmas. For example, although rabbinic sources dating back two thousand years refer to the practice of the melodic recitation of the Bible, we still do not know the sound of that recitation. Some scholars imagine that Jews from Yemen have faithfully practiced their tradition of cantillation throughout this two-thousand-year period and insist that Yemenite biblical recitation in the twentieth century is an exact replication of the past.[4] Such claims are without merit. They are based on conjecture and are not provable.

An ongoing question that needs to be addressed involves the usefulness of contemporary oral traditions to understanding music of the past.[5] To what extent do present Ashkenazic and Sephardic traditions represent the continuation of oral traditions rooted in the past or the establishment of new practices? Each situation must be considered on its own merits. Today, ethnomusicology, the academic discipline that seeks to explore music and culture, stresses the in-depth understanding and unraveling of the complexities of a single tradition rather than trying to postulate broad, and often unprovable, theories about the universal nature of music in various cultures or across time. Documentation of an oral tradition should be placed in perspective and any attempts to project the antiquity of an oral musical tradition should be carefully considered.

History

I Contexts of music in the Bible and Temple

There are hundreds of references to music in the Bible and rabbinic sources related to the Temple in Jerusalem. The biblical references discussed below provide a few examples (for further discussion, see Chapter 5 in this volume). Events that refer to music include miraculous moments where God's power is praised and exalted, for example Moses's and Miriam's songs after the Egyptians were destroyed in the Red Sea (Exodus 15:1–18, 21). Important events accompanied by musical instruments include the transport of the ark to Jerusalem (2 Samuel 6:5; 1 Chronicles 13:8), the establishment and reconstitution of the Temple service (2 Kings 12:14; 1 Chron. 15:16–28), and the anointment of kings (1 Sam. 10:5; 1 Kings 1:34, 19–41; 2 Kings 11:14). Music's role in prophecy is deduced from David's playing of the harp, which cured Saul's depression (1 Sam. 16:14–23). Biblical passages also mention mourning (1 Kings 13:30; Jeremiah 48:36), newly composed laments by men and women (2 Chron. 35:25), and the ceasing of music after the destruction of the Temple (Lamentation 5:14; for a discussion in the Mishnah see Shabbat 23:4; Baba Metzia 6:1; Ketubot 4:4; Moed Katan 3:8). Other contexts of music include entertainment for the rich and the kings' courts (2 Sam. 19:36; Amos 6:5; Ecclesiastes 2:8), the inclusion of bells on the tunic of the high priest (Ex. 28:33–4, 39:25–6), and farewell ceremonies (Genesis 31:27). Although these and other references mention music, no specific detail is given about the type of music or its sound.

Music's role in the Temple is discussed in rabbinic literature as well. Surprisingly, no description of music's use for the *avodah* (worship or Temple sacrifice) is given in the Bible. Statements can be made concerning the following aspects of music in the Temple: instrumental and vocal practices, music's role in the service, and the application of the psalms. Instrumental playing and vocal singing constituted the medium of music in the Temple. The Bible names King David's chief musician as Asaph (1 Chron. 16:5). Many references are given to the number and type of instruments and voices used in the service (Arachin 2:3–6). The instruments can be divided into three categories: percussion, wind, and string. The one percussion instrument used was the *tsiltselim* (a pair of cymbals). The *tof* (drum) was not played in the Temple, most likely due to its use during noisy celebratory purposes.[6] The wind instruments include the *shofar* and *ḥatsotserah* (trumpet) to signal events. The *ḥalil* (flute) was also used but restricted to the twelve festal days (Ar. 2:3). The *ugav* (reed pipe), mentioned in Genesis 4:21, was not played in the Temple, perhaps due to the plethora of post-biblical references to the use of the *ugav* for ritually unclean purposes. String instruments include the *kinnor* and the *nevel*. Both are forms of lyre, with strings fastened to a frame, and most likely originated in Asia Minor. The *nevel* was the larger of the two, with a deeper tone,[7] and the *kinnor* was considered more regal because it was played by David (1 Sam. 16:23, 18:10, 19:9). The singers of the Temple were the Levites. During the Temple services this included adults between the ages of thirty and fifty, and young boys who added "sweetness" (Ar. 2:6). It is unclear if the Levites sang with the instruments or if they sang a cappella. Discussion is given to the training of Temple singers (Hullin 24a), vocal tricks (Yoma 3:11), and responsorial singing style (Sotah 5:4, B. 30b; Sukkah 3:11, B. 38b). The rabbinic sources for the Temple service dictate a minimum of twelve instruments for a regular weekday service: two *nevel*, nine *kinnor*, and one cymbal. This was matched by a minimum of twelve Levitical singers; the balance of instruments to singers was intentional (Ar. 2: 3–6).

The Mishnah Tamid (chapters 5–7) illustrates music's use within the service. After opening benedictions from the priests, sacrifices were offered. The *magrepha* (a large rake used for clearing the ashes) was thrown forcefully to the ground to summon other priests and Levites into the Temple, and ritually unclean members were sent to the east gate. Two priests stood by the altar and blew trumpets with the sounds of *tekiah*, *teruah*, and *tekiah* (*tekiah* is a single deep, sustained blast; *teruah* consists of nine short notes). The priests stood on both sides of the cymbal player, who sounded the instrument after the trumpet blasts. The Levites next sang a text from the Psalms. The trumpet blowing was then repeated, participants prostrated themselves, and the Levites continued singing. The psalm texts of the daily singing are indicated in Tamid 7:4. A psalm's *incipit* (introductory line) can provide a possible clue to the use of that psalm within the service, and may also offer evidence of melodic description, direction or place of use, and performance practice. Melodic description includes psalms beginning with indications of a song of a particular person or group, for example Korah (Psalm 87) and Asaph (Ps. 77); a style of performance in the melodic scale *al ha-sheminit* (Pss. 6, 12), or the use of an instrument such as *nehilot* (flute) (Ps. 5), *shigayon* (Ps. 7), *gitit* (Pss. 8 and 81), or *alamot* (Ps. 46);[8] and cue words of a known song, such as "Ayelet ha-shaḥar" (The Hind of the Dawn) (Ps. 22) or "Shoshanim" (Roses) (Pss. 45, 80). The issue of the performance practice of psalms is inferred from the portions of psalm texts that indicate a specific use, such as responsorial psalmody (leader-group alternation), as seen in the verse parallelism of Psalm 47, the antiphonal psalmody (alternation between two groups) suggested in certain passages (see Ps. 103 verses 20–2), and the litanies with repeated refrains such as Psalm 80 verses 4, 8, and 20. The 150 psalm texts are a rich source of material awaiting further analysis to reveal more about music's role in the Temple.[9]

II Development of liturgy and the ḥazzan

Music's role in liturgy was developed during the same period of time as the canonization of the liturgy text (between 100 and 1000 CE). After the destruction of the Second Temple in 70 CE the focus of Jewish ritual practices shifted to the synagogue. Even during the latter period of the

Second Temple synagogue rituals had begun to develop, and the practice intensified after the Temple's destruction. The recitation of the liturgical text replaced the requirement for ritual sacrifices. The primary canonization of the text of the liturgy was a process that developed between the eighth and eleventh centuries CE. The earliest compilation of prayer, known as *Seder Rav Amram*, dates to the ninth century, and includes biblical (particularly psalmodic), rabbinic, and poetic texts.

Passages drawn from the Bible and rabbinical prayers encompass the core of Jewish liturgy. Two portions of the morning service, the *Shema* and the *Amidah*, and the prayers of their environs are mandatory according to Jewish Law. The *Shema*, taken from three biblical passages (Deuteronomy 6:4–9, 11:13–21; Numbers 15:37–41), is the creed affirming the unity of one God. The *Amidah* is said in place of the daily sacrifices once performed in the Temple; this text evolved slowly and was defined, as it is known today, in the seventh century CE.

In general, the history of Jewish liturgy is divided into two rites: Ashkenazic and Sephardic.[10] The major distinguishing features between the two rites entail small changes in the order of the prayers and in the inclusion or exclusion of psalms and liturgical poems. The statutory prayers of the two major rites are the same, with only slight differences in wording. The Sephardic rite, a development originally from Spain, influenced the local rites of those European and Middle Eastern communities that received an influx of Spanish Jews after the expulsion from Spain in the sixteenth century.

Prior to the circulation of known settings of liturgical texts in the seventh century and thereafter, the non-statutory positions of the liturgy were textually improvised. Presumably the melodic recitation was also improvised. It was the task of the *ḥazzan* to create texts spontaneously. The term *ḥazzan* is presently applied to the leader of the prayers. The term first appeared in Mishnah sources and was used variously to indicate the teacher of children (Shabbath 1:3), the superintendent of prayer (Yoma 7:1, Sot. 7:8), and the one who announces the order of the proceedings (y. Berakoth 4:7d). Some speculate that the term *ḥazzan* comes from the word *ḥarzan* (to versify).[11] It was not until the ninth century that the *ḥazzan* became the religious officiant who led prayers. Interestingly, the role of the office of the *ḥazzan* was standardized at the same time that the liturgical text was codified (the eighth to eleventh centuries). Thus, the musical expression of the liturgy grew out of liturgical need, function, and aesthetics.

Three musical types in the reading of sacred texts

Cantillation, psalmody, and liturgical chant are liturgical musical practices formed in the medieval period. Cantillation refers to the melodic recitation of biblical texts during the service. Psalmody refers to the practice of reciting psalm texts within the liturgy that could include a single text or a grouping of multiple texts. Liturgical chant encompasses a broad range of melodic styles set to the non-biblical portions of the liturgy. The melodic styles mentioned here include rhythmic and non-rhythmic melodies. Later generations built upon these three types in culturally specific musical styles.

I Cantillation: Recitation of Torah

Biblical cantillation occurs whenever the Bible is read publicly. The indication that the Bible was read publicly is inferred from Deuteronomy 31:12: "Gather the people – men, women, children, and the strangers in your communities – that they may hear and so learn to revere the Lord your God and to observe faithfully every word of this Teaching." The yearly cycle of the biblical reading begins on the Sabbath following the Simchat Torah holiday. The process of cantillation was formalized into a system by Aaron Ben Moses Ben Asher during 900–30 CE. Ben Asher lived in Tiber and his system of cantillation symbols, *te'amei ha'mikrah*, is referred to as the "Ben Asher" or "Tiberian" system. These signs (*te'amim*), placed above or below the biblical text, were intended to provide grammatical indications for proper syntax and sentence division. The shapes of the signs indicate grammatical or musical function, visual representations of melodic contour, or the shapes of hand signs used to indicate the melody.[12] This later practice of hand signals is mentioned in the Gemara (Ber. 62a), and Rashi comments that even in his time, the eleventh century, the practice remained in effect. The practice is still found in some Yemenite communities.

Sephardic and Ashkenazic communities differ in their melodic interpretation of these cantillation symbols. The shape of the sign does not determine a fixed pitch or melodic phrase. Avigdor Herzog defines five regional styles in cantillation: Yemenite, Ashkenazic, Middle Eastern, North African, Jerusalem-Sephardic, and North Mediterranean.[13] Some traditions supply the specific melodic unit for each sign, while others use larger melodic units for a phrase. The Yemenite, Middle Eastern, North African, and Jerusalem-Sephardic are more recitative in style and some follow an Arabic *maqām* (mode) and are not in a Western scale. The Ashkenazic and North Mediterranean have the broadest melodic contours and most commonly have a different musical phrase for each melodic sign.

II *Nusaḥ*

Psalmody is the practice of melodically rendering psalm texts mostly used within the introductory part of the liturgy. The melodies are known as *pesuke dezimrah* in Ashkenazic liturgy and *zemirot* in Sephardic liturgy for the Sabbath morning service. Typically, psalm chanting consists of an introductory phrase, a medial recitation note, and a final phrase. The use of

Example 6.1 *HaShem Malakh* mode.

Example 6.2 *Magen Avot* mode.

psalms in Christian liturgy led many scholars to believe that the early music of the church based itself on Jewish models.[14] Eric Werner expounded upon this topic in his seminal work *The Sacred Bridge*.[15] Werner's conclusions have been the subject of greater scrutiny by chant scholars who see his work as speculative.[16] Several attempts have been made to note the similarities of Jewish and Christian traditions without specific focus on the uncertain origins of these practices, due to the lack of sufficient evidence.[17]

The mainstay of Ashkenazic liturgy is made up of the Jewish prayer modes, referred to as *nusaḥ*.[18] The prayer modes operate like other musical modes, which are defined by two parameters: scalar definition and a stock of melodies variously applied. The number of modes used in the Jewish tradition is a matter of scholarly debate.[19] The generally accepted practice today that is a part of the pedagogy in American cantorial schools is the adoption of three prayer modes, named *HaShem Malakh* (The Lord Reigns), *Magen Avot* (Shield of Our Fathers), and *Ahavah Rabbah* (Great Love).[20] The name of each prayer mode is taken from the opening words of the liturgical passage that marks one of the first usages of that particular mode in the Sabbath liturgy. Hence, music and text are closely associated.

The *HaShem Malakh* mode is similar intervallically to the Western major scale, but with a lowered seventh scale degree (Example 6.1). In most instances the four lowest notes (or tetrachord) of a melody's scale pattern determine a Jewish prayer mode. As the *ḥazzan* continues reciting *Kabbalat Shabbat*, the *HaShem Malakh* prayer mode is developed. An additional feature of the musical modes is an affective association, and grandeur and God's strength are connotations of the *HaShem Malakh*.

Magen Avot has intervallic similarity to the Western minor scale (Example 6.2). Recited towards the end of the Friday evening Sabbath prayer, the text of *Magen Avot* refers to the forefathers guarding the Sabbath. The mode is also heard in cantor's prayers on the Sabbath morning service, in the setting of the text *Shokhen Ad Maron* (He Who Dwells Forever). The typical ending of this mode emphasizes the fourth and final

Example 6.3 *Ahavah Rabbah* mode.

notes of the mode (F to C). *Magen Avot* is known as the didactic mode because it is used for extended declamations of text and does not make use of melodic elaboration.

Ahavah Rabbah has often been called the most "Jewish" of the Jewish Prayer modes, because of its distinctive sound. The essential feature is the augmented second interval between the second and third notes of the mode (Example 6.3). There is no Western equivalent to this mode. The broad augmented second is produced by the lowering of the second scale degree (here, from D, as it appears in *HaShem Malakh* and *Magen Avot*, to Db) while the third scale degree remains in place (here, on E). Expressive liturgical texts use this mode. The common example is heard on the Shabbat morning in the setting of the text *Tsur Yisrael* (Rock of Israel) that precedes the *Amidah*. *Ahavah Rabbah* means "great love," aptly reflecting the affective association of this mode, which musically expresses the "great love" for God through a unique musical sound.

In other sections of the cantor's recitation of prayers, all three Jewish prayer modes are used. The differing quality of each mode expresses the unique subtleties of the text. This modal modulation helps to heighten the meaning of the text through emotional expression associated with the use of the *nusaḥ*. The three modes are used to express the text of the Sabbath morning *Kedushah*, recited during the *ḥazzan*'s repetition of the *Amidah*, making it an important liturgical highlight. Ashkenazic liturgical music without harmony, performed by solo voice, demonstrates how the Jewish prayer modes aptly express the meaning of the text and provide a symbolic commentary. *Ḥazzanut* (the cantorial repertoire) is filled with intricate details combining textual and musical meaning.

III Liturgical chant

As the *ḥazzan*'s role became formalized with the development of the liturgy, so too did the liturgical chant. It is important to view the standardization of the texts, the need for the *ḥazzan*, and the growth of liturgical chant as coterminous, because they were simultaneous developments. The *ḥazzan* became the prayer leader for the congregation, known as *sheliaḥ tsibur* in Hebrew, who facilitated the prayers through musical recitation. This role was established during the eighth to tenth centuries CE. Musical developments kept pace with textual innovations, although we know more about the latter than the former. The development of the *piyyut* during this period saw the growth of new poetic forms to include the use of rhyme and meter. Music served as a means to express the text.

Attitudes about music began to change. Although there is quite limited musical notation from the year 1000 to 1750, we do know from written evidence that *ḥazzanim* and community members wanted to create new tunes while others, most notably rabbis, desired the preservation of older tunes, presumably to slow the rate of continued influence from surrounding non-Jewish musical practices. Cantors were known by name for the individual musical personalities that they brought to their musical recitation of prayers, and in some communities composers of music were identifiable.

Liturgical melodies in the Ashkenazic practice can be divided into two categories: *Mi-Sinai nigunim* (melodies from Mount Sinai) and metrical tunes. These two categories contain known melodies that are sung by the *ḥazzan*, the congregation, or both, and are associated with particular liturgical sections at specific times during the calendar year. The *Mi-Sinai nigunim* represent the oldest body of melodies in the Ashkenazic tradition and encompass the recurrent melodies of the High Holidays and the Three Festivals. No collection or tabulation of all the melodies exists. The term *Mi-Sinai nigunim* is not fully understood by cantors. Many have noted the similarity to the phrase "*halakhah le-Moshe mi-Sinai*" (a law given to Moses at Mount Sinai); in Talmudic discourse this phrase is used to denote a law put into Jewish practice with no originating biblical source. Hanoch Avenary has stated that the present musical application of the term *Mi-Sinai nigunim* is attributed to Abraham Zvi Idelsohn.[21] *Mi-Sinai nigunim* differ from Jewish prayer modes in that the former comprise set tunes of greater length whereas the latter are shorter musical fragments. Both musical types are similar in that they flexibly apply the melody or melodic fragment to the text. There is no exact correspondence between text and melody, so interpretations vary.

Ashkenazic tradition

I Pre-modern practices

During various periods preceding the *Haskalah* (the Jewish Enlightenment of the eighteenth and nineteenth centuries), different communities sought unique musical innovations in Jewish prayer. Most noteworthy are the Italian Jewish composers of the early seventeenth century and the Amsterdam composers of the early eighteenth century. These two communities provide the first examples of metrical tunes. Leon Modena (1571–1648), a rabbi in Ferrara, sought to reestablish artistic beauty in the synagogue, fueled by his enthusiasm for the ancient Temple music, and he supported a number of musical innovations. In 1605, for example, eight singers in the synagogue performed polyphonic (multi-voiced) music, a style that was contemporary for his time. The best-known composer of Jewish religious music during this era was Salamone Rossi (c. 1570–c. 1630), whose synagogue composition *Ha-shirim asher lishlomo* (Venice, 1622–3) displays the High Renaissance musical style (see Chapter 9). Rossi interweaves polyphonic musical lines with block chords in a manner similar to that found in the works of Giovanni Gabrieli (c. 1554–1612). The composers of music for Jewish occasions in Amsterdam, principally Christian Joseph Lidarti (1730–after 1793) and Abraham Caceres (Casseres, fl. early eighteenth century), were not Jewish. Although the development of Jewish music in Italy and Amsterdam during these eras was short-lived and the repertoire was not maintained in the tradition, the music shows the desire of those in Jewish religious circles to engage in the creation and performance of artistic music like that of their Christian contemporaries. Later generations continued to draw from the outside as a basis for innovation in synagogue music, and this music reached new heights.

II The early *Haskalah*

Ideological proponents of the *Haskalah*, who resided in large central European cities, sought to integrate the totality of Judaism (philosophy, culture, and religious practice) into the Western sphere of knowledge. Opponents favored an inward approach to Judaism seeking to solidify traditional Jewish practices with greater intensity. Musical practices, likewise, reflected a desire for incorporating external influence while, at the same time, keeping elements of traditional Jewish music, such as the *Mi-Sinai nigunim*. Synagogue compositions of this period added Baroque-like musical interludes to traditional melodies. These interludes were excesses and can be seen as an elaboration of the *meshorerim* practice – in which two assistants, a boy soprano and a male bass, traveled and sang with the cantor – with each of the three participants given an opportunity for melodic embellishments. Most often the boy soprano and bass were given this role in the interludes. An important individual who sought to incorporate secular musical practices was Israel Levy (1773–1832), also known by the last name Lowy and Lovy in France. Synagogue music gradually grew to include occasional harmonizations, and finally choral settings. Choral music for the synagogue originated in Italy and France and later moved into Germany, where it spread quickly.

During this time Hasidim sought spiritual beauty not through culturally elite practices but through ecstatic experience intent on elevating the soul. Hasidic music also borrowed from its cultural surroundings, incorporating folk tunes and many other sources, but artistry was not the goal. For

Hasidim, singing in the synagogue, at home, and at other occasions offered opportunities to engage in a deeper commitment to Judaism.

III Central European cantorial and synagogue music

The most significant development in central European cantorial and synagogue music resulted from the liturgical and aesthetic changes of the Reform movement (see Chapter 12). Although changes in various central European cities began in the late 1700s and early 1800s, reform did not take shape in an established fashion until the mid-nineteenth century. Israel Jacobson (1768–1829), a merchant by profession, initiated various changes to the synagogue service. These included the elimination of the *ḥazzan*, the use of Protestant hymns with Hebrew words, sermons in German, confirmation for boys and girls, and the reading, not cantillation, of the Bible. With the exception of the elimination of the *ḥazzan*, most of Jacobson's changes were incorporated into the Reform service later in the nineteenth century and thereafter. Many congregations replaced traditional Jewish music with hymnal singing in the Protestant style and in some cases literally supplanted known German Protestant hymns with Hebrew words. Jacobson introduced the first organ in Seesen in 1810. These reforms were initially seen as too drastic and later further developed with the central European cantorial style of Salomon Sulzer (1804–90) who from 1926 officiated at the New Synagogue in Vienna. Further developments took shape in the work of synagogue composer Louis Lewandowski (1821–94). Together with Samuel Naumbourg (1815–80), Lewandowski had a significant impact on central European synagogue music. Eastern European cantors also developed synagogue music from the nineteenth into the twentieth century. This includes the work of Nissan Blumenthal (1805–1903), Abraham Baer Birnbaum (1864–1922), and Eliezer Gerovich (1844–1913), a student of Blumenthal. Where the central European cantors were more innovative using secular musical styles of the Classical and early Romantic eras, the eastern European cantors retained modal influences of *nusaḥ* with modal harmonization. The eastern European synagogue tradition can also be distinguished from the central European tradition by the use of more vocal embellishments.

American Reform synagogues in the nineteenth century drew on the work of contemporary European composers, predominantly Sulzer and Lewandowski, as well as of American composers. Nineteenth-century American synagogue innovators included Sigmund Schlesinger (1835–1906) and Edward Stark (1863–1918), whose music was devoid of traditional prayer modes. An organist at a synagogue in Mobile, Alabama, Schlesinger set texts for the synagogue service to operatic excerpts from Bellini, Donizetti, and Rossini. Stark, a cantor at Temple Emanuel in San Francisco, used some traditional melodies. The Hungarian-born Alois Kaiser (1840–1908), an apprentice to Sulzer who had performed stints in Vienna (1859–63) and Prague (1863–6), immigrated to Baltimore, where he served as cantor to Congregation Ohab Shalom. His collections of synagogue music include hymnal compositions, melodies with four-part chorale settings following the Lutheran model of J. S. Bach.

These cantors and composers, though largely forgotten today, were instrumental in the emergence of *Minhag* America, a term coined by Isaac Mayer Wise, the mid-nineteenth-century progenitor of American Reform Judaism, to refer to a new and specifically American form of Jewish tradition. Originally the title of a prayerbook in 1856, *Minhag* America has been adopted more generally to refer to the Americanization of European Jewish traditions. Convinced that the communal singing of hymns was the quintessential religious experience, the Central Conference of American Rabbis resolved in 1892 to adopt Wise's publication as the official hymnbook of American Jewish Reform Congregations. Abraham W. Binder (1895–1966), professor of Jewish liturgical music at Hebrew Union College and founder of the Jewish Music Forum, became the editor of the third edition of the hymnal, which appeared in 1932. Although a part of many Reform congregations through the 1950s, hymn singing eventually fell out of fashion. The new approach in America was to write in a more modern idiom while still retaining elements from the past. Binder championed this approach, found in some of his liturgical settings for the Friday night service and Three Festivals. He also encouraged other aspiring composers in America to apply their talents to the synagogue. These included Herbert Fromm (1905–55) and Isadore Freed (1900–60). Freed was trained in America but spent some time studying in Europe, including as a composition pupil of Ernest Bloch (1880–1959), whose own major contribution to synagogue music, the *Sacred Service* (1933), was a monumental work for cantor, choir, orchestra, and narrator. The *Sacred Service* showed the most advanced musical styling in composition for the synagogue, inspiring synagogue composers for decades.

Music in Sephardic liturgy

Due to the diversity of Sephardic liturgical music, its study presents significant difficulties. The problem is compounded when one considers that the Sephardic practices are still maintained orally and only a limited amount of the repertoire has been notated and collected. In addition, Sephardic liturgical music has not received the same amount of study as Ashkenazic liturgical music and, hence, the research to draw upon is limited.

One other point deserves discussion. The term "Sephardic" has been variously understood in Judaic studies. The word *Sepharad* appears in the Bible in Obadiah 1:20 and is thought to refer to the Iberian Peninsula. The term "Sephardic" refers to Spanish Jews and their descendants in various points of relocation. Use of the term becomes problematic when these descendants relocated to other existing communities. In some cases the Spanish Jewish traditions replaced existing practices, while over time these immigrant Jews intermixed with the local Jewish culture. Through the remainder of this entry the term "Sephardic" may be better understood to refer to non-Ashkenazic Jews, as Sephardic Jewry has never been a single community that has remained unchanged over time.

I Influences of Arabic music and poetry

Arabic culture richly influenced medieval Jewish life in Spain, most significantly during the Spanish Golden Age (the eleventh to thirteenth centuries), a period in which Jewish culture flourished in an unprecedented way. Every dimension of Jewish religious and cultural life during this time drew from free interaction with non-Jewish cultures, which provided a fertile source of traditions that could be adapted for Jewish purposes.

Most notably, theoretical writings on the nature of music had a lasting influence on the manner in which music was viewed. Islamic scholars followed the ancient Greeks in conceiving of musical phenomena namely through acoustics and other abstract principles. In his *Emunot ve-Deot* (Beliefs and Opinions), from 933, Saadiah Goan wrote that there are eight types of musical rhythm that affect the human temper and mood. Similar concepts can be found in the works of Arabic writers on music including Al-Kindi (died c. 874). Other Jewish writers applied Saadiah's ideas to overlapping musical and moral phenomena and biblical events such as David's harp playing for Saul. In such ways, the discussion on the nature of music by Arabic music theorists was fused with Jewish concepts.

An area of innovation that significantly impacted music was the creation of liturgical poetry, the *piyyutim*. Arabic poetry increased in prominence through new rhyme schemes and a consistent use of meter. Hebrew poetry was likewise influenced through the poetry of Dunsah Labrat (tenth century) and others. After the 1492 expulsion from Spain, descendants of this rich tradition brought these cultural processes of creation with them. One significant figure was Israel Najara (1550–1620), who created new Jewish songs by replacing the lyrics of Turkish, Arabic, Spanish, and Greek songs with Hebrew. In this process of adaptation some of the sounds or assonances of the text were incorporated into his Hebrew poetry. The melody was often adapted to fit this new text. Thus, Sephardic music, both past and present, is comprised of adaptation. The adaptation of thought in theoretical writings about music parallels the adaptation of music and text found in the *piyyutim*. The wealth of Sephardic musical material to study is taken from the *piyyut* and paraliturgical traditions. The few purely liturgical sources have only been available recently due to new ethnographic studies.

II Musical influences and major regional styles

The discernable musical styles of Sephardic cantillation, liturgical prayers, and *piyyutim* can be classified according to four geographic regions: Spanish and Portuguese, Moroccan, *Edot hamizraḥ* (Middle Eastern or Arabic), and Yemenite.[22] The first two of these styles are more Westernized than the others. Spanish and Portuguese descendants who traveled to Western Europe, England, and Amsterdam, as well as the Americas, both North and South, brought their traditions with them and began to adapt them in their new homes. Moroccan Jewry received a large number of Spanish Jewish refugees during the fifteenth and sixteenth centuries. Jewish musical traditions from Morocco have been continually influenced by regional Spanish traditions such as Andalusian. The two other musical styles, *Edot hamizraḥ* and Yemenite, are marked by the influence of Arabic music. Spanish elements within these two traditions are faint or nonexistent. The *Edot hamizraḥ* include the Jews of the Levant (Syrian, Lebanon, Iraq, Iran, Egypt, and other neighboring locales). The Arabic modal system, known as *maqāmāt*, is deeply incorporated into their liturgical and paraliturgical practices. The Yemenite tradition also makes use of Arabic musical practices. Other traditions, such as Turkish, a practice that perpetuates Jewry from the Ottoman period, combine some of these styles. The geographic position between Morocco and the Middle East also characterizes Turkish Jewish music, which contains Spanish and Arabic elements.

The practice of lively congregational singing describes Sephardic liturgy. While many portions are recited by the *ḥazzan* as required by Jewish law, congregational participation is enthusiastic and joyful. Unlike the Ashkenazic practice, which intones the last two to three lines of a liturgical text, known as a *hatima*, Sephardic *ḥazzanim* recite the entire liturgical text out loud. Congregants may join in the recitation, and some do so in an undertone. The unique quality of the Sephardic tradition is displayed not only by the melodies they use, but also by the liturgical performance practice, which combines both active and passive participation from the congregation.

III Music in paraliturgical contexts

Many liturgical melodies are adaptations of melodies used elsewhere within each tradition. Most often the melodies are adapted from *piyyutim*. The venerable tradition initiated by Najara has been kept alive in Yemenite,

Moroccan, Turkish, and Syrian communities up to the present. In many of these regions, Jewish practices involve adaptations of local melodies from the surrounding cultures. Only recently have the musical practices of *piyyutim* been studied.[23] In many instances, liturgical melodies, following the past practices of Najara, were taken from known non-Jewish melodies, but these tunes became so popular that one finds their use in a variety of secular and religious contexts. In general, distinctions between sacred and secular use are arbitrary, since many melodies are used in both contexts.

The singing of *piyyutim* occurs mainly in celebrations of holiday and life-cycle events. Specific texts are associated with particular holidays and are sung in the synagogue or at home during meals. On some recurring paraliturgical occasions, the singing of *piyyutim* is the main source of the ritual. One such occasion, the *baqqashot*, or *nuba* in the Moroccan tradition, is practiced in some Syrian and Moroccan communities. Participants go to the synagogue at midnight or early in the morning before sunrise and sing supplications to elevate their spirits prior to the formal morning prayers.

A venerable tradition among Sephardic Jews, whose ancestry is from Spain, is their Ladino culture. The Judeo-Spanish written and spoken dialect of Jews of Spanish descent, Ladino represents the synthesis of Jewish and Spanish culture for Sephardic Jews (see Chapter 7). The rich tradition of this cultural interconnection from the Golden Age of Spain has continued. The amount of preservation versus new influence varies among Sephardic Jews over the past 500 years. The Spanish influence has been ongoing for Jews in Morocco, whereas Jews in Turkey and Greece have incorporated more Middle Eastern influence. Some historians hold that the venerable musical forms of these Sephardic Jews, namely the *ballad* and *romancero*, were time-honored traditions untouched by new cultural influence and thus faithfully transmitted. Modern scholars, however, have been unable to validate this claim.[24] Nevertheless, Ladino music has deep historic roots, and as with other forms of Jewish music, this musical tradition is both perpetuated and innovatively revitalized by modern performers.

Ladino music has long been conserved by women. In fact, many of the song texts of the *romancero* and *ballad* deal with women's experiences in life-cycle events, passionate or erotic courtly poetry, and epic tales or stories. Dirges related to the death of individuals in untimely and other circumstances are known as *endechas*. The *coplas*, short holiday songs, also complement the Ladino musical repertoire. The wedding context in particular has been a rich source of music for Sephardic women. The preparation of the bride for the *mikva* (ritual bath) prior to the wedding, the bride's dowry, and her relationship with her mother-in-law are some subjects of the texts of Ladino wedding songs.

Each performer has personalized the Ladino repertoire because no standard forms exist. Musicologist Israel Katz has devoted his scholarly efforts to understanding Ladino songs through viewing present manifestations of this tradition. He sees a distinction between two musical types with respect to the *ballad*. The Western Mediterranean, or Moroccan, Ladino singing style includes regular phrases and rhythms with few embellishments. Many performers of Judeo-Spanish music within this style incorporate Spanish and Moorish musical styles into their song renditions. The Eastern Mediterranean, or Turkish and Balkan, Ladino singing style includes more melodic embellishments in a freer and, often, less regular rhythm. Over time these two styles have merged.

The role of new music in modern synagogue life

The music of the American synagogue has undergone distinct changes in the last century. The present musical traditions of the synagogue can be seen as both a continuation of their European legacy and a reaction to influences from America culture. Although the seventeenth-century settlers in America were Sephardic, their influence was overshadowed by the European immigration of the nineteenth century. German Jews were the first to arrive after 1820. It was the mass migration of eastern European Jews in 1880 that led them to dominate American Judaism at the turn of the century. The predominant liturgical music during this immigrant period was known as the Golden Age of the Cantorate, which lasted from 1880 until around 1930, when it began to wane. Most of the cantors associated with the Golden Age were born and trained in eastern Europe and then came to America around the turn of the century through the 1930s. Some had regular pulpits for the entire year and others were only engaged for the High Holidays, when they commanded large salaries. Radio broadcasts, in addition to 78-rpm recordings and live concerts, proliferated this musical liturgical artistry. The discs provide a lasting record, freezing the sound of the Golden Age of the Cantorate for future generations. Great cantors of this period include Yossele Rosenblatt (1882–1933), Leib Glantz (1898–1964), Mordecai Hershman (1888–1940), Leibele Waldman (1907–69), Pierre Pinchik (1900–71), and Moshe Koussevitzky (1899–1966) and his brother David (1891–1985). So admired were these cantors that people came from long distances to hear them sing at concerts and services. The Golden Age of the Cantorate was a brief but significant period in the history of Jewish liturgical music that uniquely fused vocal artistry and impassioned prayer in a distinctive style that has become the definitive form of *ḥazzanut*.

As described above, the Reform movement that began in central Europe, and the music of Sulzer and Lewandowski, came to America and spread throughout the country. In the second quarter of the twentieth century, American composers sought to innovate the music of the synagogue according to contemporary styles. Musicians such as Binder, Freed, and Lazar Weiner (1897–1982) arranged traditional European melodies in accordance with the Jewish prayer modes, producing harmonies not typically found in Western music. Towards the middle of the twentieth century, two composers, Max Helfman (1901–63) and Max Janowski (1912–91), wrote compositions that have become standards for the High Holidays, Helfman's *Sh'ma Koleinu* (Hear Our Voice, Lord) and Janowski's *Avinu Malkeinu* (Our Father, Our King). During the second half of the twentieth century musical tastes have preferred more accessible music. In this context, Michael Isaacson adapts a variety of musical styles, both classical and contemporary, for his synagogue compositions. He and others also borrow from folk, popular, and Israeli-style songs. Cantors in Reform synagogues today draw from these diverse musical compositions encompassing the last 150 years, to provide interest and variety to their congregations.

The three denominations of American Judaism, Reform, Conservative, and Orthodox, deal with similar concerns with respect to new music in the synagogue. At issue are congregational involvement and the role of the cantor as prayer facilitator. The history of the rhythmically precise central European and the rhythmically free eastern European traditions have been combined in varying practices in American congregations. Where Reform synagogues were once the source of artistic innovation, the trend has diminished in favor of participatory services. Trained cantors and some congregants seek to draw from the rich musical history of the Jewish tradition. Other congregants desire a more accessible musical service that facilitates their participation in an idiom they prefer. Music within this sphere may draw from the Jewish tradition, including the use of Hasidic and Israeli melodies, but folk and popular styles are predominant. The songs of Debbie Friedman (1951–2011), whose popularity increased in the 1980s and 1990s, amply represent this trend.

The dynamics of the use of music in Conservative synagogues is similar. Traditional melodies may be more commonly heard in Conservative synagogues, but these melodies are less than one hundred years old. Abraham Goldfarb (1879–1956) arrived in the United States in 1893 from Poland and studied at the Jewish Theological Seminary. He produced many books and pamphlets of synagogue melodies that are regularly sung today in synagogues and at home rituals. The Havurah movement, begun in the 1970s, sought to empower laity to participate in services and further their education. The result has been an increase in congregational involvement throughout a service. The cantor often functions as an educator and facilitator of congregational participation. But, particularly on the High Holidays and for special events, the rich legacy of liturgical music can be heard combining the artistry of cantorial recitatives, taken from or inspired by the Golden Age of the Cantorate, in compositions based on the traditional use of prayer modes and liturgical chants. Volunteer and professional choirs are also used.

Within Orthodox synagogues music serves a more functional purpose. A paid professional cantor is rare in these synagogues, whereas it is much more common in Reform and Conservative synagogues. The prayer leader in an Orthodox synagogue assumes the role of *baal tefilah*, and vocal embellishments are kept to a minimum. Congregational involvement is interspersed throughout the service. Like in the other movements, traditional melodies are more commonly heard on the high holidays. In many Orthodox synagogues, a *ḥazzan* may only be employed during the holidays and on the other days of the year a congregant serves in this role. Orthodox congregations also differ in their incorporation of *nusaḥ*. Some prefer the use of Israeli melodies or tunes from songs popular in the community for the highlighted portions of the prayer such as the *Kedushah* in the Sabbath morning service.

While some are critical of the lack of artistry in the continual influence of popular genres on liturgical music, others embrace it as a way of encouraging synagogue attendance. The popular trends and changes reflect the influences and gradual adaptation of contemporary American cultural surroundings. The process of adapting musical influences has long been a part of Jewish synagogue music's history.

Prior to the formation of cantorial training programs after World War II, individuals learned *ḥazzanut* through apprenticeship and life experience, and many sang in synagogue choirs during their youth. The first program to be developed was the Reform movement's School of Sacred Music at Hebrew Union College-Jewish Institute of Religion New York Campus, founded in 1948. The Jewish Theological Seminary of America, affiliated with the Conservative movement, opened its Cantors Institute in 1952. The Cantorial Training Institute at Yeshiva University began training cantors to serve Orthodox synagogues in 1964.

Other examples include a wide variety of folk and art contexts. Religious and secular summer camps and programs throughout the year make use of a wide variety of music to educate children and teenagers in Jewish concepts and religious practices. For nearly sixty years new religious music has been composed in Israel. The range of music includes children's songs, popular music, and folk songs associated with Zionist themes. Folk singer Naomi Shemer captivated the feeling of solidarity in the country and the enduring importance of Israel as the home of the Jewish people with her songs

"Al kol eleh" (All These Things) and "Yerushalayim shel zahav" (Jerusalem of Gold). The synthesis of traditional Jewish musical styles and forms in both sacred and secular contexts, combined with a contemporary classical idiom, has been the goal of several noted composers in Israel (see Chapter 15). The most significant figure was Paul Ben-Haim (1897–1984) who drew from a wide variety of Jewish and non-Jewish musical styles. Many have debated the "Jewish" elements in Israeli music, raising the question whether Israeli music is a national or Jewish musical form. The same debate is cast in regards to American Jewish composers of note such as Leonard Bernstein (1918–90), whose "Jeremiah" (1942) and "Kaddish" (1963) Symphonies make use of Jewish themes but also seek acceptance as works of mainstream Western art music.

Many art music composers and popular songwriters seek the goal today that has long been a part of Jewish music history: to compose music that draws from the Jewish tradition and that respects the past and inspires one in the present to perpetuate Judaism.

Notes

1 The earliest manuscripts of Jewish music are the notations of the twelfth-century cleric Obadiah the Norman Proselyte, found in the Cairo *Genizah*. For studies and transcription of these manuscripts, see Israel Adler, "The Notated Synagogue Chants of the 12th Century of Obadiah, the Norman Proselyte," in Eric Werner (ed.), *Contributions to a Historical Study of Jewish Music* (New York: Ktav, 1976), 166–99, translated from French, *Journal de Musicologie* (1967). For recordings of musical items in the manuscript, see *Chants Mystiques: Hidden Treasures of a Living Tradition* (PolyGram Special Markets, 1995) 314 520 340 2, track 5, "Mi al har chorev." Biblical cantillation was first notated melodically by Johannes Reuchlin in his *De accentibus et orthographia linguae hebraicae* (Haguenau, 1518). For a valuable study of early cantillation, see Hanoch Avenary, *The Ashkenazi Tradition of Biblical Chant between 1500 and 1900: Documentation and Musical Analysis*, Music Documentation and Studies Series 2 (Tel Aviv University, 1978).

2 This collection appears in three languages. The complete ten-volume work was published in German under the title *Hebräisch-orientalisher Melodienschatz*. Volumes 1–5 were also published in Hebrew under the title *Otser neginot yisrael*. The English version, under the title *Thesaurus of Hebrew-Oriental Melodies*, consists of only seven volumes: 1, 2, 6, 7, 8, 9, and 10. For a useful guide to this collection, see Eliyahu Schleifer, "Idelsohn's Scholarly and

Literary Publications: An Annotated Bibliography," in Israel Adler, Bathja Bayer, and Eliyahu Schleifer (eds.), *The Abraham Zvi Idelsohn Memorial Volume*, Yuval Studies of the Jewish Music Research Center 5 (Jerusalem: Magnes, 1986), 53–180.

3 The "Jerusalem-Sephardic" tradition refers to the Sephardic Jews of the Levant who immigrated to Israel during the late nineteenth and early twentieth centuries. After their arrival in Israel they developed a unified and identifiable musical and liturgical tradition rather than seeking to differentiate themselves by the country of their diaspora.

4 Abraham Zvi Idelsohn, *Jewish Music in Its Historical Development* (New York: Henry Holt, 1929), 35–71.

5 Amnon Shiloah, *Jewish Musical Traditions* (Detroit: Wayne State University Press, 1992), 21–33, 96–109.

6 Musicologist Eric Werner suggests that the *tof* was excluded from the Temple because of its associations with women's activities (Exod. 15:21 and 1 Sam. 18:6–7), at a time when women were prohibited from participating in the service; see Eric Werner, "Jewish Music," in Stanley Sadie (ed.), *The New Grove Dictionary of Music and Musicians*, 20 vols. (London: Macmillan, 1980), ix:614–34 (619).

7 See Bathja Bayer, "The Biblical *Nebel*," *Yuval*, 1 (1968): 89–131.

8 *Shigayon*, *gitit*, and *alamot* are often left untranslated in non-Hebrew editions of the

psalm text. The exact meaning of these words is uncertain. They are understood to be types of musical instruments.

9 Bathja Bayer, "The Title of the Psalms – A Renewed Investigation of an Old Problem," *Yuval*, 4 (1982): 29–123.

10 Lawrence Hoffman, *Beyond the Text: A Holistic Approach to Liturgy* (Bloomington: Indiana University Press, 1987), 46–59.

11 See Macy Nulman, *Concise Encyclopedia of Jewish Music* (New York: McGraw Hill, 1975), 102.

12 Hanoch Avenary, *Studies in the Hebrew, Syrian and Greek Liturgical Recitative* (Tel Aviv: Israel Music Institute, 1963).

13 Avigdor Herzog, "Masoretic Accents," in *Encyclopedia Judaica*, 16 vols. (Jerusalem: Keter; New York: Macmillan, 1971–2), xi:1098–112.

14 Idelsohn, *Jewish Music*, 62–4.

15 Eric Werner, *The Sacred Bridge*, vol. I (New York: Columbia University Press, 1959); idem, *The Sacred Bridge: The Interdependence of Liturgy and Music in Synagogue and Church during the First Millennium*, vol. II (New York: Ktav, 1984).

16 Peter Jeffery, "Werner's *The Sacred Bridge*, Volume 2: A Review Essay," *Jewish Quarterly Review*, 77.4 (April 1987): 283–98.

17 Hanoch Avenary, "Contacts between Church and Synagogue Music," in Judith Cohen (ed.), *Proceedings of the World Jewish Congress on Jewish Music, Jerusalem 1978* (Tel Aviv: Institute for the Translation of Hebrew Literature, 1982), 89–107; James W. McKinnon, "On the Question of Psalmody in the Ancient Synagogue," *Early Music History*, 6 (October 1986): 159–91.

18 In addition to its musical usage, the term *nusah* also refers to Ashkenazic and Sephardic liturgical traditions, the *nusah Ashkenaz* and *nusah Sepharad*. The Yiddish term for Jewish prayer modes is *shteyger*.

19 Hanoch Avenary, "The Concept of Mode in European Synagogue Chant," *Yuval*, 2 (1971): 11–21.

20 This accepted practice is based on the naming and categorization of the modes by Baruch Joseph Cohon. See his "The Structure of the Synagogue Prayer-Chant," *Journal of the American Musicological Society*, 3.1 (Spring 1950): 17–32; reprinted in *Journal of Synagogue Music*, 11.1 (June 1981): 58–73.

21 Hanoch Avenary, "The Cantorial Fantasia of the Eighteenth and Nineteenth Centuries: A Late Manifestation of the Musical Trope," *Yuval*, 1 (1968): 65–85.

22 This discussion is based upon the observation of present practices during the twentieth century. Due to the lack of historic sources these comments focus on a comparative approach, where it is instructive to understand the music of these traditions through their similarities and differences. Similarities between two Jewish cultures separated by large geographic distances do not necessarily indicate that their practices stem from one "original" practice.

23 Edwin Seroussi, "The Turkish *Makam* in the Musical Culture of the Ottoman Jews: Sources and Examples," *Israel Studies in Musicology*, 5 (1990): 43–68; Kay Kaufman Shelemay, *Let Jasmine Rain Down: Song and Remembrance Among Syrian Jews* (Chicago University Press, 1998).

24 Israel J. Katz, "The 'Myth' of the Sephardic Musical Legacy from Spain," in Avigdor Shinan (ed.), *Proceedings of the Fifth World Congress of Jewish Studies in Jerusalem*, 4 vols. (Jerusalem: World Union of Jewish Studies, 1973), iv: 237–43.

7 The traditional performance of Sephardic songs, then and now

SUSANA WEICH-SHAHAK

Introduction

In trying to understand how the Sephardic musical repertoire was performed in the past, we must take into consideration the relationship of each song to two important defining parameters: genre and social function. This question arises in the study of the repertoire in the two main areas of the Sephardic diaspora, namely, the Eastern Mediterranean (the Ottoman area, later Turkey and the Balkan countries, Yugoslavia, Bulgaria, and Greece) and the Western Mediterranean (Northern Morocco), as well as in Israel and the many places to which Sephardim later dispersed, and where the Judeo-Spanish musico-poetic repertoire has been maintained until the present day. The subject of the performance practices associated with Sephardic music involves both the traditional ways the repertoire was once performed, and the ongoing styles and techniques of its performance today.[1]

This chapter explores the songs that are either secular (non-religious in content) or paraliturgical (related to religious matters but with texts that are not in Hebrew but in Judeo-Spanish). The repertoire is predominantly vocal, sung in the Judeo-Spanish language, which is a Spanish dialect based on the language that the Jews spoke in Medieval Spain, where they had lived for many centuries before their final expulsion in 1492. The Judeo-Spanish language developed as its speakers borrowed from Hebrew and from the languages of their new surroundings. It flourished in two parallel dialects, one called "Judezmo" or "Ladino" in the Eastern area (with additions from Turkish, Greek, and Slavic languages), and the other called "Haketia" (with additions from Berber, Arabic, and Moroccan Arabic dialect) in the Western area.

In this chapter, we will consider the following questions in regard to the performance of Sephardic songs: What is the genre of the song? Who sings it, men or women? Where is it sung? When is it sung? And how is it sung, as a solo or in group singing, and with or without instrumental accompaniment? We will consider the function of examples from each genre in the lives of the individual and of the community, and as part of the repertoires of songs for the year cycle and for the life cycle.

Traditional performance

Modes of performance, as well as characteristics of text and music, differ in the cases of each of the Sephardic traditional genres, the *romance*, *copla*, and *cantiga*, collections of which are known as the *romancero*, *coplas*, and *cancionero*. These genres vary in: 1) their rendering, whether by solo or group; 2) the presence or absence of instrumental accompaniment; and 3) their gender definition, that is, whether they belong to the male or the female repertoire.[2]

I Romancero

The term "Romancero" means a collection or corpus of romances, which are narrative poems with a well-defined textual and musical structure.[3] Their texts typically relate to the Spanish Middle Ages, involving kings, queens, princesses and galant knights, prisoners, and faithful (or unfaithful) wives. Other romances' texts involve classical, historical, and even biblical themes.

Several old romances reflecting historical events have been forgotten in Spain but preserved in the oral tradition of the Sephardic Jews. One such romance relates the struggle between the children of King Fernando I of Castile and León (1016/18–65), Sancho, Alfonso, and Urraca: Sancho II from Castile puts his brother Alfonso (King of León) in prison, and his sister Urraca (of Zamora) intervenes to achieve Alfonso's freedom (Song 1).[4]

> Song 1: *Fernando in France + Sancho and Urraca*. Elvira Alfasi, et al.
>   (Larache, Morocco).
> Rey Fernando, rey Fernando   de Toledo y Aragón,
> y al pasar con los franceses   dentro de la Francia entró.
> Halló la Francia revuelta,   no hubo quien la apaciguó;
> metió a su hermano en la carcel   y a su hermano cautivó.
> Y, después de cautivado,   mandó a soltar un pregón:
> todo el que por él rogare   mérito no le quedó,
> sea monja o sea fraile,   le quito su religión [volunta].
> Doña Inacia, doña Inacia,   doña Inacia, antes que el sol,
> quitó las ropas de siempre,   las de la Pascua pusó,
> con ciento de sus doncellas   dentro de la corte entró.[5]

Romances are rendered as solo songs, with no instrumental accompaniment, and it is predominantly women who perform the repertoire and are responsible for its transmission. The music of the romances often has an ornamented melody and uses Eastern modes (the Arabic and Turkish *makamat*) that include microtonal intervals (narrower than the half-step) not found in the Western diatonic scale.

The next example, from Saloniki, Greece, has a melody in a free rhythm (without repeating accent patterns) built on a *makam* called *Husseyni*

Example 7.1 "The Husband's Return."

(with a lowered second degree), and features melismas (series of different pitches sung to a single syllable) at the end of each musical phrase (Song 2; Example 7.1). The romance tells the story of a fidelity test. A husband returns after many years away at war and asks a woman washing at a well for a cup of water; he asks why she is crying, and she explains that her husband has not returned from battle. She gives him her husband's description, after which he declares that her husband has died and told him to marry her. When she refuses, he reveals that he is her long-lost husband.[6]

> Song 2: *The Husband's Return.* Renée Bivas (Saloniki, Greece).
> Lavaba la blanca niña,   lavaba y espandía,
> con lágrimas la lavaba   y con suspiros la 'spandía.
> Por ahí pasó un caballero,   'n copo d'agua le demandó,
> de lágrimas de sus ojos   siete cantaricas le hinchó
> – ¿Por qué lloras, blanca niña?   mi siñora, ¿por qué lloras?
> – Todos vienen de la guerra,   al qu'aspero non hay tornar.
> – Dáme siñal, mi siñora,   siñal del vuestro balabay.
> – Alto, alto como'l pino,   derecho como es la flecha,
> su barbica roya tiene,   empezándol' a despuntar.[7]

The Romancero belongs to the women's repertoire, and its most common function is that of a lullaby, except in the case of a few romances that are included in the wedding repertoire, sung by groups and accompanied by percussion instruments. The previous example was a romance sung on the occasion of the preparations for the new couple, when the wool for the pillows and mattresses was washed by members of the community. The following song is also from the wedding repertoire, and its text relates the story of a married woman wooed by a young man who sends her love letters and presents, but she sends all of them back and remains true to her husband (Song 3). This narrative seems appropriate as advice for a bride.

(Because the whole group sang it, men knew this song as well as women, as is evident from the name of the singer of this romance.) The romance closes by quoting a liturgical text with verses in Hebrew and their translation into Spanish.

> Song 3: *Rahel lastimosa.* Moises Abitbul (Tetuán, Morocco).
> Esta Rahel lastimosa,   lástimas que Dios la dio,
> siendo mujer de quien era,   mujer de un gobernador.
> Un dia salió al paseo   con sus damas de valor,
> se encontró con un mancebo   que la trataba de amor:
> la mandara muchas joyas,   alhajas de gran valor,
> la mandara un anillo,   solo una ciudad valió.
> Y todo se lo volvía   porque casada era yo.
> Hodu l'Adonai ki tov,   ki leolam hasdo,
> alabado sea su nombre   su merced nunca falto,
> y en los cielos y en la tierra   mucho bien siempre nos dio.[8]

An interesting trait of the performance of the previous two examples is that they are sung in a special manner referred to as "concatenation." To demonstrate this technique clearly we can consider two musical strophes of the Saloniki romance, "Lavaba la blanca niña," in which the second half of the text in one strophe is repeated at the beginning of the next. (Thus, the music is structured in four phrases, repeated, as usual: *abcd, abcd...*; but the text, with its repetitions, follows the scheme 1234, 3456...) In this way the listener can participate every time the text is repeated in the next strophe.

A few other romances may be sung as dirges or for Tisha B'Av (literally, the ninth of the month of Av, a day of fasting to commemorate the destruction of the First and Second Temples in Jerusalem). On the occasion of a death in the family, professional women referred to as *endechaderas* or *oinaderas* used to perform a special repertoire of dirges called *endechas* or *oínas*. From this repertoire the *endechadera* selected those dirges whose subjects were the most appropriate to be dedicated to the deceased's memory.[9] More recently, in Israel as well as abroad, this function declined, dislocated by the uniformity of the official death rites in modern times. According to my informants, in the late 1980s the last *endechadera*, from Alcazarquivir (Morocco), died in Eilat. The *endechas* as such became obsolete songs, seldom performed, and then only on request and not by everyone, for it is considered a bad omen to sing them.[10] Some of the *endechas*, such as "David Mourns for Absalon" (Song 4, about King David's grief for the death of his rebel son Absalom) have retained part of their function as dirges: they are kept among the corpus of *endechas* or *qinot* for Tisha B'Av and are still sung on this fast day (Example 7.2). The text of "David Mourns for Absalom"

Example 7.2 "David Mourns for Absalon."

describes a scene in which King David receives a messenger who brings sad news: David's son Absalom, who took arms against his father, died when his long hair became caught in a tree and he was stabbed there. David calls upon each of his family members to mourn for Absalom.[11]

> Song 4: *David Mourns for Absalon.* Regina Israel-Cohen (Izmir, Turkey).
> Triste está el rey David,   triste está de corazón,
> por endechar las sus angusias   subióse al mirador,
> vido a sus campos vedres   como los envicia el sol,
> vido venir de un pajico,   más negro que el carbón,
> demandando y preguntando: – ¿Onde está el emperador?
> – El emperador sta en su palacio,   asentado en el salón.
> Se echó de rodillas fuertes,   pieses y manos le besó,
> – ¿D'onde vienes, el mi hijo?   – Vengo de rogar al Dio,
> la novedad que vos traigo   es más negra que el carbón,
> que vos mataron al vuestro hijo,   vuestro hijo Absalón.[12]

II Coplas

Coplas (or complas) represent a distinct repertoire, clearly differentiated from the Romancero and the Cancionero. They are strophic songs, with varied but consistently patterned textual structures, sung to repeating melodies that show clearly the influence of the surrounding musical cultures. Their textual content, unlike the romances', is related to Jewish tradition, history, and social and political events, and it always exhibits characteristics of continuity and coherence – a feature shared with the romances – but in strophic structures (in which the poetry is divided into stanzas of the same repeated form, and the music is equivalent for each stanza of poetry), a point of difference from the romances. This genre flourished in the seventeenth and eighteenth centuries, when many coplas were published in Constantinople, Saloniki, Vienna, and Livorno.[13]

In regard to their performance, the coplas are mostly rendered in group singing, often accompanied by hand-clapping. Since many coplas are passed down in writing, they belong to the realm of men, unlike the Romancero, which, being mostly of oral transmission, belongs to the female repertoire. Thus, the coplas are mostly sung by men or, when the group participates, it is led by a man, as it is the men who are (or were) able to read the Hebrew Rashi letters (a Sephardic semi-cursive script) used for writing Ladino in printed texts. This is most evident in the repertoire of paraliturgical coplas for the festivities of the Jewish year cycle, sung from printed booklets and performed at home, in performances led by the man in the family. The main goal of the coplas was didactic, to provide information about the Jewish festivities and the transmission of Jewish knowledge and values to those (predominantly women and children) who could not read Hebrew and therefore had no access to original sources.

The Jewish feast most often celebrated in the coplas repertoire is Purim, a holiday in the Jewish month of Adar (around February) that commemorates the salvation of the Persian Jews by the intervention of the Jewish queen Esther, following her uncle Mordechai's advice. Even the duties to drink and be merry on Purim are reflected in the copla texts.[14] Coplas are very long, especially when they are sung from printed texts, and in the following example only a few strophes are presented (Song 5). The text is structured in four-line strophes, in which three lines rhyme (they have the same vowels at the end of each line), while the fourth rhymes with the fourth line of each of the other strophes.[15]

> Song 5: *Manjares y dádivas de Purim*. Abraham Benhamu (Tetuán,
>   Morocco).
> Con ayuda del Dios Alto,
> no nos haga nada falto,
> le alabo y le canto,
>   que le tenemos que deber.
>
> Todos juntos alabemos,
> porque mucho le debemos,
> despues de esto beberemos,
>   que así se debe hacer.[16]

III Cancionero

The songs of the cancionero are called *canticas* or *cantigas* by the Eastern (Ottoman Balkan) Sephardim, and *cantares* or *cantes* by the Moroccan Sephardim. Like the coplas, they have great versatility of texts and music, and are deeply influenced by the surrounding local cultures. Some Sephardic songs are known to be translations or adaptations of Turkish, Greek, or Bulgarian songs.

The songs of the cancionero differ from the two other genres – romancero and coplas – in textual and musical structure, involving mostly quatrains

Example 7.3 "Morenica."

(four-line strophes, with a rhyme scheme of *abab* or with only the second and fourth lines rhyming), very often with a refrain; accordingly, the
melodies are strophic, with a different tune for the refrain. The texts of these
songs are not continuous, either according to a narrative or by any other
means, and the order of the strophes is not fixed (as in the Turkish *şarkı*).
Their subject matter is mostly lyric.

In its performance the Cancionero has more variable traits. The canticas
or cantigas are sung either as solos or by groups, and by men and women.
A distinct corpus of songs from the Cancionero forms an important part of
the nuptial repertoire (*cantigas de novia* or *de boda*), as they are performed
at the various ceremonies of the Sephardic wedding and are accompanied,
in both Eastern and Western communities, by percussion instruments,
especially the tambourine, which is called *pandero* or *panderico* in the
Eastern area and *sonaja* in Morocco. The most common metric pattern for
the accompaniment in both areas is the duple 2/4; in the Balkan states,
7/8 and 9/8 are more typical, and in the Moroccan repertoire, 6/8 is found
(often in the "hemiola" type: 3/8 + 3/8 + 2/8 + 2/8 + 2/8).

The wedding songs are sung or led mostly by the women, especially
those for specific wedding rituals at which only women are present, such
as the bathing or dressing of the bride. A common manner of performing
the wedding repertoire in both the Ottoman and the Moroccan areas is to
sing a series of different songs that share a common rhythmic organization.
One well-known song in this genre is about a beautiful brunette (*morena* or
morenica) who, as is described in the biblical Song of Songs, had white skin
that darkened in the summer sun (Song 6; Example 7.3). The many strophes
(only some of them are presented here) have no specific relationship to one
another and may be sung in any order, although there are parallel subjects
and similar enunciations in some pairs of strophes (and in other versions,
even in more than two strophes) in a serial literary structure: as can be
observed in the text, the first two stanzas have the same first line (the call

to the brunette); likewise, in the third and fourth stanzas, we find the same first line ("tell the brunette"); and the fifth and sixth stanzas again share the same opening line ("the brunette gets dressed") and a similar formulation about what colors the brunette wears, with comparisons to different varieties of fruit. Each strophe is followed by a refrain ending in the Greek words *mavra matiamu*, meaning "black eyes" (probably inherited from a Greek song). The melody is in *makam Bayati* (a mode with the second scaled degree, lowered to half mol – an interval smaller than the half-step – with the dominant occurring on the fourth degree).

> Song 6: *The call to the brunette*. Rahel Altalef-Brenner (Izmir, Turkey).
> Morenica a mi me llaman
> Blanca yo nací:
> El sol del en verano
> M'hizo a mi ansí.
> Morenica, graciosica sos,
> Morenica y graciosica y mavra matiamu.
>
> Morenica a me llaman
> Los marineros,
> Si otra vez me llaman
> Me vo con ellos.
> Morenica, graciosica sos,
> Morenica y graciosica y mavra matiamu.[17]

Weddings commonly involved the participation of a semi-professional female singer called a *cantadera*, and the accompaniment of *pandero*-players called *tañederas*. These performers were specially invited to every joyful event, such as weddings and circumcisions. They were not payed directly for their participation, but cash donations from the public were collected during their performances to benefit causes such as the dowry of a poor bride, or the purchase of children's clothing for families in need. In terms of status, there was great pride in being a *cantadera* or a *tañedera*.

In addition to playing the tambourine as instrumental accompaniment, Moroccan Sephardic women add the castanets, which are often held on the middle finger of one hand and stroked by the fingers of the other hand. In the Turkish area the women often use the *parmak zili* (in Turkish: finger-cymbals), two pairs of tiny cymbals attached to the thumb and middle finger of each hand. The *darbuka* or *dumbelek* (a cup-shaped drum made of clay or metal, with one skin) are played in both regions, and Bulgarian Sephardic men also play a large cylindrical double-skin drum called a *baraban*.

The last example is from Bulgaria (Song 7). It is a wedding song performed at the marriage feast, and its music has a rhythmic structure in 9/8 meter, ordered as 2+2+2+3, a pattern widely used in Balkan folklore.

Song 7. *Las casas de la boda* – Group of Sephardim (Sofia, Bulgaria).
Oy, que casas tan hermosas,
para que bailen las novias
para bodas,
para bodas, las mis siñoras,
ésta y otra.
Tra la la . . .

Adientro bailan las damas
afuera bailan galanas
para bodas,
para bodas, la mi siñora,
esta y otra.[18]

In Jewish wedding feasts, celebrants hired professional musicians, some of whom were gentile performers. In such cases, instrumentalists (violin, 'ud, daire, kanun) of different origins participated: there were ensembles of gypsies, known as *ziganos*, or of Greeks, called *banda de gregos*, or Turkish players called *chalguí* (Tur.: *çalgı*) or *chalguigís* (Tur.: *çalgıcı*) who, through their frequent participation at such occasions, knew the Judeo-Spanish repertoire and could accompany the *cantigas de boda* in addition to playing dance music (including Turkish dances, as well as the waltz, foxtrot, tango, and other Western genres).

Performance of Sephardic songs today

The preceding descriptions of traditions associated with the performance of Sephardic songs reflect musical practices in Sephardic communities before the twentieth century, when modernity and European influence brought about changes in the preservation and performance of Sephardic songs, and, in most cases, caused the tradition to be almost forgotten. As is well known, the preservation and continued performance of any musical tradition depends on its functionality, but the practices sustaining the Sephardic musico-poetic repertoire began to decline by the middle of the nineteenth century, with the modernization of society. The new generations, especially those born in the new settings to which their parents had immigrated, tried to fit in amid their new surroundings, learning the local languages and customs, and in most cases they did not maintain the Judeo-Spanish languages or the cultural treasures of their elders. It seemed that there would be no continuity to the Sephardic musico-poetic tradition. Thus, the performance of the Judeo-Spanish repertoire found its place on stage, in the renditions of professional artists interested in this repertoire in a great wave of Sephardic renaissance.

The deep interest in the Sephardic musico-poetic repertoire inspired the appearance of an astonishing number of professional performers. Many soloists and ensembles (mostly not of Sephardic descent) chose to specialize in the Sephardic repertoire in stage performances and on sound recordings. I will not get into a discussion about the necessity, importance, or desirability (questioned by some scholars and even entirely denied by others) of this phenomenon, nor shall I touch on its sociological aspect (including its impact on the public and questions of the cultural backgrounds and ages of audiences, etc.), but its buoyant and thriving existence must be acknowledged.

Such performances of the Sephardic repertoire on the stage and in sound media often involved a very small part of the rich Judeo-Spanish repertoire and were based on careless transcriptions of the authentic sources. Furthermore, these performances were accompanied by instrumental arrangements for ensembles that were absolutely alien to the original style and required (and – alas! – achieved) a pitiful simplification of the rich melodic ornamentation and varied rhythmic structures that characterized the music of the Sephardic repertoire, ignoring even the Oriental modal organization that was the basis of its melodies.

I will consider here some of the aspects of this phenomenon that I might name the "stage-recycling of the Sephardic repertoire," and point out its problems. In order to understand the problematics of stage performance it is important to consider the wide gap between what we could call "the natural situation of the traditional event," and this "stage-recycling of the repertoire." This gap is related to the dichotomy between *performer* and *public* in contemporary performance, a dichotomy that does not exist in the traditional setting, where, even if the audience members do not know all the songs performed, they feel a sense of belonging in relation to the event. Even if they cannot sing along to every verse, they are involved in a sort of "passive participation," based, 1) on the general knowledge of the repertoire and the outline of its contents; and 2) on the learned ability to recognize the context of and feelings expressed in each song.

Especially important among the general traits of contemporary "stage-recycling" performances is the loss of the musical context, through the separation of the songs from the activities they used to accompany. An example of this decontextualization is the romance of "The husband's return," with the incipit "Lavaba la blanca niña" (see Song 2 above), which used to be sung in Saloniki when the women of the bride's family assembled to wash the wool for the mattresses and pillows for the new couple; this romance has now become a nostalgic souvenir, as this activity is no longer necessary and all the dowry can be bought ready-made. Despite the ethnomusicologist's expectations of professional performers, it is certainly very difficult for them to build a new bridge over the abyss opened by the loss of context.

The question of how close one can come to reproducing the original performance practice is not an easy one. Two aspects are to be considered here: voice and instruments. The first is the most difficult, because the professional artist probably had vocal training that does not correspond to the typical vibrant singing voice of the Sephardim. Recognizing this challenge, I most enthusiastically applaud the efforts of some contemporary groups to lower the register of their voices and change their timbre. The second aspect, instrumental accompaniment, is one method by which professional artists attempt to make their Sephardic songs more likeable for their audiences. The accompaniment practices of today's professional performers of this song repertoire can be classified into four groups:

1) those that prefer the "old look," with medieval or Renaissance instruments and corresponding vocal settings (and sometimes even costumes from those eras);
2) those that turn to the eastern sources, using instruments such as the 'ud, qanun, darbuqa (a globlet-shaped drum), and, of course, tambourines of different sizes;
3) those that perform solo and do not budge, setting all kinds of Sephardic tunes to the ill-suited and limiting chords of the guitar; and
4) those that choose their instrumental accompaniment according to the song, considering its social function, its original mode of performance, and the time of its origin: medieval instruments for epic romances, 'ud for certain songs and coplas from the life-cycle repertoire, guitar for the more modern canzonetta-style love songs, or just *panderos* (tambourines) for the eastern Sephardic wedding songs, with the addition of castanets for the Moroccan Sephardic wedding repertoire.

Thus the contemporary professional performance of this repertoire is varied, and the performers' choices testify to their musical sensibility and historical and cultural knowledge.

The impossibility of recreating the tightly knit form of communication between the singer and the group (as it occurred in the traditional performance settings) has led professional performers to seek different solutions, many of which are ill-advised. One technique for attracting the public's attention, shared by stage performers of all sorts, involves the use of lighting to define the spaces of the performer and the public. We know, however, that lighting, most certainly, does not bring the audience any closer to the singer on stage, nor does it enhance the feeling of belonging that characterizes the traditional setting. Many performers also sing selections of a reduced and stereotyped repertoire, ignoring the best jewels of the Sephardic musico-poetic heritage in favor of a set of five or six well-known pieces, almost all of them lyric songs (about the sufferings and joys of love), and learned mostly from earlier commercial records.

One bright light shines from those groups that, having a greater sensibility for the tradition, have started to look for authentic sources, renewing the repertoire on stage with songs from local repertoires, with no fear concerning the acceptance of this "new" material by their audience.[19] Audiences, following these groups' choices with interest, seem to have begun to open up and enjoy gratefully the "new" gifts from the Sephardic repertoire. And here we will conclude this chapter by allowing the subject of how to perform Sephardic songs on stage today to remain an open question.

Notes

1 This study is based on materials collected during my fieldwork in the context of my research at the Jewish Music Research Centre, of the Hebrew University of Jerusalem. I am thankful for the support granted by the Spanish Government (Subdirección General de Promoción de Investigación del Ministerio de Educación y Ciencia) to conduct my project at the Consejo Superior de Investigaciones Científicas, at the Institute of Anthropology.

2 The definition of each of these three genres also considers the different parameters used in the analysis of their music (pitch and duration, formal structure, and melodic character) and text (content, subject, structure, i.e., versification, and rhyme), as well as the interaction between them.

3 A romance consists of an indefinite number of sixteen-syllable rhyming verses, each divided by a cesura into two isometric eight-syllable hemistichs (half-line verses). (The rhyme scheme of all the verses, between each line's second hemistich, is maintained throughout the song.) The series of rhyming verses is divided by the musical stanzas into a strophic structure: one musical strophe is repeated, with slight variations, throughout the entire romance.

4 In the Romancero, the names are frequently altered, and in this Sephardic version the queen Urraca's name is changed to Doña Inacia. But what is stressed is that she gets her wish by reminding her brother Sancho of a promise he made to her when they were children.

5 The text continues:

  – Buenos días, do[n] mi hermano,   do[n]
    mi hermano y mi señor:
  t'acordás, cuando chiquita,   me dates un
    bofetón;
  lloraba y no me callaba,   vos me
    prometiste un don,
  y ahora que ya soy grande   quiero que me
    le deis vos.

  – Quieres Sevilla, o Granada,   o Toledo, o
    Aragón?
  – No quiero ciudá ninguna,   todas a mi
    mando son;
  lo que quiero es a mi hermano,   sano y
    libre y sin prisión.
  – Mañana por la mañana   vo le mandaría
    yo.

This romance was sung by Elvira Alfasi, with a group of women, all of them from Larache, Morocco. I recorded their rendition in Qiryat Malakhi (16.6.1979, NSA Y 2854/13). The text combines two subjects. In the first part, in the course of battle King Fernando arrives in France, and succeeds in appeasing the French (according to historical data it was his knight Don Rodrigo de Vivar, called El Cid, who heroically achieved a sort of peace). The second part, from the fourth line on, is translated as follows: "He [the eldest son, Sancho] captured his brother [Alfonso], put him in prison, and declared that anyone who intercedes on his behalf will be punished. However, their sister Urraca [here named Doña Inacia] changed her everyday clothes and put on the festive [Pascual] dresses, and with 100 of her female companions she entered the court of her brother [Sancho]. – Good morning, my brother, my lord: you remember, when I was little you slapped me; I cried and cried and wouldn't stop, so then you promised me a gift, and now that I am grown up, I want you to give it to me. – Do you want the cities of Seville, Granada, Toledo, or Aragón? – No, I don't want any city, I rule over many of them, I only want my brother, free and healthy, out of prison. – Tomorrow morning I will send him to you."

6 The theme of the husband returning and testing his wife's fidelity is widely repeated across Europe. This particular variant seems to be an adaptation of a Greek ballad, but the text keeps the romance's structure. On this romance, see Susana Weich-Shahak, "Social Functions of the Judeo-Spanish Romances," in Joachim Braun and Uri Sharvit (eds.), *Studies in*

Socio-Musical Sciences (Ramat-Gan: Bar-Ilan University, 1998), 245–56.

7 The text continues:

– Ya lo vide yo, mi siñora,   a la guerra matado sta,
una hora antes que muriera   tres palavricas me habló:
mujer hermosa yo tengo,   hijicos como es el sol,
y la de tres, mi siñora,   que me casara yo con vos.
– Onde siet'años l'asperí,   otros siete lo vo 'sperar,
si al de ocho non viene,   bivdica quedara ella.
– Non llores más, blanca niña,   non llores no quieres llorar:
yo s'el vuestro marido,   el qu' asperas de la guerra.
– Si sos el mi marido   siñal de mi puerpo darés.
– En el pecho de ezquiedro   ahí tenes un buen lunar.

The Husband's Return was sung by Renée Bivas (born in Saloniki, Greece, arrived in Israel after World War II, after imprisonment in Auschwitz, and died in 2012). This is one of many songs I collected from her, as I recorded her repeatedly at her house in Tel Aviv. I recorded this romance on January 31, 1996 (NSA Y 5283c/4). The text is translated as follows: "The fair woman was washing and putting linens out to dry, with her tears she washed and with her sighs she dried. A knight passed by and asked her for a cup of water and she filled for him seven jugs from her tears. – Why do you cry, fair maiden? Milady, why do you cry? – Everyone comes back from the war and the one I wait for does not return. – Give me a sign, milady, a sign from your husband [*balabay*, Hebrew: *baal habait*] – He is tall like a pine tree, straight as an arrow, his beard is blond, just starting to appear [indicating how young he is]. – I saw him, milady, he was killed at war; three things he told me one hour before he died: first, I have a beautiful wife, second, I have children [that shine] like the sun, and third, that I should marry you. – I have waited for seven years and seven more I will wait, and if by then he does not come, she [instead of saying 'I', to shield herself from a bad omen] will remain a widow. – Do not cry, milady, I am your husband for whom you waited to return from the war. – If you are indeed my husband, you should have a sign from my body. – Under your left breast you have a nice freckle."

8 This romance was sung by Moises Abitbul (born in Tetuán, Morocco) and recorded in Ashdod, on September 25, 1983 (NSA Y 3997/4). The text is translated as follows: "Pitiful Rahel, who was the governor's wife. One day while out promenading she met a young man who wooed her: he sent her many jewels of great value, and a ring worth as much as a city. And she sent back everything because she was a married woman. Praise God for his mercy and in heaven and on earth He always provides us well."

9 These professional performers are discussed in Michael Molho, *Uso y costumbres de los sefardíes de Salónica* (Madrid and Barcelona: Consejo Superior de Investigaciones Científicas, 1950), 180–3. Molho writes about the mourners, or *plañideras*, of the Talmudic era, in pre-exilic Spain, and among the Sephardim in Saloniki. In the Sephardic diaspora, the *endechaderas* sang their dirges and cried only at home, but did not accompany the family to the cemetery. According to Molho, this custom has been obsolete in Saloniki since the second half of the nineteenth century.

10 I was able to record the version presented here as Song 4 when I arrived at the Old Peoples' Home Karataş Hastanesi in Izmir, Turkey, precisely on the day of Tisha B'Av, for which occasion Regina was prepared to sing this dirge.

11 A similar text appears in a setting for voice and vihuela (an early guitar) by the sixteenth-century Spanish composer Alonso Mudarra.

12 The text continues:

– Vinid aquí, la mi mujer,   y lloraris de corazón,
que vos mataron nuestro hijo,   al mi hijo Absalón.
– Vinid ahora, aquí, mi elmuera,   que arrelumbras más que el sol,
quitadvos ales y vedres,   de preto vestidvos vos,
que vos mataron al marido,   al mi hijo Absalón.
– Vinid aquí, mi inietos,   huerfanicos muevos sos,
vos mataron al padre,   al mi hijo Absalón.
– Vinid aquí, los mis mozos,   y lloraris de corazón,
que vos mataron a el amo,   al mi hijo Absalón.

This romance was performed by Regina Israel-Cohen (born and living in Izmir, Turkey) on July 28, 1996 (NSA Y6313/40). The text is translated as follows: "King David is sad, and sad is his heart, and because of his anguish he went up to the balcony; he looked at his green fields, blessed by the sun; he saw a messenger, black as coal, who asked and demanded: Where is the Emperor? – The Emperor is in his palace, sitting in his living room. He fell on his knees and kissed his [the king's] hands and feet. – Where do you come from? – I come from praying to God, because the message that I bring to you is blacker than coal, that your son has been killed, your son Absalon. – Come here, my wife, and you will cry with all your heart, because they killed your son, my son Absalon. – Come here, my daughter-in-law, you that shine more than the sun, take down white and green [dresses] and put on black, because they killed your husband, my son Absalon. – Come here, my grandchildren, you just became new orphans, because they have killed your father, my son Absalon. – Come here my servants and you will cry from your heart, because they have killed your owner, my son Absalon."

13 For general discussion about the Coplas structure and performance, see Susana Weich-Shahak, "Stylistic Features of the Sephardic Coplas," in Michel Abitbol, Galit Hasan-Rokem, and Yom Tov Assis (eds.), *Hispano-Jewish Civilization after 1492: Proceedings of the Misgav Yerusalayim's Fourth International Congress, 1992* (Jerusalem: Misgav Yerushalayim, 1997), 101–24.

14 According to Elena Romero's *Bibliografía analítica de ediciones de coplas sefardíes* [Analytical Bibliography of Printed Sephardic Coplas] (Madrid: Consejo Superior Investigaciones Científicas, 1992), this Purim copla was first printed in a booklet published in Constantinople in 1745, and then again eighteen additional times, with the most recent printing in 1923.

15 This form, *aaax-bbbx-cccx*, is very common both in Hebrew prayers and in the old Arabic poetry, where it is called *zejel*; the form is therefore called "*zejel*-like rhyme" (*rima zejelesca*). In our example the last strophe of the text is quoted from another Purim copla where it functions as a refrain.

16 The text continues:

> Mordejai manda y dice:/ todo judío que se
>   avise,/ en Adar catorce y quince// miren
>   mucho de beber.
> Vivas tú y viva yo,/ vivan todos los judios,/
>   viva la reina Ester// que tanto placer nos
>   dio.

This Purimic copla was performed by Rabbi Abraham Benhamu, born in Tetuán, Morocco, who was then the Rabbi of the Sephardic community in Lima (Peru), where I recorded him on October 1, 1975 (NSA Yc 931/25). The

text is translated as follows: "With High God's help we shall lack nothing, I praise Him and sing to Him as is our duty. Let us praise all together, because we owe Him very much, and afterwards we will drink as it has to be done. Mordechai ordered and said that every Jew must pay attention and on the fourteenth and fifteenth of the month of Adar to drink a lot. Blessings to me and to you, and to all the Jews, and long live Queen Esther who gave us so much pleasure."

17 The text continues:

> Decilde a la morena/ Si quere vinir/ La
>   nave ya sta'n vela,/ Que ya va a partir.//
>   Morenica . . .
> Decilde a la morena:/ ¿por qué no me
>   querés?/ Con oro y con tiempo/ A mí
>   me rogarés.// Morenica . . .
> Ya se viste la morena/ Y de yul yaguí/
>   Ansina es la pera/ Con el šiftilí.//
>   Morenica . . .
> Ya se viste la morena/ De amarillo,/ Ansi es
>   la pera/ Con el bembrillo.//
>   Morenica . . .

This song was performed by Rahel Altalef-Brenner, born in Izmir, Turkey, living in Yahoud (near Lodd), where I often recorded Izmirli liturgy performed by her father, Abraham Altalef. This is based on a studio version recorded at the National Sound Archives of the National Library in Jerusalem, on August 27, 1986 (NSA Yc2774/22). The text is translated as follows: "They call me brunette, but I was born fair, the summer sun made me this way. They call me brunette, the sailors; if they call me again, I will go with them. Tell the brunette if she wants to come, the ship has its sails ready to part. Tell the brunette: why don't you love me? With gold and time, you will beg me. The brunette gets dressed in the color of flowers, just like the pear with the apricot. The brunette dresses in yellow color, just like the pear with the quince." Refrain: "Morenica brunette, you are charming and black-eyed" (Greek: *mavra* means black, *matia* means eyes; *matiamu* means my eyes).

18 This wedding song was performed by a group of Bulgarian Sephardim: Rachel Levy, Sarah Cohen, Milka David, Yosef Buco, Mosé Capón, Shalom Hayaari, and Sara Mashiah, accompanied by percussion instruments (*baraban* and *panderos*) played by Berto Yom-tov, Yaacov Hizkiyah et al. Most of these performers were born in Sofia and arrived in Israel soon after 1948. I recorded them at the Senior Citizen's Club *Moadon Tiferet* in Yaffo on February 1, 1978 (NSA Yc 1332/21). The text is

translated as follows: "These houses are so beautiful for the brides to dance there on weddings, for weddings, my lady, this one and another. Inside the ladies are dancing and outside dance the young girls, for weddings, my lady, this one and another. La lara la la la..."

19 Ensembles and performers include Arboleras and Alia Musica (Spain), The Voice of the Turtle (Boston), Elias Ladino Ensemble (New York), Gerineldo (Canada), and, in Israel, Orit Perlman's Trio Ladino, Esti Kenan Ofri, Etty ben Zaken, Ruth Yaakov, and Ventanas altas de Saloniki (based at Haifa University).

8 Klezmer music – a historical overview to the present

JOEL RUBIN

Introduction

In contemporary usage, klezmer music designates various genres of vernacular music associated with the Yiddish-speaking Jews of eastern Europe and their descendents. Klezmer music has undergone a worldwide revival since the 1970s, becoming one of the most popular world music genres, generating numerous hybrid forms, and influencing and interacting with musics as diverse as indie rock, avant-garde jazz, and contemporary art music.

In rabbinic Hebrew the compound *kley-zemer* meant "musical instruments."[1] By the sixteenth century, klezmer was used by Yiddish-speaking Jews in eastern Europe to signify instrumentalists.[2] More specifically, klezmer (pl. *klezmorim*, *klezmer*, or *klezmers*) referred to the largely hereditary socioeconomic group of professional and semi-professional Jewish instrumentalists who performed at weddings and other family and communal celebrations in the Jewish life and calendrical cycles of eastern Europe. Often viewed from within traditional Jewish society as religiously suspect because of their frequent contacts with women and non-Jews and their generally lower standard of religious knowledge, klezmorim enjoyed a low social and economic status historically.

In Yiddish, klezmer was used to describe the repertoire and style of the music performed by klezmorim at least as early as the mid-1920s.[3] In English, such usage dates to 1970–1,[4] but its widespread popularity first came through the late-1970s recordings of early American klezmer revivalists such as The Klezmorim (*East Side Wedding*, 1977) and Andy Statman and Zev Feldman (*Jewish Klezmer Music*, 1979).

As a result of the klezmer revival, the meaning of the term klezmer music has broadened in common usage over the past four decades. Today it is used to describe not only the music performed by klezmorim of various periods historically, but also a panoply of genres and styles that have emerged since the revival, as well as a number of hybrid genres that have been influenced by klezmer music.

The origins of klezmer music lie in twelfth-century Ashkenaz.[5] There, wedding music and entertainment was provided by all-around Jewish entertainers known as *Spielleute* (minstrels) or *letsonim*,[6] who sang, clowned, and played instruments. An early form of klezmer music was likely brought to eastern Europe by Jewish refugees from Ashkenaz fleeing Christian persecution from the mid-fourteenth century onwards. There, the klezmer tradition developed across approximately 500 years in inter-action with the traditional musical cultures of the lands where Jews set-tled. Over the course of several centuries, these included parts of Imperial Russia (Congress Poland, Lithuania, Latvia, western Belorussia, western Ukraine, and Bessarabia), the Austro-Hungarian Empire (Galicia, Bukov-ina, Máramaros, Slovakia, Subcarpathian Rus), and Romania (Moldavia).

Klezmer in eastern Europe

The earliest evidence of klezmorim in eastern Europe is from sixteenth-century Poland. Klezmorim were an urban phenomenon, with the vast majority of them living in the Jewish towns (*shtetls*),[7] as opposed to in villages or in the countryside. They formed bands known as *kapelyes*, *khavrusas*, or *kompanyes*, and were present in most towns and cities with a sizable Jewish population by the eighteenth century.[8]

Developed in a society guided by religious principles with gender separa-tion, klezmer music was a male dominion until the early twentieth century, at which point it became possible, but never typical, for women to play prior to the klezmer revival. Until the second half of the nineteenth century (and into the twentieth in some regions), klezmorim were organized into close-knit guilds.[9] They had their own specific lifestyle (*lebns-shteyger*), as well as their own secret argot, known as *labushinske, klezmer-loshn*, or *klezmer-shprakh*.[10] *Klezmeray* (the klezmer profession), with its attendant musical repertoire and style and lifestyle was passed on in oral tradition within families of musicians, often over the course of many generations. Receiving no formal training, the typical klezmer received his first music lessons from a male family member, later apprenticing to a klezmer in another town.[11] The *kapelyes* were organized along the lines of a partnership with aspects of a mutual aid society. The bandleader, who was usually the first violinist, took the largest share of the earnings and each other member received a proportional share, and they took care of their ill and retired.[12]

Klezmorim appeared especially at celebrations associated with the tra-ditional wedding, the most important ritual in the Jewish life cycle, which would normally last for an entire week and sometimes longer.[13] Klez-morim performed for disparate groups, a result of their professional status and their reputation for having a high level of skill on their instruments, as well as their not being able to make an adequate living from playing for Jewish weddings and festivities alone. They thus performed for the mostly

Polish landowning aristocracy as well as for peasants of a number of ethnicities, including Ukrainians, Ruthenians, Lithuanians, Poles, Belorussians, Romanians, Czechs, Slovaks, Hungarians, and Germans, depending upon their geographical location. Within the Jewish context, klezmorim also had to know repertoire appropriate for specific holy days (Purim, Sukkot, Simchat Torah, and Hanukkah), for dedications of new Torah scrolls, and especially for the various Hasidic dynasties.

The ascendancy of Hasidism had a profound effect on the development of klezmer music.[14] Among Hasidim, music, singing, and dance were central because they were considered to be even more important than prayer itself in attaining *devekut*, a state of communion between man and god.[15] Many klezmorim were themselves Hasidim or stemmed from Hasidic families. In addition, klezmorim acted as mediators and transmitters of music not only between the various Hasidic groups, but also between Hasidic and non-Hasidic Jews. These included the ultra-orthodox opponents of Hasidism known as *mitnagdim*, less strictly observant factions within communal life that emerged in the wake of the *Haskalah*,[16] and even followers of the myriad secular political movements that took hold in eastern Europe over the course of the nineteenth century, such as socialism, anarchism, and Zionism.

Seventeenth- and eighteenth-century klezmer ensembles comprised primarily combinations of violin, string bass, and a hammered dulcimer known as the *tsimbl*. Most of our knowledge about klezmorim regarding instrumentation, repertoire, and style begins in the nineteenth century. By the first half of the nineteenth century, the eastern European klezmer bands typically ranged from three to five instruments in varying combinations of violin, *tsimbl*, transverse flute, clarinet, and a Turkish-style bass drum with attached cymbal, known as *poyk mit tatsn*. By the 1870s, the size of the typical ensemble had generally increased, especially in the larger towns. Small orchestras of from ten to fourteen men were common. These larger groups consisted typically of several violins, viola, cello, contrabass, clarinets, wooden flutes, trumpets or cornets, valve trombones and other low brass, and *poyk*.[17] By the end of the century, snare or field drum had been introduced as well.[18] The lead melodic instruments in the nineteenth century were violin and flute, and later, clarinet and trumpet. The *tsimbl* appears to have been used primarily as a solo melodic instrument. The relationship of the klezmer to his audience, the wedding guests, was particularly close. The best players were valued for their "philosophizing" or "moralizing" on their instruments, and were known to have deeply moved their listeners.[19]

Although klezmorim were often depicted as wandering musicians, the territory covered by the typical *kapelye* in the nineteenth and early twentieth centuries was usually limited to a radius of thirty to forty kilometers.

The musicians had families and typically returned home for the Sabbath. There are accounts, however, of klezmorim traveling as far as Constantinople to perform.[20] The fame and influence of a few instrumentalists was national or, even, international in scope, although most klezmorim were not known outside their own region or even their own town and its environs. The klezmer *kapelyes* in the Ukraine and other areas did not always consist of Jews only. The orchestras typically employed non-Jewish musicians for a specific purpose, such as for their knowledge of regional repertoires like various Ukrainian or Polish peasant styles. Besides the klezmorim, the other group of professional entertainment musicians in eastern Europe, particularly in the southeastern regions, were Roma (Gypsies). Klezmorim and Romani musicians (*lăutari*) interacted with one another and sometimes were members of each other's ensembles, especially in areas such as Russian Bessarabia (now Republic of Moldova) and Romanian Moldavia.[21]

Early popular performers of klezmer included the xylophonist Mikhoel-Yoysef Guzikov (Shklov, Belarus, 1806–37), who became one of the most famous European concert artists of the 1830s, as well as the violinists Arn-Moyshe Kholodenko ("Pedotser," Berditchev, Ukraine, 1828–1902) and Yosele Druker ("Stempenyu," Berditchev, Ukraine, 1822–79).[22] By the late nineteenth century many klezmorim were musically literate. Klezmer music and, especially, style continued to be a primarily orally transmitted tradition. Many musicians born in the last quarter of the nineteenth century began their training as klezmorim, but as teenagers moved into classical music via the Russian conservatories. Such was the case with cellist and popular bandleader Joseph Cherniavsky (1894–1975), reputedly a relative of Stempenyu. In an era of music making where there was no clear differentiation between high and low culture,[23] Cherniavsky enjoyed conservatory training as a cellist and conductor in Russia and Germany, performed as a chamber musician, and later composed Yiddish theater scores and popular songs, was associated with Hollywood film studios, and led popular dance bands and klezmer orchestras in the US.[24] In addition, a number of well-known classical virtuosi stemmed from klezmer families, including violinist Mischa Elman (1891–1967) and cellist Emanuel Feuermann (1902–42).

The emergence of a Yiddish popular music culture in the mid-nineteenth century in the urban centers of eastern Europe represents the beginning of a process by which klezmer music began to transform itself into a popular and increasingly secularized genre. The existence of popular song brought new possibilities for klezmer musicians, and a number of instrumentalists toured as the musical accompaniment to troupes of café house entertainers (*broder-zinger*), or became involved as performers and/or composers in the new professional Yiddish theater that was founded in 1876 in Romania and rapidly spread throughout the Yiddish-speaking world.

The influence of this repertoire is already apparent in the first commercial European recordings of klezmer music made in the years immediately preceding World War I,[25] which contain instrumental versions of popular songs from the Yiddish theater in addition to traditional instrumental numbers. Klezmorim and descendents of klezmer families also became prominent within the realm of general entertainment musical culture. In interwar Poland, for example, performer-composers such as Jerzy Petersburski (1895/97–1979), Henryk Gold (1898/1902–77), Arthur Gold (1903–43), and Władysław Szpilman (1911–2000) – all descendents of klezmer families – dominated Polish popular music,[26] composing in particular many original tangos.[27] During this period, the flexibility of the professional klezmorim enabled them to expand their repertoire and their performance venues to please an increasingly secular audience. The same wedding musicians who performed *nigunim* (tunes of spiritual elevation) for Hasidic *rebbes* (dynastic leaders) and paraliturgical pieces prior to the wedding ceremony might appear at a May Day rally and were familiar with the latest waltzes and tangos, as well as jazz and other vernacular styles imported from the US.

The klezmer profession essentially had come to an end in the Soviet Union after the Revolution. The main exception appears to have been the State Ensemble of Jewish Folk Musicians of the Ukrainian SSR, assembled in 1937 during a brief period of Soviet support for Yiddish culture as part of its nationalities policy. The ensemble, which was dissolved in 1939, made recordings, performed on the radio, and appeared live in Culture Houses, at health resorts, on Jewish collective farms, and in cities with large Jewish populations, as well as at mass political events such as those commemorating the anniversary of the October Revolution.[28]

Due to a complex series of factors, including World War I, the Russian Revolution and Civil War, the Holocaust, and Stalinism, the klezmer tradition in Europe all but ceased to exist after the late 1930s. The few surviving klezmorim who returned to their countries of origin had lost their audience and context. Marian Fuks writes, for example, about the Polish klezmer violinist Marek Goldman, who survived the war in the Soviet Union, later settling in Wrocław, where he died in 1981,[29] and the life of Leopold Kozłowski, a nephew of clarinetist Naftule Brandwein (see below), has been documented on CD and in the film, "The Last Klezmer" (1994).

Remaining Yiddish culture in the Soviet Union was actively suppressed during the Stalinist purges of 1948–53. In the aftermath of Stalin's death in 1953, Jewish orchestras did reappear in the Soviet Union, but unofficially. These musicians do not appear to have been descendants of the pre-Revolution klezmer families. They performed primarily at Jewish weddings in the Ukraine, Moldavia and other regions with large Jewish populations. Their repertoire included traditional klezmer and Moldavian tunes, as well as popular Yiddish folk, thieves', and theater songs, Israeli tunes, and American popular songs and dances. A number of these musicians emigrated to the US, Western Europe, and Israel since the 1970s, most notably the clarinetist German Goldenshteyn (1934–2006) from Mogilev-Podolsk, Ukraine, who settled in New York and became well known as a collector, teacher, and performer of Soviet klezmer repertoire.

Klezmer in the US

Included among the Russian and other eastern European Jews who settled abroad during the great immigration wave of 1881–1924 were many musicians who would bring traditional klezmer music to the US and other countries where they settled. During that time, the center of Yiddish cultural production shifted largely to New York. There Yiddish-speakers developed a transitional immigrant culture over a seventy-year period that created an amalgam of eastern European and American religious and secular attributes.[30] Whereas in eastern Europe Jews had lived predominantly in the *shtetl,* in North America they settled voluntarily in the crowded immigrant quarters of large cities. By 1915, there were 140,000 Jews in New York, representing 28 percent of the total population and creating the largest single concentration of Jews in history.[31] Other urban areas with significant Jewish populations included Philadelphia, Chicago, Boston, St. Louis, Cleveland, and Baltimore, and each had its own smaller community of Jewish wedding musicians.[32]

Jewish immigrants in New York and other North American cities enjoyed a rich musical and entertainment culture, within which klezmer music occupied a small but specific niche, the dominant Jewish musical forms being cantorial music and Yiddish-language operetta. The existence of a Jewish Musicians Union in the late 1880s shows that Jewish musicians were active in New York from the earliest years of immigration.[33] Klezmer musicians were quick to diversify their playing opportunities, and the music began to be heard even more frequently in non-ritual contexts. By then, a number of wine cellars, cafés, and restaurants had sprung up on the Lower East Side of Manhattan. Many of these had musical entertainment, as did the many dance halls, and klezmorim got involved performing at such establishments, as well as at parades, picnics, benefit concerts, and even strikes of the various unions and political parties.[34] In the US context, the term klezmer gradually took on a negative connotation among upwardly mobile musicians who were trying to assimilate and broaden their professional realm. To them, "klezmer" referred to a player of limited abilities, who was unable to learn new styles of music and only capable of carrying out the function of Jewish wedding musician. Depending on their level of musical literacy and flexibility, they may have played in the Yiddish theater and vaudeville, on Yiddish-language radio, and in a plethora of mainstream musical contexts such as in hotel dance orchestras, accompanying silent films, in vaudeville and burlesque theaters, on Broadway, in brass bands and symphony orchestras, and on radio and film, as well as in the recording studios. Continuing a pattern already established in Europe, New York klezmorim often performed for and sometimes with members of various European ethnic communities, including Ukrainians, Poles, Russians, Hungarians, Roma, Greeks, Turks, Germans, and Italians, as well as for Sephardic Jews.

The leading klezmer musicians during the immigrant era were the clarinet soloists Naftule Brandwein (1884–1963) and Dave Tarras (1895–1989). Both of them had been fully experienced, professional klezmorim and members of established klezmer families in eastern Europe prior to their emigration. They were highly respected by musicians and audiences alike for their abilities in interpreting traditional klezmer music.

It was the *landsmanshaftn* and similar immigrant organizations that formed the center of klezmer activity in New York and other cities.[35] The members of such organizations tended to be older, Yiddish-speaking, working class, and orthodox or of an orthodox background, and they generally acculturated less rapidly, and were most likely to organize traditional weddings and other celebrations where klezmer music was likely to be heard. The musical tastes of the members seem to have remained distinctly European, and the music the immigrants favored comprised largely the down-home Yiddish and European dances they had known prior to emigration.[36]

The issue of acculturation became an increasing factor as the first generation of American-born Jews came of age and, especially, after the virtual stop in immigration in 1924 brought about by restrictive legislation. It gradually affected all aspects of immigrant life, including religious observance, communal organizations, Yiddish literacy, and theater attendance. In the midst of the acculturational process, klezmer music reached the zenith of its popularity from the late 1910s to the late 1930s. It was during this period that the classic recordings of musicians such as Brandwein and Tarras, as well as of clarinetist Shloimke Beckerman (1883–1974) and bandleader Abe Schwartz (1881–1963) in New York, and bandleader Harry Kandel (1885–1943) in Philadelphia, were made for Columbia, Victor, Brunswick, Emerson, Pathé, and other labels.[37]

Wedding bands in New York consisted of an overlapping membership drawn from a limited pool of perhaps 200 accomplished players. Klezmer music, which appears to have had a relatively uniform repertoire and style over a large geographic area in eastern Europe, became even more homogeneous in New York, due to the close physical proximity of the musicians and the freelance structures of the engagements. Within this framework, though, some klezmer groups were still organized along family lines – for example the Brandweins, the Levitts (Levinskys), and the Kutchers – and members of the families attempted to guard their repertoire zealously.

Changes in the composition of klezmer bands in America consisted of several elements. New instruments were introduced to the ensemble, most notably the saxophone (which was usually played by the clarinetist), the piano, and, in the 1930s, the piano accordion. The *poyk* and the small drum were replaced by the modern drum set, which could be played by one musician; the slide trombone replaced the valve trombone; silver flutes replaced the wooden ones; and, in some cases, Boehm system clarinets replaced the Albert (Müller) system clarinets used in Europe. The B-flat clarinet gradually replaced the C clarinet as well. Finally, the tendency throughout the 1920s was towards smaller ensembles. This, in combination with a stronger emphasis on dance music, led to the gradual disappearance of violins from the ensemble. Throughout the 1920s and 1930s, the standard small wedding band consisted of a quartet of clarinet doubling on saxophone, trumpet, piano, and drums.

At the same time that these changes were taking place, bandleaders perceived the need to be seen as popular entertainers and began to incorporate elements of showmanship into their performances. During the 1920s, musicians in the vanguard of this process included Cherniavsky, who, together with his Yiddish American Jazz Band, performed on the vaudeville circuit dressed up as Hasidim or Cossacks, and Brandwein, who was known for wearing an electric "Uncle Sam" suit on the bandstand or performing the clarinet under a spotlight wearing a pair of white gloves.

During the early decades of immigration, the traditional wedding in North America continued to occupy an important place in the Jewish life cycle, and it was still to remain the most important occasion for the performance of music by klezmorim. The entire wedding, which was now mostly reduced in length to one-day events, most often took place in a catering hall. The music performed at early American Jewish weddings does not appear to have differed significantly from that which had been played at weddings in eastern Europe. In addition, the musicians also performed the same repertoire in a number of other Jewish settings, most notably the bar mitzvah, the importance of which increased dramatically after the 1920s.[38] The mountainous region north of New York known as the Catskills became the most popular resort area for immigrant Jews and their children, burgeoning especially between the years 1883 and 1906.[39] In the 1920s, the resort hotels began to bring in cabaret performers, and musicians such as

Schwartz, Brandwein, and Tarras would also appear during summers in the Catskills.

The New York klezmer tradition began to decline in the 1930s, yet even into the 1950s and 1960s, the musicians performed annually for the surviving members of the *landsmanshaftn*. The decline may be attributed to a combination of factors that included acculturation among the American-born, restrictive immigration legislation, and the Great Depression. While most of the children of the European-born players became musicians and carried on their family traditions to a certain extent, almost all were multi-musical, equally versed in klezmer music and various American vernacular styles. Almost without exception, the members of the second American-born generation either left the realm of klezmer music or did not become musicians at all.

Despite the general decline in Yiddish culture, for a time the musicians regrouped, developed new styles and repertoires, and created new markets. A new type of American klezmer music flowered briefly in the 1930s and 1940s, fostered in part by the popularity of Yiddish radio and a revival in ethnic music recording in New York. The new style was fuelled by the composition of new Romanian- and Greek-influenced dance tunes by Tarras and his contemporaries. In addition, the influence of popular songs from the American-Yiddish operettas, as well as the entry into the Jewish wedding bands of American-born musicians, were contributing factors to changes in klezmer repertoire and style beginning in the 1930s. It was also during the 1930s that the percentage of American music performed at Jewish weddings dramatically increased. Typical repertoire of that period included foxtrots and other American dances, the Yiddish dances *sher*, *freylekhs*, and *bulgar*, as well as Russian and Polish tangos, waltzes, the Hungarian *csárdás*, polkas, polka mazurkas, and Polish *obereks*. Jewish bands also began to hire singers to perform American pop songs.

By the late 1930s, immigrant bandleaders were competing with a younger generation of American-born clarinet musicians who were equally competent in the American repertoire, especially the clarinetists Max Epstein (1912–2000) and Tarras' son-in-law Sam Musiker (1916–64). In order to remain competitive, they would hire such American-born musicians to play in their bands. Some of the American-born musicians, most notably Musiker, experimented with fusions of klezmer and swing jazz.

By the 1940s, a number of the Jewish wedding orchestras in New York consisted entirely of American-born children of eastern European Jewish immigrants, many of them from klezmer families. What these musicians brought to klezmer music was a rhythmic and harmonic sense shaped by their experiences playing in hotel and society dance orchestras, and big bands. This coincided with the emergence of so-called "club date" orchestras, generic bands that played at celebrations such as weddings, bar mitzvahs, and anniversary parties. Here it was the *type* of event, and not the religion or ethnicity, that became the determining factor, and the music we now know as "klezmer" was largely subsumed within the general club date field.

The founding of the State of Israel in 1948 brought about a general shift in orientation among the American Jewish community from its eastern European past and Yiddish culture to the nascent Hebrew-Israeli culture. The creation of a new Hebrew folk music as a unifying factor played an important role in the establishment of the new state,[40] and the new orientation brought about a dramatic shift in repertoire at American Jewish weddings as well: the older, eastern European and European-style repertoire was quickly replaced in many contexts by Israeli *horas* of recent vintage. Despite this shift in orientation, however, klezmer music continued to be performed in cities like New York and Philadelphia after 1948 to an aging and rapidly dwindling audience.

The US saw an influx of Holocaust survivors in the aftermath of World War II. Among these were followers of various Hasidic dynasties, who settled predominantly in Brooklyn, New York. With their traditional Judaism and high birth rates, these new immigrants provided a significant new market for European- and, especially, American-born Jewish wedding musicians, who had to learn a repertoire of *nigunim* that was almost entirely new to them directly from the immigrants and their children. In addition to the Hasidim, many of the non-Hasidic survivors had grown up in an interwar Europe radically different from that of pre-war immigrants. Among other things, they listened and danced to music that represented the significant and rapid changes the Jewish communities had undergone in Europe during the interwar years. Several musicians capitalized on that repertoire, especially bandleader and clarinetist Marty Levitt (1930–2008).[41]

The period of revitalization among the New York klezmer musicians was, however, short-lived. The advent of rock and roll in the 1950s and changing musical aesthetics – also among the ultra-orthodox – led to the gradual obsolescence of even the American-born musicians. Although a few of these performers are still alive and playing today, their music would not really be appreciated again until after the emergence of the klezmer revival movement in the mid-1970s.

Klezmer music in Israel and elsewhere

In Israel, a parallel, yet separate klezmer tradition developed from the mid-eighteenth century onwards, as Hasidic pilgrims to the Holy Land settled in the northern Galilee in Safed and Tiberias, and in Jerusalem.[42] There klezmer has enjoyed a continuous development to the present day.[43] In Israel the clarinet had already become the most important instrument in the klezmer ensemble before the turn of the twentieth century. At that time, the ensembles were small, usually not more than three instruments, which typically comprised combinations of clarinets, violins, trumpets, and drums. Later, accordion was added to the ensembles. While this music also based on the eastern European klezmer tradition, it is not clear whether the Israeli klezmorim were descendants of European klezmer families or not. Style and repertoire were also strongly influenced by local musical traditions, such as that of Arab Druze, and of the Ottoman Turkish military bands. The founder of the modern Israeli klezmer tradition, which exists almost exclusively within Haredi (ultra-orthodox) and National Religious (orthodox Zionist) circles, is considered to be the clarinetist Avraham Segal (1908–93). After his retirement in the early 1970s, the leading role in Israeli klezmer music has been taken on by Segal's protégé, Moshe "Moussa" Berlin (b. 1938), who since 1992 has made numerous recordings of klezmer and Hasidic music.[44] Today the Israeli klezmer ensembles typically consist of clarinet (saxophone), electric guitar, synthesizer, and drums. The most prominent member of the younger generation of Israeli klezmer musicians is clarinetist Chilik Frank, in Jerusalem.

Although no systematic study in other countries has been carried out to date, klezmer music appears to have been performed in virtually all large immigrant communities where eastern European Jews settled, such as Toronto, Santiago de Chile, Rio de Janiero, and Buenos Aires. For example, the clarinetist Sam Liberman, originally from Safed, Israel, settled in Buenos Aires sometime after World War I, where he led Argentinian jazz bands and Jewish dance bands and became a well-known recording artist. Also from Buenos Aires was the clarinetist Leo Feidman (d. 1980) and his son, Giora (b. 1936), who both settled in Israel. Buenos Aires became the second largest recording center for Yiddish music in the Americas after New York. In Toronto, klezmer music was dominated by members of the Szpilman (Spellman), Barsht (Barsh), Baigelman, Levak, and Lustig families, who were mostly interrelated.

The klezmer revival

Following a relatively brief period of decline, already in the late 1960s there was an incipient revival of interest in Yiddish language and culture in the United States.[45] The klezmer revival can trace its roots to the same period, and by the mid-1970s, the first klezmer bands began to perform publicly and record. As folklorist Barbara Kirshenblatt-Gimblett has pointed out, this development coincided with the end of what historian Haim Soloveitchik termed "self-evident Jewishness,"[46] in which the klezmer revival was one possible outcome of the tension between tradition and ideology that existed at that time.[47]

The klezmer revival had its beginnings among a small number of young American Jews on the West and East Coasts of the United States, almost all of whom were born in the 1950s and most of whom neither stemmed from klezmer families nor had intimate prior knowledge of klezmer or other Yiddish musical traditions. The revival can be viewed as the outgrowth of both a climate of American Jewish reassessment in the aftermath of the Holocaust and a general ethnic roots seeking and empowerment in the wake of the civil rights and black power movements.[48] Its emergence coincided roughly with the US Bicentennial celebrations and, among other things, the publication of both Alex Haley's *Roots* and Irving Howe's *World of Our Fathers* in 1976.[49] The revival began largely outside Jewish communal structures in the counterculture. The climate of large-scale acceptance after 1948 of the new Hebrew-Israeli culture as *the* valid expression of postwar secular Jewishness caused most of an entire generation of American Jews to become alienated from the richness of their eastern European Jewish heritage. Early klezmer revivalists were often surprised to find that their own ethnic group had a musical heritage comparable to Balkan and other traditional music forms with which they already had experience.[50]

Some cite the klezmer revival as an attempt by these young American Jews, mostly secular and well educated, and often from families where Yiddish was no longer spoken at home, to forge an ethnic identity apart from Israel, at the same time rejecting the notion that the center of Jewish history is occupied by the Holocaust. The increasingly right-wing politics of the Israeli government in the post-Six-Day War period did not sit well with the left-liberal ideologies of many of the 1960s generation, and one solution was to look to the eastern European past for suitable cultural models. Furthermore, within the general trend towards reaffiliation with Jewishness since the 1960s, klezmer was a simple route to Jewish self-identification, since it required no knowledge of religion or language.[51] Finally, the emergence of the klezmer revival can be interpreted as a means of healing the multiple ruptures of Jewish cultural continuity,[52] be it from the destruction of Yiddish-speaking, Eastern European Jewry in the Holocaust, the crisis in American Judaism resulting from the presumed diminishing of tribal connections, or the apparent failure of Jewish assimilation in the wake of the advent of US multiculturalism.

The klezmer revival was initially popularized by LP releases by the groups The Klezmorim (*East Side Wedding*, 1977; *Streets of Gold*, 1978) in Berkeley, Andy Statman and Zev Feldman (*Jewish Klezmer Music*, 1979) and

Kapelye (*Future & Past*, 1981) in New York, and the Boston-based Klezmer Conservatory Band (*Yiddishe Renaissance*, 1981).[53] The concerts and tours they generated garnered considerable media attention,[54] helping to spawn a much larger movement that continues to thrive to this day. What differentiated the klezmer revival from the other "named-systems revivals,"[55] such as blues, folk, or Balkan, was that here the majority of the participants were reviving their own cultural traditions.

Statman, already a prominent bluegrass mandolinist at the time, and Feldman, a linguist and ethnomusicologist, began to study with Tarras in the mid-1970s. Their work with him led to a US National Endowment for the Arts-funded project under the auspices of the Center for Traditional Music and Dance in New York (then Balkan Arts Center), which included performances and a recording (*Music for the Traditional Wedding*, 1979). The efforts of the Center for Traditional Music and Dance led to Tarras being one of the first recipients of the prestigious National Heritage Fellowship in 1984.

The performance styles of the Klezmorim and Statman and Feldman defined early on the extreme parameters of the klezmer revival. Taken together with the contributions of the Klezmer Conservatory Band and Kapelye, the core of most of the trends that would later develop in the klezmer revival was already present.[56] The early revival was dominated by the commercial success of the Klezmorim, formed in 1975. Their two high-profile LPs enabled them to tour nationally by 1978. Their combination of street music sensibility, new vaudeville aesthetic, and energetic and witty delivery enabled them to tap into college and festival audiences, as well as the fine arts circuit. Highlights of their career are indicative of the impact klezmer was beginning to have in mainstream popular culture: an onscreen performance in the Neil Diamond remake of *The Jazz Singer* (1980), a Grammy nomination in 1982 in the Best Ethnic or Traditional Folk Recording category for *Metropolis* (1981), and two sold-out shows at Carnegie Hall in 1983.[57] The band's European tours in the mid- to late 1980s and early 1990s brought them popularity particularly in France. At the other extreme, Statman and Feldman's performances on clarinet and mandolin with *tsimbl* accompaniment, sometimes augmented by string bass, were serious and intimate, highlighting virtuosity and expressive intensity. Their repertoire emphasized both the European roots of the klezmer tradition and their connection to their mentor Tarras. Their single LP was a critical success and pointed in a direction that would not be taken up again until the early 1990s with the emergence of a historically informed performance practice aesthetic. The main innovation of both the Klezmer Conservatory Band and Kapelye was the introduction of vocals as a central part of their repertoire into what had essentially been an instrumental tradition. The vocal repertoire of both groups drew on a wide array of sources, including Yiddish musical theater and vaudeville, so-called "Yinglish" comedy,[58] Yiddish folk songs, and workers' songs.

The period from the mid-1980s to the mid-1990s was one of both consolidation and innovation for the klezmer revival. The focus of the movement broadened from mere imitation and emulation of the klezmer music of various historical periods to include innovation and the creation of new forms. The number of performers continued to grow rapidly.[59] Whereas the early revival period had been characterized by informal networks of musicians and collectors trading tunes via cassette recordings, jamming, and sharing the joy of discovering what was for most of them a still largely unknown heritage, the mid-1980s saw the beginning of institutionalized frameworks. Perhaps most significant was the founding by Henry Sapoznik of the first annual Yiddish Folk Arts Program (KlezKamp) under the auspices of the YIVO Institute for Jewish Research in 1985. For the first time, perhaps, klezmer style and repertoire were transmitted in a formalized group setting. A whole scene began to develop around klezmer music nationally and, eventually, internationally. A number of similar workshops and gatherings emerged in the US, Canada, and western and eastern Europe over the ensuing decades, in particular KlezKanada near Montréal (since 1996) and Yiddish Summer Weimar in Germany (founded in 2000).

Beginning in the late 1980s, new groups with more innovative agendas came to the fore. Certainly the two most important of those were the internationally based Brave Old World (Germany-USA), and the New York-based Klezmatics. Formed in 1989, Brave Old World was dedicated to creating a new, concert-oriented music based on the roots of instrumental klezmer, Yiddish song, and other eastern European Jewish and non-Jewish musical forms. The band's five CDs chart its development of what musical director Alan Bern terms "New Jewish Music," abandoning the term klezmer entirely and incorporating also elements of jazz, art music, free improvisation, and other world musics into the mix. More than any other group, the Klezmatics, formed in 1986, have been responsible for both popularizing klezmer music to a general audience internationally and moving klezmer and Yiddish music in the direction of global popular music.[60] German world music pioneer Christoph Borkowsky Akbar invited them in 1988 to perform at the new *Heimatklänge* world music festival in Berlin and to record for his label, Piranha. The Klezmatics became the first klezmer band to tap into the then-incipient world music market that had emerged in the wake of the success of Paul Simon's *Graceland* (1986) and similar projects. The group's CD *Rhythm + Jews* (1991) was the first to mix traditional klezmer music and Yiddish song with elements as disparate as jazz-fusion, Arabic belly-dance music, and acid rock, and contains all of the elements that the group would perfect over the course of twenty-five years. They were also at the forefront of the introduction of instrumental soloing (of the types common in rock, jazz, or Balkan and Middle Eastern music) to a genre that had previously been based on the ornamenting of and slight variations in pre-composed melodies. Through collaborations with artists as diverse as playwright Tony Kushner, Israeli singer Chava Alberstein, choreographer Twyla Tharp, and poet Allen Ginsberg, and performances on the sound-track of the HBO television series *Sex and the City*, the Klezmatics have helped to steer klezmer music into the sphere of mainstream culture. They are the first klezmer band to be awarded a Grammy, winning in 2007 in the Best Contemporary World Music Album category for their CD *Wonder Wheel*, albeit a recording that largely featured the sounds of American folk music in original compositions set to the lyrics of Woody Guthrie.

In the mid-1980s, leading American klezmer musicians and bands started performing regularly in Europe, beginning with tours in 1984 by Kapelye and Andy Statman. German audiences were particularly receptive to klezmer. Initially this appears to have been mostly part of the process of coming to terms with historical responsibility for the Holocaust (*Vergangenheitsbewältigung*). Germany has become over the course of the past thirty years perhaps the most important market for klezmer internationally. Through his onstage performances in the Berlin production of Joshua Sobol's play *Ghetto* in 1984, and then via an extended touring and recording schedule, Giora Feidman established, with his message of forgiveness and reconciliation, an almost continuous presence in Germany, and was largely responsible for popularizing the genre among German and then general European audiences.[61] He was awarded the Order of Merit of the Federal Republic of Germany, the nation's highest honor, in 2001. The black hole that the Holocaust left in the middle of Europe has been filled with the sounds of klezmer music. The appearances of Feidman and the American bands inspired the formation of hundreds of German klezmer bands over the past twenty-five years, the vast majority of them comprising non-Jews. Workshops such as Yiddish Summer Weimar have proved to be both meeting grounds for klezmer musicians transnationally as well as instrumental in training a series of serious German and European students of klezmer. Some of them, such as clarinetist Christian Dawid, have gone on to national and international careers. This has provided a counterbalance to Feidman's numerous workshops, where klezmer is taught as a non-specific but empowering universal feeling that can be played by anyone.

It was not a klezmer musician, but classical violin virtuoso Itzhak Perlman, who brought klezmer music its greatest notoriety and widest audience yet with his Great Performances PBS television documentary *In the Fiddler's House* (1995), the best-selling CD of the same name (1995), and the touring show in collaboration with the Klezmatics, Brave Old World, Andy Stat-man, and the Klezmer Conservatory Band (1995–7), with performances from Radio City Music Hall to Tanglewood and the Hollywood Bowl.

Clearly, by the 1990s, klezmer music had moved far beyond its originally Jewish audience and into the musical mainstream, and it is not only in Ger-many and Europe that a significant portion of the music's audience as well as its players are non-Jews. At the same time, within Jewish circles in the US and elsewhere, the focus of the klezmer revival has shifted from its original left-liberal secularity towards the center as it has been accepted, embraced, and, some would argue, co-opted by the various wings of organized Jewry, from Reform to Conservative and, in some cases, Orthodox. Klezmer may now be seen as being firmly ensconced in American Jewish communal life. Many Jewish community centers and synagogues have amateur and youth klezmer bands, and hardly a fundraising event takes place without musical accompaniment by a local or nationally known klezmer group.

Already by the mid-1990s, klezmer had expanded in so many musical directions that it had become difficult to speak of it as a unified musical genre. Some speak now of post-revival klezmer or even "postklezmer."[62] Since the mid-1990s, the focus of the klezmer revival has largely shifted away from the recordings and concert activities of the handful of musicians with international tours and record distribution to a more grassroots, com-munity level. While cities and regions such as New York, Berlin, the San Francisco Bay Area, Boston, and Toronto have continued to be important magnets for klezmer activity, the revival has no specific geographic center, and regionalism plays an important role.[63] The scene is dominated by jam sessions, the activities of synagogue community and youth groups, and the endeavors of a myriad of local amateur, semiprofessional, and profes-sional groups. Participants in the revival congregate physically at annual and biannual gatherings such as KlezKamp, KlezKanada, or Yiddish Summer Weimar, at festivals such as Ashkenaz in Toronto and the Jewish Culture Fes-tival in Cracow, Poland, and in the virtual community that has emerged on the Internet, such as on the Jewish-Music electronic mailing list (founded in 1992). In addition, websites and podcasts such as www.klezmershack.com and klezmerpodcast.com cover bands, review and preview events, CDs, and other publications, and provide links to resources.

The revival in its latest phase is characterized by a great deal of eclec-ticism, with a variety of approaches ranging from attempts at the re-creation of a nineteenth-century eastern European performance style and an original-instruments aesthetic to contemporary improvisations often inspired only peripherally by klezmer and Yiddish music, and includes numerous attempts at fusing klezmer music with genres as disparate as salsa, flamenco, bebop, reggae, and bluegrass.

Historically informed performance practice is an important stream within the klezmer revival that began to emerge in the early 1990s, focusing especially on earlier eastern European repertoire and style. A key recording signalling this development was *Bessarabian Symphony: Early Jewish Instrumental Music*.[64] Some of the key groups and performers include the Joel Rubin Jewish Music Ensemble, Budowitz, Khevrisa, Veretski Pass, the Chicago Klezmer Ensemble, and the violinists Alicia Svigals, Steven Greenman, and Deborah Strauss. In recent years, a younger generation of neo-traditional musicians has emerged, creating dynamic new music featuring original compositions based on traditional forms, most notably the clarinetist Michael Winograd and violinist Jake Shulman-Ment. In addition, the fall of the Iron Curtain opened up possibilities for musicians from the former Soviet Union to interact with musicians from the West, and a significant Russian klezmer scene has emerged since the mid-1990s. In addition, the fall of the Iron Curtain opened up possibilities for musicians from the former Soviet Union to interact with musicians from the West, and a significant post-Soviet klezmer scene has emerged since the mid-1990s with groups such as Dobranotch (St. Petersburg) and Forshpil (Riga/Berlin).

In the popular realm, perhaps the most significant voices to have emerged since the late 1990s are clarinetist David Krakauer (ex-Klezmatics) as soloist and bandleader of Klezmer Madness! and Ancestral Groove, with a mixture of traditional klezmer, rock, and funk, and Frank London, a founding member of the Klezmatics. More than any other artist besides Giora Feidman, Krakauer has also contributed to bringing klezmer music together with Western art music, performing and commissioning numerous concertos and chamber works. London has formed a number of popular ensembles that are pushing the envelope in various directions, most notably the Klezmer Brass All Stars, which mixes klezmer with Balkan music and other world musics, and the Nigunim Project with Lorin Sklamberg that presents klezmer-influenced settings of Hasidic *nigunim*.

Further recent trends have included the entry of klezmer onto the dance floor, especially in Europe via DJs and groups such as Yuriy Gurzhy (Berlin) and his Shtetl Superstars project and the Amsterdam Klezmer Band's work with DJ Shantel and others, as well as the emergence of klezmer bands with a punk sensibility, such as Golem (New York) and the Russian band Nayekhovichi (Moscow).

The Radical Jewish Culture movement around composer-saxophonist John Zorn emerged in the early 1990s. Originally conceived as a community of improvising musicians based primarily in Lower Manhattan, Radical Jewish Culture has become more inclusive through Zorn's founding of the Tzadik label in 1995 and networking among experimental improvising musicians internationally. The movement has been instrumental in creating a body of new music influenced by klezmer among a whole host of musical influences drawing on jazz, classical, rock, Jewish, and other world traditions. Klezmer has played a greater or lesser role in the output of the Radical Jewish Culture movement, depending on the musicians. A handful of key players are intensively involved in both, most notably London and Krakauer, and a number of musicians working at the fringes of contemporary klezmer have released their music on the Tzadik label.[65] In that musical space, the boundaries between what is klezmer and what is Radical Jewish Culture are becoming increasingly irrelevant.

At the further fringes of klezmer exist a wide variety of groups that are not expressly klezmer bands and, in most cases, are not limiting their musical framework to an eastern European Jewish one. Some are expressly Jewish-oriented groups that include klezmer influence in various degrees, such as Pharaoh's Daughter (New York); others are singer-songwriters, like Daniel Kahn and The Painted Bird (Berlin) and Geoff Berner (Vancouver), who use the energy of klezmer to infuse their song-based, cabaret-style repertoire – both cite klezmer as a major influence. Hundreds of not specifically Jewish bands, especially in the new cabaret and indie scenes, now include klezmer as one of a myriad of musical influences in their musical mix. To make things more complicated, a number of groups are drawing on klezmer, Balkan, and "Gypsy" (Romani) influences in varying combinations.[66]

On the one hand, it would seem to be a misconception to consider the contemporary klezmer revival to be a direct continuation of the pre-revival tradition as it had developed over the course of centuries. Disparities in modes of transmission, language milieus, musical and religious milieus, social structures, and repertorial demands, as well as artistic intentions and aspirations account for the major differences. On the other hand, the style and repertoire of the klezmorim have served as the primary inspiration for the movement, and several leading musicians have apprenticed themselves to tradition bearers such as Dave Tarras (Andy Statman) and Max Epstein (Joel Rubin), so that one can also not speak of a complete rupture in the tradition.

The European klezmorim developed patterns of professionalism, virtuosity, flexibility, and eclecticism that would make it possible for them later to adapt easily to musical life on other continents through immigration, and it is this flexibility and eclecticism that has served as a model for the development of contemporary klezmer music by musicians of the revival. What tie all of this together musically are characteristic performance practice techniques, and typical modal and melodic patterns that are at the core of the klezmer tradition. Klezmer music makes use of a small number of modal scales with characteristic motifs, which contain elements of Ottoman Turkish modal scales known as *makams*, eastern Ashkenazic Jewish prayer modes known as *shteygers* or *gusts*, as well as Western major and minor scales. As they are employed in klezmer music, they function as a coherent and unique system.[67] More than anything else, perhaps, it is the *manner* in which klezmer tunes are ornamented and varied that forms the most characteristic aspect of the genre. It is the stereotypical sound of the ornaments, especially on instruments like violin and clarinet, with their characteristic note bends, trills, and grace notes, as well as the timbre of the instruments that make the music instantly recognizable as klezmer even to the untrained ear. In addition, klezmer music is traditionally heterophonic, and the basic texture along with the melodic conflicts and dissonances that may arise form a basic element of the sound of the music.[68]

Notes

1 The literal translation is vessels or instruments of song.

2 Walter Salmen, *"Denn die Fiedel macht das Fest": Jüdische Musikanten und Tänzer vom 13. bis 20. Jahrhundert* ["For the Fiddle Makes the Party": Jewish Musicians and Dancers from the Thirteenth to the Twentieth Century] (Innsbruck: Edition Helbling, 1991), 15.

3 *Yoysef Tshernyavski un zayn khsidisher dzhezz bend bageystert tsendliker toysender mentshn* [Joseph Cherniavsky and His Hasidic Jazz Band Enthrall Tens of Thousands] (clipping from an unidentified Yiddish-American newspaper, early to mid-1920s).

4 Hanoch Avenary, "Music," in *Encyclopedia Judaica* (Jerusalem: Keter; New York: Macmillan, 1971–2), xii: 566–664, 675–8 (632).

5 Ashkenaz is the Hebrew name for the German-speaking lands along the banks of the Rhine and its tributaries, as well as the Danube, where Jews had settled as early as Roman times.

6 *Letsonim*, also *letsim* (sing. *leyts*), is a Yiddish word of Hebrew origin and literally means clowns, pranksters, scoffers.

7 On the Jewish towns, see Barbara Kirshenblatt-Gimblett, "Introduction," in Mark Zborowski and Elizabeth Herzog, *Life Is with People: The Culture of the Shtetl* (New York: Schocken Books, 1995), ix–xlviii.

8 Joachim Stutschewsky, *Ha-Klezmorim: Toldotehem, orakh-hayehem, v'yezirotehem* [Klezmorim: History, Folklore, Compositions] (Jerusalem: Bialik Institute, 1959).

9 Salmen, *"Denn die Fiedel"*; Walter Zev Feldman, "Remembrance of Things Past: *Klezmer* Musicians of Galicia, 1870–1940," *Polin: Studies in Polish Jewry*, 16 (2003): 29–57.

10 Robert A. Rothstein, "Klezmer-Loshn," *Judaism*, 47.1 (Winter 1998): 23–9.

11 Moshe Beregovski, *Jewish Instrumental Folk Music: The Collections and Writings of Moshe Beregovski*, trans. and ed. Mark Slobin, Robert Rothstein, and Michael Alpert (Syracuse University Press, 2001, orig. 1938).

12 *Ibid.*

13 Samuel Weissenberg, "Eine jüdische Hochzeit in Südrussland" [A Jewish Wedding in Southern Russia], *Mitteilungen zur jüdischen Volkskunde*, 15.1 (1905): 59–74.

14 Hasidism is a populist Jewish mystical movement credited to Israel ben Eliezer (Ba'al Shem Tov, c. 1700–60) that emerged in Podolia (Ukraine) during the second half of the eighteenth century and spread throughout eastern Europe, especially in the nineteenth century.

15 Ellen Koskoff, *Music in Lubavitcher Life* (Urbana, IL, and Chicago: University of Illinois Press, 2000).

16 The *Haskalah* (Hebr.) was the Jewish Enlightenment originating from philosopher Moses Mendelssohn (1729–86) in Berlin. The ideas of the *Haskalah* began to spread to eastern Europe by the late eighteenth century.

17 In some regions, such as East Galicia, *tsimbl* continued to be used into the 1930s (Feldman, "Remembrance of Things Past").

18 Beregovski, *Jewish Instrumental Folk Music*.

19 Israel Rabinovitch, *Muzik bay yidn un andere eseyen af muzikalishe temes* [Music among the Jews and Other Essays on Musical Topics] (Montreal: Eagle Publishing, 1940), 203–6.

20 Martin Schwartz, *Klezmer Music: Early Yiddish Instrumental Music, The First Recordings: 1908–1927, From the Collection of Dr. Martin Schwartz* (El Cerrito, CA: Folklyric Records, 1997, compact disc).

21 Moshe Bik, *Klezmorim be-Orgeev/Jewish Wedding*, ed. M. Gorali (Haifa Music Museum and Library, 1964).

22 While his background was as a klezmer musician, it is not clear how much klezmer music made up the concert programs of Guzikov, which were replete with eighteenth- and nineteenth-century classical works,

theme-and-variation numbers, and fantasies on eastern European folk melodies. Dov Sadan, *Ha-menagen ha-mufla: Chai Yosef Michel Guzikov u-svivehem* [The Great Player: Joseph Michael Gusikov and His Environment] (Tel Aviv: M. Newman, 1947). The lives of all three musicians generated numerous legends and were immortalized in works of Yiddish fiction, e.g. Sholem Aleichem, "Stempeniu, A Jewish Romance," in Joachim Neugroschel (ed. and trans.), *The Shtetl: A Creative Anthology of Jewish Life in Eastern Europe* (New York: Perigree/G. P. Putnam's Sons, 1982), 287–375 (original Yiddish edition 1888); Irme Druker, *Klezmer* (Moscow: Farlag "Sovetski pisatel," 1976); idem, "Mikhoel-Yoysef Guzikov," *Sovetish Heymland*, 11 (November 1981): 20–81, and 12 (December 1981): 12–89.

23 Lawrence W. Levine, *Highbrow/Lowbrow: The Emergence of Cultural Hierarchy in America* (Cambridge, MA, and London: Harvard University Press, 1988).

24 Zalmen Zylbercweig, *Leksikon fun yidishn teater* [Lexicon of the Yiddish Theater], 6 vols. (New York: Hebrew Actors Union of America, 1934), ii:904.

25 Jeffrey Wollock, "European Recordings of Jewish Instrumental Folk Music, 1911–1914," *Association for Recorded Sound Collections Journal*, 28.1 (1997): 36–55; Michael Aylward, "Early Recordings of Jewish Music in Poland," *Polin: Studies in Polish Jewry*, 16 (2003): 59–69; Joel Rubin and Michael Aylward, *Chekhov's Band: Eastern European Klezmer Music from the EMI Archives 1908–1913* (London: Renair Records, 2015), liner notes.

26 Szpilman was author of *The Pianist: The Extraordinary True Story of One Man's Survival in Warsaw, 1939–1945* (New York: Picador, 2003) (orig. Śmierć miasta, Warsaw, 1946).

27 Issachar Fater, *Yidishe muzik in Poyln tsvishn beyde velt-milkhomes* [Jewish Music in Poland between the World Wars] (Tel-Aviv: Velt-federatsye fun poylishe yidn, 1970).

28 Jeffrey Wollock, "The Soviet Klezmer Orchestra," *Eastern European Jewish Affairs*, 30.1 (Summer 2000): 1–36.

29 Marian Fuks, *Muzyka Ocalona: Judaica Polskie* [Rescued Music: Polish Judaica] (Warsaw: Wydawnictwa Radia i Telewizji, 1989).

30 Gerald Sorin, *A Time for Building: The Third Migration, 1880–1920*, vol. III of H. L. Feingold (ed.), *The Jewish People in America*, 5 vols. (Baltimore and London: Johns Hopkins University Press, 1992).

31 Moses Rischin, *The Promised City: New York's Jews, 1870–1914* (Cambridge, MA, and London: Harvard University Press, 1977).

32 See, for example, Hankus Netsky's study of Philadelphia's klezmer community, *Klezmer: Music and Community in Twentieth-Century Jewish Philadelphia*, (Philadelphia: Temple University Press, 2015).

33 James B. Loeffler, *A Gilgul fun a Nigun: Jewish Musicians in New York 1881–1945* (Cambridge, MA: Harvard College Library, 1997); idem, "Di Rusishe Progresiv Muzikal Yunyon No. 1 fun Amerike: The First Klezmer Union in America," *Judaism*, 47.1 (Winter 1998): 29–40.

34 *Ibid.*

35 A *landsmanshaft* was a mutual aid society formed by immigrants from the same town, city, or region.

36 Daniel Soyer, *Jewish Immigrant Associations and American Identity in New York, 1880–1939* (Cambridge, MA, and London: Harvard University Press, 1997).

37 Richard K. Spottswood, *Eastern Europe*, vol. III of *Ethnic Music on Records: A Discography of Ethnic Recordings Produced in the United States, 1893 to 1942*, 7 vols. (Urbana, IL: University of Illinois Press, 1990).

38 Jenna Weissman Joselit, *The Wonders of America: Reinventing Jewish Culture, 1880–1950* (New York: Hill and Wang, 1994).

39 Stefan Kanfer, *A Summer World: The Attempt to Build a Jewish Eden in the Catskills, from the Days of the Ghetto to the Rise and Decline of the Borscht Belt* (New York: Farrar, Straus, and Giroux, 1989).

40 Jehoash Hirshberg, *Music in the Jewish Community of Palestine 1880–1948: A Social History* (Oxford: Clarendon Press, 1995).

41 Joel E. Rubin, "'They Danced It, We Played It': Adaptation and Revitalization in Post-1920s New York Klezmer Music," in *Studies in Jewish Civilization*, vol. XIX, *"I Will Sing and Make Music": Jewish Music and Musicians Throughout the Ages*, ed. Leonard J. Greenspoon, Ronald A. Simkins, and Jean Cahan (Omaha: Creighton University Press, 2008), 181–213.

42 These areas were part of the Ottoman Empire until 1919 and from 1919–48 were ruled under the British Mandate.

43 Joel Rubin, "*Rumenishe shtiklekh* (Romanian pieces). *Klezmer* Music among the Hasidim in Contemporary Israel," *Judaism*, 47.1 (Winter 1998): 12–23; Yaacov Mazor, *The Klezmer Tradition in the Land of Israel: Transcriptions and Commentaries*, Yuval Music Series 6 (Jerusalem: Magnes Press, 2000) (book and CD, Anthology of Music Traditions in Israel 11).

44 Mazor, *Klezmer Tradition*.

45 Milton Doroshkin, *Yiddish in America: Social and Cultural Foundations* (Rutherford,

Madison, and Teaneck, NJ: Fairleigh Dickinson University Press, 1969).

46 Haym Soloveitchik, "Rupture and Reconstruction: The Transformation of Contemporary Orthodoxy," *Tradition*, 28.4 (Summer 1994): 64–130.

47 Barbara Kirshenblatt-Gimblett, "Sounds of Sensibility," *Judaism*, 47.1 (Winter 1998): 49–78.

48 Marilyn Halter, "Ethnic and Racial Identity," in Reed Ueda (ed.), *A Companion to American Immigration* (New York: Wiley VCH, 2005), 161–76.

49 Alex Haley, *Roots* (Garden City, NY: Doubleday, 1976); Irving Howe, with the assistance of Kenneth Libo, *World of Our Fathers: The Journey of the East European Jews to America and the Life They Found and Made* (New York: Simon & Schuster, 1976).

50 Mark Slobin, "The Neo-Klezmer Movement and Euro-American Revivalism," *Journal of American Folklore*, 97.383 (1982): 98–104.

51 Mark Slobin, *Fiddler on the Move: Exploring the Klezmer World* (Oxford University Press, 2000).

52 Kirshenblatt-Gimblett, "Sounds of Sensibility."

53 In the early 1970s, before the American klezmer revival had fully emerged, Israeli clarinetist Giora Feidman began to popularize what he called "Jewish soul music," bringing out several LPs by 1975. After resettling in New York in 1974, Feidman enjoyed success performing mostly for American Jewish communities, but his eclectic repertoire – which also included Israeli folk songs, *Fiddler on the Roof* medleys, and Gershwin arrangements – and sentimental aesthetic were unappealing to most of the younger American revivalists. He has had tremendous success in Europe, especially Germany, as shall be discussed below. Other important centers of the early klezmer revival included Los Angeles, Seattle, and Portland on the West Coast.

54 See, for example, Nat Hentoff, "Indigenous Music," *The Nation*, January 14, 1978, 28–9; Ari L. Goldman, "Reviving Yiddish 'Klezmer' Music," *New York Times,* November 17, 1978; Bob Norman, "Echoes from the Shtetl: Reviving Jewish Klezmer Music," *Sing Out!*, 28.4 (July/August 1980): 2–7. Scholars, too, began to take note of the phenomenon by the early 1980s (e.g., Slobin, "Neo-Klezmer Movement").

55 Neil V. Rosenberg (ed.), *Transforming Tradition: Folk Music Revivals Examined* (Urbana, IL, and Chicago: University of Illinois Press, 1993).

56 The latter two groups are featured in the documentary film *Jumpin' Night in the Garden of Eden* (1987).

57 Richard F. Shepard, "Klezmer Music Makes Leap to Carnegie Hall," *New York Times*, February 18, 1983.

58 Yinglish is often used to describe the mixed-language comedy songs of musicians such as Mickey Katz (1909–85). Herbert J. Gans, "The 'Yinglish' Music of Mickey Katz," *American Quarterly*, 5.3 (Autumn 1953): 213–18.

59 Ethnomusicologist Lynn (Shulamis) Dion had documented thirty-four groups by 1986, all but one in the US. Lynn Dion, "Klezmer Music in America: Revival and Beyond," *Jewish Folklore and Ethnology Newsletter*, 8.1–2 (1986): 2–8.

60 Timothy D. Taylor, *Global Pop: World Music, World Markets* (New York: Routledge, 1997).

61 Joel E. Rubin, "Music without Borders in the New Germany: Giora Feidman and the Klezmer-Influenced New Old Europe Sound," *Ethnomusicology Forum*, 24.2 (August 2015): 205–29.

62 Jonathan Freedman, *Klezmer America: Jewishness, Ethnicity, Modernity* (New York: Columbia University Press, 2008).

63 Christina L. Baade, "In Response to 'Freylekhe Felker: Queer Subculture in the Klezmer Revival' by Dana Astmann," *Discourses in Music*, 5.1 (Spring 2004), http://library.music .utoronto.ca/discourses-in-music/v5n1a3.html (accessed June 25, 2013).

64 Joel Rubin and Joshua Horowitz, *Bessarabian Symphony: Early Jewish Instrumental Music*, Wergo SM-1606-2, 1994, compact disc.

65 Through interlocking band memberships and musical collaborations, many of the same musicians are involved in the full range of contemporary klezmer music stylistically, whether neo-traditional or avant-garde.

66 Due to misunderstandings among numerous journalists, some groups that are working with Balkan and Romani materials (or even simply central or eastern European-sounding materials), but *not* klezmer, are often mistakenly attributed as "klezmer" bands. The confusion seems to stem largely from the fact that in the New Europe, both Jews and Roma are seen as symbols of the quintessential ethnic Other, and more generally of a powerful emotionalism, symbolizing the exotic or "Oriental," and transcending cultural and national borders. Within this framework, it becomes easy to confuse or substitute the one for the other. Carol Silverman, "Gypsy/Klezmer Dialectics: Jewish and Romani Traces and Erasures in Contemporary European World Music,"

Ethnomusicology Forum, 24.2 (August 2015): 159–80.

67 Joel E. Rubin, *The Art of the Klezmer: Improvisation and Ornamentation in the Commercial Recordings of New York Clarinettists Naftule Brandwein and Dave Tarras 1922–1929*, Ph.D. thesis, City University of London (2001).

68 In heterophonic music, when more than one melodic voice is present, each player interprets and ornaments the melody independently.

PART THREE

Periods, places, and genres of Jewish music composition

9 Art music and Jewish culture before the Jewish Enlightenment

Negotiating identities in Late Renaissance Italy

JOSHUA R. JACOBSON

> By the rivers of Babylon we sat down and wept when we remembered Zion. There by the willows we hung up our harps... How could we sing the Lord's song on foreign soil?
>
> — PSALM 137:1–4

For centuries, the musical soundscape of the Ashkenazi synagogue remained essentially insular. The core of the service was the "reading" of the Bible utilizing a set of fixed traditional cantillation motifs, performed modally and monophonically by a soloist in free rhythm. The rest of the service, the chanting of prayers, allowed for slightly more improvisation, but, like biblical cantillation, was based on traditional modes, in free rhythm, with no harmony or instrumental accompaniment.[1] The emphasis was on piety rather than on beauty. At the same time, music in Catholic churches was evolving in a strikingly different direction, with the addition of new compositions by professional composers complementing the ancient chant, with harmony and counterpoint in performances by trained choirs, organists, and other instrumentalists.

Christians visiting synagogues were often puzzled by a music that seemed primitive, alien, even ugly in comparison with what they were used to hearing in church. The Frenchman François Tissard wrote of his experience visiting a synagogue in Ferrara, Italy, around 1502, "One might hear one man howling, another braying and another bellowing. Such a cacophony of discordant sounds do they make! Weighing this with the rest of their rites, I was almost brought to nausea."[2]

The eighteenth- and nineteenth-century Enlightenment (*Haskalah*) would bring tremendous changes to the synagogue ritual and its music. But several centuries before that, in the early modern era, there were a few isolated instances of musical innovation in Jewish worship, the most striking of which occurred in Mantua, Italy, at the end of the sixteenth century. Italy had a relatively large Jewish population, and was home to the oldest diaspora community in Europe. The original indigenous population had recently been enlarged by immigrations from

Spain and from the lands of Ashkenaz. In the city of Mantua at the beginning of the seventeenth century there were nine synagogues for a population of 2,325 Jews, representing about 4 percent of the general population.[3]

Under the influence of the humanistic spirit of the Renaissance, many Italian Christians expressed more tolerant attitudes towards their Jewish neighbors. There was also a growing amount of commerce connecting the two communities, with Jews rising to significant positions as bankers, moneylenders, pawnbrokers, and traders of second-hand merchandise. In 1516 Jews were permitted for the first time to establish permanent residences in the city of Venice, on an island that was the former site of a foundry, called "ghetto" in Italian (or "getto" in the Venetian dialect).

Many Jews were becoming increasingly bicultural, fluent in the language, customs, literature, dance, and music of Italy, while at the same time retaining adherence to their ancestral religious traditions. Perhaps the most famous of these bicultural Jews was Rabbi Leon Modena (1571–1648), who served as an intermediary between the Jewish and Christian communities.[4] Modena was a skilled author of poetry and prose in both Hebrew and Italian. He was well-versed in rabbinic literature, as well as the Christian Bible, philosophy, scientific theory, and Renaissance literature. He advocated for reforms in the synagogue liturgy but also passionately defended traditional Jewish practice. His *Historia de gli riti hebraici*, commissioned by an English lord, was the first book to explain the Jewish religion to a general audience. He experimented with alchemy, magic, and astrology, and was a compulsive gambler. Modena was also an accomplished amateur musician, and is credited with encouraging his friend, Salamone Rossi, to compose an unprecedented collection of polyphonic motets in Hebrew for the synagogue.

We don't know very much about Salamone Rossi. He was born circa 1570. His first published music is a book of nineteen canzonets printed in 1589.[5] His last published music is dated 1628, a book of two-part *madrigaletti*. And after that there is nothing. Perhaps he died in the plague of 1628. Perhaps he died during the Austrian invasion in 1630. We just don't know. His published output consists of six books of madrigals, one book of canzonets, one *balletto* from an opera, one book of *madrigaletti*, four books of instrumental works (sonatas, sinfonias, and various dance pieces), and a path-breaking book of synagogue motets – in all, some 313 compositions between 1589 and 1628.

* * *

> Most people are principally aware of one culture, one setting, one home;
> exiles are aware of at least two, and this plurality of vision gives rise to an
> awareness of simultaneous dimensions, an awareness that – to borrow a
> phrase from music – is *contrapuntal.*
>   – Edward Said, "The Mind of Winter: Reflections on Life in Exile"[6]

In sixteenth- and seventeenth-century Italy, religion was a significant
marker of identity. And those who were not situated within the borders
of Catholicism were required to signify their status of alterity in their clothing, in their locus of residence, and in their name. Salamone Rossi enjoyed
a contrapuntal life in two distinct domains, each set off by its boundaries,
both physical and political.

Rossi was employed at the ducal palace in Mantua, where he served as a
violinist and composer. He was quite the *avant-garde* composer. He was the
first composer to publish trio sonatas.[7] Rossi's madrigals are based on texts
by the most modern poets of his time, and he was the first composer to
publish madrigals with continuo accompaniment.[8] There were many other
notable musicians at the Mantuan court, including Claudio Monteverdi
(1567–1643) and Giovanni Gastoldi (1554–1609). But as far as we know,
Rossi was the only Jew. In August 1606, acknowledging Rossi's stature, the
Mantuan Duke Vincenzo Gonzaga (1562–1612) issued an edict that stated,
"As we wish to express our gratitude for the services in composing and
performing provided for many years by Salamone Rossi Ebreo, we grant
him unrestricted freedom to move about town without the customary
orange mark on his hat."[9] And yet, as we see in the edict, Rossi still bore the
epithet "Ebreo" – Jew.

At the Mantuan court, Rossi worked alongside as many as thirty
Christian composers, instrumentalists, and singers. Then each night Rossi
switched to his Jewish identity, returning to his home in the Jewish ghetto
of Mantua, where he lived, and where he worshipped.[10] But influenced by
Rabbi Modena, Rossi would poke a hole in the cultural boundary line. In a
daring innovation, Rossi introduced polyphonic music into the synagogue,
bringing the extramural music of the Christian world into the ghetto. In
1622, thirty-three of Rossi's Hebrew motets were published in Venice. The
title of the collection, *Ha-shirim asher lishlomo* (The Songs of Solomon),
not only refers to the name of the author (Salamone is the Italian form
of Shelomo, or Solomon), but also, by playing on the name of a book of
the Hebrew Bible, *Shir ha-shirim asher lishlomo* (The Song of Songs of
Solomon), gives the music an implied intertextual stamp of approval.

As far as we know there were no precedents for Rossi's innovation. Certainly the composer himself believed that was the case. Figure 9.1 shows the

Figure 9.1 Title page of Salamone Rossi, *Ha-shirim asher lishlomo* (1622).

title page of Rossi's 1622 publication of his thirty-three polyphonic motets for the synagogue. Notice the words "an innovation (Hebrew: ḥadashah) in the land." The title page, like the rest of the book, is written almost totally in Hebrew. Here is a translation:

> Bass
> The Songs of Solomon
> Psalms, songs, and hymns of praise
> that have been composed according to the science of music

for three, four, five, six, seven, and eight voices
by the honored master Salamone Rossi, may his Rock
keep him and save him,
a resident of the holy congregation of Mantua,
to give thanks to the Lord, and to sing His most
exalted name on all
sacred occasions. An innovation
in the land.
Here in Venice, 1622
at the command of their Lordships
Pietro and Lorenzo Bragadini
in the house of Giovanni Calleoni.
By the distinguished Lords
Pietro and Lorenzo Bragadini

We can see on this title page some of the challenges of a bi-cultural identity. To describe what they were creating, the authors had to borrow or invent words that did not exist in the Hebrew language. The first word on the page is *basso*, the Italian word meaning bass, spelled out in Hebrew letters.[11] There was no word for harmony or polyphony in Hebrew, so the authors used the Italian word "musica," again spelled with Hebrew letters. Elsewhere in the book, in order to express musical terminology, Hebrew words were given new meanings. Thus meter was translated as *mishkal* and music theory as *hokhmat ha-shir*. This macaronic text with its linguistic code-switching reflected a radical change of culture and musical style.

Indeed the very concept of this book is predicated on both its authors' and its readers' ability to negotiate multiple identities. In these polyphonic motets the lyrics are in Hebrew, and the context is the synagogue worship service. But the musical styles, the convention of notation, the musical terminology, and the performative aspect are all borrowed from the culture of Christian Europe.

Rossi's bilingual (or bi-directional) identity can be seen most strikingly in a page of music from the 1622 publication (Example 9.1). The musical notation is read from left to right; each word of the Hebrew lyrics, however, must be read from right to left. This manifestation of battling orthographies made for very complicated code-switching.

Code-switching also occurs in several of the motets in which the choir would sing certain parts of the prayer in the new polyphonic Italian style, while other sections of the prayer would be chanted by the congregation or the cantor using the traditional monophonic modal melodies. In accordance with the conventions of church music of his time, Rossi inserted double bar lines in the middle of a composition as a signal for the choir to pause while the cantor or the congregation sang the traditional chant. Example 9.2 shows

Example 9.1 Rossi, *Keter*, canto part book.

a portion of the present author's attempt to reconstruct a performance of Rossi's *Keter*.[12] Rossi composed music for only a portion of the liturgical text, leaving the rest to be chanted by cantor and congregation in the traditional manner. Rossi's original is shown in Example 9.1.

Example 9.2 Pages 1 and 2 of Rossi's *Keter*, edited by Joshua Jacobson. Reproduced by permission of Broude Brothers Limited.

Other conventions of Italian polyphony can be found in *Ha-shirim*. Nine of the thirty-three motets are in the style of *cori spezzati*, a polychoral format in which singers are divided into two groups in physical opposition, singing at times in alternation, and at times together. This style is commonly associated with the Cathedral of San Marco in Venice, and was widespread in churches throughout Italy and beyond. One of Rossi's polychoral motets, the wedding ode *Lemi eḥpots*, is set in the "echo" format, well known to choral singers from Orlando di Lasso's "Echo Song" (1581). *Lemi eḥpots* also features intriguing wordplay between its Hebrew lyrics and Italian homophones. For example, one of the Hebrew lines ends with the phrase *kegever be'alma*, "as a man with a maid." The echo chorus then repeats just the last two syllables, *alma*, which in Italian means "soul."

One of Rossi's motets suggests a style of dance music that was extremely popular in his time. The *Kaddish* a5 was composed as a *balletto*, modeled after his colleague Giovanni Giacomo Gastoldi's 1591 collection *Balletti a*

Example 9.2 (*cont.*)

cinque voci con li suoi versi per cantare, sonare e ballare, which was among the best-selling sheet music of the sixteenth century. Like many *balletti*, but unique among Rossi's motets, *Kaddish* is in strophic form, with sharply defined rhythms in a largely homophonic texture. It is also the only motet in the collection in triple meter, which was often used for joyous dancing.

Some of Rossi's melodies link him to his Christian contemporaries. The main theme of Rossi's *Elohim hashivenu* bears a strong resemblance to Lasso's *Cum essem parvulus* (Examples 9.3a–b). And the bass line of Rossi's *Al naharot bavel* is nearly identical to that of his colleague Lodovico Viadana's *Super flumina Babylonis*, a setting of the same text (Psalm 137) in Latin (Examples 9.4a–b).

There was bound to be a conflict between modern Jews who had been influenced by the Italian Renaissance, and those with a more conservative theology and praxis. Rabbi Leon Modena described what happened when Rossi's choral music was sung in a synagogue in Ferrara in 1605:[13]

Example 9.3a Rossi, *Elohim Hashivenu* (first phrase).

Example 9.3b Orlando Lasso, *Cum essem parvulus* (first phrase).

Example 9.4a Rossi, *Al naharot bavel, basso* (first phrase).

Example 9.4b Lodovico Viadana, *Super flumina Babylonis* (first phrase).

> We have six or eight knowledgeable men who know something about the science of song, i.e. "[polyphonic] music," men of our congregation (may their Rock keep and save them), who on holidays and festivals raise their voices in the synagogue and joyfully sing songs, praises, hymns, and melodies such as *Ein keloheinu, Aleinu leshabeah, Yigdal, Adon olam*, etc. to the glory of the Lord in an orderly relationship of the voices according to this science [music].
>
> Now a man stood up to drive them out with the utterance of his lips, answering [those who enjoyed the music], saying that it is not proper to do this, for rejoicing is forbidden, and song is forbidden, and hymns set to artful music have been forbidden since the Temple was destroyed.[14]

The objections to choral singing were based on several rabbinic rulings. Living as a tiny minority community in exile, Jews were expected to maintain their unique ancestral culture, and refrain from imitating the practices of the Gentiles among whom they lived. Furthermore, as a sign of mourning for the destruction of the Temple in Jerusalem and its renowned music, Jews were expected to refrain from performing or listening to any joyous music. Mar 'Ukba (early third century) is quoted in the Talmud decreeing, "it is forbidden to sing [at parties]."[15] And his contemporary, Rav, ruled, "The ear that listens to song should be torn off."[16]

The great philosopher Moses Maimonides (late twelfth-century Spain and Egypt) stressed the historical reasons for Jews refraining from music:

> [The rabbis at the time of the destruction of the Second Temple] prohibited playing all musical instruments, any kind of instrument, and anything that makes any kind of music. It is forbidden to have any pleasure therein, and it is forbidden to listen to them because of the destruction [of the Temple].[17]

But there were exceptions to this ban on music. Music was allowed, even required, to enhance a religious imperative (*mitzvah*). The medieval Rabbis known as the Tosafists clarified that there are no restrictions on singing at a wedding: "Singing which is associated with a mitzvah is permitted: for example, rejoicing with bride and groom at the wedding feast."[18] Nor would there be any restriction on singing God's praises in a liturgical service, as this Midrash makes clear: "If you have a pleasant voice, chant the liturgy and stand before the Ark [as leader], for it is written, 'Honor the Lord with your wealth' (Proverbs 3:9), i.e. with that [talent] which God has endowed you."[19]

But the antagonism towards music, especially non-traditional music, remained strong. Anticipating objections over the publication of Rossi's music, Rabbi Modena wrote a lengthy preface in which he refuted the arguments against polyphony in the synagogue:

> To remove all criticism from misguided hearts, should there be among our exiles some over-pious soul (of the kind who reject everything new and seek to forbid all knowledge which they cannot share) who may declare this [style of sacred music] forbidden because of things he has learned without understanding, I have found it advisable to include in this book a responsum that I wrote eighteen years ago when I taught the Torah in the Holy Congregation of Ferrara (may He protect them, Amen) to silence one who made confused statements about the same matter.[20]

He immediately cites the liturgical exception to the ban on music:

> Who does not know that all authorities agree that all forms of singing are completely permissible in connection with the observance of the ritual commandments? I do not see how anyone with a brain in his skull could cast any doubt on the propriety of praising God in song in the synagogue on special Sabbaths and on festivals. The cantor is urged to intone his prayers in a pleasant voice. If he were able to make his one voice sound like ten singers,

would this not be desirable? . . . And if it happens that they harmonize well with him, should this be considered a sin? Are these individuals on whom the Lord has bestowed the talent to master the technique of music to be condemned if they use it for His glory? For if they are, then cantors should bray like asses and refrain from singing sweetly lest we invoke the prohibition against vocal music.[21]

But Modena goes even further in his defense. He argues that if Jews are imitating the music of Christians, it is only to reclaim their own lost heritage. Modena is using here a classic Renaissance argument. Restoring the glorious culture of antiquity was at the heart of the Italian Renaissance. The Florentines who invented opera claimed that they were reviving the art of ancient Greek theater. Modena claimed that Rossi was actually reviving the musical practice of the ancient Temple in Jerusalem, "restoring the crown of music to its original state as in the days of the Levites on their platforms."[22] Modena asserted that the music of Christian churches was derived from the practice of the Levitical choir and orchestra in the ancient Temple in Jerusalem. He quotes Immanuel of Rome, who wrote that Christian music "was stolen from the land of the Hebrews."[23] Therefore, he and Rossi were merely reclaiming the lost heritage of the ancient Israelites.[24]

Modena indulges in hyperbolic praise in his description of the culture of ancient Israel:

> For wise men in all fields of learning flourished in Israel in former times. All noble sciences sprang from them; therefore the nations honored them and held them in high esteem so that they soared as if on eagles' wings. Music was not lacking among these sciences; they possessed it in all its perfection and others learned it from them. However, when it became their lot to dwell among strangers and to wander to distant lands where they were dispersed among alien peoples, these vicissitudes caused them to forget all their knowledge and to be devoid of all wisdom.[25]

There is no record of Rossi after 1628, when there was an outbreak of the plague in Mantua. In 1630 the ghetto was evacuated during the Austrian invasion, and some of the residents relocated to Venice. Leon Modena established a Jewish musical academy in Venice that functioned from 1628 until around 1638, but there is no mention of Salamone Rossi.

There is no evidence of any other collection of polyphonic synagogue music of the size and quality of *Ha-shirim* until the nineteenth century. The musicologist Israel Adler discovered several isolated instances of art music that were performed in the seventeenth and eighteenth centuries in the synagogues of Venice, Siena, Casale Monferrato, Amsterdam, and Comtat Venaissin.[26] These are delightful works, most of them composed by Christian musicians for special occasions, but none having the depth of Rossi's *Ha-shirim*.

Ha-shirim seems to have been largely forgotten after Rossi's death until the middle of the nineteenth century. While on vacation in Italy, Baron Edmond de Rothschild was given an unusual collection of old part books of music with Hebrew lyrics. Rothschild thought they might be of interest to his synagogue choir director Samuel David, who passed them along to Samuel Naumbourg, Cantor of the Great Synagogue of Paris. With the assistance of a young music student named Vincent D'Indy, Naumbourg prepared the first modern edition of Rossi's music in an anthology that included thirty of the thirty-three motets and was published in 1876. Naumbourg chose modernization over historical accuracy. In accord with nineteenth-century standards, he felt free to add his interpretations for tempo and dynamics, transpose to a different key, rearrange for a different number of voice parts, alter rhythms, even substitute different lyrics. But his edition did instigate a revival and brought Rossi's music to a wider audience. In the twentieth century several new editions of *Ha-shirim* were published, for both scholars and performers, and numerous recordings were issued. The most significant scholarship on Rossi to date has come from musicologist Don Harrán, who has written an impressive monograph, and edited all of Rossi's music for the American Institute of Musicology's Corpus Mensurabilis Musicae.

Notes

1 In some synagogues the cantor would assemble a few singers to improvise a primitive harmonic accompaniment to his chanting. These singers, generally known as *meshorerim*, would hum drones, sing in parallel thirds or sixths with the cantor, and lead the congregation in appropriate responses.

2 François Tissard, *De Iudeorum ritibus compendium*, Paris, 1508, Fol. 17b. Cited in David Ruderman, *The World of a Renaissance Jew: The Life and Thought of Abraham ben Mordecai Farissol* (Cincinnati: Hebrew Union College Press, 1981), 101.

3 Don Harrán, *Salamone Rossi: A Jewish Musician in Late Renaissance Mantua* (Oxford University Press, 1999), 11.

4 Modena's fame is due in part to the publication of his autobiography, *Life of Judah*, reprinted in Mark R. Cohen (ed. and trans.), *The Autobiography of a Seventeenth-Century Venetian Rabbi: Leon Modena's Life of Judah* (Princeton University Press, 1988).

5 Some musicologists think that Rossi chose to publish nineteen compositions because he was nineteen years old, and if so he would have been born nineteen years before 1589.

6 Edward Said, "The Mind of Winter: Reflections on Life in Exile," *Harper's*, September 1984, 49–55 (55).

7 Rossi's sonatas were published in 1613, Biagio Marini's not until 1617.

8 Rossi's madrigals with continuo were published in 1600, Monteverdi's in 1605 (book five).

9 Mantua, Archivo Storico, Archivio Gonzaga, Mandati 97, fol. 62. Cited in Harrán, *Salamone Rossi*, 16.

10 The first ghetto was established in nearby Venice in 1516. Mantua did not legislate a closed area for Jews until 1612, after the death of Duke Vincenzo. However, the Jews of Mantua had already been living in their own enclave for many years.

11 Each part-book begins with the name of its voice part, transliterated and spelled in Hebrew characters: *canto, alto, tenore, basso, quinto, sesto, setto, ottavo.*

12 The traditional chants are taken from Elio Piatelli, *Canti liturgici ebraici de rito italiano* (Rome: Edizioni De Santis, 1967).

13 Modena does not specifically name Rossi as the composer, but from the context and from

the absence of any evidence to the contrary, we may safely assume that to be the case.

14 Salamone Rossi, *Ha-shirim* (Venice: Bragadini, 1622), fol. 5.

15 Babylonian Talmud, Gittin 7a.

16 Babylonian Talmud, Sota 48a.

17 Moses Maimonides, *The Laws of Fasting*, 5:14.

18 Tosafot to Gitin 7a.

19 Midrash Tanḥuma, Re'eh, ch. 9.

20 Rossi, *Ha-shirim*, fol. 4.

21 *Ibid.*, fol. 5.

22 *Ibid.*, fol. 4.

23 *Ibid.*, fol. 3. Immanuel of Rome (1261–1328) was a Jewish scholar and poet. This quote, playing on the words of Genesis 40:15, is found in Immanuel's *Notebooks* 6/341.

24 Modena's predecessor in Mantua, Rabbi Judah Moscato (c. 1530–90), also sang the praises of harmony. On Simchat Torah one year he delivered a sermon devoted entirely to music, *Aley higgayon bekhinor*, expounding on the harmony of the spheres and the Israelite origins of music. See Moscato, *Nefutsot Yehudah* (Venice, 1889), in Israel Adler (ed.), *Hebrew Writings Concerning Music* (Munich: G. Henle, 1975), 221–39.

25 Rossi, *Ha-shirim*, fol. 3.

26 Israel Adler, *La pratique musicale savante dans quelques communautés juives en Europe aux XVIIe et XVIIIe siècles* (Paris: Mouton & Co., 1966). Some of the scores have been published by the Jewish Music Research Centre at the Hebrew University, Jerusalem.

10 A new song

Jewish musicians in European music, 1730–1850

DAVID CONWAY

Sing unto him a new song; play skilfully.
— PSALM 33.3

A new meaning for "Jewish music"

From February 1850 onwards a series of increasingly vituperative articles, attacking the opera *Le prohète* by Giacomo Meyerbeer (1791–1864) following its debut (in German) in Dresden, began to appear in the *Neue Zeitschrift für Musik*. They were written by the friend, disciple, and correspondent of Richard Wagner (1813–83), the Dresden musician Theodor Uhlig (1822–53). They culminated in a series of six essays, *Zeitgemässe Betrachtungen* (Contemporary Observations), attacking Meyerbeer's pretensions to the creation of musical drama or beauty; as opposed, of course, to the compositions of Uhlig's hero Wagner. The first of these "Observations," entitled "Dramatic,"[1] swiftly highlights the writer's objective; despite his success, the "false Prophet" Meyerbeer, as a Jew, can be no true German, and his music is a betrayal of German art. Uhlig cites three two- or three-bar snippets from the opera's last act, which he claims "belch out" (*aufstossen*) at us, for their allegedly unnatural word-setting and crudity of expression. These are scarcely representative of the opera as a whole (and no worse than similar examples that could be extracted from Wagner's *Lohengrin*). Uhlig then comments:

> If that is dramatic song, then Gluck, Mozart, and Cherubini carried out their studies at the Neumarkt in Dresden or the Brühl in Leipzig [i.e., in those cities' Jewish quarters] . . . [T]his way of singing is to a good Christian at best contrived, exaggerated, unnatural and slick [*raffinirt*] . . . [I]t is not possible that the practised propaganda of the Hebrew art-taste [*hebräisches Kunstgeschmack*] can succeed by such means.[2]

It is perhaps needless to say that none of the musical examples cited by Uhlig bear the slightest resemblance to Jewish music, either of the synagogue or the *klezmorim*. But when Wagner adopted Uhlig's formulation of a "Hebrew art-taste" in his anti-Jewish assault "Das Judentum in der Musik"[3] (initially published anonymously in the *Neue Zeitschrift* as a "response" to Uhlig), he shrewdly refrained from giving examples or even attempting to define this concept in musical terms; instead he relied on traditional Jew-baiting principles. Just as a Jew cannot speak German properly, but can only produce a "creaking, squeaking, buzzing snuffle," Wagner concludes that inevitably his attempts at creating song, which is "talk aroused to highest passion," must be even more insupportable.[4] Music produced by Jews, decreed Wagner, was thereby inherently corrupted into "Jewish music," and hence a false art, even in the more sophisticated compositions of Felix Mendelssohn (whom Wagner oleaginously damns with faint praise).[5] Moreover, Jews treat art just like any other commercial commodity and are only interested in exploiting the public's lack of taste by making money from it.[6]

Thus was initiated a concept of "Jewish music," quite independent of Jewish musical traditions, and musicologically indefinable, that would lead ultimately to the bible of National Socialist musicologists, the *Lexikon der Juden in der Musik*,[7] and, ironically by the same process, to the quasi-martyrological status in the present day of those musicians who, whether or not they had any interest in or knowledge of Judaism, perished as a consequence of their ancestry and Nazi Germany's criminal racial politics. The genesis of this concept must be sought, therefore, not in any definable characteristics observable in the music of those concerned, but in the remarkable success of Jews in making a reputation for themselves in the world of music in the period from the late eighteenth-century onwards, and the reception of this success among their contemporaries.

Advent of Jews to the world of art music

Taste and employment in the arts, in an age predating global publicity, were determined by patronage. It is therefore no surprise that while such patronage was monopolized in Europe by the Church and the aristocracy, Jews were not to be found in the realm of art music. They had no means of learning or acquiring its techniques, and in any case their semi-feudal status in most of the continent would not have permitted employment outside their permitted trades. Indeed the only notable manifestation of Jews in the world of *musique savante* before the eighteenth century was the brief period 1600–30 when the community of Mantua was indulged by the Gonzaga family and produced not only the composer Salamone Rossi (c. 1570–c. 1628), whose Monteverdian output included both secular madrigals and settings of Hebrew prayers (see Chapter 9), but a host of other Jewish musicians, singers and dancers.[8]

As a caste living at the fringes of Western European society, Jews were moreover held to be beyond the cultural pale, a people, as Voltaire put it, "without arts or laws."[9] Music of the synagogue was caustically derided by

Gentile commentators who bothered to investigate it with comments such as "a Hebrew gasconade . . . a few garbled and conjectural curiosities,"[10] or "It is impossible for me to divine what idea the Jews themselves annex to this vociferation."[11] As to Jewish folk music, it was, like all others, overlooked by the cognoscenti. The cliché that the Jews were a "musical people," commonplace by the end of the nineteenth century, would have seemed absurd at its commencement.

The disdain evinced towards Jewish music was not only an expression of traditional Jew-hatred. Parts of the synagogue services had remained "icons" of those of the Temple, and still retained (and retain today) elements of chants, modes, inflexions, and rhythms not reducible to the ideas of harmony and form that musical theoreticians were beginning to systematize in the eighteenth century. This "otherness" was more simply dealt with by dismissal than analysis. It was also easy to equate this non-conformity with an immoral betrayal of the duty of music to purvey a noble *Affekt*; this "moralistic" distaste for music of the Jews can still be found underlying Wagner's "Judentum in der Musik."[12] It is in this context that we must read the genuine surprise of Carl Zelter (1758–1832) at the talent of his new pupil Felix Mendelssohn (1809–47) in an 1821 letter to his friend Goethe: "It would really be something special if for once a Jewboy [*Judensohn*] became an artist."[13]

Nonetheless, from around the beginning of the eighteenth century we begin to see an increasing interplay between Jewish urban communities and the musical life of their hosts in western Europe. At the end of the seventeenth century, the synagogue at Altona issued a series of decrees deterring members from attending the opera at nearby Hamburg (where *Singspiels* – works of musical theater combining German singing and speech – in the early eighteenth century featured caricature Jews speaking in *mauscheln*, the crude word used by non-Jewish Germans to discuss Jewish-German speech mannerisms).[14] In the same period Jews in Frankfurt and Metz began to complain about the inclusion of music from the theater in synagogue services,[15] and wealthy Sephardic Jews in Amsterdam became noted musical patrons (and even commissioned settings for their synagogues from Gentile composers).[16] It is scarcely surprising that early evidence of Jews as active in the world of Gentile music comes from the two urban centers, Amsterdam and London, within states whose constitutions were least prejudiced against Jews.

As with many immigrant communities seeking entry to society (even today), musical entertainment was a popular career option for Jews. For such a profession capital requirements are low and all that may be necessary for success is some talent (and perhaps chutzpah). The very exoticness of the aspirant may be in itself an advantage where an audience, freed from the restrictions of ordained taste, seeks novelty. We see a harbinger of this in "Mrs. Manuel the Jew's wife," who caught the eye and ear of Samuel Pepys in 1667/8 (just some ten years after Cromwell allowed the Jews to return to England following the 1290 expulsion) – "[she] sings very finely and is a mighty discreet, sober-carriage woman."[17] Hanna Norsa (c. 1712–84), the daughter of a Jewish tavern-keeper, made the classic transition from stage success in 1732 (as Polly in John Gay's *Beggar's Opera*), to mistress of an aristocrat (the Earl of Orford, Horace Walpole's brother).[18] David Garrick introduced Harriett Abrams (c. 1760–1821) as the title role in his 1775 *May Day: or the Little Gypsy*, causing a newspaper to exclaim, "The Little Gipsy is a Jewess . . . the numbers of Jews at the Theatre is incredible." This was the start of a long and distinguished profession for Abrams as a singer and a songwriter – and also an early example of Jewish audiences in London "supporting their own."[19] The notable operatic careers of the *ḥazzan* (cantor) Myer Lyon (c. 1748–97) (who appeared at Covent Garden as "Michael Leoni" and was allowed Friday nights off for his synagogue duties) and his protégé and sometime *meshorer* (descant) John Braham (c. 1774–1856) arose from their singing at London's Great Synagogue; the unusual qualities of their voices are likely to have arisen from the synagogue musical tradition.[20] Yet another form of musical fame founded in the synagogue was that of the egregious Isaac Nathan (c. 1792–1864), son of a *ḥazzan*, who, cashing in on the trend for esoteric folk music, was able to publish his arrangements of synagogue tunes through his improbable partnership with Lord Byron, whom he persuaded to write the words for his *Hebrew Melodies* (published in 1815). Cannily, Nathan persuaded Braham to allow his name to be placed in the front page in return for 50 percent of the profits. Nathan's turbulent career led to his retreat to Australia, where his musical pioneering earned him the accolade of "the father of Australian music."[21]

Jewish musicians of Germany and France

While after the 1820s we find few significant home-grown Jewish musicians in England, a new generation of Jewish musicians emerged on the Continent of a very different type from those who, from Norsa to Braham, had chanced their way up virtually from the pavements. Typically they were, like the opera composer Giacomo Meyerbeer (born Jakob Beer, 1791–1864) or Felix Mendelssohn and his sister Fanny (1805–47), the offspring of merchant or extremely wealthy German-Jewish families whose parents had provided them with a musical education as part of an increasing fashion for acculturation with their host country. Lesser lights in this category include Ferdinand Hiller (né Hildesheim, 1811–85), Julius

Benedict (1804–85), and the Prague-born Ignaz Moscheles (1794–1870), who became a close colleague of Mendelssohn.

The trend to German culture in this class had commenced in the mid-eighteenth century with the advance of Enlightenment ideas amongst progressive Jewish thinkers, notably Felix's grandfather Moses Mendelssohn (1729–86), which flourished amongst the wealthy Jewish elite in Germany and Austria who had associated themselves with Court and state finances. This movement inevitably accelerated as the French Revolutionary Army moving through continental Europe opened the ghettos and transformed the previous status of Jews, which had been virtually feudal, to that of (more or less) equal citizens. The education of the new generation of privileged Jews (for the mass of European Jewry was still extremely poor) coincided with a transfer of patronage in the arts towards the moneyed bourgeois – thus providing many opportunities for change, access, and career opportunities, notably (for Jews) in literature and music. In the fashionable Jewish salons of Berlin and Vienna of the early nineteenth century (among which the Mendelssohn and Beer families, and their Austrian relatives the Arnsteins and Eskeleses, were prominent), Gentiles from the worlds of the arts and politics mingled with the social newcomers, testifying to these changes. In the fashion of Romanticism, the exotic Jews, newcomers to cultured society, became a fashionable trend before the vogue of *völkisch* nationalism from the 1820s onwards began to disturb their status.

In these circumstances it is scarcely surprising that traditional Jewish music played little or no part in the musical upbringing of this generation. Felix Mendelssohn and his sister were brought up as Christians; most others of a German background (with the notable exception of Meyerbeer) converted to Christianity at some stage, as a matter of convenience if not deep belief. Moreover it was clear from an early stage that the traditional synagogue turned its back on contemporary Western culture. When the Vienna congregation commissioned a cantata to celebrate the Treaty of Paris in 1814 from the young Moscheles, the Pressburg (Bratislava) Rabbi Moses Schreiber issued a ruling that it was quite unacceptable for women's and men's voices to be heard together in a synagogue.[22] It was left to the Jewish Reform movement to later populate synagogue services with quasi-Schubertian or Mendelssohnian strains such as those penned by the cantors Salomon Sulzer (1804–90) or Louis Lewandowski (1821–94) (see Chapter 12).

In France, a different route to musical careers was enabled by the confirmation of full citizenship to Jews following the decision of the National Assembly in 1791. This entitled those with the ability, even if from poor backgrounds, to attend the Paris Conservatoire; amongst those to take advantage of this opportunity were the opera composer Fromental Halévy

(1799–1862) and the piano virtuoso and composer Charles-Valentin Alkan (1813–88) (neither of whom converted).

It is the latter who, in some of his *Préludes* op. 31 (1844), and in the melodies of his *Sonate de concert* for cello op. 47 (1857), created perhaps the first published artworks based on Jewish music.[23] That is not to say that other Jewish composers ignored such music. We know from correspondence that Mendelssohn, who it appears never so much as entered a synagogue, and his sister Fanny were fascinated by the music of the *klezmer* Joseph Gusikov (1806–37),[24] and that Hiller was to introduce his (non-Jewish) pupil Max Bruch (1838–1920) to the Yom Kippur (Day of Atonement) hymn *Kol Nidre*, which in 1881 the latter made into one of his greatest successes.[25] But, other than in the works of Alkan, we may seek in vain, despite the most energetic efforts of some scholars, to find a note of Jewish melody, or even idiom, in works of this generation. The search for such links ranges from Eric Werner's exotically optimistic attribution of a key melody in Mendelssohn's 1847 *Elijah*,[26] to the quite unfounded statement that the Passover meal scene in Halévy's 1835 opera *La Juive* "reflect[s] an awareness of traditional Jewish practice" and is "an authentic treatment... of ceremony"[27] (although indeed Halévy, who came from a practicing Jewish household, certainly knew how a *seder* ought to be conducted). Indeed the libretto of *La Juive*, in its presentation of the vengeful, money-obsessed, and secretive Eléazar, seems to truckle to the basest prejudices of Judaeophobia. Significantly, contemporary reviews of the opera do not relate the storyline in any way to the social situation of Jews of France in the 1830s (or even mention that the composer is a Jew), being more concerned with its attitude to the Church.[28]

Where a "Jewish" sympathy may be found in the operas of Meyerbeer is not in their music, but in their storylines. Meyerbeer's *Robert le diable* came to the stage the year after the July Revolution of 1830, which ushered in a new era for France of bourgeois liberalism in reaction to the conservative world of Charles X. Nothing could have been more attuned to the new spirit than this brash, novel, and spectacular work, produced with the finest singers of the day, using all the technical resources of the Opéra stage; Meyerbeer became an instant Europe-wide celebrity, and remained as such with the similar successes of his further grand operas, all to librettos by Eugène Scribe: *Les Huguenots* (1826), *Le prophète* (1849), and the posthumously produced *L'Africaine* (1864). Uniquely, because of his wealth and authority, Meyerbeer had the opportunity to choose and shape his libretti; and it is no accident that each of his works in this form has a hero (in sequence Robert, Raoul, Jean of Leyden, and Vasco da Gama) who, for reasons of birth, religion, or belief is a neurotic outsider in his own society – Meyerbeer himself retained with his Judaism an excessive sensitivity to slights, both real and imagined, to his origins, as his diaries and correspondence reveal.

Reception of Jewish musicians

The German writer and convert Ludwig Boerne (1786–1837; born Judah Loew Baruch) wrote in 1832, "Some people criticize me for being a Jew; others forgive me for being one; a third even praises me for it; but all are thinking about it."[29] This is the atmosphere in which all musicians of Jewish extraction operated throughout the nineteenth century and beyond. Inevitably this was to affect their careers, status and public perception – and their music – in ways both direct and indirect.

"Jewishness" is not merely a matter of practiced religion, but also of *yiddishkeit* – the secular customs, use of Yiddish, shared humor, and mutual identification – which persisted as much amongst those who, like Felix Mendelssohn, were never circumcised, as those who, like Meyerbeer, remained (more or less) practicing Jews. Not least of the consequences was the tendency of such musicians, whether they attended church or synagogue, to associate closely with friends and collaborators of a similar status. Felix and the Mendelssohn family continued to have in their circle Moscheles, Benedict, Hiller, the violinists Ferdinand David (1810–73) and Joseph Joachim (1831–1907), the composer and writer Adolf Bernhard (né Samuel Moses) Marx (1799–1866) and many other *Neuchristen*; not only that, they can still be found in the company of many of their contemporary *Neuchristen* in the same section of the Dreifaltigkeit Cemetery in Berlin. Also striking was the connection of many Jewish composers to the successful music publisher Adolf Martin (né Aron Moses) Schlesinger (1769–1838) in Berlin (and to his son Maurice Schlesinger [1798–1871] in the Paris branch of the business). Schlesinger, who began his bookselling business in 1810, became the publisher of many of Beethoven's late masterpieces, made a fortune from his early "spotting" of Carl Maria von Weber,[30] and was Mendelssohn's first publisher. Schlesinger-owned music journals in Berlin (edited by A. B. Marx) and Paris naturally supported "house" composers.[31] Apart from publishing Meyerbeer and Halévy, Maurice also published works of Liszt, Berlioz, and many other leading Parisian musical celebrities. He incidentally employed the impoverished Wagner in 1840–1 to write articles for his *Gazette musicale* and to make arrangements of opera arias; and indeed he was responsible for introducing Wagner personally to Liszt in his shop.[32] It was perhaps this sense of an extra-musical cartel amongst his contemporaries that prompted Robert Schumann to comment in his wedding diaries that he was fed up with promoting Mendelssohn:

"Jews remain Jews: first they take a seat ten times for themselves, then comes the Christian's turn."[33]

Apart from this clannish dimension of *yiddishkeit*, other factors demarcated these musical newcomers in the minds of their Gentile colleagues; notably, as regarded the German musicians, their often wealthy (or at least comfortable) origins. Whereas, for example, Wagner was only able to dream of traveling to Italy to study,[34] Meyerbeer was comfortably subsidized by his family to study and write his early operas there for seven years. Berlioz noted, "I can't forget that Meyerbeer was only able to persuade [the Paris Opéra] to put on *Robert le diable* . . . by paying the administration sixty thousand francs of his own money"[35] (an allegation that is in fact unfounded). Robert Schumann wrote to Clara Wieck of Mendelssohn in 1838, "If I had grown up under circumstances similar to his, and had been destined for music since childhood, I'd surpass each and every one of you."[36]

Not only this, but in the growing ethos of musical nationalism, Jews were difficult to "place." When Meyerbeer's friend Weber had written, in 1820, about the former's Italian operas, "My heart bleeds to see how a German artist, gifted with unique creative powers, is willing to degrade himself in imitation for the sake of the miserable applause of the crowd,"[37] he could of course hardly have foreseen how such comments could be recast under the more strident nationalism of later decades, when the "Germanness" of the artist concerned might become the crux of the issue. Once again, it is Schumann, in his vituperative 1837 review of Meyerbeer's *Les Huguenots*, who gives a foretaste of the critique of Uhlig and Wagner: "What is left after *Les Huguenots* but actually to execute criminals on the stage and make a public exhibition of whores? . . . One may search in vain for . . . a truly Christian sentiment . . . It is all make-believe and hypocrisy . . . The shrewdest of composers rubs his hands with glee."[38]

And of course the extraordinary success of Jewish musicians was bound to excite pure envy. Following the successes of *La Juive* and *Les Huguenots* at the Paris Opéra, the truculent opera composer Gaspare Spontini (1774–1851) (whom Meyerbeer was in fact to replace as *Kapellmeister* in Berlin in 1842) was satirically said to have been observed weeping at the mummies of the Pharaohs at the Louvre, complaining that they had let the Jews go free.[39] Mendelssohn's appointments as musical director in Düsseldorf (1833) and later Leipzig (1835), and the appointments of both Meyerbeer and Mendelssohn at the more liberal court in Berlin of Frederick William IV after 1843, signified their influence in Germany, where the support of Meyerbeer enabled the production of Wagner's *Rienzi* in Dresden in 1842, and the indifference of Mendelssohn to Wagner's offer of his Symphony in Leipzig in 1836 was another source of the latter's sense of grievance.[40]

What Jewish musicians contributed to European musical life was indeed to some extent associated with a change of public taste to grandeur and sensation. The works of Meyerbeer, whose musical innovation was to combine the colorful orchestral romanticism of Weber with the vocal pyrotechnics of Italian opera, fitted well with this trend. So did the pianists who became, in the words of Heine, "a plague of locusts swarming to pick Paris clean" in the 1830s and 1840s, many of them as juvenile prodigies – amongst the Jewish-born exemplars being Jakob Rosenhain (1813–94), Julius Schulhoff (1825–98), Louis Gottschalk (1829–69), and Anton Rubinstein (1829–94) (who partnered Halévy's student Jacques Offenbach [1819–80] in the latter's debut Paris recital as a cellist in 1841). It may be that the status of Jews as "newcomers" freed them to some extent both from allegiance to the supposedly more refined tastes of earlier generations, and from the dictates of the self-appointed bearers of the standards of "true art" of German nationalist romanticism, so as to meet the demand and taste of the expanding audiences of the bourgeois. Perhaps this is part of what suggested Wagner's accusation of commercialism (the word "Judentum," in the title of his tirade, in colloquial German of the time carried not only the meaning of "Jewry," but also "haggling").[41]

But on the other hand the serious and scholarly approach of Mendelssohn, Moscheles, and their school – to whom, in fact, the music of Meyerbeer and the piano virtuosi were anathema – scarcely fitted this characterization of commercialism. Mendelssohn himself was indeed a prime mover in the rehabilitation of the music of the great German masters, Bach and Handel, and Moscheles was a pioneer of the "historical recital," including performances on the harpsichord.[42] To Wagner, and to other advocates of new music, however, such "classicism" was as much a threat as the popularity of grand opera in alienating the affection of potential audiences for their own art. Wagner indeed succeeded in coupling this dedication to tradition with his more traditional Jew-baiting approach in a repulsive metaphor of the decaying flesh of German art dissolving into "a swarming colony of insect-life."[43]

Despite all the above, however, only in Germany is there significant evidence of Jewish musicians and their music being a source of contention for their contemporaries. Berlioz in an 1852 article derided the notion of "Hebraic elements" compromising Mendelssohn's music.[44] In Britain, Mendelssohn became an honored guest in his ten visits, and his descent from Moses Mendelssohn was noted with approval. Indeed after his death he was incarnated in thin disguise as the Chevalier Seraphael, in the very popular novel *Charles Auchester* (1855), by the teenaged Elizabeth Sheppard, in which his Jewishness was cited as the source of his musical genius.[45] In the concert halls and opera houses of London and Paris, music that Jews wrote or played was not distinguished as a separate category. Only later in the century, with the birth of political anti-Semitism as a mass movement, and Wagner's later return to the fray in 1869 with a lengthened version of his attack (this time published under his own name), began the transformation of the notable musical achievements of Mendelssohn, Meyerbeer, and their generation into a stick with which to beat them. And not until the end of the century, and partly in reaction to this development, would Jewish musicians, notably the activists of the St. Petersburg Society for Jewish Folk Music, begin at last a musical exploration of their own ancestral heritage.

Notes

1 Theodor Uhlig, "Dramatisch," *Neue Zeitschrift für Musik*, 32.33 (April 23, 1850): 169–71.

2 *Ibid.*, 170 (my translation). Uhlig was perhaps not aware that Wagner was in fact born in the Brühl.

3 Often referred to in English, following its first translation, as "Judaism in Music" – but see n. 41 below.

4 Richard Wagner, *Judaism in Music and Other Essays*, trans. William Ashton Ellis (Lincoln, NE, and London: University of Nebraska Press, 1995), 84, 86.

5 *Ibid.*, 93–6.

6 *Ibid.*, 82: "What the heroes of the arts . . . have wrested from the art-fiend of two millennia of misery, today the Jew converts into an art-bazaar"; and 96 (of Meyerbeer): "[He] has addressed himself and products to a section of our public whose total confusion of musical taste [can be] worked out to his profit."

7 Theo Stengl and Herbert Gerigk, *Lexikon der Juden in der Musik mit einem Titelverzeichnis jüdischer Werke* (Berlin: Berhard Hahnefeld Verlag, 1941).

8 See Don Harrán, *Salamone Rossi: Jewish Musician in Late Renaissance Mantua* (Oxford University Press, 1999).

9 In the 1772 *Essai des moeurs*, cited in Jacob Katz, *From Prejudice to Destruction: Anti-Semitism, 1700–1933* (Cambridge, MA: Harvard University Press, 1980), 47.

10 Johann Mattheson, in *Das neu-eröffnete Orchester* (1713), cited in Jacob Hohenemser, "The Jew in German Musical Thought before the Nineteenth Century," *Musica Judaica*, 3.1 (1980–1): 63–73.

11 Charles Burney, *An Eighteenth-Century Musical Tour in Central Europe and the Netherlands*, ed. Percy A. Scholes, 2 vols. (Oxford University Press, 1959), ii:229. (On the Amsterdam Ashkenazi synagogue in 1772.)

12 "Who has not had occasion to convince himself of the travesty of a divine service . . . in a real Folk-synagogue? Who has not been seized with a feeling of the greatest revulsion, of horror mingled with the absurd, at hearing that sense-and-sound-confounding gurgle, yodel and cackle." Wagner, *Judaism in Music*, 90–1.

13 Johann Wolfgang von Goethe and Carl Friedrich Zelter, *Briefwechsel zwischen Goethe und Zelter in den Jahren 1799 bis 1832*, ed. Hans-Günter Ottenberg and Edith Zehm, 3 vols. (Munich: Hanser, 1991–8), i:679 (my translation). Interestingly, for "something special," Zelter writes "*eppes Rores*," in imitation of Jewish jargon or *mauscheln*, for the German "*etwas Rares.*"

14 Jeanne Swack, "Anti-Semitism at the Opera: The Portrayal of Jews in the Singspiels of Reinhard Keiser," *Musical Quarterly*, 84.3 (2000): 389–416 (390–4).

15 Abraham Zvi Idelsohn, intr. Arbie Orenstein, *Jewish Music: Its Historical Development* (New York: Dover, 1992), 208–9.

16 Israel Adler, *Musical Life and Traditions of the Portuguese Jewish Community of Amsterdam in the XVIIIth Century*, Yuval Monograph Series 1 (Jerusalem: Magnes Press, 1974).

17 Samuel Pepys, *The Diary of Samuel Pepys*, ed. Robert Latham and William Matthews, 13 vols. (London: Bell and Hyman, 1974), vii:384, ix:128.

18 David Conway, *Jewry in Music: Entry to the Profession from the Enlightenment to Richard Wagner* (Cambridge University Press, 2012), 69–70. Orford died before his promised marriage to Norsa, but not before running through her money.

19 *Ibid.*, 80–1.

20 *Ibid.*, 75–90.

21 *Ibid.*, 91–100.

22 Hanoch Avenary, Walter Pass, and Nikolaus Vielmetti, *Kantor Salomon Sulzer und seine Zeit* (Sigmaringen: J. Thorbecke, 1985), 39–43, 48.

Moscheles was to convert to Christianity in England in 1832, having married in a synagogue in Frankfurt in 1824. Conway, *Jewry in Music*, 106.

23 *Ibid.*, 235–7.

24 *Ibid.*, 179.

25 "Kol Nidrei" for cello and orchestra (1881). Bruch wrote in 1882, "The success of 'Kol Nidrei' is assured, because all the Jews of the world are for it *ipso facto*." Christopher Fifield, *Max Bruch: His Life and Works*, 2nd edn. (Woodbridge: Boydell Press, 2005), 168.

26 Eric Werner, *Mendelssohn: A New Image of the Composer and His Age*, trans. Dika Newlin (London: Collier-Macmillan, 1963), 471. For the tense, disorderly, and ultimately futile scholarly battle waged over Mendelssohn's supposed religious allegiances in recent decades, see Conway, *Jewry in Music*, 173–84.

27 Diana R. Hallman, *Opera, Liberalism and Antisemitism in Nineteenth-Century France: The Politics of Halévy's* La Juive (Cambridge University Press, 2002), 177, 176. It is true that the melody of Eléazar's Act IV aria "Rachel, quand du Seigneur" is thought by some to have a "Jewish" tinge; it may, however, in fact have been written by its first interpreter, the (Gentile) Adolphe Nourrit. *Ibid.*, 34–6.

28 Conway, *Jewry in Music*, 215–18.

29 "Letter from Paris," no. 74. Cited in Sander L. Gilman and Jack Zipes (eds.), *Yale Companion to Jewish Writing and Thought in German Culture, 1096–1996* (New Haven: Yale University Press, 1997), 130.

30 Conway, *Jewry in Music*, 185–6.

31 *Ibid.*, 188–9.

32 Ernest Newman, *The Life of Richard Wagner*, 4 vols., vol. I, *1813–1848* (Cambridge University Press, 1976), 285–91.

33 Robert and Clara Schumann, *The Marriage Diaries of Robert and Clara Schumann*, ed. Gerd Nauhaus, trans. Peter Ostwald (London: Robson, 1994), 31–2.

34 See, for example, his 1834 letter to Theodor Apel, in Richard Wagner, *Selected Letters of Richard Wagner*, ed. and trans. Stewart Spencer and Barry Millington (London: Dent, 1987), 23–4.

35 Cited in David Cairns, *Berlioz*, 2 vols., vol. II, *Servitude and Greatness, 1832–1869* (London: Allen Lane, 1999), 104.

36 Robert and Clara Schumann, *The Complete Correspondence of Robert and Clara Schumann*, ed. Eva Weissweiler, trans. Hildegard Fritsch and Ronald Crawford, 2 vols. (New York: Peter Lang, 1994), i:152.

37 Letter to M. Lichtenstein of 27 January 1820, cited in Reiner Zimmermann, *Giacomo Meyerbeer: Eine Biographie nach Dokumenten* (Berlin: Parthas, 1991), 90 (my translation).

38 Robert Schumann, *The Musical World of Robert Schumann*, ed. and trans. Henry Pleasants (London: Gollancz, 1965), 139.

39 An added twist is that this jibe was written by the Jewish writer Heinrich Heine. Heinrich Heine, *The Works of Heinrich Heine*, trans. C. G. Leland, 12 vols., vol. IV, *The Salon* (London: W. Heinemann, 1893), 435–6.

40 See John Deathridge, *Wagner: Beyond Good and Evil* (Berkeley and Los Angeles: University of California Press, 2008), 180–8.

41 And hence William Ashton Ellis's translation of *Judentum* in Wagner's essay's title as "Judaism" – implying the centrality of religious concepts – is misleading; see Conway, *Jewry in Music*, 9, 261–3.

42 *Ibid.*, 108–9.

43 Wagner, *Judaism in Music*, 99.

44 Cairns, *Berlioz*, 68 (n.).

45 Conway, *Jewry in Music*, 111.

11 From biblical antiquarianism to revolutionary modernism

Jewish art music, 1850–1925

JAMES LOEFFLER

Introduction

In his memoirs, the Russian Jewish poet and translator Leon Mandelshtam (1819–89) describes an 1840 visit he paid to the legendary Minsk cantor Sender Poliachek (1786–1869). A musical illiterate, Poliachek had won fame for his liturgical compositions that were said to evoke the "soul" of the Jewish past. Mandelshtam himself had fled a small-town life of religious traditionalism for Moscow, where he would become the first Jew to graduate from a Russian university. Yet he felt compelled to stop en route in Minsk to ask the venerable cantor a question: Where did this music of the Jews come from? Was it a product of the East, signifying that the Jews of Russia were descended from the medieval Khazars who had converted to Judaism? Or was it derived from Western Europe, proving that the Jews had migrated to eastern Europe from Spain and Germany, pushed on by the violence of the Crusades? Perhaps, Poliachek replied, since the Jews had lived under both Muslims and Christians, their music was a cultural hybrid: East and West had fused together to produce the distinctive "binational Jewish melody."

The conversation did not end there. For the cantor then surprised Mandelshtam with a question of his own. Why, he wished to know, would such a nice and talented young man abandon his people to go live in Moscow like a Christian? Mandelshtam replied with a pithy rabbinic maxim: "Better to be last among lions, than first among hares." Poliachek was unimpressed. He too had once felt the lure of Western music, he explained, before concluding that such a career would have ruined his distinctive Jewish voice: "A spring quenches the thirsty man if he is on dry land; let him be in the sea, and it is of little use. The moonlight dazzles your eyes at night; during the day it is but a pale patch in the sky. In my primitive national form I am distinct; mixed together with all the colors, I would become lost in the crowd." Undeterred, Mandelshtam countered that the modern world did not scare him: "A country is only a miniature image from space; a year is only time in a smaller form; the same is true of virtue, which, similar to genius, lies above space and time, and fears neither foreign lands on the road of wandering nor temptation in the era of modern life."[1]

This exchange between the cantor and the poet neatly summarizes the main themes of the history of Jewish art music from the middle of the nineteenth century through the first quarter of the twentieth. Before 1800, only a handful of European Jews had ventured beyond the confines of the Jewish community into the world of European art music. Many rabbinical authorities frowned on secular musical education as a dangerously seductive pathway to heresy. Even knowledge of Western musical notation was regarded in some quarters with suspicion. In turn, Christian Europeans looked on Jews as an alien culture whose musical practices threatened to contaminate Western art. Yet, at the same time, late eighteenth- and early nineteenth-century Jewish liturgical and folk music professionals – cantors and klezmorim – exhibited increasing interest in Baroque vocal genres, opera and operetta, and European court dances. The allure of art music proved quite strong. From the middle of the nineteenth century onwards, Jewish musicians flocked in extraordinarily high numbers to conservatories across Europe with profound consequences for both Western music and modern Jewish identity.

Mandelshtam's query about the historical origins of the music of the Jews and the cantor's expansive yet curious reply (Christian-Muslim "binational Jewish melody") also point to the ambiguous place of "Jewish music" in the modern European imagination – both Jewish and Christian. From Richard Wagner's famous 1850 anti-Semitic essay "Das Judentum in der Musik" to the racialist theories of fin-de-siècle French and Russian critics, ideological fantasies about the essentialist character of Jewish music – and its indelible imprint in the works of composers of Jewish origin, and even in the styles of Jewish performers – surfaced repeatedly in European culture. Likewise, early twentieth-century Jewish nationalists produced elaborate musical theories of their own. Indeed, the entire project of modern Jewish art music can be characterized as an ongoing search for an answer to the question of how to define the genre of Jewish music horizontally – belonging to the "Oriental" East or Christian West – and vertically – as an autochthonous tradition extending from biblical antiquity to the modern times. Just as Mandelshtam's anecdote suggests, the modern dialogue with the Jewish musical past emerged as a constant theme across the first several generations of Jewish composers. For some of these artists, Jewish religious sonorities required delicate refinement to meet the new aesthetic dictates of Enlightenment rationalism in nineteenth-century Europe ("the era of modern life"). For others, modernity demanded a radical re-imagination of Jewish vernacular and liturgical traditions into a secular form of national art music (at once "primitive" and "modern"). Still other composers gravitated to modernism as a utopian quest to liberate all art and artists – from the particularistic confines of nation and religion ("above time and space").

This chapter explores these developments through a chronological survey of the period between 1850 and 1925, highlighting major figures as well as shifts in cultural ideas of Jewish music and musicianship down through time. It is divided into three sub-periods: Hebrew Melodies: Virtuosity and Antiquarianism, 1850–1900; Aural Emancipations: Renaissance and Modernisms, 1900–17; and Revolutionary Echoes: Affirmations and Ambiguities, 1917–25.

Hebrew melodies: virtuosity and antiquarianism, 1850–1900

At the dawn of the nineteenth century, the idea that a Jew might excel in the realm of European art music constituted an odd, if not unnatural, proposition. Over the next half-century, however, western and central European Jews began a dramatic ascent into the ranks of professional musicians. This socio-cultural trend, already visible *in nucleo* before 1800, swelled into a remarkable – and much remarked upon – pattern of Jewish virtuosos by the middle of the nineteenth century. Jewish child prodigies became the norm for the next seventy-five years, with hundreds upon hundreds of pianists, violinists, cellists, and other musicians concertizing across Europe at very young ages. Some of these notable performers went on to notable careers as composers, including the likes of Ignaz Moscheles (1790–1870), Giacomo Meyerbeer (1791–1864), Charles-Valentin Alkan (1813–88), and Anton Rubinstein (1829–94). Many others swelled the ranks of the new conservatory faculties, symphony orchestras, and other musical institutions that emerged as prime features of nineteenth-century European musical life.[2] All contributed to an image of Jews as singularly talented in the field of art music, though contemporary observers differed widely in their estimation of the sources and meaning of that talent.

In hindsight, historians have explained the rapid gravitation of Jews to art music and extraordinary professional success as stemming from the confluence of several factors: the long-established pattern of music as a hereditary profession in pre-modern European Jewish life; the relative openness of new cultural spheres that catered to a newly ascendant urban bourgeoisie with a strong appetite for secular entertainment; the concrete economic opportunities represented by these new cultural realms, which also attracted a considerable quotient of Jewish musical entrepreneurs, sheet-music publishers, concert impresarios, and critics; the broader pattern of Jewish embourgeoisement, reflected in the popularity of both childhood musical training and amateur chamber music performance as key features of European salon life; and the identification of many leading classical musical figures (though certainly not all) with the cause of political liberalism. In a larger sense, the Jewish movement into art music was a legacy of the late eighteenth-century Enlightenment, which framed music as a secular activity, musical talent as an innate human gift irrespective of particular origin, and art as a path to moral self-cultivation and modern individualism.[3]

Significantly, what does *not* appear to have played a strong role in this process, contrary to popular perception, was the force of Jewish religious tradition or traditional rabbinic cultural values. In spite of its significance in pre-modern Jewish life, including in synagogue and wedding rituals, music remained a low-status profession with musicians occupying an ambivalent position in the social hierarchy of the Ashkenazic Jewish community.[4] Nor, with a few notable exceptions, did most of these first few generations of nineteenth-century concert musicians evince much direct self-consciousness about their Jewish musical heritage or active compositional engagement with Jewish themes. Indeed, music beckoned precisely as an ostensibly unobtrusive path of acculturation and social advancement in mainstream European bourgeois society.

That religion was not the motivating force drawing Jews to classical music did not mean that art lacked spiritual significance. On the contrary, for many Jews – both professional performers and dedicated concert patrons – classical music constituted a veritable alternative religion. A case in point is the legendary Hungarian-born violinist Joseph Joachim (1831–1907). A pioneering force in European concert life and musical pedagogy, long a fixture of German musical life, and a close collaborator of Brahms, Schumann, and others, Joachim redefined the nature of violin playing and chamber music during his long career. A nominal convert to Christianity, he remained identified as Jewish yet practiced neither religion. Listening to Beethoven's music, he once wrote, was like listening to the "Religion of the Future" (*Zukunftsreligion*).[5] In this way, absolute music – instrumental music without words – offered an attractive ideal of a universalist realm beyond language, religion, and national differences that otherwise defined so much of the Jewish experience in modern Europe. A later quip retold by the German Jewish humorist Alexander Moszkowski, brother of the noted composer and pianist Moritz Moszkowski, conveyed a similar sentiment: "[I have] no sympathies for any ritual aspects of our religion. Of all the Jewish holidays the only one I keep is the concert of Gruenfeld [a famous Austrian Jewish pianist]."[6]

When Jewishness did surface as a specific theme in nineteenth-century European art music it came clothed in the Romantic garb of a virtuous antiquarianism. Like Jewish visual artists of the day, Jewish composers looked backwards to biblical antiquity in search of religious themes suitable for a modern era of rational religion and improved Jewish-Christian relations. This trend might be said to have officially begun with the British Jewish composer Isaac Nathan's 1815 collection of song settings of the poet Lord Byron's "Hebrew Melodies," a common touchstone for many later composers of Jewish-themed music, both Jewish and Christian.[7] Like Nathan's work, these aural imaginaries often took the form of compositions that addressed the historic borderlines and commonalities between Judaism and Christianity, such as Felix Mendelssohn's oratorios *Elijah* (1846) and *St. Paul* (1836), Jacques-François-Fromental-Élie Halévy's opera *La Juive* (1840), Ferdinand Hiller's oratorios *The Destruction of Jerusalem* (1840) and *Saul* (1858), Joachim's "Hebrew Melodies" (1854) for viola and piano, Karl Goldmark's opera *The Queen of Sheba* (1875), and Friedrich Gernsheim's Symphony No. 3 in C minor, "Miriam" (1888), inspired by Handel's *Israel in Egypt* oratorio.

Particularly notable exemplars of this pattern came in the works of two of the greatest pianist-composers of the nineteenth century: Anton Rubinstein (1829–94) and Charles-Valentin Alkan (1813–88). Born in the Jewish Pale of Settlement and baptized in the Russian Orthodox Church as an infant, Rubinstein went on to global fame as a concert performer, composer, and artistic celebrity. At the same time, he introduced a modern conservatory system into the Russian Empire that generated a unique social pathway for two generations of Russian Jewish musicians to achieve an unprecedented professional status and legal freedom in an otherwise tightly regimented, illiberal society with onerous legal restrictions on its Jewish population. In his art, Rubinstein opposed both the Romantic nationalism of his Russian contemporaries and the growing cult of Wagner. Instead he often stressed biblical themes such as in his various "spiritual operas," including *Sulamith* (1883), *The Maccabees* (1884), *Moses* (1894), and *Christus* (1895). In the end, his oft-quoted self-evaluation came to summarize his estrangement from a musical world that increasingly insisted on assigning composers to national and religious categories: "To the Jews I am a Christian. To the Christians – a Jew. To the Russians I am a German, and to the Germans – a Russian. For the classicists I am a musical innovator, and for the musical innovators I am an artistic reactionary and so on. The conclusion: I am neither fish nor fowl, in essence a pitiful creature!"[8]

In contrast to Rubinstein's restless performance career, colorful personality, and complex personal identity, Alkan lived his entire life as a traditionally observant religious Jew who abandoned public performance. He rarely, if ever, left his native Paris, and for much of his later life lived as an enigmatic recluse. A graduate of the Paris Conservatoire, he emerged early on as one of the great pianistic talents of French musical life. He became close friends with Chopin, Liszt, and George Sand. Though he vanished from public view, Alkan produced a large body of technically demanding piano music that sits comfortably alongside that of Liszt and Chopin as some of the most expressive, technically forbidding piano music of the Romantic era. Alkan's piety surfaced in his work with the main Paris synagogue and his compositional efforts to set both the Hebrew Bible and the Christian Bible to music. He framed his Jewishness nearly exclusively in terms of religious referents, chiefly in the form of synagogue texts – and occasionally liturgical melodies – transposed for voice and piano or integrated into biblically themed works such as his "By the Rivers of Babylon" (1859).[9]

The notion of re-harmonizing Jewish and Christian sonorities took a much different form in the music of nineteenth-century Jewish cantor-composers, who reshaped the Jewish liturgical repertoire to reflect the contemporary norms of Romantic style and Christian liturgical music. Chief among these was Salomon Sulzer (1804–90), "father of the modern cantorate," whose career as a prominent cantor in Vienna stretched from the 1820s to 1880s. In his compendium *Schir Zion*, he created an enormously influential style of modern liturgy that amounted to a wholesale aesthetic reformation of Jewish synagogue music.[10] Sulzer trimmed Jewish liturgical music of its perceived Oriental characteristics, such as melisma, extended recitative, modal character, and flowing meter, in favor of a style that conformed more to Christian church hymnody. He adopted fixed meters, four-part choral singing, and conventional European tonal practices for the arrangements of Hebrew-language prayers. His talents as a composer and cantorial soloist earned the respect, praise, and curiosity of the leading critics and composers of his day. Outside the synagogue, Sulzer's career also epitomized the other growing artistic links between central European cantors and the world of modern classical music. He was a well-respected vocal interpreter of Schubert's *Lieder* and served as professor at the Imperial Conservatory in Vienna.[11]

Sulzer's pattern of liturgical reform spread gradually throughout European Jewish synagogue music, particularly in larger urban communities identified with the nascent Jewish Reform religious movement. Across England, France, and the Netherlands, cantors introduced four-part chorale-style singing, organ instrumental accompaniment, and standard Western harmonic practices.[12] Under the leadership of Cantor Samuel Naumbourg (1817–80), the Paris synagogue became a second major center for liturgical composition, and the composers Alkan, Halévy, and Meyerbeer all contributed choral settings of liturgical texts for use there.[13] So too in Berlin, where Louis Lewandowski (1821–94) emerged as a formidable choral composer, putting his German conservatory training to use in building a repertoire of psalm settings that became staples of synagogue music in his

generation and long after.[14] The transformation of oral traditions into tex-
tualized repertoires through musical notation had a profound effect on the
self-understanding of Jewish communities in nineteenth-century Europe.
This was equally true of the Sephardic religious communities of France, Germany, and Austria, which followed the same pattern of assimilating orally
based liturgical traditions into the stylistic conventions of the surrounding
European musical culture.[15]

Alongside this Jewish recasting of cantorial music in terms of modern European aesthetics, nineteenth-century Christian composers turned
to the Jewish musical corpus in search of source material with which to
color biblical-themed works and other exotic Oriental fantasies. This phenomenon appeared most strikingly in the Russian Empire, where from
Mikhail Glinka onwards, composers transcribed contemporary Jewish
melodies for use in their compositions, frequently titled "Hebrew Melody"
or "Hebrew Song." These typically elegiac compositions by the likes of
Rimskii-Korsakov, Balakirev, Mussorgsky, and others evoked a lost Hebraic
melos from antiquity sometimes contrasted implicitly with a calcified or
degenerated present-day Jewish folklore.[16] Though this philo-Semitic trend
of Jewish folkloric melodies set by Christian composers continued on in later
compositions such as "Chanson hébraïque" (1910) and "Deux mélodies
hébraïques" (1914) by Maurice Ravel (1875–1937), a key turning point
emerged with the 1881 "Kol Nidrei" of Max Bruch (1838–1920). Bruch's
setting of the traditional Yom Kippur prayer for cello and piano, inspired by
his musical contacts with the Jewish communities of Berlin and Liverpool,
achieved tremendous popularity as a concert piece and aural symbol of
Jewish identity (so much so that Bruch, a German Protestant, has often
been erroneously claimed as a Jew by birth). Its continued presence in the
classical repertoire speaks to its potent appeal as a document of Jewish
liturgical tradition refashioned as modern art music.

Even as Romanticism prompted composers to experiment with elements
of Jewish musical folklore, the idea of a distinctively Jewish strain of modern
art music did not appear until the end of the nineteenth century. It would
take two further developments for the notion of "Jewish music" to emerge in
European discourse: the rise of Jewish ethnic nationalism and a hardening
of the racial lines in European thought. A decisive factor in this process
was the appearance of the explosive modern anti-Semitic musical myth
propagated by Richard Wagner. In his 1850 essay "Das Judentum in der
Musik," published anonymously in the *Neue Zeitschrift für Musik*, then
again under his own name in 1869, Wagner presented a brutally racist
diatribe against the alien Jewish presence in the world of European music
and the other arts. For decades before Wagner's pamphlet the concentration
of acculturated Jews in the classical music profession as both performers

and composers – and the ambiguous relationship between composition and performance as ideational poles in the Romantic artistic imagination – had existed as a locus for anti-Jewish ideologies. So too did the medieval "music libel" of Jewish musicians as noise polluters of Christian harmony persist into the modern era.[17] Wagner amplified these preexisting negative tropes, blending them with Romantic nationalism and modern racism to craft a new ideology of full-blown musical anti-Semitism.[18] For Wagner, Jewish racial identity was inescapable in music. Further, since diasporic Jews possessed no common national language or authentic folk culture of their own from which to generate original art, they were doomed to be imitators, manipulators, and defilers of German, French, and other European music. He thus condemned Mendelssohn and Meyerbeer for their Judaic limitations as composers and mocked the idea of Jewish music.

Wagner's essay was not the only such ideological expression regarding the links between Jews and art music to appear at mid-century. Franz Liszt's *The Gypsies and Their Music in Hungary* (1859; rev. ed. 1881), though not entirely written by the composer himself, presented a similar tranche of anti-Semitic stereotypes.[19] In Russia, England, and elsewhere, influential writers also proffered elaborated theories about Jewish musical talent.[20] Popular English novels such as Benjamin Disraeli's *Coningsby* (1844), Elizabeth Sara Sheppard's *Charles Auchester* (1849), and George Eliot's *Daniel Deronda* (1876) further engrained the cliché of an innate Jewish musical talent in the Western imagination – but with a significant difference.[21] Almost a mirror image of their anti-Semitic counterparts, these philo-Semitic theories often ascribed to Jewish composers a discernible Semitic character reflected in their compositions by linearity, ornamentation, or lyricism and a conversant weakness in terms of larger musical thematism.[22] Yet for all the parallels and overlap between the various nineteenth-century anti-Semitic and philo-Semitic theories of Jewish musicality, Wagner's essay stood out for its lasting influence on European musical thought. Buoyed by Wagner's towering reputation as a composer and cultural figure, "Das Judentum in der Musik" cast a long shadow over the critical reputations and public receptions of multiple generations of European Jewish composers, notably Mendelssohn and Mahler.[23] It also distinctly impacted the ways later Jewish composers attempting to forge a national style of Jewish art music understood their own relationship to the Western tradition.[24]

Aural emancipations: Renaissance and Modernisms, 1900–1917

After 1900, a new generation of Jewish musicians came of age in European musical life. With urbanization and secularization making ever-faster inroads into central and eastern Europe, the pattern of Jewish demographic overrepresentation in classical music only intensified. Jewish residents of Vienna were three times more likely to study music than non-Jews, while Russian Jews constituted roughly one out of every three conservatory-trained musicians in their country. Indeed, the conservatories of Vienna, St. Petersburg, Moscow, Berlin, Odessa, and other European cities became extraordinary breeding grounds for a generation of Jewish violinists, pianists, and other musicians who would predominate in the concert world of the twentieth century.[25] Of particular note is the impressive roster of violin prodigies that emerged from the St. Petersburg Conservatory studio of Hungarian-born violinist and master pedagogue Leopold Auer (1845–1930), himself a student of Joachim. Auer's pupils included the likes of virtuosos Jascha Heifetz (1901–87), Mischa Elman (1891–1967), Nathan Milstein (1903–92), and Efrem Zimbalist (1890–1985). The careers of European Jewish virtuosos would in many respects parallel those of their nineteenth-century forebears. Highly mobile individuals in an age of war, revolution, and emigration, these musical celebrities came to be heralded as the international torchbearers for the cultural prestige of classical music and objects of affection for European audiences nostalgic for the vanishing world of the nineteenth century. So too would Jews continue to play a significant role in Western art music as publishers, critics, and scholars.[26]

The post-1900 generation of European Jewish composers was the first to appear on the historical stage with an intensely ideological, self-conscious determination to break with the past. This revolutionary ethos took two distinct forms. In the Russian Empire, an explicitly Jewish national renaissance movement centered in the Russian Empire rejected the putative absorption of Jewish musicians into a universalist European culture. These Jewish nationalist composers called for the renewal of Jewish national identity through freeing a previously silenced Jewish voice within Western music. At virtually the same moment, a looser central European avant-garde school appeared, comprised of composers who aspired to emancipate music itself from the aesthetic conventions of nineteenth-century realism in favor of an abstract modernism. What linked these two cohorts – along with those Jewish composers who bucked both trends – was an acute awareness of the passage of European Jewry into a new historical era. In response to tremendous societal change, modernist nationalists and cosmopolitan modernists alike called for an immediate radical reconstruction of Jewish identity in music. Yet both found that the long shadows of the Jewish past continued to define Jewish identity in Western music.

In the Russian Empire, a number of conservatory-trained Jewish composers experimented with Jewish musical ethnography in the late 1890s and early 1900s. Inspired by the new spirit of secular Jewish nationalism, emboldened by the Russian, Finnish, and other national schools, and encouraged by Russian musical mentors such as Rimskii-Korsakov, Balakirev, and the critic Vladimir Stasov, these composers began to collect and arrange Yiddish and Hebrew folk songs, traditional liturgical selections, Hasidic spiritual chants, and klezmer dance tunes.[27] The key figure in this process was the Russian critic, ethnographer, and composer Joel (Iulii Dmitrevich) Engel (1868–1927). A Moscow Conservatory graduate, Engel presented a concert of Yiddish folk song arrangements in 1900 in Moscow that subsequently came to be regarded by many as the first-ever concert of Jewish art music. With the stature that came as one of Russia's leading music critics, Engel went on to advocate a Jewish national movement in classical music. He also published several influential song collections, and pioneered the use of early sound recording technology to document *shtetl* musical traditions *in situ*.[28]

Engel was joined in his efforts by a group of young composers, among them Mikhail Gnesin (1883–1957), Solomon Rosowsky (1878–1962), Lazare Saminsky (1882–1959), and Moyshe Milner (1886–1953), who had all met in Rimskii-Korsakov's composition class at the St. Petersburg Conservatory. In 1908, these St. Petersburg musicians launched the Society for Jewish Folk Music (*Obshchestvo evreiskoi narodnoi muzyki*). The new organization pursued a campaign on multiple fronts to encourage explicitly Jewish art music composition, to promote Jewish cultural nationalism among Russian Jewish conservatory musicians, and to define through research and polemical debate the legitimate paternity and national contours of Jewish music. Engel was named the organization's first honorary member, and in 1913 he opened a branch in Moscow.[29]

In the decade after 1908, the Society for Jewish Folk Music produced nearly 1,000 concerts across Russia and eastern Europe, launched branches in many cities, and issued a very popular songbook for schools and homes. Most crucially, they published a number of compositions by multiple composers that used Yiddish and Hebrew folk songs and klezmer instrumental dance melodies in vocal arrangements and small chamber music formats. Many of these early compositions reflected the tenets of Russian Romanticism and common-practice harmonies. The Russian influence could also be detected in performance practices and other extra-musical referents that signaled Jewish music to be simultaneously a recovered Jewish national voice, an enriching contribution to European culture, and a coveted object of Russian imperial patrimony. Building on Russian Orientalism and European antiquarianism, the Russian Jewish School also pioneered new techniques of Jewish auto-exoticism. Composers such as Engel, Ephraim Shkliar, Rosowsky, and Leo Zeitlin (1884–1930) pioneered a genre of musical miniatures that sought to preserve the folkloric qualities of ethnographically sourced melodies in the lead instrumental voices with modern harmonic accompaniments and novel instrumentations.[30] Just as in other spheres of modern Jewish culture, many composers also imbibed the influence of pan-European modernism and French Impressionism. Composers such as Joseph Achron (1886–1943), Gnesin, and Alexander Krein (1883–1951) married the chromaticist experiments, intense tonal lyricism, and extended harmonies of modernist composers like Scriabin and Debussy to Jewish scales and intonational gestures.[31] They also moved easily back and forth between the larger European artistic milieu and the world of modern Jewish culture. It was not uncommon for these composers to set both Russian Symbolist poetry and modern Hebrew and Yiddish lyrics to music. They thus positioned Jewish art music simultaneously as one genre within a larger universe of Jewish cultural expression and as a stream within modern Russian and European art music.

The young Jewish composers of late Tsarist Russia balanced an attraction to the new universalist aesthetics of modernist abstraction with a particularistic commitment to representing Jewish identity in music. A similar phenomenon appeared in the Sephardic musical realm in the form of the Alexandrian-born Turkish-Jewish composer Alberto Hemsi, who collected and arranged Sephardic Jewish song texts and melodies in his landmark collection *Coplas Sefardies* (1932–73). By contrast, the central European Jewish exponents of modernism dispensed with all Romantic folklorism and realism alike in favor of a new avant-garde ideology of tonal experimentation and formal abstraction. In the eyes of composers such as Gustav Mahler (1860–1911) and Arnold Schoenberg (1874–1951), modern art demanded that artists transcend ethnic or religious parochialisms. Yet this utopian goal proved difficult to achieve in practice.

Born in the Austrian Bohemian hinterlands, Mahler rose to become arguably the leading conductor and symphonist of the fin-de-siècle. As a composer, he drew acclaim for his music's psychological intensity, ruminative beauty, and tonal complexity. Yet he also faced a series of devastating crises in his personal life, including illness and infidelity. He additionally possessed a vexed identity as an ambivalent convert to Christianity and an ongoing target of anti-Semitism. His aching sense of inner conflict, emotional displacement, and powerful longing for transcendence permeated his deeply lyrical, expressionist style. Scholars have differed about the presence of explicitly Jewish influences in his brooding modernist textures. Yet there is little disagreement that Mahler's life and art epitomized the mixture of triumph and tragedy, inclusion and exclusion that characterized the larger experience of generations of Jews in the fin-de-siècle world of European classical music.[32] He summed up his own fate with his famous remark: "I am thrice homeless, as a native of Bohemia in Austria, as an Austrian among Germans, and as a Jew throughout the world. Everywhere an intruder, never welcomed."

Similarly, Schoenberg launched a musical revolution over the course of 1908 and 1909 with works that stretched tonality outwards in pursuit of what he termed the "emancipation of dissonance." An Austrian Jew who converted to German Lutheranism, Schoenberg rejected realism for extreme chromaticism, unconventional rhythms, and eventually, the serialist approach of tone-rows. Paradoxically, Schoenberg extolled his anti-parochial aesthetic universalism as a German cultural achievement. This complicated utopianism represented a dialectical response to the dilemmas of Jewishness in art music. Yet it did not prevent European anti-Semitic ideologues from collapsing Jewishness and modernism into a single essentialist view of Jews as arch-modernists when it came to music. This anti-Semitic attack on modernism grew even stronger after the rise of Nazism. This prompted Schoenberg to publicly renounce his Germanism and Christianity and formally re-embrace Jewish religion, politics, and eventually musical thematics in his own idiosyncratic way.[33]

The Jewish currents of nationalism and modernism were never completely sealed off from one another. A case in point is the Swiss Jewish composer Ernest Bloch (1890–1959). Bloch composed his first Jewish-themed works shortly before World War I. He soon attracted international fame. Indeed, to many Western observers, Bloch stood out as the "first Jewish composer." Yet in contrast to the Russian Jewish composers, he opted not to draw directly on Jewish folkloric material in most of his compositions. In iconic works such as his *Schelomo Rhapsody* for cello and orchestra (1914/1915), he avoided quotation from Jewish liturgical or folkloric music. Instead he spoke of himself as a composer whose Jewish essence simply bubbled up, flowing organically into his works. In this scheme of self-racialization or auto-exoticization, Bloch imagined his own "Jewish soul" to be an inescapable and defining element of his work. In works such as his Piano Quintet (1921–3), which employed a complex hybrid of expressionism and neoclassicism, avoiding any explicit Jewish quotations or musical markers, the quarter-tone intervals and Jewish scalar intervals gestured obliquely towards an East European Jewish melody. At times Bloch encouraged a Jewish reading of his work, while at other moments he bristled at this artificial demarcation of his music as Jewish and himself as a "Jewish composer." This ambiguity points to both the possibilities and the perils of modernism for Jewish art music in the World War I era.[34]

Other variations on Bloch's racialized Jewish modernism echoed across the Jewish musical world in important ways during the 1910s. In the Russian Empire, composer Lazare Saminsky denounced the "assimilated" Jewish composers who avoided their racial destiny. He urged his fellow Jewish composers to employ only purely Jewish liturgical melodies with an authentic biblical paternity instead of modern Yiddish melodies borrowed from surrounding non-Jewish cultures of eastern Europe.[35] The Zionist music critic Max Brod (1884–1968) argued influentially that Mahler's music must be understood in terms of the composer's Hasidic soul. In Ottoman Palestine, Russian-born musicologist and pedagogue Abraham Zvi Idelsohn (1882–1938) conducted a massive scholarly project to collect the true specimens of Hebrew music – ancient melodies uncorrupted by millennia of exposure to the diaspora – primarily from the "Oriental" sections of the Jewish nation, those Jewish communities in the Arab Middle East. He articulated the concept of a musical Hebrewism – an ideological rejection of exilic Western culture for a reborn Hebrew aesthetic based on authentic elements indigenous to the Middle East. In polemical writings in Hebrew, German, and English, Idelsohn called for a global racial awakening among Jewish composers. Though few responded directly to his manifestos, his ideas still cast a long shadow over the fields of Israeli and diasporic Jewish art music for decades to come. Idelsohn's massive ten-volume *Thesaurus of Hebrew-Oriental Melodies* became a chief source of motivic material and artistic inspiration for Jewish composers of modern Israeli, European, and American Jewish art music.[36]

Revolutionary echoes: affirmations and ambiguities, 1917–1925

The traumas of World War I and post-war revolutions had an explosive impact on Jewish art music. The displacement of individual musicians led to a collapse of many large-scale cultural projects, particularly in the Russian context. Yet the waves of emigration and resettlement also brought Jewish art music to new corners of the globe. So too did it lead to new attempts to institutionalize and propagate compositional efforts and novel forms of artistic collaboration. As a result, the period from 1915 to 1925 saw a great rise in the global profile of Jewish art music combined with increasing political pressures and ideological conflicts over its meaning.

For the Russian Jewish composers associated with the Society for Jewish Folk Music, the events of 1917 unleashed a tumultuous creative period. Emboldened by the Balfour Declaration's salutary effect on Zionism and early encouragement from Bolshevik revolutionary leaders, composers such as Engel, Krein, and Gnesin threw themselves into a new phase of activity. Socialist political themes commingled with settings of modern Hebrew poetry and modernist scores for the experimental Yiddish theater studios of Moscow and Petrograd. A new burst of chromaticist and harmonic abstraction in the first Jewish-themed piano sonatas and symphonic works by Krein and Gnesin signified a striking convergence between Russian revolutionary avant-garde, Jewish musical nationalism, and European modernism as a whole. Works such as Gnesin's 1919 *Symphonic Fantasia à la Juif* and Krein's First Symphony (1921) also signified a trend of expanding musical forms. By the mid-1920s, Jewish symphonic works were commonly found on the programs of Soviet orchestral concerts as well as in Vienna, Berlin, and New York.

Jewish popular composers in the Yiddish theaters of eastern Europe, London, and New York had long experimented with light operetta forms, mixing liturgical motifs with Yiddish folk songs and Wagner and Verdi arias to form a musical pastiche. The 1910s and 1920s witnessed a flurry of unsuccessful attempts to compose the first full-fledged Jewish national opera. These included London cantor-composer Samuel Alman's Yiddish-language *King Ahaz* (1912); Gnesin's unfinished Hebrew-language work *Abram's Youth* (1923), begun while he was living near Jerusalem; Milner's Yiddish-language opera *The Heavens are Burning* (1923), briefly premiered in Leningrad; Idelsohn's never-performed Hebrew-language *Jephta* (1921); and Jacob Weinberg's 1925 Hebrew-language work *He-ḥalutz* (The Pioneers), composed in Jerusalem shortly before the Odessa-born musician's departure for the United States.

No less impactful than war, revolution, and migration on Jewish art music was the rise of new technologies of music publishing and recorded sound. The first commercial recordings of Yiddish and Hebrew art songs began to appear in the Russian Empire and the United States in the late 1910s, along with an important early recording of Joseph Achron's "Hebrew Melody," issued in 1917 by Jascha Heifetz. International music publishing earned the works of Jewish composers new audiences as reprint series and new editions carried the music across the world, inspiring other publishing initiatives in Vienna, Berlin, and elsewhere.[37] These publishing efforts were hallmarks of a new phase of the institutionalization of Jewish art music prompted by the consolidation of the Soviet Bolshevik state and the boost in fortunes of the international Zionist movement. The Society for Jewish Folk Music was reorganized in 1923 in Moscow as the Society for Jewish Music. Parallel organizations appeared in Vienna, Paris, Berlin, and eventually New York and Jerusalem.[38] In Riga, Vilnius, Jerusalem, and Tel Aviv, music conservatories were started to train Jewish concert musicians.

In central Europe, the modernist avant-garde began to cross paths directly with the Jewish musical movement. The Russian-born cellist Joachim Stuchevsky (1891–1982), already a fierce proponent of Jewish art music based on the klezmer repertoire of Jewish eastern Europe, launched the *Verein zur Förderung jüdischer Musik* in Vienna. At the same time, he served as first cellist of the Kolisch Quartet, where he befriended Schoenberg and performed the premieres of path-breaking modernist works by Berg and others. The Berlin-born Erich Walter Sternberg (1891–1974) wrote his first String Quartet (1924) in an Expressionist style with shades of Hindemith and Schoenberg. Yet he also incorporated a Yiddish popular song and the *Shema* prayer into the work. Similar cross-pollinations reflected a new interest in Jewish themes among modernists elsewhere in western Europe and the United States. In France, the bitonality of Darius Milhaud (1892–1974) included Jewish musical settings beginning with his 1916 *Poèmes juives*. The Russian-born Polish-French Jewish composer Alexandre Tansman (1897–1986) achieved renown for his mixture of neoclassicism with modernism, and Polish and Jewish folk influences, as evidenced by his *Rapsodie hébraïque* for orchestra (1933). In the United States, young Russian-born composers such as Lazar Weiner (1897–1982) and Solomon Golub (1887–1952) continued the development of a new genre of Yiddish art songs. In 1919 the Zimro Ensemble formed in revolutionary Petrograd by clarinetist Simeon Bellison (1881–1953) arrived in New York City after a round-the-world tour to raise funds for a Jewish national conservatory in Palestine. Their Carnegie Hall debut inspired Serge Prokofiev to compose his "Overture on Hebrew Themes" (1919).

By the mid-1920s, Jewish art music seemed to be on the verge of a new status in the larger world of classical music. Soviet and American critics wrote positively of a Jewish national school now emerging into view. In the United States, composers such as Saminsky, Bloch, Achron, and Leo Ornstein (1893–2002) pushed forward an artistic agenda that pledged equal parts loyalty to both European modernism and Jewish nationalism. In the Soviet Union, state support encouraged those composers who had remained. In central Europe, a larger Jewish cultural renaissance engulfed many composers and performers. British Palestine continued to attract a stream of Zionist immigrants and saw the launch of a music department at the Hebrew University of Jerusalem in 1925. For Jewish nationalist composers, the rise of a generation of international Jewish concert virtuosos who incorporated Jewish-themed compositions into their repertoires added to the prestige of their efforts to forge a distinct national school.

Yet the very factors that had stimulated the spread of Jewish musicians and musical ideas across the globe also contributed to their weakness and divergence. The politicization of musical life in the Soviet Union introduced discordant notes into the dialogue between avant-garde modernists, Bolshevik populists, and neo-nationalist Jewish composers. The success of Schoenberg, Bloch, and other more abstract modernists inspired envy and frustration among Russian Jewish composers committed to Romanticist folklorism. The currents of anti-Semitism in central Europe continued to unleash torrents of attack on the Jewish presence in European musical life. Opponents of modernism blamed Jews as the agents of Western music's atonal demise. In the Jewish community of Palestine, the economic stagnation and political violence frustrated attempts to build a substantial European-style concert music culture. A mass exodus of recently arrived Russian Jewish composers only added to the disruption in the development of a national musical culture.

These contradictory trends inspired mixed reactions among contemporary observers. By 1925, some critics and composers spoke of Jewish art music as a coherent nationalist project still in its infancy. They proclaimed the dawn of a new era in which de-assimilation would produce a new generation of creative artists and reborn sounds. Still others saw nationalism as a trap for Jewish composers. For them the enduring ambiguity of Jewish identity in Western music was an insurmountable fact. It was also a dangerous mark of difference in a classical musical world increasingly defined by racism and fascism. They feared the increasingly loud claims of anti-Semites about the political meaning of Jewish music in Europe and, to a lesser extent, the United States. Both anxiety and optimism, affirmation and ambiguity would continue to mark Jewish art music in the ensuing decades leading up to World War II and even afterwards. In the meantime, the larger intertwined fates of Jews and modern classical music would change dramatically in ways that few in 1925 could even imagine.

Notes

1 Shaul M. Gintsburg, "Iz zapisok pervogo evreia-studenta v Rossii (Lev Iosifovich Mandelshtam, 1819–89)," *Perezhitoe*, 1 (1909): 29–31.

2 On the entrance of Jews into European musical life, see James Loeffler, *The Most Musical Nation: Jews and Culture in the Late Russian Empire* (New Haven: Yale University Press, 2010), 1–14; David Conway, *Jewry in Music: Entry to the Profession from the Enlightenment to Wagner* (Cambridge University Press, 2012); Daniel Jütte, "Juden als Virtuosen: Eine Studie zur Sozialgeschichte der Musik sowie zur Wirkmächtigkeit einer Denkfigur des 19. Jahrhunderts," *Archiv für Musikwissenschaft*, 66.2 (2009): 127–54; David Schoenbaum, "Fiddlers on the Roof: Some Thoughts on a Special Relationship," in Henning Tewes and Jonathan Wright (eds.), *Liberalism, Anti-Semitism, and Democracy: Essays in Honour of Peter Pulzer* (Oxford University Press, 2001), 273–87; Ezra Mendelsohn, "On the Jewish Presence in Nineteenth-Century European Musical Life," and Judit Frigyesi, "Jews and

Hungarians in Modern Hungarian Musical Culture," in Ezra Mendelsohn (ed.), *Modern Jews and their Musical Agendas*, Studies in Contemporary Jewry 9 (Oxford University Press, 1993), 3–16, 40–60.

3 On the social, cultural, and economic factors drawing Jews into European art music, see Leon Botstein, *Judentum und Modernität. Essays zur Rolle der Juden in der deutschen und österreichischen Kultur, 1848 bis 1938* (Vienna: Böhlau, 1991), 126–48; idem, "Music, Femininity, and Jewish Identity: The Tradition and Legacy of the Salon," in Emily D. Bilski and Emily Braun (eds.), *Jewish Women and Their Salons: The Power of Conversation* (New York: Jewish Museum under the auspices of the Jewish Theological Seminary of America; New Haven: Yale University Press, 2005), 159–69; Daniel Jütte, "Die Grenzen der Musik: Verbürgerlichung, Antisemitismus und die Musikästhetik der Moderne im Kontext der Geschichte jüdischer Interpreten (1750–1900)," in Beatrix Borchard and Heidy Zimmermann (eds.), *Musikwelten – Lebenswelten: Jüdische*

Identitätssuche in der deutschen Musikkultur (Vienna: Böhlau, 2009), 227–49; Ruth Katz, "Why Music? Jews and the Commitment to Modernity," in Shulamit Volkov (ed.), *Deutsche Juden und die Moderne* (Munich: Oldenbourg, 1994), 31–8; Michael Steinberg, *Judaism Musical and Unmusical* (University of Chicago Press, 2007); Philip V. Bohlman, *Jewish Music and Modernity* (Oxford University Press, 2008).

4 Moisei Beregovskii, *Jewish Instrumental Folk Music: The Collections and Writings of Moshe Beregovski*, ed. and trans. Mark Slobin, Robert Rothstein, and Michael Alpert (Syracuse University Press, 2001), 21–35.

5 Beatrix Borchard, "Von Joseph Joachim zurück zu Moses Mendelssohn. Instrumentalmusik als Zukunftsreligion?," in Borchard and Zimmermann, *Musikwelten – Lebenswelten*, 31–58 (32). Cf. Beatrix Borchard, *Stimme und Geige. Amalie und Joseph Joachim: Biographie und Interpretationsgeschichte* (Vienna: Böhlau, 2005).

6 Alexander Moszkowski, *Der jüdische Witz und seine Philosophie: 399 Juwelen echt gefaßt* (Berlin: Eysler, 1922), 51, quoted in Till van Rahden, "'Germans of the Jewish *Stamm*': Visions of Community between Nationalism and Particularism, 1850 to 1933," in Neil Gregor, Nils Roemer, and Mark Roseman (eds.), *German History from the Margins* (Bloomington: Indiana University Press, 2006), 27–48 (31).

7 Frederick Burwick and Paul Douglass (eds.), *A Selection of Hebrew Melodies, Ancient and Modern, by Isaac Nathan and Lord Byron* (Tuscaloosa: University of Alabama Press, 1988); Graham Pont, "Byron and Nathan: A Musical Collaboration," *The Byron Journal*, 27 (1999): 51–65; Conway, *Jewry in Music*, 91–100; Ruth HaCohen, *The Music Libel against the Jews* (New Haven: Yale University Press, 2012), 171–8.

8 Loeffler, *Most Musical Nation*, 14–55; Annakatrin Täuschel, *Anton Rubinstein als Opernkomponist* (Berlin: Ernst Kuhn, 2001).

9 Brigitte François-Sappey (ed.), *Charles Valentin Alkan* (Paris: Fayard, 1991); William Alexander Eddie, *Charles Valentin Alkan: His Life and His Music* (Aldershot, UK, and Burlington, VT: Ashgate, 2007); Annie Kessous-Dreyfuss, "D'un 'Psaume' de Benedetto Marcello à une 'Mélodie juive' de Charles Valentin Alkan: le parcours d'un 'Air,'" *Acta Musicologica*, 77.1 (2006): 55–74.

10 Salomon Sulzer, *Schir Zion: ein Zyklus religiöser Gesänge zum gottesdienstlichen Gebrauche der Israeliten* (Vienna, 1840), and *Schir Zion II: Gottesdienstliche Gesänge der Israeliten* (Vienna, 1865).

11 Tina Frühauf, "Jewish Liturgical Music in Vienna: A Mirror of Cultural Diversity," in Leon Botstein and Werner Hanak (eds.), *Vienna: Jews and the City of Music 1870–1938* (Annandale-on-Hudson, NY: Bard College, 2004), 77–91; Hanoch Avenary (ed.), *Kantor Salomon Sulzer und seine Zeit: Eine Dokumentation* (Sigmaringen: J. Thorbecke, 1985); Tina Frühauf, *Salomon Sulzer: Reformer, Cantor, Icon* (Berlin: Hentrich & Hentrich, 2012).

12 Geoffrey Goldberg, "Jewish Liturgical Music in the Wake of Nineteenth-Century Reform," in Lawrence A. Hoffman and Janet R. Walton (eds.), *Sacred Sound and Social Change: Liturgical Music in Jewish and Christian Experience* (University of Notre Dame Press, 1992), 59–83; Hanoch Avenary, "The Cantorial Fantasia of the Eighteenth and Nineteenth Centuries," *Yuval*, 1 (1968): 65–85. On the organ, see Tina Frühauf, *The Organ and Its Music in German-Jewish Culture* (Oxford University Press, 2009); David Ellenson, "A Disputed Precedent: The Prague Organ in Nineteenth-Century Central European Legal Literature and Polemics," *Leo Baeck Institute Year Book*, 40 (1995): 251–64.

13 Samuel Naumbourg (ed.), *Zemiroth Yisrael: chants religieux des Israélites* (Paris, 1847–64).

14 Louis Lewandowski, *Todah w'simrah: vierstimmige Chöre und Soli für den israelitischen Gottesdienst* (Berlin, 1876–82); idem, *Kol rinnah u't'fillah: ein und zweistimmige Gesänge für den israelitischen Gottesdienst* (Berlin, 1871).

15 Edwin Seroussi, "Sephardic fins des siècles: The Liturgical Music of Vienna's 'Türkisch-Israelitische' Community on the Threshold of Modernity," in Philip V. Bohlman (ed.), *Jewish Musical Modernism, Old and New* (University of Chicago Press, 2008), 55–79; idem, *Spanish-Portuguese Synagogue Music in Nineteenth-Century Reform Sources from Hamburg: Ancient Tradition in the Dawn of Modernity* [Heb.], Yuval Monograph Series 11 (Magnes Press of the Hebrew University of Jerusalem, 1996); idem, "Two Spanish-Portuguese 'Cantorial Fantasias' from Hamburg (1838)," in Michael Studemund-Halévy and Peter Koj (eds.), *Die Sefarden in Hamburg: zur Geschichte einer Minderheit* (Hamburg: Buske, 1994), 171–84.

16 Loeffler, *Most Musical Nation*, 35–41; Klára Móricz, *Jewish Identities: Nationalism, Racism, and Utopianism in Twentieth-Century Music* (Berkeley and Los Angeles: University of California Press, 2008), 38–81; Richard Taruskin, *On Russian Music* (Berkeley and Los

Angeles: University of California Press, 2009), 190–201; Ilia Kheifets, "Evreiskaia muzykalnaia idioma i kompozitsionnaia tekhnika (na primere dvukh proizvedenii M. I. Glinki i M. P. Musorgskogo)," *Vestnik evreiskogo universiteta v Moskve*, 5.23 (2001): 49–76; Boris Schwarz, "Musorgsky's Interest in Judaica," in Malcolm Hamrick Brown (ed.), *Musorgsky, in Memoriam, 1881–1981* (Ann Arbor: UMI Research Press, 1982), 85–94.

17 HaCohen, *Music Libel*.

18 Annkatrin Dahm, *Der Topos der Juden. Studien zur Geschichte des Antisemitismus im deutschsprachigen Musikschrifttum* (Göttingen: Vandenhoeck & Ruprecht, 2007); Jacob Katz, *The Darker Side of Genius: Richard Wagner's Anti-Semitism* (Hanover, NH: University Press of New England, 1986); Paul Lawrence Rose, *Wagner: Race and Revolution* (New Haven: Yale University Press, 1992); Marc A. Weiner, *Richard Wagner and the Anti-Semitic Imagination* (Lincoln, NE: University of Nebraska Press, 1995); Conway, *Jewry in Music*, 258–66; Jens Malte Fischer, *Richard Wagners "Das Judentum in der Musik." Eine kritische Dokumentation als Beitrag zur Geschichte des Antisemitismus* (Frankfurt am Main: Insel, 2000); Benjamin Binder, "Kundry and the Jewish Voice: Anti-Semitism and Musical Transcendence in Wagner's *Parsifal*," *Current Musicology*, 87 (Spring 2009): 47–131.

19 Klara Hamburger, "Understanding the Hungarian Reception History of Liszt's *Des Bohémiens et de leur musique en Hongrie* (1859/1881)," *Journal of the American Liszt Society*, 54–6 (2003–5): 75–84; Leon Botstein, "A Mirror to the Nineteenth Century: Reflections on Liszt," in Christopher H. Gibbs and Dana Gooley (eds.), *Liszt and His World* (Princeton University Press, 2006), 517–68.

20 Yaacov Shavit, *Athens in Jerusalem: Classical Antiquity and Hellenism in the Making of the Modern Secular Jew*, trans. Chaya Naor and Niki Werner (London: Frank Cass, 1997), 220–71.

21 Conway, *Jewry in Music*, 257–8.

22 Daniel Khvol'son, *The Semitic Nations* (Cincinnati, 1872), 29; Sander L. Gilman, "Are Jews Musical? Historical Notes on the Question of Jewish Musical Modernism," in Bohlman (ed.), *Jewish Musical Modernism*, vii–xvi.

23 K. M. Knittel, *Seeing Mahler: Music and the Language of Antisemitism in Fin-de-Siècle Vienna* (Farnham, UK, and Burlington, VT: Ashgate, 2010); Leon Botstein, "The Aesthetics of Assimilation and Affirmation: Reconstructing the Career of Felix Mendelssohn," in R. Larry Todd (ed.), *Mendelssohn and His World*

(Princeton University Press, 1991), 5–42; idem, "Whose Gustav Mahler? Reception, Interpretation, and History," in Karen Painter (ed.), *Mahler and His World* (Princeton University Press, 2002), 1–54; Karen Painter, "Jewish Identity and Anti-Semitic Critique in the Austro-German Reception of Mahler, 1900–1945," in Jeremy Barham (ed.), *Perspectives on Gustav Mahler* (Aldershot, UK, and Burlington, VT: Ashgate, 2005), 175–94; Jane Fulcher, *The Composer as Intellectual: Music and Ideology in France, 1914–1940* (Oxford University Press, 1998); Ernst Kuhn, Jascha Nemtsov, and Andreas Wehrmeyer (eds.), *"Samuel" Goldenberg und "Schmuyle." Jüdisches und Antisemitisches in der russischen Musikkultur* (Berlin: Ernst Kuhn, 2003).

24 James Loeffler, "Richard Wagner's 'Jewish Music': Antisemitism and Aesthetics in Modern Jewish Culture," *Jewish Social Studies*, 15.2 (Winter 2009): 2–36; Daniel Jütte, "'Mendele Lohengrin' und der koschere Wagner. Unorthodoxes zur jüdischen Wagner-Rezeption," in Mark H. Gelber, Jakob Hessing, and Robert Jütte (eds.), *Integration und Ausgrenzung. Studien zur deutsch-jüdischen Literatur- und Kulturgeschichte von der Frühen Neuzeit bis zur Gegenwart* (Tübingen: Niemeyer, 2009), 115–29; Karen Painter, "From Biography to Myth: The Jewish Reception of Gustav Mahler," *Jahrbuch des Simon-Dubnow-Instituts*, 11 (2012): 259–81; Henrik Rosengren, "'A Wagner for the Jews': Moses Pergament, Richard Wagner and Anti-Semitism in Swedish Cultural Life in the Interwar Period," *Scandanavian Journal of History*, 38.2 (2013): 245–61.

25 Leon Botstein, "Social History and the Politics of the Aesthetic: Jews and Music in Vienna 1870–1938," in Botstein and Hanak (eds.), *Vienna*, 43–64; Loeffler, *Most Musical Nation*, 43–7, 94–133.

26 Pamela Potter, *Most German of the Arts: Musicology and Society from the Weimar Republic to the End of Hitler's Reich* (New Haven: Yale University Press, 1998); Nicholas Cook, *The Schenker Project: Culture, Race, and Music Theory in Fin-de-Siècle Vienna* (Oxford University Press, 2007); Bennett Zon, *Representing Non-Western Music in Nineteenth-Century Britain* (University of Rochester Press, 2007), 159–248.

27 On Jewish musical ethnography, see Loeffler, *Most Musical Nation*, 56–93; Bohlman, *Jewish Music and Modernity*, 73–145; Karl E. Grözinger (ed.), *Klesmer, Klassik, jiddisches Lied: jüdische Musikkultur in Osteuropa* (Wiesbaden: Harrassowitz, 2004); Philip V. Bohlman, *Jüdische Volksmusik: Eine mitteleuropäische*

Geistesgeschichte (Vienna: Böhlau, 2005); Beregovskii, *Jewish Instrumental Folk Music*.

28 Loeffler, *Most Musical Nation*, 56–93.

29 *Ibid*.; Jascha Nemtsov, *Die Neue Jüdische Schule in der Musik* (Wiesbaden: Harrassowitz, 2004); Jascha Nemtsov and Ernst Kuhn (eds.), *Jüdische Musik in Sowjetrussland: Die "Jüdische Nationale Schule" der zwanziger Jahre* (Berlin: Ernst Kuhn, 2002).

30 On the notion of Jewish auto-exoticism, see Assaf Shelleg, "Israeli Art Music: A Reintroduction," *Israel Studies*, 17.3 (Fall 2012): 119–49 (126–7); idem, *Jewish Contiguities and the Soundtrack of Israeli History* (Oxford University Press, 2014). On the question of genre and miniature, see Joshua S. Walden, "Music of the 'Folks-Neshome': 'Hebrew Melody' and Changing Musical Representations of Jewish Culture in the Early Twentieth Century Ashkenazi Diaspora," *Journal of Modern Jewish Studies*, 8.2 (July 2009): 151–72.

31 For discussion of compositional style, see Móricz, *Jewish Identities*, 26–91; Paula Eisenstein Baker and Robert S. Nelson (eds.), *Leo Zeitlin: Chamber Music*, Recent Researches in Music of the 19th and Early 20th Centuries 51 (Middleton, WI: A-R Editions, 2009), xvi–xviii; Beate Schroeder-Nauenburg, *"Der Eintritt des Jüdischen in die Welt der Kunstmusik": Die Anfänge der Neuen Jüdischen Schule: werkanalytische Studien* (Wiesbaden: Harrassowitz, 2007); Joshua S. Walden, *Sounding Authentic: The Rural Miniature and Musical Modernism* (Oxford University Press, 2014).

32 For recent works that focus on the Jewish dimension of Mahler's music and persona, see Daniel Jütte, "His Majesty's Mahler: Jews, Courts, and Culture in the Nineteenth Century," *Jahrbuch des Simon-Dubnows-Institut*, 11 (2012): 149–62; Jens Malte Fischer, *Gustav Mahler* (New Haven: Yale University Press, 2011); Norman Lebrecht, *Why Mahler? How One Man and Ten Symphonies Changed Our World* (New York: Random House, 2011); Francesca Draughon and Raymond Knapp, "Gustav Mahler and the Crisis of Jewish Identity," *Echo*, 3.2, http://www.echo.ucla.edu/ Volume3-issue2/knapp_draughon/knapp_ draughon1.html (accessed February 18, 2014); Carl Niekerk, *Reading Mahler: German Culture and Jewish Identity in Fin-de-Siècle Vienna* (Rochester: Camden House, 2010); Karen Painter, "Contested Counterpoint: 'Jewish' Appropriation and Polyphonic Liberation," *Archiv für Musikwissenschaft*, 58.3 (2001): 201–30.

33 Steven J. Cahn, "Schoenberg, the Viennese-Jewish Experience and Its Aftermath," in Jennifer Shaw and Joseph Auner (eds.), *The Cambridge Companion to Schoenberg* (Cambridge University Press, 2010), 191–206; Juliane Brand and Christopher Hailey (eds.), *Constructive Dissonance: Arnold Schoenberg and the Transformations of Twentieth-Century Culture* (Berkeley and Los Angeles: University of California Press, 1997); William Kangas, "The Ethics and Aesthetics of (Self)Representation: Arnold Schoenberg and Jewish Identity," *Leo Baeck Institute Year Book*, 45.1 (2000): 135–70; Móricz, *Jewish Identities*, 201–336; David Schiller, *Bloch, Schoenberg, and Bernstein: Assimilating Jewish Music* (Oxford University Press, 2003), 74–126.

34 Joshua S. Walden, "'An Essential Expression of the People': Interpretations of Hasidic Song in the Composition and Performance History of Ernest Bloch's *Baal Shem*," *Journal of the American Musicological Society*, 65.3 (Fall 2012): 777–820; Móricz, *Jewish Identities*, 95–200; Schiller, *Assimilating Jewish Music*, 12–73; David Kushner, *The Ernest Bloch Companion* (Westport, CT: Greenwood Press, 2002).

35 Lazare Saminsky, *Music of the Ghetto and Bible* (New York: Bloch Publishing, 1934), 227–52; Izalii Zemtsovskii, "Muzykalnyi idishizm: K istorii unikalnogo fenomena," in Leonid Gural'nik (ed.), *Iz istorii evreiskoi muzyki* (St. Petersburg: Evreiskii obshchinnyi tsentr Sankt-Peterburga, 2001), i:119–24.

36 James Loeffler, "Do Zionists Read Music from Right to Left? Abraham Tsvi Idelsohn and the Invention of Israeli Music," *Jewish Quarterly Review*, 100.3 (Summer 2010): 385–416; Edwin Seroussi, "'Yesod 'eḥad lahen.' Gilui ha-mizraḥ ve-'aḥdutan shel mesorot ha-musikah ha-yehudiot ve-mishnat 'Avraham 'Idelson," *Pe'amim*, 100 (2004): 125–46; Shai Burstyn, "'Shirah ḥadashah-atikah': Moreshet Avraham Tzvi Idelson ve-zimrei 'shorashim,'" *Katedrah*, 128 (Tammuz 2008): 113–44; Bohlman, *Jewish Music and Modernity*, 44–70; Abraham Zvi Idelsohn, *Hebräisch-orientalischer Melodienschatz*, 10 vols. (Leipzig: Breitkopf and Härtel, 1914; Jerusalem, Berlin, and Vienna: Benjamin Harz, 1922–9; and Leipzig: Friedrich Hofmeister, 1932); idem, *Jewish Music in Its Historical Development* (New York: Henry Holt, 1929).

37 Loeffler, *Most Musical Nation*, 134–72; Nemtsov, *Die Neue Jüdische Schule*, 93–130.

38 Nemtsov, *Die Neue Jüdische Schule*, 131–84; Jascha Nemtsov, *Der Zionismus in der Musik. Jüdische Musik und nationale Idee* (Wiesbaden: Harrassowitz, 2009); Verena Bopp, *Mailamm*

1932–1941. Die Geschichte einer Vereinigung zur Förderung jüdischer Musik in den USA (Wiesbaden: Harrassowitz, 2007); Philip V. Bohlman, *The World Centre for Jewish Music in Palestine, 1936–1940: Jewish Musical Life on the* *Eve of World War II* (Oxford University Press, 1992); Jehoash Hirshberg, *Music in the Jewish Community of Palestine 1880–1948: A Social History* (Oxford: Clarendon Press, 1996); Shelleg, *Jewish Contiguities.*

12 The reform of synagogue music in the nineteenth century

TINA FRÜHAUF

An overview of synagogue music reform

Rooted in the *Haskalah* (Jewish Enlightenment) and Jewish emancipation, movements that had an important role in the development of modern Judaism, reform-minded Jews in central Europe began to develop ideas toward a modernized worship service in the first decades of the nineteenth century. In the course of these reforms, synagogue music underwent radical changes to make it appear more current and sophisticated to a public that was increasingly educated in Western art music, however not without the resistance of traditionalists. The *ḥazzan* was succeeded by what was now termed the "cantor." With the shift in nomenclature came changes in the profession as well. The cantor possessed a thorough knowledge of liturgy like the *ḥazzan*, but had a more profound knowledge of music from outside the synagogue as well, and was able to write music and conduct, but his role throughout the nineteenth and twentieth centuries would continuously change. Congregational singing in unison became a central part of Jewish worship; known in German under the umbrella term *Synagogengesang* (synagogue song), it emphasizes commonality and processes of exchange that are key elements of the reforms. Larger communities employed a (semi-)professional chorus (depending on the congregation, either mixed voices or male voices only, to avoid *kol isha*, the prohibition against women singing in the presence of men) and later sometimes hired instrumentalists as well.

Torah cantillation was only practiced in a very few Reform congregations in Germany, because the reformers believed that cantillation and biblical chant no longer had validity, as both were a "post-biblical invention."[1] Besides, the Reform movement found cantillation to be antiquated and unattractive, and not in line with the current fashion of synagogue song. The elimination of selected elements from worship was common, indeed, as is also evident in the prayer *Kol Nidre*, which from the mid-nineteenth century onward was substituted by Psalm 130 or replaced with new texts that redigested its basic themes through key words and some original phrases, albeit using the traditional melody. If until the nineteenth century vocal music was mostly orally transmitted, from the early nineteenth century it began to be written down, thereby pressed into the "novel" scheme of notation and regular meter. Hence the improvisation inherent to *hazzanut* slowly vanished, replaced by rhythmically and structurally fixed melodies. Classical and Romantic styles began to infiltrate the structure and expression of synagogue music, raising questions concerning the authenticity of the new compositions. One of the most strident markers of a new musical identity, however, was the organ as accompaniment and solo instrument.

The orientation towards Western models of music had profound consequences for synagogue music, and became tied to new movements and branches of Judaism variously known also as Progressive, Reform, Liberal, or Neolog. The reform of synagogue music was a long and gradual process, bound up in complex ways with cultural, societal, and religious changes that originated in central Europe (in England it made little headway) and extended eastwards to Hungary, Bohemia, Galicia, Russia, and Poland, and spread to parts of North America, South America, and the Caribbean, and as far as South Africa.

The origins of reform in the early nineteenth century

During the first half of the nineteenth century musical reforms in Jewish worship services were limited to only a few synagogues in Germany. The banker Israel Jacobson (1769–1863), a vehement advocate of reforms who aimed at improving the social position of the Jews through education, opened schools in Seesen and Kassel in Westphalia. He also presided over the Royal Westphalian Consistory of the Israelites (1808–13), which in 1810 published an official pronouncement roughly equivalent to today's synagogue bylaws, which among other things details the role and function of music, promoting order and decorum.[2] For the Kassel school, Jacobson arranged well-known Protestant melodies to be sung to Hebrew texts, with the music set from right to left. The synagogue of his school for Jewish children at Seesen saw the installment of an organ in July 1810. The first reformed Jewish worship took place there with choral music following Protestant models.[3] Upon moving to Berlin in 1815, Jacobson continued holding Reform services in his house with organ music and choral and congregational singing in German. These changes in synagogue music joined liturgical changes: German-language sermons filled the void of the abbreviated or omitted Torah readings. These services proved to be so popular that they continued in the much larger home of Jacob Herz Beer (1769–1825; father of the composer Giacomo Meyerbeer, 1791–1864).

After the Jewish community appealed to Emperor Friedrich Wilhelm III to close the private synagogue, on the grounds that the Reform schism was detrimental to the established rights of Judaism, the Prussian government banned the service, reasoning that prayer meetings outside of community synagogues were not allowed in accordance with existing regulations. Two years later, in December 1817, preacher Eduard Kley (1789–1867) brought the reforms from Berlin to Hamburg, where he co-founded the New Israelite Temple Association. Its synagogue, the First Temple on Brunnenstraße, was consecrated on October 18, 1818. The First Temple brought a completely new order to the worship service, including the official introduction of the sermon, German-language hymnal, and choral music provided by a boys' choir with organ accompaniment for the first time in a synagogue open to the public (as opposed to school or private services); a loft had been specially built for the organ and choir. Cantillation practices, however, are not transmitted.

Moderate approaches: the cantor and his repertoire

Even as the First Temple on Brunnenstraße adopted the organ, early radical reforms elsewhere in Germany initially stalled due to the introduction of the instrument, which provoked controversies that will be discussed below, while other countries and communities embraced more moderate reforms. Beginning in 1819, the Viennese Jews began to demand modernization of their religious service. In addition to a preacher, a cantor, an organist, choir singers, and choirboys, the reformers wanted to build an attractive place for worship and to develop a prayer book, thus following the German radical reforms beginning in 1810. But the need both to work together with traditionalists and to deal with the opposition in the government forced the Viennese reformers to compromise on some of the earliest proposed reforms. In the end, no radical changes were introduced in Vienna, in contrast to Germany, due to protests from parts of the community. In fact, the Viennese Jewish community rejected the changes that were gaining popularity in Germany. Indeed, the most notable sign that Vienna's Jews compromised on their proposed reforms was the absence of the most radical marker of modernization, the organ. In 1821, some Jewish leaders had hinted that an organ should be used in Vienna, but resistance was fierce and the decision was not carried out. Still, in the following years, the formation of a high-quality musical program was of special concern to the community.

With the appointment of Salomon Sulzer (1804–90) as Obercantor of the newly consecrated Stadttempel in 1826, the Viennese reformers found their musical architect. Together with the preacher Isaac Noah Mannheimer (1793–1865), Sulzer developed what is commonly known as the Viennese rite. Although it differed from prevalent customs, the new service balanced traditional and modernizing elements while adhering to Jewish law. It was characterized by what the reformers viewed as greater decorum and aesthetically pleasing music. The new service included edifying sermons in German, while the Hebrew language and the traditional text of the prayers for the service were retained in a slightly abbreviated liturgy. Sulzer and Mannheimer also revised certain texts, regulated their Ashkenazic pronunciation, and adapted them to traditional prayer melodies. Sulzer preserved the custom of employing two assistants, but did not use them in the common style of the *meshorerim* (singers who traditionally serve to support the *hazzan*, accompanying him in parallel intervals and providing vocal interludes). He also worked with a chorus of Jewish boys and young adolescents.

Initially, Sulzer faced an almost insurmountable task. There was hardly any available liturgical repertoire that would have fit the new aesthetic and liturgical ideals. There was no immediate example on which to model his arrangements, perhaps with the exception of the work of the famous *hazzan* Israel Lovy (1773–1832) who at the time worked in Paris.[4] Thus Sulzer had to create a suitable repertoire. He began by selecting traditional melodies of the Ashkenazic *minhag* (custom) and reinterpreted them by renouncing the coloraturas in the cantorial solo, and the imitation, absorption, or parody of late Baroque instrumental and operatic music, or dance melodies that had "pervaded" *hazzanut*. He adapted these melodies for solo and chorus in accordance with the harmonic rules of his time – later his application of major and minor tonality to melodies in original Jewish modes was heavily criticized.

Sulzer produced a significant written repertory of liturgical music, bringing into motion a musical development with a lasting effect on synagogues worldwide. By 1838, the first part of this endeavor was nearly finished: *Schir Zion I.* Although it initially existed only in autograph form, various communities in Europe were well aware of the collection in its early stages, among them Berlin, Copenhagen, and Stuttgart. By September 1840, the final version of *Schir Zion I* appeared in print, self-published by Sulzer, and perhaps motivated by increasing demand from congregations and *hazzanim* for his scores and the competing publication of the collection assembled by cantor and teacher Maier Kohn, *Vollständiger Jahrgang von Terzett- und Chorgesängen der Synagoge in München.*[5]

Schir Zion I consists of 159 cantorial solos and five- to eight-part choral pieces for Sabbath, the Three Pilgrimage Festivals, the High Holidays, Purim, and Tisha B'Av, as well as miscellaneous occasions such as bar mitzvahs and weddings. Sulzer included thirty-six traditional and eighty-six newly composed melodies. While *Schir Zion* displays a variety of musical practices and settings, Sulzer often treats the chorus as a nucleus of the congregation and the solos as an extension of the cantor's soloistic role in the service. The solos receive harmonic accompaniment through choral setting with a vocally light texture, while the congregational responses are rendered by the chorus, an approach criticized by Mannheimer, who wished for more congregational participation in the liturgy through singing. For the remaining thirty-seven numbers, Sulzer commissioned seven different composers, most of them not Jewish, among whom were Joseph Drechsler (1782–1852), Franz Schubert (1797–1828), and Ignaz, Ritter von Seyfried (1776–1841). As most of them were not familiar with the Hebrew language, Sulzer or another member of the Jewish community must have instructed them in Hebrew text declamation, or provided them with a text that indicated metrical patterns and also included translation. Unusual as it may seem, the contributions by non-Jewish composers do not stand alone and have immediate precedence in the *Vollständiger Jahrgang von Terzett- und Chorgesängen der Synagoge in München*.

Schir Zion I is one of the first attempts to balance reform and tradition in an artistically motivated edition of synagogue song. Sulzer remained rooted in the past by setting texts in Hebrew only, yet he departed by destroying the free rhythmic styles of ḥazzanut, forcing it into regular meter that does not fit Hebrew prosody. He provided clean-cut melodic lines without excessive coloratura, and refrained from repeating words, thus giving the meaning of the text the highest priority. Indeed, his sensible phrasing and word stress reveals his deep knowledge of the text. Yet he broke with the past when he began to harmonize these melodies largely according to the rules of Western tonality, thus compromising the modality of traditional ḥazzanut. Many of the settings relate to the choral style of the period, strongly influenced by contemporaneous secular and ecclesiastical styles. What remained traditionally Jewish was the stylized cantorial recitative and the responsorial alternation between cantor and choir or congregation.

As *Schir Zion I* became a great success in Europe and beyond, Sulzer conceived a second part, which finally appeared in print in 1865. It provided pieces for all occasions including special services, and offered some organ and harp accompaniment to serve as "a mediatory mission between the past and the future."[6] Only in the second volume of *Schir Zion* did the mature Sulzer approach traditional ḥazzanut for cantor and choir on a larger scale, as seen in many of the cantorial solos, but also in certain choral settings. To date, *Schir Zion* has gone through several editions.[7] Numerous selections from the monumental *Schir Zion* were, and still are, sung throughout the occidental Jewish world, and served as models for countless Jewish composers.

Embracing moderate reform as a bridge from the old to the new, Sulzer made further proposals of a musical, liturgical, and pedagogical nature at the 1869 First Jewish Synod in Leipzig: the main pieces of the Hebrew service shall be sung in the same melody in all synagogues; multi-part choral singing and other musical performances are recommendable, but only where sufficient forces exist; singing in unison is preferable; instrumental accompaniment of synagogue song shall be adopted everywhere; secular music shall be excluded. The Kaddish prayer shall be spoken by the mourners only once and with the addition of a sentence that remembers the deceased relative; the weekly chapters of the Torah should be divided into multiple parts to be read across various days of the week; calling the community to the Torah, which should awake the word of God, shall be abolished. Sulzer also encouraged communities to teach Jewish pupils liturgical singing and proposed the establishment of schools for the training of cantors. Sulzer's proposals met with weak response, and only some of them gained acceptance. At the Second Jewish Synod in Augsburg, in 1871, his visions regarding the education of cantors were approved.[8]

Through his position as Obercantor, Sulzer also redefined the position of the *ḥazzan*, bringing concern and attention to issues of vocal technique. The new type of "*ḥazzan*" was schooled in traditional Jewish learning, Western music, music theory, and composition. Sulzer also introduced a declamatory style of singing, emphasizing the inner meaning of the liturgical word, in contrast to older *ḥazzanut*, which stressed the overall mood of the prayers or the particular liturgical occasion. It was Sulzer's style of singing that encouraged *ḥazzanim* from all over Europe to learn from him and ultimately disseminate his style far and wide. His students consisted of choirboys who worked closely with him and later became renowned cantors themselves, among them Alois Kaiser (1840–1908) and Moritz Goldstein (1840–1906), who later exerted significant influence on the Reform repertoires in the United States. Innumerable trained cantors came to Vienna to study with Sulzer, some at the request and expense of their own communities; the most famous of them were Moritz Deutsch of Breslau (1840–4), Louis Lewandowski (1821/23–94) and Abraham Jakob Lichtenstein of Berlin (1855), and Eduard Birnbaum of Königsberg (1874–7). Even eastern European cantors, particularly from the Odessa community, made their way to Vienna.

What is remarkable about the Sulzerian reforms is their reception and appeal. Sulzer's creative output became a model, and his compositions soon made their way across the ocean, becoming a standard part of the cantorial repertoire in many American synagogues. Even communities further east embraced some of the changes that took place in the West, most notably parts of Silesia, Cracow, Lemberg (Lviv), Königsberg (Kaliningrad), Odessa, and the St. Petersburg's Choral Synagogue. The extent to which the reforms were accepted differed from congregation to congregation. Königsberg, the capital of East Prussia, was a major link between central and eastern Europe and thus served as a meeting point between Jewish cultures, enabling the community to easily absorb changes that took place in the West. The Jewish community in Odessa, one of the largest and most flourishing in all of Russia until the Bolshevik Revolution, was equally receptive to Western Jewish culture and was home to the first liberal synagogue in the Russian Empire, the Brodsky Synagogue in Odessa, whose services had featured instrumental accompaniment since 1869. There is no doubt that Sulzer's approach to synagogue music was instrumental in creating a stylized and formal structure in these communities.

The organ and its controversies

As noted above, the reforms of the New Israelite Temple Association, and in particular the organ, set off fierce controversy within the community and beyond. The debates surrounding the introduction of the organ into the synagogue began with two responsa advocating it, *Nogah ha-Ẓedek* (Brightness of Righteousness, 1818) and *Or Nogah* (The Bright Light, 1818), and one rejecting it, *Eleh Divrei ha-Berit* (These are the Words of the Covenant, 1819). The *Nogah ha-Ẓedek*, published by the Austrian Talmudist and agent of the patrons of the First Temple Eliezer Liebermann, is a collection of the opinions of different European rabbis.[9] Originally composed in response to inquiries by Jacob Herz Beer, the collection is controversial in many respects. For one, Liebermann exaggerated the importance of some rabbis; for another he only published those views that permitted the organ without setting too many conditions on its use.[10] The advocates of the organ argued on the basis of *Shulḥan Arukh* (Oraḥ Ḥayyim 338:2 and 560:3) that organ playing by a non-Jew would be permitted for weddings or for the Sabbath. With regard to the general prohibition on music in the synagogue after the destruction of the Second Temple in Jerusalem by the Romans in 70 CE, they insisted that vocal music was allowed for religious purposes, and the reformers merely wished to extend this compromise to instrumental music. There was also a precedent for instrumental music in the synagogue from earlier periods, for example in Prague, Venice, Corfu, and Modena.[11] Finally, in *Nogah ha-Ẓedek* the organ is viewed as not explicitly Christian, since it is not played in all churches.

Following the *Nogah ha-Ẓedek* Liebermann wrote *Or Nogah*, in which he gives a lengthy and learned exposition of his own views in favor of changes, claiming that organ playing had been the Jewish custom in the Temple prior to the Christian adoption of the organ. In refutation of this book, the Hamburg rabbinate published the views of twenty-two prominent central European rabbis, *Eleh Divrei ha-Berit*. The collection also contained a declaration by the Hungarian rabbi and pioneer of religious reform, Aaron

Chorin, revoking his former opinion published in *Nogah ha-Zedek*. The rabbis argued that playing a musical instrument is prohibited on Sabbaths and holy days, if only because it might need to be adjusted or repaired, which would constitute forbidden work (*shevut*). Other concerns raised in *Eleh Divrei ha-Berit* were the general prohibition of any music in the synagogue as a sign of mourning for the destruction of the Second Temple, and the prohibition against imitating the worship of other religions. The opponents of the organ saw in its introduction a Christianization of the service and, with that, a loss of Jewish tradition and identity.

It was probably because of these early debates that few other Jewish congregations in the subsequent three decades followed the Hamburg model. One exception could be found in the United States, in the originally Sephardic congregation Kahal Kadosh Beth Elohim in Charleston, South Carolina. In 1824, some members of this congregation formed the Reform Society of Israelites to promote a shorter service, use of the vernacular, and choir and organ to beautify the service. But the older members of the congregation objected to the reforms. When, in 1841, the congregation – at this point no longer Sephardic in orientation – acquired an instrument (the first synagogue in the United States to do so) and used it at all liturgical celebrations, a dispute arose, and in 1844 the matter ended up in court. The decision ruled against the minority, who appealed the case; and the higher court affirmed the decision in 1846. The court held that being unable to decide the merits of this religious controversy, it must rely upon the judgment of the majority of the congregation. This affair led to the permanent breakup of the congregation.[12]

This example of an American congregation adopting the organ and other aspects of Reform was a rare case at this time. In other instances, efforts toward musical reform were only indirectly adopted at first. For example, at the Berlin synagogue on Heidereutergasse in 1837, violins were played at one service, and *meshorerim* imitated an orchestra. In this synagogue the installation of an organ was already being planned.[13] Concrete plans only materialized several decades later, however, when the congregation expanded to the Neue Synagoge on Oranienburger Straße.

During the early 1840s, when the Bingen Jewish community announced its intention to acquire an organ, it triggered broader and more formal discussions at the Second Rabbinical Conference held in Frankfurt am Main, July 15–28, 1845, concerning whether the organ could be permitted in Jewish worship services and who should play it.[14] These questions were once again debated under familiar banners of whether the organ was to be regarded as a neutral or a specifically Christian instrument, and whether it should be disallowed on the basis of the traditional mourning for the loss of the Second Temple.[15] The discussion closed with the statement that the organ was a foreign element in the Jewish liturgy and thus not quite recommended. The conference nevertheless consented to its use on the grounds that it was needed to encourage the mood of devotion. It also established a new order of service in which the organ was to be integrated.

The unanimous decision at the Second Rabbinical Conference to permit organ playing in Jewish worship services – not only on weekdays but also on the Sabbath and holy days – did little to stop further debates. For example, later in 1845, a group of rabbis from Upper Silesia sent an address opposing the organ to Zacharias Frankel (1801–71), the chief rabbi at Dresden, who had seceded from the conference on the grounds that its reforms were too radical. Despite the continuing controversy, a number of Jewish congregations began to acquire a pipe or reed organ, among the earliest being in Koblenz and Heidelberg in 1845, Berlin in 1846 and 1848, Hildesheim in 1850, Mainz in 1853, the Berlin Reform Congregation in 1854, Mannheim and Alzey in 1855, and Leipzig in 1856.

The introduction of the organ in synagogues was debated in other European countries as well. In France, the Consistoire Centrale, in a ruling of May 1846, assented to the use of the organ in synagogues in the celebration of all "religious" and "national" occasions. Thereafter, the synagogues of Besançon, Lille, Lyons, Marseilles, Nancy, and Strasbourg acquired instruments. Austria-Hungary (with the exception of Vienna, at first), Belgium, Denmark, Italy, Luxembourg, the Netherlands, and Sweden all followed, as did England and Switzerland. Though not every congregation used the organ on the Sabbath, it was at least played for weddings and other special occasions.

New debates began in 1861 with the plan for the construction of an organ in the Neue Synagoge on Oranienburger Straße in Berlin. The arguments in this case are representative of discussions of the issue in individual communities. The congregation's board of directors collected various responses to the permissibility of the organ. Two responsa by local rabbis, Elkan Rosenstein and Michael Sachs, rejected and condemned the introduction of the organ. The Berlin congregation then solicited the advice of a larger committee that included the music directors Julius Stern and Louis Lewandowski, and five well-known rabbis who were all in favor of the organ.

Lewandowski's statement takes musical aspects into consideration for the first time, rather than depending on the premise of *halakha* (Jewish law). In his response, *Gutachten betr. den Antrag wegen Bewilligung der Geldmittel zur Herstellung eines Orgelwerkes in der Neuen Synagoge* (1862), Lewandowski states that there is no greater appropriate support for the newly introduced congregational and choral singing, because only the organ is in a position to "control and to lead large masses in large spaces." Lewandowski's unambiguously positive attitude toward the organ as a synagogue instrument, and his strategically cunning arguments, may have had a strong influence on the decision to introduce it to the Berlin congregation.

The introduction of the organ in the Neue Synagoge at Oranienburger Straße in 1866 was the harbinger of a moment of change that became truly evident in June and July 1869, at the First Jewish Synod in Leipzig, headed by philosopher Moritz Lazarus and Rabbi Abraham Geiger. For the first time rabbis from all over Europe, the United States, and even the West Indies assembled to discuss the views and opinions of an "enlightened" liberal Judaism. The sole representative of the cantors and synagogue musicians in the synod was Sulzer, Obercantor at the Stadttempel in Vienna's Seitenstettengasse. According to the official report of the deliberations, in a well-received speech he argued in favor of the introduction of the organ.[16] The synod accepted Sulzer's conclusions, and at the Second Jewish Synod in Augsburg, 1871, the decision was broadened with the addition that even Jews were permitted to play the organ on Sabbath and holy days. Sulzer's stance seems surprising considering his role in developing the so-called Viennese rite, a moderate revision of the liturgy and traditional synagogue music. The most notable sign that Vienna's Jews eschewed drastic reforms in their quest for modernity was the absence of an organ in their new synagogue. Although the Viennese Jews rejected the ideological changes that were gaining popularity in German-Jewish communities, the question of Reform was nevertheless constantly being renewed. Though blocked at first, the organ eventually made its way into Vienna's Turkish Temple[17] and some Ashkenazic temples while the controversy continued.

Further repertoires

Sulzer's *Schir Zion* inspired other cantor-composers to enlarge and expand the repertoire for liberal or reformed synagogues. In 1843, the Synagogue de Nazareth in Paris hired Samuel Naumbourg (1817–80) in order to reorganize the worship service, which was in disarray after the death of Israel Lovy in 1832.[18] Upon his appointment Naumbourg immediately began compiling an anthology of traditional liturgical songs. He also commissioned songs for soloists and mixed chorus from professional composers. Among the hundreds of settings published in the first two volumes of his *Zemirot Yisrael* of 1847 and the third volume published in 1865 under the subtitle *Shirei Kodesh*, there were two or three by Charles-Valentin Alkan, né Morhange, one by Meyerbeer, and several by Fromental Halévy (1799–1866). His 1874 anthology *Aggudat Shirim* posthumously included three more Halévy settings.[19]

When Sulzer's style no longer fit the ideals of the Berlin community, Louis Lewandowski, one of the first to serve a synagogue as music director, conceived new liturgical pieces. While Sulzer's *Schir Zion*, for example, reflected his own liturgical practice by linking choral music with virtuoso cantorial solos, Lewandowski limited himself to much simpler means, at least initially. In *Kol Rinnah u-T'fillah* of 1871, which predominantly features the cantorial recitatives Sulzer had neglected, Lewandowski based his compositions on the liturgical tradition of the Old Synagogue, specifically the eastern European melodies he learned from Berlin's cantor Abraham Lichtenstein. The choir parts were all written for two voices, and the ambitus, or vocal range, was relatively narrow. Thus smaller congregations could easily use his work as well. The artistic conditions at the Neue Synagoge on Berlin's Oranienburger Straße inspired Lewandowski to create an entirely new service with organ accompaniment in two parts, *Toda W'simrah* (1876/82), a collection of the entire liturgical cycle for four-part mixed choir, solo cantor, and organ ad libitum. In *Toda W'simrah*, Lewandowski reproduced the traditional melodies in a more classical form and gave greater attention to organ music.

Of the communities farther east, the Brodsky Synagogue is noteworthy due to its unique position as a satellite, musical and otherwise, of German-Jewish culture. There, David Nowakowsky (1848–1921) served from 1869 on as choral director and assistant to ḥazzan Nissan Blumenthal. Nowakowsky composed a considerable amount of music during his tenure, with an especially productive period around 1891, after Blumenthal's retirement. His successor Pinchas Minkowsky was more supportive of Nowakowsky's emerging style and included the repertoire in the religious service. Nowakowsky's output was vast; among his over 1200 works are oratorios, sacred chamber music, and choral works with instrumental accompaniment. Nowakowsky employed a variety of vocal combinations (with choral textures of five to eight voices predominating) and experimented with techniques of counterpoint and fugue. Only two volumes of his liturgical compositions were published during his lifetime, *Schlussgebet für Jom-Kippur für Cantor Solo und gemischten Chor* (1895) and *Gebete und Gesänge zum Eingang des Sabbath für Cantor Solo und Chor, mit und ohne Orgelbegleitung* (1901). For solo organ, Nowakowsky composed approximately 100 pieces of three basic types: music for the Jewish service, music for concert settings, and compositional exercises.[20]

In the US, Alois Kaiser joined forces with two fellow immigrant cantors, Moritz Goldstein and Samuel Welsch (1835–1901), to compile, arrange, and edit a four-volume anthology of music for the American Synagogue, *Zimrat Yah – Liturgic Songs, Consisting of Hebrew, English and German*

Psalms and Hymns, Systematically Arranged for the Jewish Rite with Organ Accompaniment (1873–86). *Zimrat Yah* contains compositions by all three compiler-editors, as well as a number of individual works from Sulzer, Naumbourg, and others – though often rearranged or re-adapted and given organ accompaniments where none existed in the original. Kaiser, who, beginning in 1866, served the congregation Oheib Shalom in Baltimore as cantor, established a solid role for the *ḥazzan* and served as president of the Society of American Cantors, which he founded in 1895. Commissioned by the Central Conference of American Rabbis (the rabbinical arm of the official Reform movement), Kaiser also created and edited a new unified hymnal, published in 1897, with adaptations from non-Jewish secular classical pieces by French, German, and English composers; some traditional tunes; and Kaiser's own contributions.[21] The *Union Hymnal* went through several subsequent editions that reflect the changing aesthetics and tastes of American Reform; the third edition of 1932 by Abraham W. Binder (1895–1967), music director at the Stephen S. Wise Free Synagogue in New York, leaned more toward traditional tunes.

Processes of change in synagogue music occurred throughout early modernity, particularly in the seventeenth and eighteenth centuries, but never in ways as radical, visible, and lasting as in the nineteenth century. Several stages of reform took place simultaneously in different communities, ranging from extreme acculturation to assimilatory tendencies that preserved some traditions. Although the organ's use was not widespread and was embraced by some congregations that did not consider themselves reformed, it nonetheless became a symbol for the schism between Orthodox and Reform. Choral music of different styles and arrangements, however, became an integral part of many synagogues' music.

By the early twentieth century the reform of synagogue music faced new challenges. If early reforms broke with older traditions by combining or replacing them with new and "foreign" elements, synagogue music in the subsequent century became increasingly pluralistic. While some communities adhered to the nineteenth-century repertoires, others embraced processes of a dissimilative nature by retrieving older traditions and integrating them into contemporary musical forms. The reasons that reformed music lost some importance in central Europe after 1945 are historic. In the US, however, social movements and folk music influenced Jewish liturgical music to grow in new directions, especially during the 1960s. An informal congregationally active mode of worship became popular, influenced to some extent by the worship style of Jewish summer camps with singalongs accompanied by guitar, in order to provide an ever-stronger sense of community.

Notes

1 See *Protokolle und Aktenstücke der zweiten Rabbinerversammlung* (Frankfurt am Main: E. Ullmann, 1845), 133.

2 This document is published in *Sulamith: Eine Zeitschrift zur Beförderung der Kultur und Humanität unter den Israeliten*, 3.1 (1810): 366–80.

3 The event is documented in an anonymous contemporary account; see "Feyerliche Einweihung des Jacobs-Tempels in Seesen," *Sulamith: Eine Zeitschrift zur Beförderung der Kultur und Humanität unter den Israeliten*, 3.4 (1810): 298–303.

4 There was a precedent of earlier composers aiming at combining Jewish tradition with contemporaneous musical aesthetics: Salamone Rossi (c. 1570–c. 1628) and Carlo Grossi (c. 1634–88) in Italy, Ludovico (Louis) Saladin (seventeenth century) in southern France, and Christian Joseph Lidarti (1730–after 1793) and Abraham Caceres (fl. 1718–38) in Amsterdam.

5 Announced in August 1938, this volume was published in September 1939 with settings of synagogue songs for three- and four-part chorus by prominent local musicians, both Jewish and non-Jewish. A digital copy of this volume can be found at http://sammlungen.ub.uni-frankfurt.de/freimann/content/titleinfo/1357314 (accessed March 1, 2014).

6 See Salomon Sulzer, "Vorwort (Zum II. Theile)," in *Schir Zion: Gesänge für den israelitischen Gottesdienst*, 2nd edn. (Frankfurt am Main: J. Kauffmann, 1922), 7.

7 Heavily edited by his youngest son Joseph, the second edition, of 1905, interlaces pieces from the two parts of *Schir Zion* together and adds optional organ accompaniments to the newly arranged choral settings. This revised edition served as the model for all subsequent issues. The fifth edition appeared in New York in 1954 on the occasion of the 150th anniversary of the Salomon's birth. The first critical edition of forty excerpts of *Schir Zion I* appeared in 1983 and is based on an earlier print of 1839.

8 See *Die Beschlüsse der ersten und zweiten israelitischen Synode* (Mainz: J. Gottleben'sche Buchdruckerei, 1871), 8.

9 The two collections *Nogah ha-Ẓedek* and *Eleh Divrei ha-Berit* are discussed in detail with focus on the Italian involvement in the Reform controversy by Lois C. Dubin, "The Rise and the Fall of the Italian Jewish Model in Germany: From Haskalah to Reform, 1780–1820," in Elisheva Carlebach, John M. Efron, and David N. Myers (eds.), *Jewish History and Jewish Memory: Essays in Honor of Yosef Hayim Yerushalmi*, Tauber Institute for the Study of European Jewry Series 29 (Hanover, NH: University Press of New England, 1998), 271–95.

10 See *ibid.*, 276–8.

11 For a detailed discussion of the Prague organ case, see David H. Ellenson, "A Disputed Precedent: The Prague Organ in 19th-Century Central-European Legal Literature and Polemics," *Leo Baeck Institute Yearbook*, 40 (1995): 251–64.

12 See in this connection the exhaustive study of Allan Tarshish, "The Charleston Organ Case," *American Jewish Historical Quarterly*, 54.4 (1965): 411–49.

13 See Eliezer Ehrenreich, "Der erste Synagogenchor in Berlin (Aus alten Akten)," *Gemeindeblatt der jüdischen Gemeinde zu Berlin*, 19 (February 1929): 66–7.

14 See *Protokolle und Aktenstücke*, 146.

15 *Ibid.*, 326. Although the argument of organ playing being work was and continued to be a general concern, the subject of who should supply the organ wind by means of bellow-blowing never came up in the early debates. Until the mid-nineteenth century manpower was the only means of operating the blowers, and it was not until the second half of the century that human efforts could be replaced by alternative mechanical systems and later by electricity. Treading the bellows was not considered a devotional part in Jewish worship, and may have been performed by a non-Jewish person employed to perform activities forbidden to Jews on the Sabbath, so perhaps rabbis never felt compelled to address this issue.

16 Sulzer, in contrast to Lewandowski, refers to the organ as having a function as a solo instrument in the Jewish worship service. For a detailed discussion of the repertoire for organ solo used in Jewish worship, see Tina Frühauf, *The Organ and Its Music in German-Jewish Culture* (Oxford University Press, 2009).

17 The organ of the Sephardic community in Vienna was played predominately at weddings. Further Sephardic congregations that adopted the organ, always with controversy, were those of Bayonne in France, London, and New York.

18 In 1822, the synagogue had introduced the use of a choir and organ and commissioned Israel Lovy to compose a new rendition of the service to compliment these reforms. These compositions for male chorus with organ accompaniment, along with other earlier works, were published in 1862 in the posthumous collection *Chants religieux, composés pour les prières hébraïques*.

19 For details on the French Reform, see Eric Werner, *A Voice Still Heard: The Sacred Songs of the Ashkenazic Jews* (University Park, PA: Pennsylvania State University Press, 1976), 199–205.

20 With the exception of the two volumes published during his lifetime, Nowakowsky left behind much of his oeuvre in manuscript form. The Nowakowski collection is held, in part, at the YIVO Institute for Jewish Research in New York, location number 1594, and in part at the Nowakowsky Foundation in California.

21 For details on hymnal reforms in the US, see Benjie-Ellen Schiller, "The Hymnal as an Index of Change in Reform Synagogues," in Lawrence A. Hoffman and Janet R. Walton (eds.), *Sacred Sound and Social Change: Liturgical Music in Jewish and Christian Experience* (University of Notre Dame Press, 1992), 187–212. For a general overview of nineteenth-century synagogue music, see in the same volume Geoffrey Goldberg, "Jewish Liturgical Music in the Wake of Nineteenth-Century Reform," 59–83.

13 Under pressure

Jewish art music, 1925–1945

LILY E. HIRSCH

The musicologist Anneliese Landau (1903–91) lectured on Jewish composition for Jewish audiences in Nazi Germany, within the Berlin Jewish Culture League (*Jüdischer Kulturbund*), which supported theater and music performances by and for Jews from 1933–41. Her focus was in many ways dictated by the Nazi context, and, more specifically, the Nazi in charge of the League, Hans Hinkel, who enforced the organization's national/racial orientation. In 1977, after her emigration and eventual work to establish serious engagement with classical music in Southern California,[1] she was asked to write a history of the Jewish contribution to music, a return in some ways to her work in Germany. She understandably hesitated: "I had just freed myself from evaluating composers and performers according to their birth and inheritance in a national sense – and now I should go back again and limit my outlook only [to] Jewishness."[2]

Landau's reluctance points to the problem of category in discussions of Jewish art music, 1925–45, underscored in blood by the Nazis. How do we explore music connected to Jewishness during an era disgraced by the Nazi regime's own circumscription of Jewish music – a musical persecution that went hand in hand with the segregation and extermination of Jewish people? Not only that, more recently the Holocaust itself has been viewed as a methodological pitfall, with the ability to overshadow or taint how we think about Jewish music. In *Historians of the Jews and the Holocaust*, David Engel examines a traditional separation between Jewish studies and the history of the Holocaust in academia. He credits this division in part to academic concerns about the Holocaust's power to divert "attention from how Jews themselves lived and what they created to the awful circumstances of their death."[3] Ismar Schorsch, former chancellor of the Jewish Theological Seminary of America, has voiced similar unease. The Holocaust, for him, represents a "stain of passivity and submissiveness" within Jewish history.[4] How can we reconstruct Jewish musical activities with direct connections to the Nazi era and thus this perceived overwhelming specter of murder?

With an awareness of these larger issues, this chapter traces moments of Jewish art music, 1925–45. I first outline the roles of Jewishness in musical activities immediately preceding the Nazi era, in Germany, the United States, and Russia. I then focus on the operation of the Jewish Culture League during the Third Reich and its debate on Jewish music. To close, I highlight the evolution of several composers' musical relationship to Jewishness during the Holocaust, in exile and internment. Essentialized thinking about Jews, and arguably Jewish music, worked toward murderous ends from 1925 to 1945. This period thus supports and extends Landau's concern about category while, yes, forcing us to confront Jewish victimization in the musical realm. And yet, in the moments I highlight, this period brings to the fore the impossibility of any fixed definition of Jewish music in practice, underlining the negotiation surrounding Jewish music in this particular time and place. As I will show, it also offers examples of agency and choice for individuals composing in an evolving reality of extremes.

Degrees of choice

The Weimar era in Germany (1918–33) witnessed unprecedented innovation in the arts, propelled by prominent musicians with varying degrees of Jewish connection and self-identification. Arguably the greatest pianist and cellist of the early twentieth century, Artur Schnabel (1882–1951) and Emanuel Feuermann (1902–42), respectively, taught in Berlin during the late 1920s. Bruno Walter (1876–1962), who was famous across Europe, conducted the Leipzig Gewandhaus Orchestra, and Otto Klemperer (1885–1973) championed new music at Berlin's Kroll Opera. Arnold Schoenberg (1874–1951) and Kurt Weill (1900–50) composed in accordance with their distinct thinking about music and its purposes.

Berlin was the epicenter of much of this musical activity. Indeed, "Weimar was Berlin. Berlin Weimar."[5] But in Berlin, German Jews could also choose to contribute to Jewish-only endeavors – part of what some have termed a Jewish Renaissance.[6] During the 1920s, Jewish leaders in Berlin established the United Synagogue Choirs, the Society of the Friends of Jewish Music, and the Juwal Publishing Company for Jewish Music.[7] And there were also those individuals who worked to bridge these two porous circles, entangling Jewish with more mainstream trends, through the reform of synagogue music and reevaluation of the Jewish prayer service.[8] To this end, Heinrich Schalit (1886–1976), who took the position of music director and organist at the Munich synagogue in 1927, produced music both modern and anti-modern, building on tradition while responding to the groundbreaking compositional ideas of the time. Arno Nadel (1878–1943), composer, writer, and choir director of the Kottbusser Ufer Synagogue, saw Schoenberg's atonality as the perfect model in this respect. In 1923, he wrote, the "new music (especially Schoenberg!) attempts to free itself from the harmonic basis and to proceed in new contexts in ways similar to what we assumed of the ancient."[9] Weill and Weimar-era *Zeitoper* – opera that incorporated contemporary themes, popular music, and technology – served as similar inspiration for Hugo Adler (1894–1955), the chief cantor in Mannheim, in the composition of his Instructional Cantatas.[10]

But this musical invention was not without opposition. Anti-Semitism grew alongside Jewish involvement in cultural as well as commercial spheres. This hate was not of a single variety. For some, socioeconomic concerns inspired anti-Jewish attitudes.[11] For others, anti-Semitism was a cultural code. Jews were seen as a threat to social status, prestige, and cultural hegemony.[12] Even amid increasing anti-Semitism, though, German Jews enjoyed success and freedom, a freedom of choice. German Jews could participate in the era's general cultural creativity, embrace Jewish undertakings, or both, depending on their ideals.

German Jews enjoyed this tenuous freedom for slightly longer than Jews in Russia. James Loeffler, in this volume, has highlighted the contribution of the Society for Jewish Folk Music, founded in St. Petersburg in 1908 (see Chapter 11). Government support of Jewish national culture, however, began to fade in the late 1920s. By 1931, the state exercised total control of Soviet cultural life. At this time, private organizations, such as the Society's Moscow branch, were officially dissolved.[13] Individual artists were then subject to accusations of political crimes. Mikhail Gnesin (1883–1957), an original member of the Society, eventually lost close colleagues and even his own brother to arrest and execution. Gnesin himself sought a certain protection in composition centered on the folk music of other Soviet minorities, for a time shifting his musical agenda away from Jewish music.[14]

In the United States, on the other hand, attitudes toward Jewish identity in music were less overt. During the 1920s, a substantial block from within New York's International Composers' Guild (ICG, 1921), which supported modern American composition, left to join the newly formed League of Composers (1923), including Louis Gruenberg (1884–1964), who grew up in America though he was Russian-born, and Lazare Saminsky (1882–1959), another former member of the Society in St. Petersburg. Though historical explanations of the split have focused on the first American performance of Schoenberg's *Pierrot lunaire*, musicologist Rachel Mundy has recently brought to light the role of Jewishness in this rupture. She cites Virgil Thomson's reference to the new organization as "the League of Jewish Composers," given the prominence of Jewish composers among the founding group.[15] She ties this perception to a general xenophobia at the time. Though the US was heralded as the so-called land of immigrants, its government had actually sought to legislate against immigration in the early

1920s, particularly with the Immigration Act of 1924. Discourses surrounding anti-immigration in conjunction with a latent rhetoric of anti-Semitism played an implicit, if not explicit, role in American musical life during the 1920s and early 1930s. Aaron Copland (1900–90), who aligned with the League, was often depicted then as a "shrewd" commercial composer, recycling stereotypes of Jewish music making from the past.[16] For many during and after the Nazi era, the United States would seem a haven from such discrimination. The reality was far more complex.

Negotiation in segregation

In 1933, the Weimar era's promise of choice ended for those termed Jewish. On January 30, Adolf Hitler was officially appointed chancellor. His party, the National Socialist German Worker's Party, or NSDAP, continued to grow in power during the early months of 1933. With the burning of the Reichstag on February 27, Hitler had the state of emergency he needed to demolish parliamentary government. One of the earliest results was the Law for the Reconstitution of the Civil Service of April 7, 1933, passed six days after a boycott of Jewish businesses. By means of the Law's Aryan paragraph, "civil servants who are not of Aryan ancestry" were to be dismissed. This measure effectively prevented so-called non-Aryans – defined at that time as any person descended from a Jewish parent or grandparent – from holding positions in the public sphere, at state-run music conservatories, opera houses, concert halls, and theaters.

Even before this legislation, there were high-profile acts to exclude "non-Aryan" musicians. On March 16, Bruno Walter arrived for rehearsal at the Gewandhaus only to find himself locked out. Fearing he might have similar problems at an upcoming concert in Berlin with the Philharmonic Orchestra, Walter requested police protection for the event. His request was denied and it was made clear that his safety was in jeopardy. Walter Funk, the secretary in the Propaganda Ministry, explained that the concert could only take place with an Aryan conductor. And it did, with Richard Strauss in Walter's place.[17] Walter canceled his German engagements and eventually emigrated from Austria to the United States.

At this time, Schoenberg was similarly forced to resign from his position in Berlin at the Prussian Academy and leave Germany. Many composers, including Schoenberg, ended up in the United States, mostly in New York or Southern California: Erich Wolfgang Korngold (1897–1957), Kurt Weill, Paul Hindemith (1895–1963), Ernst Toch (1887–1964), Ernst Křenek (1900–91), Paul Dessau (1894–1979), and Alexander von Zemlinsky (1871–1942), among others. Some, like Korngold and Weill, in many ways prospered there.[18] Korngold enjoyed success composing for films in Hollywood while Weill thrived with work on Broadway. (Both have, however, paid a price in reception, with condemnations of their participation in "mass culture" and accusations of "selling out.")[19] Others, such as Schoenberg, who earned a formidable reputation as a teacher if not a composer, endured a notoriously contentious professional relationship with the University of California, Los Angeles, and the city of Los Angeles in general.[20] Landau recalls visiting him during those years: "No kindness or any form of hospita[lity] expected me at Schoenberg's house. I felt like an intruder into the sanctuary of an embittered man."[21] Hanns Eisler (1898–1962), a former student of Schoenberg, struggled for different reasons in the United States. He emigrated only to fall victim to a comparable climate of intolerance, encouraged by Senator Joseph McCarthy's Communist witch-hunts. In 1948, he decided to return to the newly formed German Democratic Republic.[22]

Though I stress the United States, displaced Jews were hardly confined to a single destination; they found themselves exiled in and out of Germany, far and wide, including, in one example, Shanghai, as the ethnomusicologist Tang Yating has recorded. After Kristallnacht in 1938, Jewish refugees arrived as a third wave to the Chinese city and brought with them musical traditions from the Reform service that would prove influential.[23] Ethnomusicologist Philip V. Bohlman identifies the publication of books of Jewish repertory in the 1930s as an essential means for emigrants from Germany to reestablish and reconstruct cultural activities. He specifically notes their importance in Israel as well as North and South America.[24]

The Nazi regime generally banned the music left behind by composers termed Jewish as well as music by those deceased, such as Felix Mendelssohn (1809–47), Giacomo Meyerbeer (1791–1864), and Gustav Mahler (1860–1911). With some degree of error, given a certain measure of disorganization and competition within Nazi offices, anything that could be called Jewish music disappeared from "Aryan" concert venues. Accepted Germans were only allowed a glimpse into the rich world of forbidden music in 1938, at the propaganda exhibition "Entartete Musik" (Degenerate Music), presented in conjunction with the first "Reichsmusiktage" (Reich Music Days) in Düsseldorf by Hans Severus Ziegler, the director of the German National Theatre at Weimar. Modeled after Munich's "Degenerate Art" exhibit, the music exhibition reused the German term "Entartung," which blends in definition a Darwinian sense of the decline of the species with an immoral quality of degeneration or pollution.[25] Emblematic of the event was its booklet cover, emblazoned with what Michael H. Kater has described as "a monkeylike Negro," wearing the Star of David and playing the saxophone.[26] This image hinted, not so subtly, at Ernst Křenek's opera *Jonny spielt auf!*

(Johnny Strikes Up), a 1927 hit that incorporated the composer's understanding of jazz. Nationalistic writers at the time despised jazz for its link
with Africans or African-Americans and the United States, its sexual power,
and the unsuitability of jazz rhythms for marching. When Nazi scientists
concluded that Jews had large proportions of "negroid blood," enemies of
jazz also had enough justification to link jazz with the Jews, connecting in
some ways the non-Jewish Křenek with Jewish music.[27]

Much of the music featured in Düsseldorf did have one other platform
in Germany, beyond the exhibition: the Jewish Culture League. This organization, in which Landau worked until her emigration, was the musical
and theatrical home for Jewish musicians, actors, and audience members
that had remained for a variety of reasons. Michael Haas compares the
League to four Austrian musical groups: the Hakoah Orchestra, Jewish
Song Society, Symphony Orchestra of the League of Jewish Austrian Front
Soldiers, and Society for the Promotion of Jewish Music, which eventually
led the repertoire programming of the other three ensembles, though it was
established last, in 1927. These groups were created before the League in
Germany, with ties to the goals of the St. Petersburg Society. As Haas notes,
however, all five organizations performed a restricted repertoire. Until its
dissolution in 1939, a year after Austria's Annexation, the Society for the
Promotion of Jewish Music also met in protected circles in private homes,
which were likewise venues of choice and necessity in Germany.[28] But the
League in Germany, given its direct cooperation from the start with the
Nazi government – on matters large and small, from repertoire to venue
and promotion – offers a unique lens onto notions of Jewish music at the
time, as well as an extreme example of the mediation surrounding Jewish
music during this time of tremendous stress.

Kurt Baumann (1907–83), a former director's assistant in Berlin, and
Kurt Singer (1885–1944), a physician, musicologist, and the director of the
Doctors' Chorus in Berlin, developed the initial plan for the League, to be set
in Berlin, in the early months of 1933.[29] The Nazi administrator Hans Hinkel
supported the plan for several reasons: the League operated within the Nazi
propaganda machine;[30] the League functioned as a mechanism of local
social control; and, with the requirement that the League perform Jewish
works – backed by the censorship of so-called Aryan composers – the League
represented a means for the regime to end Jewish cultural appropriation
and perceived degradation of the German masterworks.

The assimilated League leaders, however, hoped simply to offer unem-
ployed Jewish musicians a means of income and a place of solace. They thus
did not initially focus on a Jewish repertoire. To some, such a repertoire
was, in fact, at odds with their sense of Germanness and threatened to turn
their Jewish organization into a ghetto. From the very start, German Zionist

writers demanded that the League confront the changing situation of Jews in Germany and the need for a repertoire connected to Jewishness. The conflict here, which the heterogeneous Jewish public only compounded, in part, explains why League leaders did not follow the example of other organizations dedicated to Jewish music, such as the St. Petersburg Society. The League lacked support for similar work but also the time. In September 1936, after three years of debate about their repertoire and Jewish music, Singer convened, at the Nazi regime's insistence, the Jewish Culture League Conference. Though League branches had been established in most major cities in Germany by this time, the conference took place in Berlin, given the centrality of the original branch in repertoire programming.

In his presentation at the conference on Jewish liturgical music and Jewish folk song, Arno Nadel insisted that "authentic Jewish music" (echte jüdische Musik) was Jewish folk song, but especially music for the synagogue.[31] Synagogue music was privileged above Jewish folk song, in part, because the authenticity of Jewish folk music, in the absence of a common Jewish nation, was questionable. Karl Adler (1890–1973), a leader in the artistic community in Stuttgart,[32] in his speech on Jewish choral music, also confronted this absence when he argued that the only logical criteria for Jewish choral music were "the religious [tradition], the language, the land" (das Religiöse, die Sprache, das Land).[33] In so doing, he further indexed a Zionist position that Jewish music could not exist outside Palestine, a position that could have effectively rendered impossible the League's immediate performance needs. But Joachim Prinz (1902–88), a Zionist rabbi, in his speech at the conference on Jewish theater, had offered a solution: he contended that without a common land, the League could only have a "national-pedagogical" function – building "a bridge from a denationalized Jewry, living remote from Jewish prime sources, to Jewish life."[34] In other words, the League could not perform authentic Jewish art, but could encourage Jewish awareness, which could foster future Jewish cultural activities in Palestine. In his presentation, Adler did not advance the same conclusion. Though he restated Prinz's basis for such a conviction, he also explained that he could "feel something" in the creations of Jews[35] – an insinuation that implies a sweeping definition of Jewish music as the composition of Jewish composers.

Anneliese Landau's speech on Jewish art song reiterated this Zionist position that Jewish music did not yet exist. But she also offered a practical course of action by accepting all art songs created by composers with Jewish roots as Jewish music. She then betrayed both of these positions by suggesting a sliding scale of Jewishness, as she discussed the songs of Mendelssohn, Meyerbeer, and Jacques Offenbach (1819–80). She explained, "These songs have nothing to do with the Jewishness of their composers. They grow from the atmosphere of the country in which they were written."[36] In contrast she listed composers such as Joel Engel (1868–1927), Heinrich Schalit, Darius Milhaud (1892–1974), and Ernest Bloch (1880–1959), and explained that, within the twentieth-century art song tradition, these composers created Jewish *Lieder* "in complete consciousness by Jews for Jews" (im völligen Bewusstsein von Juden für Juden).[37]

Hans Nathan (1910–89), a professor of musicology and music critic,[38] in his speech, similarly distinguished between the music of various Jewish composers through the organization of his speech in two parts: "Jewish orchestra and chamber music" and "General literature." Under the category of "Jewish orchestra and chamber music," he again recognized Bloch and Schalit. Under "general literature," he discussed composers of Jewish origin such as Mendelssohn and Offenbach, who he did not believe displayed Jewish musical inclinations.[39] Of Mendelssohn, he stated simply that the composer was the "purest German classicist" (reinster deutscher Klassicist).[40]

Neither Landau nor Nathan explained the grounds for their separate categorization of Jewish composers – why for example the music of Mendelssohn, the grandson of the great Jewish philosopher Moses Mendelssohn (1729–86), was not seen as Jewish art at the time – and the Jewish Culture League Conference ended with no definitive criteria of Jewish music. What the League ultimately performed then was the result of compromise. And in practice, the League actually performed and adopted certain works by non-Jewish composers as though they were Jewish, including, for example, several Handelian oratorios based on Old Testament texts and Schubert's setting of Psalm 92 to the Hebrew text.[41]

As conditions worsened for Jews in Germany, League leaders shifted their attention from notions of a national repertoire to a repertoire of entertainment and diversion. The debate on Jewish music would have to continue or begin anew elsewhere – as the German Jewish composer Stefan Wolpe (1902–72), for one, would ensure with his lecture "What is Jewish Music?" on February 29, 1940, at the invitation of the Jewish Music Forum of the Society for the Advancement of Jewish Musical Culture in New York. In March 1939, Wolpe had given a talk to the same organization, which was then called the MAILAMM (an acronym for the Hebrew for America-Palestine Institute of Musical Sciences). The MAILAMM was founded in 1931 by Joseph Achron (1886–1943), Lazare Saminsky, Solomon Rosowsky (1878–1962), Jacob Weinberg (1879–1956), and Joseph Yasser (1893–1981), and had some ties to the World Centre for Jewish Music in Palestine, which existed between 1936–40.[42] The group was reorganized and renamed the Jewish Music Forum in November 1939. In "What is Jewish Music?" Wolpe challenged those who even asked the title's question, accusing them of attempting to justify their status as Jewish composers. He then explored a tension between spontaneous and formulaic approaches to the development of national music, based in part on his experience in Palestine after his emigration from Germany.[43] The debate on Jewish music had thereby shifted in an evolving context. But, within the League, this debate represents a unique look at ideas of Jewish music under pressure. This pressure worked in unique ways on the level of the individual as well.

Shifting focus

Just as repertoire negotiations changed during the early years of the Third Reich, so too did the compositional program of individual composers. During the Holocaust, we see evidence of this evolution in internment and exile. The composer Viktor Ullmann (1898–1944), for example, turned inward by composing according to a more personal musical aesthetic during the early 1940s, while imprisoned in Terezín, along with the composers Pavel Haas (1899–1944), Gideon Klein (1919–45), and Hans Krása (1899–1944), the latter of whom composed the children's opera *Brundibár* in 1938, performed forty-four times in internment. Showcasing its artistic activities, among other techniques, the Nazi regime used Terezín, renamed Theresienstadt, as a "show camp," to deceive foreign visitors, including the Red Cross, by artificially staging a better life for prisoners. The Nazis took this strategy to the next level in the propaganda film centered in Terezín, *Der Führer schenkt den Juden eine Stadt* (The Führer Gives the Jews a City, 1944).[44]

Born in the Czech Republic in 1898, Ullmann studied law at Vienna University. During his student days, however, he also enrolled in Schoenberg's composition seminar. After ending his career as a law student, he worked with Zemlinsky at the Neues Deutsches Theater in Prague. He went on to excel as a conductor and composer, incorporating into his compositions a multitude of styles and ideas – the atonality of Schoenberg and exploration of the fringes of functional tonal harmony. After he arrived in Terezín on September 8, 1942, however, he became increasingly aware of his Jewish identity and arranged Hebrew and Yiddish songs. He also wrote the one-act opera *Der Kaiser von Atlantis*. Composed to a libretto by the poet and fellow inmate Peter Kien, the work presents the evil Emperor Überall (a stand-in for Hitler) and his manipulation of Death. Ullmann made the connections between life and music explicit with the inclusion of various musical quotations, including the Nazi anthem "Deutschland, Deutschland über alles."[45] Complementing, in some ways, the strangely positive American reception of Terezín,[46] Death ultimately ends the rule of Überall himself – a triumph for all in art, if not life.

For our purposes, Ullmann's seven piano sonatas are perhaps the most instructive. Ullmann wrote the first four before his imprisonment. The composer described the first, of 1936, as follows: "The principal subjects in three tonalities . . . [but] what apparently is happening is the linking of the twelve tonalities and their related minor keys. It seems that I was always striving for a 12-tone system on a tonal basis, similar to the merging of major and minor keys."[47] The following three sonatas, which were similarly complex, were dedicated, respectively, to Hans Büchenbucher, the president of the Anthroposophical Society in Germany at the time; the Hungarian pianist Juliette Arányi; and Alice Herz-Sommer, an active pianist in Czechoslovakia and Germany before the war. The fifth sonata was composed in Terezín. This work, dedicated to Ullmann's wife, is joyful and, unlike the earlier sonatas, achieves a new tonal clarity. Ullmann completed the final sonata, dated August 22, 1944, just a few weeks before he was sent to Auschwitz on October 16 and murdered. The piece, dedicated to his children, has an uncharacteristic amount of autobiographical allusions, including references to Czech and Slovak national songs, Ullmann's earlier work, and arguably the composer's Jewish heritage with a Hebrew folk song.[48]

Another composer who seemed to respond to a new, radically altered existence was Rosebery d'Arguto (1890–1943). This Polish Jewish composer and choir director, born Martin Rosenberg, had changed his name professionally, effectively distancing himself from his Jewish roots. In 1939, he was sent to the Sachsenhausen concentration camp, which supported diverse musical activities, including an orchestra (most of the larger camps did – Buchenwald, Dachau, Flossenbürg, Mauthausen, and Auschwitz).[49] Though musicians in Terezín performed works by Jewish composers openly, Aleksander Kulisiewicz (1918–82), an invaluable collector of music from Sachsenhausen, maintained that works by Jewish and Polish composers were smuggled into the orchestra's repertoire in Sachsenhausen.[50] While it seems unlikely that the authorities would have been unaware of this effort, Kulisiewicz's recollection points to differences between the musical activities in the various concentration camps and ghettos as well as the different functions of music therein – positive and negative.[51] After all, there was no uniform Nazi organization of music during the final years of the Third Reich.

Before his transport to Auschwitz at the end of 1942, D'Arguto acted as a choir director in Sachsenhausen, continuing in some ways his previous work. For his group, he composed "Juedischer Todessang" (Jewish Death Song), based on an old Yiddish song "Tsen brider" (Ten Brothers), which recounts the death of all the brothers but one. Though d'Arguto died in Auschwitz, Kulisiewicz survived and later made d'Arguto's song central to his performance career.[52] Musicologist Shirli Gilbert notes the significance of the song within d'Arguto's ouevre: "It is interesting that the experience of incarceration led someone like d'Arguto – a non-practicing Jew who had gone so far as to de-Judaize his name – to write an explicitly Jewish lament."[53]

An even more complicated example of personal response is Gnesin's Piano Trio, op. 63, "In Memory of Our Murdered Children" of 1943. Loeffler calls the piece, which was composed in Russia, the "earliest and certainly the most significant Soviet wartime composition about the Holocaust."[54] But the Jewishness of "our murdered children" remains enigmatic. Gnesin may have been aware of the Nazi mass murder of Soviet Jews in the Ukraine, which was at the time entering the collective consciousness of Soviet society.[55] The titular children, however, must have also included Gnesin's own son, Fabi, who had recently died. Musically, Gnesin did not incorporate elements stereotypically associated with Jewishness, remaining true in some ways to his earlier move away from Jewish music. But he did quote a well-known Yiddish folk song "Amol iz geven a yidele" (There Once Was a Little Jew). Loeffler ultimately insists, in this work, "Gnesin encoded his Jewish suffering inside the Soviet war experience."[56]

Other composers in the 1930s and 1940s, in varying states of exile in the United States, confronted Jewishness and/or their Jewish roots, or reached for music as some form of personal response or constructed comment. In Chapter 16, Amy Lynn Wlodarski discusses Schoenberg's *A Survivor from Warsaw* (1947), which, along with his *Kol Nidre* (1938), could be explored along these lines. Kurt Weill offers another case in point. America had always figured in Weill's compositional imagination. Though he could probably have remained in Paris, where he moved in 1933, he eventually relocated to the United States in 1935. Weill had considered himself German and was generally secular, and had even been critical of the Jewish diaspora in central Europe, and Germany especially.[57] Though Nazi persecution forced Weill to reflect upon his Jewish ancestry, he did not return to his family's religion, as Schoenberg did in 1933. He did, however, begin work on *The Eternal Road*, along with the dramatist Franz Werfel (1890–1945), the producer Max Reinhardt (1873–1943), and the American impresario Meyer Weisgal (1894–1977). All four men agreed in May 1934 that the work was to be "a musical biblical morality play to express the spiritual origin, the earliest mythical history and the eternal destiny of the Jewish people to whom they belong."[58] The piece also in some ways mirrored the Jews' situation during the early years of the Third Reich: at the start of the play, a rabbi warns his congregation that they are about to be expelled from the country they had long since called home. In the music, Weill was true to traditions of Hebrew cantillation in instructions for the rabbi's scriptural recitation, a compositional strategy absent from his previous work in Germany. The piece premiered in January 1937 at the Manhattan Opera House and lasted, according to the perhaps unreliable *New York Times* critic Brooks Atkinson, until three o'clock in the morning.[59]

Toward the end of his life, Weill also contributed to commemorations of the Holocaust.[60] A famous result, *We Will Never Die*, was a memorial to Hitler's Jewish victims, with music by Weill, staged in Madison Square Garden in March 1943. The climax was a recitation of the Mourner's Kaddish, in memory of the departed.[61]

The intention of composers with works pointing to the Holocaust or their own Jewish roots is rarely clear, complicated by an insurmountable distance between a composer's biography and his music. But composers at this time did respond in various ways to a rapidly changing context. This response was hardly passive or inevitable, but often an active choice. I will not recycle here clichés of resistance, which often pepper discussions of music during the Holocaust. Notions of resistance, after all, often serve contemporary agendas rather than accurate historical reconstruction.[62] But the compositional decisions I have featured, at the same time, cannot support simplistic accounts of victimization. Like the debate on Jewish music in the League, composers' compositional shifts at this time underscore variety, change, and contestation in music connected to Jewishness. Jewish art music, 1925–45, bears the burden of its horrific historical context while undermining the essential thinking on which so much of it was based.

Notes

1 Dorothy Lamb Crawford outlines the challenges to serious music making faced by the many composers who immigrated to the United States and eventually settled in Southern California. Chief among these was a general climate of anti-intellectualism, created by several factors: isolation encouraged by the climate, no established operatic or instrumental concert life, and political and social control of the city in the hands of white Republican Protestants from the Midwest and rural South, with little background in the arts. Dorothy Lamb Crawford, *A Windfall of Musicians: Hitler's Émigrés and Exiles in Southern California* (New Haven: Yale University Press, 2009), 25–8.

2 Anneliese Landau, Memoirs, donated to the author (unpublished), 150.

3 David Engel, *Historians of the Jews and the Holocaust* (Stanford University Press, 2010), 30.

4 *Ibid.*, 31.

5 Eric D. Weitz, *Weimar Germany: Promise and Tragedy* (Princeton University Press, 2007), 79.

6 See, for example, Michael Brenner, *The Renaissance of Jewish Culture in Weimar Germany* (New Haven: Yale University Press, 1996).

7 *Ibid.*, 161. The Juwal Publishing Company, which can be traced back to the Society for Jewish Folk Music in St. Petersburg, published a number of Jewish folk song arrangements. See Abraham Zvi Idelsohn, *Jewish Music in Its Historical Development* (New York: Henry Holt, 1929), 463–4; Jascha Nemtsov, *Die Neue Jüdische Schule in der Musik* (Wiesbaden: Harrassowitz, 2004), ch. 5.

8 Brenner, *Renaissance of Jewish Culture*, 155.

9 Arno Nadel, "Jüdische Musik," *Der Jude*, 7 (1923): 227–36 (235), translated in Brenner, *Renaissance of Jewish Culture*, 157.

10 Brenner, *Renaissance of Jewish Culture*, 157.

11 Amos Elon, *The Pity of It All: A History of the Jews in Germany, 1743–1933* (New York: Metropolitan Books, 2002), 356.

12 Oded Heilbronner, "From Antisemitic Peripheries to Antisemitic Centres: The Place of Antisemitism in Modern German History," *Journal of Contemporary History*, 35.4 (October 2000): 559–76 (563).

13 James Loeffler, *The Most Musical Nation: Jews and Culture in the Late Russian Empire* (New Haven: Yale University Press, 2010), 205.
14 *Ibid.*
15 Rachel Mundy, "The 'League of Jewish Composers' and American Music," *Musical Quarterly*, 96.1 (Spring 2013): 50–99 (56).
16 *Ibid.*, 62–4.
17 Erik Levi, *Music in the Third Reich* (New York: St. Martin's Press, 1994), 42.
18 Albrecht Dümling, "The Target of Racial Purity: The 'Degenerate Music' Exhibition in Düsseldorf, 1938," in Richard A. Etlin (ed.), *Art, Culture, and Media under the Third Reich* (University of Chicago Press, 2002), 43–72 (62).
19 Bryan Gilliam, "A Viennese Opera Composer in Hollywood: Korngold's Double Exile in America," in Reinhold Brinkmann and Christoph Wolff (eds.), *Driven into Paradise: The Musical Migration from Nazi Germany to the United States* (Berkeley and Los Angeles: University of California Press), 223–42 (223–4). This negative reception may have been exacerbated by European anti-Americanism. See Reinhold Brinkmann, "Reading a Letter," in Brinkmann and Wolff (eds.), *Driven into Paradise*, 3–20 (11).
20 Sabine Feisst, *Schoenberg's New World: The American Years* (Oxford University Press, 2011), 232.
21 Landau, *Memoirs*, 128.
22 Michael H. Kater, *The Twisted Muse: Musicians and Their Music in the Third Reich* (Oxford University Press, 1997), 109.
23 Tang Yating, "Reconstructing the Vanished Musical Life of the Shanghai Jewish Diaspora: A Report," *Ethnomusicology Forum*, 13.1 (January 2004): 101–18 (105–6).
24 Philip V. Bohlman, *Jewish Music and Modernity* (Oxford University Press, 2008), 92.
25 Albrecht Duemling, "Nationalism as Racism: Nazi Policies Towards Music," in *Banned by the Nazis: Entartete Musik*, program (Los Angeles Philharmonic Association, 1991), 5–6. Thank you to Steven Lacoste, archivist of the Los Angeles Philharmonic, for sending a copy of this program to the author.
26 Michael H. Kater, *Different Drummers: Jazz in the Culture of Nazi Germany* (Oxford University Press, 1992), 32.
27 *Ibid.*, 32.
28 Michael Haas, *Forbidden Music: The Jewish Composers Banned by the Nazis* (New Haven: Yale University Press, 2013), 235–7.
29 See Julius Bab's 1939 *Leben und Tod des deutschen Judentums*, ed. Klaus Siebenhaar (Berlin: Argon, 1988), 106. See also Margaret Limberg and Hubert Rübsaat (eds.), *Germans*

No More: Accounts of Jewish Everyday Life, 1933–1938, trans. Alan Nothnagle (New York: Berghahn Books, 2006), 183.
30 See Kater, *Twisted Muse*, 98; Levi, *Music in the Third Reich*, 51; and Herbert Freeden, *Jüdisches Theater in Nazideutschland* (Tübingen: J. C. B. Mohr, 1964), 51.
31 *Geschlossene Vorstellung: Der Jüdische Kulturbund in Deutschland 1933–1941*, ed. Akademie der Künste (Berlin: Akademie der Künste, 1992), 285. See also Arno Nadel, "Die Renaissance der synagogalen Musik," *Jüdische Rundschau*, September 28, 1928, 545. In this publication, he wrote, "Die synagogale Musik, das ist die Hauptmusik der Juden." Likewise, in "Jüdische Musik," he wrote, "jüdische Musik, das ist vorerst synagogale Musik" (227).
32 Adler assumed the leadership of the *Stuttgarter Jüdische Kunstgemeinschaft* after he was dismissed from his post at the Stuttgart Conservatory of Music in March 1933. Hannah Caplan and Belinda Rosenblatt (eds.), *International Biographical Dictionary of Central European Émigrés 1933–1945*, 3 vols. (Munich: K. G. Sauer, 1983), i:11.
33 *Geschlossene Vorstellung*, 289.
34 Quoted in Herbert Freeden, "A Jewish Theatre under the Swastika," *Year Book of the Leo Baeck Institute*, 1 (1956): 142–62 (149).
35 *Geschlossene Vorstellung*, 289.
36 "Diese Lieder haben gar nichts mit dem Judentum ihres Komponisten zu tun. Sie wachsen aus der Atmosphäre ihres Land, in dem sie geschrieben werden." *Geschlossene Vorstellung*, 291–2.
37 *Ibid.*, 292.
38 Caplan and Rosenblatt (eds.), *International Biographical Dictionary*, ii:845.
39 *Geschlossene Vorstellung*, 286.
40 Quoted in *ibid.*, 288.
41 See Lily E. Hirsch, *A Jewish Orchestra in Nazi Germany: Musical Politics and the Berlin Jewish Culture League* (Ann Arbor: University of Michigan Press, 2010).
42 Irene Heskes, "Shapers of American Jewish Music: Mailamm and the Jewish Music Forum, 1931–62," *American Music*, 15.3 (Autumn 1997): 305–20 (307). See also Philip V. Bohlman, *The World Centre for Jewish Music in Palestine 1936–1940: Jewish Musical Life on the Eve of World War II* (Oxford University Press, 1992).
43 Austin Clarkson, "What is Jewish Music?," *Contemporary Music Review*, 27.2/3 (April/June 2008): 179–92.
44 Eckhard John, "Music and Concentration Camps: An Approximation," *Journal of Musicological Research*, 20 (2001): 269–323 (286–9).

45 Joža Karas, *Music in Terezín, 1941–1945* (New York: Pendragon, 1985), 33–6.

46 Terezín has exercised a certain fascination in the United States, with redemptive narratives that stress the positive role of music within the camp, despite the negative memories of survivors. See Amy Wlodarski, "Musical Memories of Terezín in Transnational Perspective," in Tina Frühauf and Lily E. Hirsch (eds.), *Dislocated Memories: Jews, Music, and Postwar German Culture* (Oxford University Press, 2014), 57–72.

47 Ullmann to Karel Reiner, August 1938, quoted in John Paul Healey, *The Solo Piano Music of Viktor Ullmann: From Prague to the Holocaust*, D.M.A. thesis, University of Cincinnati (2001), 110–11.

48 See Karas, *Music in Terezín*, 111–17, 120; and Healey, *Solo Piano*, 224. This evolution was highlighted in Kristof Boucquet's presentation in London, England, on April 10, 2008, at the conference "The Impact of Nazism on Musical Development in the 20th Century."

49 Shirli Gilbert, *Music in the Holocaust: Confronting Life in the Nazi Ghettos and Camps* (Oxford: Clarendon Press, 2005), 130.

50 *Ibid.*, 131.

51 See, for example, John, "Music and Concentration Camps," 279.

52 See Barbara Milewski, "Remembering the Concentration Camps: Aleksander Kulisiewicz and His Concerts of Prisoners' Songs in the Federal Republic of Germany," in Frühauf and Hirsch (eds.), *Dislocated Memories*, 141–60 (144–6).

53 Gilbert, *Music in the Holocaust*, 139.

54 James Loeffler, "'In Memory of Our Murdered (Jewish) Children': Hearing the Holocaust in Soviet Jewish Culture," *Slavic Review*, 73.3 (Fall 2014): 585–611 (588).

55 *Ibid.*, 597.

56 *Ibid.*, 601.

57 Michael H. Kater, *Composers of the Nazi Era: Eight Portraits* (Oxford University Press, 2000), 80; Magnar Breivik, "From Surabaya to Ellis Island: On Two Versions of Kurt Weill's 'Surabaya-Johnny,'" in Erik Levi (ed.), *The Impact of Nazism on Twentieth-Century Music* (Vienna: Böhlau, 2014), 77–90 (77).

58 Quoted in Kater, *Composers of the Nazi Era*, 81.

59 Alexander L. Ringer, "Strangers in Strangers' Land: Werfel, Weill, and *The Eternal Road*," in Brinkmann and Wolff (eds.), *Driven into Paradise*, 243–60 (254–8).

60 Kater, *Composers of the Nazi Era*, 82.

61 *Ibid.*, 82.

62 See the introduction to Gilbert, *Music in the Holocaust*.

14 Music in the Yiddish theater and cinema, 1880–1950

MARK SLOBIN

Early formation of the music

The Yiddish theater and its offspring, the Yiddish-language film, flourished as modern urban entertainment genres in a short historic period, from the 1870s through the 1940s, declining sharply thereafter. It was a popular theater form that, like parallel non-Jewish media systems of its time, relied very heavily on music, alongside drama and comedy, to divert, instruct, and sometimes arouse a working-class audience. More so than many other audiences, Jews were often in a situation of extreme economic, social, and political pressure at a time of massive modernization that involved widespread emigration, immigration, and discrimination.

The historic tidal wave that struck this entertainment system doomed the enterprise: the end of mass immigration to the United States, wartime destruction of a shared transatlantic cultural space with Europe, the creation of the State of Israel as a shift of focus, and the widespread integration of North American Jewry into mainstream popular culture. It survives as remnants, nostalgic or ironic musical materials woven into new formats for successive generations of Jewish revivalists and non-Jewish cultural tourists attracted to the rich material of the golden age of Yiddish dramatic arts. A handful of songs, not reams of stilted dialogue or the performances of great actors and actresses, have endured, reappearing as part of "klezmer," in Yiddish-language training programs, or in printed and online songbooks, reference works, and blogs. Reconstruction and pastiche versions of theatrical material began in the 1970s and continue to offer current audiences some sense of this rich tradition.

Like so many streams of modern Jewish life, music of the Yiddish theater and cinema needs to be seen in at least four dimensions: 1) as the organic outgrowth of pre- and early modern Jewish expressive culture; 2) as an adaptation of co-territorial European and American performing arts genres, practices, and materials; 3) as a multiply sited Yiddish-culture form that featured both wide transnational circulation and strong regional variation; and 4) as a product of the newly emerging media of modernity, from sheet music and sound recording to radio and motion pictures.

Taking the background first, it is common to say that Yiddish theater grew out of the *purimshpil* tradition, a once-a-year relaxation of rabbinic rules that allowed for a carnivalesque popular exposition of repressed parody and irreverence.[1] Door-to-door troupes demanded access to homes and handouts, in return for skits and songs nominally based on biblical stories, including the Esther theme of the Purim holiday. The plots featured cross-dressing, heavy-handed humor, and topical satire about issues and character types of the day under the cover of seasonal Jewish expression. But much more of Jewish life than the *purimshpil* was distinctively performative, even choreographed. Women's chanting of *got fun avrom* at twilight as the Sabbath departed,[2] the swinging of a chicken over a man's head while chanting a scriptural passage, in performance of the *kapores* ritual before Yom Kippur, the knocking on the window of the synagogue assistant chanting *am koydesh* to rouse men to prayer[3] – these and many other dramatized embodiments of ritual obligations, all based on melodic intonation, were precursors of more formal stagings. Explicit and self-consciously theatrical songs and satire were the specialty of the *badkhn*, a master of ceremonies at weddings, who was in league with hereditary instrumentalists, *klezmer* musicians, to set the mood for the ritualized celebration that was a major set piece of personal transition and communal solidarity. The linkage between the theatricality of everyday Jewish life and the evolution of modern forms of drama and cinema is not arbitrary. Plays, and eventually movies, continually drew on this wellspring of well-known gestures and sounds to create a flow of credibility and emotion between the creators and receivers of popular theater.

As the eastern European Jews grew ever more urbanized, their ears opened to the emerging soundscapes around them. The increased regional mobility offered by rail travel and the transatlantic passage of populations allowed for the development of new tastes and the influence of a whole range of musical inputs. The wandering players collectively called the *broder-zinger* (named for the crossroads city of Brod) had their ears open. Opera, but more particularly its younger sister operetta, infiltrated the cities and towns in various national forms. As the birth of the Yiddish theater is usually located in Moldavia, it is worth noting the figure of Ciprian Porumbescu (1853–83), whose ears and ambitions parallel those of the founders of the Jewish system he influenced: during his studies at the Vienna Conservatory, Porumbescu was inspired by the new operettas of composers including Strauss and Offenbach to adopt modern techniques of the genre in the telling of stories that derived from Romanian culture and history. Here we see the ways that mainstream European performing arts trickled out to the East through locally available intermediaries that Jewish musicians – singers, actors, composers – could use as models. The founders of Yiddish theater and its music absorbed all these influences, as is evident from their memoirs.

Above all, Abraham Goldfaden (1840–1908), the "father of the Yiddish theater," aspired to building a respectable "national" drama in Yiddish along Porumbescu's lines, even as he assimilated the wildly eclectic singing and theatrical resources of his ragtag group of actors and musicians. Boris Thomashefsky, the domineering actor-producer of New York, also sang, as did so many actors of the early Yiddish stage, the line between the two skills being thin at best. In his memoir, he relates how he began in boyhood as a cantorial choirboy (*meshoyrer*), but was advised by the Italian music director of the Kiev Opera to do opera-house training. Another choirboy, Sigmund Mogulesco (1858–1914), who wrote some of the most important early songs while being famous for his comedic genius as "the Jewish Charlie Chaplin," recalled his patchwork musical upbringing via Jewish sacred and non-Jewish mainstream entertainment. Joseph Rumshinsky (1881–1951), the great professionalizer of Yiddish musical theater, tells of writing marches and waltzes for the provincial Russian military garrison in his hometown, a formative phase of his early career training.

The growth of city amusements such as wine cellars, beer gardens, and cabaret made it possible for newer ethnic formats to thrive. The birth of Yiddish theater is pegged at 1876 and located in a wine-garden in Iaşi, Moldavia, at a time when Jewish contractors had leisure and money while servicing the military during the Russo-Turkish war. Slowly these slapdash attempts at modern entertainment grew into more mainstream popular theater venues and genres. The musical tastes and impulses of the early founders transferred almost immediately from Romania and Ukraine to New York with the enormous wave of emigration of the 1880s, eventually spreading to all immigrant enclaves, from Capetown to Buenos Aires to Melbourne. Linking the older and more modern styles, as well as several continents, were the sense of improvisation, transience of material, eclecticism of sources, and blending of pathos, pratfalls, and sweet melodies.

In many ways, this profile of the Yiddish theater fits squarely into the cross-cultural heading "popular theater," as Joel Schechter describes it: "Popular theatre forms lend themselves to adaptation, reinterpretation and changes of content because they originate in unwritten and improvised performance traditions." And, tellingly, "popular theatre performers who depend on the audience for support also usually speak for the audience by voicing its social concerns."[4] As in many world popular theater traditions, from Europe to Africa to Asia, music provides a two-way channel flowing from performers to audiences and back as both sides share similar aesthetic, as well as cultural and political, values. This allows for considerable musical conservatism, but also a hunger for novelty, particularly in the conditions of urbanization and modernization that marked the Yiddish popular theater more than those of more rural forms of global entertainment.

Sources of the music

This music has been preserved in two formats: the commercial sheet music, produced mainly by publishers in the Lower East Side of New York, and the manuscript folios of music directors and theaters, now housed in archives (principally at the YIVO Institute for Jewish Research). As definitive as the print versions look, they offer little performance information, being limited to simple voice and piano transcriptions (sometimes with added violin part) of what would have been played by a pit band. These music products formed a central node in a chain of marketing that started with sales of pianos on installments to immigrant families and music lessons given primarily to the girls of the household, and extended to gramophone players for cylinders and records, which offered leisure-time, domestic reinforcement of the repertoire, and ideals of live performance. Much of this material came directly from theater productions, as indicated on the packaging of the sheet music and recordings. Small-scale marketing synergy was part of the propagation of a coherent ethnic musical subculture.

The music directors' handwritten versions varied markedly from these commercially standardized products. There were no full scores for conductors, so just individual instrumental parts and the occasional piano score survive. This gives some sense of orchestration, which varied considerably. Sets of parts, often signed out by particular theater companies, allow us to trace the flow of show folios from place to place on the Yiddish circuit. We learn that pieces might have been played in Krakow by possibly non-Jewish trumpeters of military bands, or that "this opera was performed nine times" (with dates given) in 1894 in Chicago. There is a good deal of scattered explicit and implicit data that sheds light on performance style, often in marginalia, and a considerable amount of non-Jewish music, ranging from orchestrated galops in Romania to "My Rainbow Coon" and "Ol' Man River" in New York. One 1899 assemblage includes a very mixed bag of sources: Rossini, von Suppé, Russian and Romanian folk tunes, and "Chinese" and "Neiger" melodies.

Music of the early period

We have almost no record of the great variety of music churned out by the street musicians and vaudevillians of Yiddish-speaking cities. The only surviving text of an extended skit ("playlet," in American vaudeville parlance) survives as the program of a show of 1895, preserved possibly because the libretto ends as an advertisement for a dry goods dealer who paid for the publication. *Tsvishn indianer* (Among the Indians), by I. Minikes, contains several song texts, but no tunes are specified. The songs are as satirical and burlesque as the plot, which finds two peddlers in what was then the western "Territories" of the Midwest, trying to sell suits to a canny farmer's wife, a black field hand, and American Indians.[5]

If this was the normal proletarian entertainment of the streets, it seems hard today to understand why the pejorative Yiddish term *shund*, or "trash," was widely applied to the "legitimate" theater productions of the early era. Two types of writers had a stake in their scorn: high-minded critics, and dramatists who wanted to follow the trends of European modernist "art" theater by decreasing the comedy and music quotients of their plays. But popular theater audiences care little for "trash talk." What interests them is the embodiment of their own values and aspirations, and also the fascination of a star system, a modern addition to earlier Jewish genres. A classic example is Boris Thomashefsky in *Alexander; or, the Crown Prince of Jerusalem* (1892),[6] written by the indefatigable Joseph Lateiner (1853–1935; Lateiner penned some 200 shows), which set the tone for the passionate fandom and gossip that swirled around the leading singer-actors of the day in New York. Personality and lyrics even trumped musicality, as early recordings of songs from the Yiddish stage show. The actors who initiated the roles, and revealed their sketchy vocal training, sometimes recorded them. The associated sheet music from the heyday of the New York scene begins with modest covers that describe the contents. Line drawing, sometimes archetypally depicting imagined scenes of biblical times or the immigrant home, gave a general sense of context, but by 1910, sheet music covers were increasingly laid out to stress the centrality of the performers or the actual action of the play, in photographic form, to emphasize the lived experience of the theater world. The frequent depictions of the songs' composers reveals how seriously they were taken as creators of beloved songs and associates of star actors and producers.

As indicated above, there are no standard performing editions of *shund* plays, so versions do not even agree on the cast of characters, let alone a fixed list of songs, not to speak of interpolations such as one instruction to include "Janke dudil [Yankee Doodle] in G." The published sheet music folios with multi-song lineups similarly did not give a sense of the total musical layout of a standard show, and many popular vehicles never produced these spinoff products. As an example of how music worked scene by scene, Lateiner's *Shloyme Gorgel* (Shloyme the Throat), which came to New York at the beginning of the immigration wave (1882), is useful, since it is documented by a published version of the text that appeared in Warsaw in 1907. Lateiner's method included adaptation of non-Jewish plays (German, Romanian) by inserting songs, dances, and comedy to match the portrayal of the characters, who were given Jewish names and concerns. The music was similarly eclectic. Plays about musicians, like this one, about a down-and-out cantor, or another Lateiner vehicle, *Dovids fidele* (David's Fiddle, of 1897), about a klezmer-turned-classical violinist who bests his arrogant nouveau-riche brother, allowed authors to include a full range of music of many genres. They also created long-lasting stereotypes of musicians, cantors, and other social types, many of whom got to sing or dance – the matchmaker, the *shlemil*, the yeshiva student, the crude Americanized immigrant, the tough street kid, the sweatshop worker – that carried over into Jewish-American fiction, television, and even Broadway and Hollywood.

Despite the seemingly ramshackle method of play construction, the songs in the published version of *Shloyme Gorgel* are well placed to define characters, enhance narrative, and provide sentiment, all combining to produce an effect of *yidishkayt*, downhome Jewish folksiness. For example, Shloyme sings the first song in a courtroom for his daughter Hadassah, who has been unjustly imprisoned. This number achieves three dramatic goals: 1) Gorgel, previously depicted as a rambling drunkard, is shown to have a better nature, as well as impressive cantorial talent; 2) Hadassah recognizes her long-lost father through the music, offering the general move of sentimental recognition, a major trope of the European melodrama, to be located ethnically through musicality; 3) the situation of Jews in a Polish courtroom plays up the plight and strengths of *yidishkayt* more generally. These broader themes recur repeatedly, as in the love duet for the couple Solomon and Shifra, who sing about the hypocrisy of the world, or when Shloyme sings a solo satirizing wicked women, but ending by praising the virtuous, long-suffering working wife. This echoes the scriptural ideal wife "whose worth is above rubies," so comes from the heart of Jewish tradition, but the line "such as you won't find among the rich folks" moves the model into a more modern, political space. These and other songs masterfully appeal to the proletarian urban audience of the Yiddish stage while at the same time supporting Jewish ideals and experiences. Meanwhile, knock-about comic songs, dances, and the almost obligatory closing wedding (a double one here) afford the opportunity to introduce ritual and entertainment genres from across the Yiddish world's spectrum of expressive culture, from prayers to klezmer, drunken ditties that satirize the nations and anti-Semites of Europe to appeals to God to ease the suffering of the Jews.[7]

While all stage music of the early era was eclectic, as mentioned above, some playwrights strove to "elevate" the discourse, beginning already in the 1880s with the historic music dramas of Abraham Goldfaden. In his seminal work *Shulamis* (c. 1880) and the important follow-up *Bar Kochba*, Goldfaden tried to show that even while drawing on Verdi and other non-Jewish sources, he could create dramas set in ancient times that expressed lofty sentiments and sustained the national, didactic tone of the *Haskalah* (Jewish Enlightenment) modernizing movement of which he was a part.[8]

Music of the second phase of Yiddish theater

Joseph Rumshinsky is credited with bringing a more professional training and tone to the Yiddish operetta. In his many works and very popular songs, as well as his training of actors, singers, choruses, and orchestras, he set benchmarks for the developments of the 1920s and 1930s in theater and film.[9] His memoirs, a major source for understanding the evolution of Yiddish theater music, describe a moment that crystallizes his attitude towards the scene he was determined to change. He has encountered the great Ester-Rokhl Kaminska, the doyenne of Polish Yiddish drama: "Madame Kaminska ... gave me some music from the opera *Shulamis*. It was on torn scraps of paper, with stains and erasures. I found it very upsetting."[10] Nevertheless, it is not easy reconstructing Rumshinsky's own work. One opus of his more than 100 productions, *Di goldene kale* (The Golden Bride, 1922), has been fully worked up in a modern critical edition by Michael Ochs and can represent this phase.[11] The show, set in Russia just after the Russian Revolution, discusses such weighty topics as whether life for Jews is better in Russia or the US (with characters from both places carrying on romantic relationships), and the usual playing-out of family relations. Elements of both traditional and modern Jewish life allow for a rich variety of musical input. Ochs had a wide and varied set of sources to draw on for his work of assemblage and editing. Three commercial recordings were pressed of just one love duet, as part of a set of fourteen recordings of seven different numbers. Two sheet music folios made the music available outside of the theater, for further home performance. These commercial sources, along with a variety of lead sheets, orchestral parts, typescripts of lyrics, a piano-vocal score, a radio script, and the libretto, as deposited for copyright, form parts of the puzzle that Ochs has worked with. The linguistic mix needed for these shows is also considerable, as it includes five languages, Yiddish, Russian, Ukrainian, and Hebrew, with English words assimilated into the Americanized characters' dialogue and songs. Stitching all this together is Rumshinsky's carefully constructed musical language, doubtless enhanced by his stable of stars, who combined the versatility and flexibility with material of the older phase of theater music with a book and music that were no longer improvised on the fly, but still culturally multiple and emotionally rich enough to satisfy the increasingly sophisticated ears of a mass audience.

Those listeners were now fully tuned into mainstream American popular music, knew increasingly less Yiddish, and probably had less patience for European themes and performance styles. By the mid-1920s, it was a second or even third generation of immigrants who were taking their parents and grandparents to the theater. With the closing of mass immigration in 1924, the American audience was ever more distanced from its roots. This was increasingly the case in Europe as well, as Sovietization shifted Yiddish culture into new channels[12] and assimilation in the large cities of Poland downgraded Yiddish tradition and elevated more cosmopolitan forms of cabaret, film, and pop song. Polish Jews also played a large role in the newer forms of mass marketed media for mainstream audiences, as did the American Jewish songwriters of the era of American standards, or their French and German counterparts in Western Europe. Even in the USSR under state socialism, the most important creators of the hugely popular mass songs, largely disseminated through films, were Jews who came from a generation that shifted its creative work from Yiddish to dominant linguistic, political, and musical trends.

The culminating phase of the 1930s

With no new influx of immigrants, the shutting down of ethnic recordings by the music industry due to the Depression, and the looming danger to the Jews of eastern Europe, one might imagine that Yiddish theater music and its rising partner, Yiddish film, would collapse. Yet the 1930s saw the culminating phase of the projects set in motion from the 1880s–1920s. Goldfaden plays did not disappear from stages. New Yiddish "art theater" productions found more modernist music to supplant the *shund*-era patchwork and circumvent the Rumshinsky-founded mainstream. A generation of immensely talented songwriters such as Alexander Olshanetsky (1892–1946), Abraham Ellstein (1907–63), and Sholom Secunda (1894–1974) sprang up who often saw their songs premiered in shows ranging from revues to dramas. Secunda wrote the song that became the greatest crossover hit from Yiddish to mainstream American popularity, "Bay mir bist du sheyn." People in Poland sang songs written in New York, the flow mainly going from the US to Europe. For this period, film music is the most interesting area to watch. Jewish-American independent film began around 1918, paralleling only the African-American effort in pioneering the idea of ethnic subcultural cinema. With the advent of the "talkies," Yiddish could take its place in both the aural and the visual imaginary of Jews worldwide, and music played its role in selling the concept. Alongside filmed versions of well-known stage plays, with their attendant melodrama and downhome music cues, the Yiddish musical emerged as an extension of the Rumshinsky enterprise. Younger songwriters jumped at the opportunity to create film scores. Meanwhile, in Poland, despite severe economic and political turmoil, the local Jewish talent pool found ways to produce a set of homegrown movies in Yiddish as well. Comparing the two sides of this transatlantic system and their overlap is instructive.

On the Polish side, the surviving film (many are lost) that has become most emblematic of Yiddish cinema is *The Dybbuk* (1937), an adaptation of the canonical play by S. An-sky (1863–1920) first seen in the early 1920s and widely translated and paraphrased in many media in various countries ever since. The movie's director, Michał Waszyński, had pioneered talkies in Poland and claimed to have studied with both Stanislavsky in theater and F. W. Murnau in film. On the set for *The Dybbuk*, he could rely on the skills of leading designers and technicians, some of whom were refugees from Nazi Germany, hence had worked in Weimar cinema. So as deeply as *The Dybbuk* delves into the fast-fading provincial Jewish life and as much as it relies on vernacular language, religious custom, music, and body movements, it is the work of a remarkably cosmopolitan crew and outlook that ranges from Stanislavsky acting and Polish literature through German expressionist cinema. Upon its release, the film was widely seen and reviewed not just by Jews, but also a general Polish audience and critics. When the movie reached America, the *New York Times* felt it needed to write a review, and found the movie "incredible in its way as a documentary film of life among the pygmies or a trip to the Middle Ages."[13]

More than in the original play, music draws the audience into Polish-Jewish life, beginning with the newly added prologue featuring the great cantor Gershon Sirota, who is heard, but not seen on camera, due to his religious scruples. The dreamy main theme, a setting of "The Song of Songs," recurs as a leitmotif of the doomed romance of the couple, and there is a conventional score as well. A klezmer band accompanies the Hasidic *rebbe* at his Sabbath gathering. Beyond even these already highly evocative music cues, a host of other gestures to small-town folklore give *The Dybbuk* a deeply local atmosphere that Jewish-American cinema tends only to gesture at. Nevertheless, it is the choreographed beggars' dances of Judith Berg that stick in most viewers' minds, and they come out of Warsaw art, not *shtetl* custom. The folklorization by composers, choreographers, set designers, and art directors is part of a "national" project that on the one hand goes back to the great Polish-Jewish writer Y. L. Peretz, but on the other, has a certain kinship to Goldfaden's ideals, much as Peretz disliked the early Yiddish theater's approach.

A Polish-Jewish film that takes a less sentimental, but still outsider, approach to the small-town past is *Freylikhe kaptsonim* (The Jolly Paupers, 1937), from the same time frame as *The Dybbuk*. As played by the great comedians Dzigan and Schumacher, the looniness of a couple of *shtetl* Jews who think they have discovered oil is portrayed satirically, almost menacingly. The music ranges from a young couple's romantic Yiddish theater song to the garbled cantorial wailing of the two hapless heroes (taken from a madman they meet in an asylum) pitting generations against each other in a commentary on modernity that in some ways parallels the subtext of *The Dybbuk*, with its focus on the breakdown of the old religious ways and the ascendance of youthful eroticism, even if expressed in much deeper, demonic ways than the satire of *The Jolly Paupers*.

The Yiddish films shot in the US stand apart from these European concerns. By the late 1920s, American Jewish popular culture had shifted into a more nostalgic view of the "Old Country" than is apparent in the early immigration-era entertainment. Recreating scenes from European life on flimsy sets in New Jersey, filmmakers used older musical styles, from folk songs to the then-popular cantorial bravado, as a foil to scenes of Americanization. It was easy for them to rely on older melodramatic plots and conventions, particularly about family life. Scores could cue tear-jerking moments of reunion or rejection in conventional fashion. But the movies also offered the possibility of lively musical comedies with up-to-date, if ethnically tinged, romantic or humorous songs by Rumshinsky or his main successors, Abraham Ellstein and Alexander Olshanetsky.

The film that is usually cited as the culmination of all these trends is *Yidl mitn fidl* (Yidl with His Fiddle, directed by Joseph Green, 1936), starring a group of American actors fortified by a large Polish-Jewish cast and technical team. It was shot on location in the town of Kazimierz Dolny, with its classic central marketplace and surrounding Jewish neighborhood, before moving out to both the Polish countryside and the big city in a panoramic presentation of European Jewry on the very eve of its destruction. It is a film that is impossible not to view ironically today, as a poignant time capsule that is at the same time very American in its music and sensibilities. Ellstein's score makes accurate nods to local non-Jewish folklore in the opening sequence as well as to traditional Jewish melodies, grounding the utopian aspirations of the movie musical in the lived reality of small-town Poland. At the film's end, the klezmer characters will board a boat towards American stardom, paralleling Hollywood's happy-ending solution to the preceding tangles of emotion and, in this case, the burdens of ethnicity. It is a format that could, and did, appeal to both sides of the transatlantic Jewish movie-going public.

Music could both support and challenge nostalgia, suppress or champion modernity in Yiddish cinema. *The Cantor's Son* (1940), starring the glamorous Moishe Oysher, who uncomfortably juggled popular song and cantorial careers, takes homesickness to the extreme by showing its immigrant singer returning to his hometown in Europe to reunite with his childhood sweetheart, despite success and a woman in New York's Jewish nightclub and radio scene. Throughout, the hero refuses to sing pop songs, sticking with cantorial and old-fashioned musical fare. In conservative films of the period, issues of assimilation and intermarriage are worked out musically. As the viewership for Yiddish-language cinema was aging, filmmakers were more likely to stay with earlier styles and issues than to Americanize the music enough to try to compete with Hollywood and attract a younger audience. Ambivalence could also creep into the use of older musical layers, as in the film *Uncle Moses*, a withering indictment of sweatshop-boss control of the garment industry and union pushback, and the first Yiddish sound film to take on hot-button up-to-date issues – but not current Jewish-American music. The main theme, tied to the protagonist, a boss who lords it over his immigrant compatriots, is the prayer *Ovinu malkenu*, learned from his old-world rabbi. While this might create an equation of religion = oppression of the working class, the sentimentality of the tune carries through to the very end, almost mitigating the dark side of Uncle Moses. Along with the klezmer and *badkhn* at the boss's wedding, the completely old-fashioned insider make-up of the plot calls to mind J. Hoberman's helpful summary of the situation: "If individual films often precipitated a conflict between tradition and modernity, the Yiddish cinema in toto can be seen as something of an extended family quarrel."[14] But the younger generation has no counterpart musical themes of any importance.

In this period, music plays its part in softening the edges of in-group hostility more than it supports strife. A fine example comes in a 1924 disc called *A yidisher heym in Amerike* (A Jewish Home in America) – one of those recorded theatrical scenes that extend the range of the topic beyond stage and cinema. The daughter of the house enters with her boyfriends, who play a lively version of a pop song, "Yes sir, that's my baby," on piano and ukulele. The father demands that they stop and sing a cantorial number with him, no less than the august "Hayom haras oylem" from the Rosh Hashanah (New Year) service. They dutifully chime in with voice and instruments – somehow they know how to function as a synagogue choir – and domestic peace is restored.

Decline and revitalization

Just as African-American "race film" withered in the 1940s when black musicians were integrated into Hollywood vehicles, most Jewish-American talent had long since migrated into the mainstream musical niches open on stage and film, achieving remarkable upward mobility at a time when Jews were socially restricted in many other avenues of public life. Still, this increasing comfort with American life also allowed for the theatricality of stage and screen to filter into the burgeoning Jewish entertainment of the "Borscht Belt," a catch-phrase for a variety of weekend and summer vacation venues that gave work to musicians, actors, and comedians. The last Yiddish film of the older era, *Catskill Honeymoon* of 1950, offers a glimpse of the eclectic and sometimes unexpected acts presented to dinner-table audiences. As Hoberman puts it, the film "dissolved Yiddish movies into canned vaudeville."[15] Nevertheless, the movie played long in Jewish neighborhoods. Framed as a golden anniversary party, the movie thus directly states its appeal to an aging audience. There is a biting Yiddish parody of "The Anniversary Waltz," an Al Jolson hit song of the period set to an old Euro-Argentine waltz. *Catskill Honeymoon*'s sixteen night-club numbers, simply staged as acts at Reeds Gap Hotel, include some archaic Yiddish comedy numbers based on stuttering or local dialect (Litvak vs. Galitsianer, an American theme decades old), some tame American torch and sentimental songs, a bit of opera, but little Yiddish music outside a couple of Ellstein-style items from an earlier era. It closes with a tribute to Israel, in Yiddish and English, graphically illustrating the shift of sentiment towards the new Zionist-based song and dance numbers that would further eclipse Yiddish as an expressive language.

Carryovers continued in the work of the 1940s–50s recording and night-spot entertainers such as Mickey Katz, the Barton Brothers, and Irving Fields, who riffed parodically and often satirically on the ambivalence of postwar Jewish-American life. Their records resounded in homes despite some communal disapproval. It is important to think of these artists as inheritors of a long lineage of in-group musical commentary on immigration, post-immigration, discomfort with American reality, and generational friction. Early Yiddish-language broadside songs, sold on the streets as early as the 1880s, gave way to comedy recordings in the form of skits with songs that carried on vaudeville traditions that have largely been lost and provide a link with the post-World War II styles and, latterly, recent revivals of those sensibilities.

By the 1970s, young Jewish-American musicians from a variety of backgrounds and training converged on the remnants of Yiddish music. Although the early klezmer revival, as it came to be called, relied heavily on the sound recordings of the 1914–32 era and thought of the repertoire as European music performed mostly in the US, as time went on, the theater and cinema sources began to emerge as a source, particularly in the work of Hankus Netsky, whose Klezmer Conservatory Band was influential. The band's vocalist, Judy Bresler, from a Yiddish theater family, consistently sang older material from stage and sheet music sources, as did other singers across the US who eventually exported the material to their European students. At workshops and institutes worldwide, on websites and recordings, the rich tradition of Yiddish theater and cinema music continues to make a meaningful contribution to contemporary music.

Notes

1 For a short introduction of the genre, see Jean Baumgarten, "Purim-Shpil," trans. Cecilia Grayson, *YIVO Encyclopedia of Jewish in Eastern Europe*, www.yivoencyclopedia.org/article.aspx/Purim-shpil (accessed February 17, 2015).

2 For a good performance and this description of the theatrical quality – "I remember her with her white shawl on her head, covered, and she drew close to her my sister and me and standing, still in darkness" – see Bella Bryks-Klein's contribution to The Yiddish Song of the Week, yiddishsong.wordpress.com/2010/05/25/ (accessed February 17, 2015).

3 For a classic recorded version, listen to "Am koydesh" from Ruth Rubin's album *Yiddish Folksong: The Old Country*, available on CD from Smithsonian Folkways Records (FW 8720, 1978, reissued 2004) or attached to Chana Mlotek and Mark Slobin (eds.) *Yiddish Folksongs from the Ruth Rubin Archive* (Detroit: Wayne State University Press, 2007).

4 Joel Schechter, "Back to the Popular Source," in Joel Schechter (ed.), *Popular Theatre: A Sourcebook* (London and New York: Routledge, 2003), 3–11.

5 For an English translation and commentary, see Mark Slobin, "From Vilna to Vaudeville: Minikes and *Among the Indians* (1895)," in Schechter (ed.), *Popular Theatre*, 202–11.

6 Ronald Robboy has written about the play and its music in "Reconstructing a Yiddish Theatre Score: Giacomo Minkowski and His Music to *Alexander; or, the Crown Prince of Jerusalem*," in Joel Berkowitz and Barbara Henry (eds.), *Inventing the Modern Yiddish Stage: Essays in Drama, Performance, and Show Business* (Detroit: Wayne State University Press, 2012), 225–50.

7 For excerpts of *Shloyme gorgel* and a full translation of *Dovids fidele*, both with suggested music, see Mark Slobin, *Yiddish Theater in America: "David's Violin" (1897) and "Shloyme Gorgl" (1899)*, Nineteenth-Century American Musical Theater 11 (New York and London: Garland, 1994).

8 A full performing edition of *Shulamis* was arranged and produced by Alyssa Quint and Zalmen Mlotek, with translation by Nahma Sandrow, in 2010, so the play continues to have its remarkable hold on the Jewish-American imagination.

9 For a modern compilation, see *Great Songs of the Yiddish Stage*, vol. III, *Joseph Rumshinsky*, Milken Archive, 2006, compact disc.

10 Joseph Rumshinsky, *Klangen fun mayn lebn* (New York: A. Y. Biderman, 1944).

11 The Ochs edition will form one of the volumes of the *Music of the United States of America* series, to be published by A-R Editions.

12 For a fine account of this process, see Anna Shternshis, *Soviet and Kosher: Jewish Popular Culture in the Soviet Union, 1923–1939* (Bloomington: Indiana University Press, 2006).

13 Frank S. Nugent, "The Continental Brings in a Film of 'The Dybbuk,'" January 28, 1938.

14 J. Hoberman, *Bridge of Light: Yiddish Film between Two Worlds* (New York: The Museum of Modern Art and Schocken Books, 1991; 2nd edn., Hanover, NH: Dartmouth College Press, 2010), 9.

15 *Ibid.*, 337.

15 Art music in the Yishuv and in Israel

JEHOASH HIRSHBERG

Introduction

Art music in the Yishuv[1] and in Israel was a latecomer to the nineteenth-century tradition of national schools. Yet it was unique in that it was established solely by immigrant Jewish composers from central and eastern Europe. Nearly all of them were anticipatory refugees who escaped the Nazi and Fascist governments in these regions.[2]

The history of art (as well as folk and popular) music in the Yishuv and in Israel was closely linked with the momentous process of the revival of Hebrew as a spoken and modernized literary language among Jews in the country. Hebrew became a principal tool for the unification of the immigrant society. Singing in amateur choruses in turn became a powerful method for spreading the use of the Hebrew language and especially the Sephardic accent, which was officially adopted in the early years of the twentieth century.

Methodological aspects

The history of art music in the Yishuv and in Israel is methodologically a unique case in the history of national schools in that it could be documented and studied from its onset; that is, we know "how it all began." Archives of works by Israeli composers have been meticulously collected and deposited in central libraries, mostly at the National Library in Jerusalem, at the Israeli music archives of Tel Aviv University, and at the publishing house Israeli Music Publications. The enormous size of the repertory of Israeli art music may be judged through Alice Tischler's valuable catalogue.[3]

Incipient attempts, 1910–1929

Musical life in the small Jewish community under Ottoman rule was motivated by the need of immigrants to get together, singing in choirs or playing in amateur orchestras. In 1910 the singer Shulamit Ruppin (1873–1912) founded a music school in Jaffa. Based on the model of the Berlin conservatory, the curriculum included individual tutoring in piano, violin, cello, and voice, as well as theory classes, a choir, and a pupils' orchestra. Additional schools soon opened in Jerusalem and Haifa. The European model of professional music instruction was thus transplanted from central Europe to the Yishuv, and then to Israel up to the present day.

World War I caused a severe crisis in the Jewish community. Recovery soon began with the establishment of the British mandate over Palestine. The 1920s were marked by over-ambitious endeavors, above all the Palestine Opera, which the conductor Mark Golinkin (1875–1963) founded in July 1923. Despite facing formidable economic difficulties, Golinkin produced seventeen mainstream operas in four seasons, with special emphasis on the Jewish-themed operas *La Juive*, by Fromental Halévy, and *The Maccabees*, by Anton Rubinstein. Golinkin insisted on performing all of them in Hebrew translation, but the Russian-speaking singers hardly spoke any Hebrew and the audience was unable to follow the awkward translations. The project collapsed in 1927, though Golinkin maintained sporadic productions later on. The state of the opera did not allow for the production of *He-ḥalutz* (The Pioneers, 1924) by Jacob Weinberg (1879–1958), the first Hebrew opera composed in Palestine, and the work in its entirety was to be premiered in New York. A naïve, idealistic opera, it was strongly influenced by the Russian orientalism of the Mighty Five.[4] Nevertheless, in this period ad hoc ensembles, mostly outdoors, performed orchestral concerts of light classics relatively frequently, with audiences of thousands attending.

The emergence of art music in the 1930s

The Nazi takeover triggered the largest wave of emigration of Jews from Europe to Palestine. The Jewish population of Palestine increased from 156,000 in 1928 to 445,000 in 1939.[5] This immigration wave included experienced and motivated concert audiences, a large group of performers who had lost their positions in leading European orchestras, and more than forty well-trained and mature composers,[6] that is, the entire tri-partite structure required for dynamic, creative musical life. It also resulted in an inverted process of absorption by which the number of immigrant musicians far exceeded that of the receiving professional community.

Many of the immigrants brought along their fine German pianos. With a ban on taking money out of Germany, the sale of the pianos provided ready cash for their first steps in the country, indirectly supporting the transplant of *Hausmusik* culture. Many children started their music instruction on these instruments, which are still found in Israeli homes to this day.

The basic professional infrastructure of musical life was formed as early as the 1930s. In 1933 the Palestine Conservatory was founded in Jerusalem with instruction on all instruments and advanced classes in music theory, composition, music history, and ethnomusicology. In March 1936 the British administration founded the Palestine Broadcast Service (PBS), alternating English, Arabic, and Hebrew broadcasts daily. The PBS included a relatively large music department, with a small ensemble that soon developed into the radio symphony orchestra (nowadays the Jerusalem Symphony). The crowning achievement arrived when international violinist Bronisław Huberman (1882–1947) accomplished his pioneer herculean project of creating the Palestine Orchestra (since 1950, the Israel Philharmonic Orchestra) in December 1936. Huberman's goal was to establish a first-rate orchestra built mostly of refugee Jewish musicians from Europe, for whom he secured immigrant certificates from the British administration. In that way he saved about seventy musicians and their families from Nazi extermination.

The conductor of the first festival concert series was the venerable Arturo Toscanini, who donated his performances as a powerful and well-publicized anti-fascist demonstration. The members of the orchestra founded multiple chamber ensembles, mostly string quartets, which were eagerly received by the discerning central European audience. The orchestra started a subscription program that was sold out, keeping the ensemble active throughout the horrible years of World War II. All this provided the infrastructure for the creation of art music. It is remarkable that despite the generally classical-romantic musical taste of the audience and Huberman's insistence on training the new orchestra of immigrants with mainstream repertory, the Palestine orchestra performed as many as 116 new compositions by immigrant composers during its first ten seasons, thus encouraging the creation of a symphonic repertory.[7]

The vision of the East versus the heritage of the West

The immigrant composers were faced with the awesome challenge of forming a new creative community under severe economic conditions, the need to recuperate from the trauma of sudden displacement, and the threat of the war that in its first stages imperiled Palestine itself. The majority of composers arrived from Germany, as well as from Czechoslovakia, Hungary, and Lithuania, which were strongly affected by German culture. The few composers from Russia and Poland received their advanced training mostly in France.

The emigration of Paul Ben-Haim (1897–1984) will illustrate the process of resettlement. Born in Munich as Paul Frankenburger, Ben-Haim graduated from the Munich Academy as a pianist, composer, and conductor, and

Example 15.1 Paul Ben-Haim, Symphony No. 1 (1940), excerpt.

in 1924 became First Kapellmeister of the Augsburg Opera. He composed more than eighty *Lieder* as well as chamber and orchestral works. In 1931 the newly appointed Nazi director of the opera did not renew his contract. In 1932–3 he composed his monumental oratorio *Joram* to a book by Rudolf Borchardt, clinging to the long tradition leading from Bach's Passions through Mendelssohn's *Elijah* and Brahms's Requiem.[8] After Hitler's takeover in February 1933, Ben-Haim decided to emigrate, and in October of the same year he settled in Tel Aviv. The move terminated his operatic career, and he devoted himself mostly to composition and teaching. His first action was to take intensive Hebrew lessons and to initiate the new genre of Hebrew art song with compositions set to verses from the Song of Songs and poems by leading modern Hebrew poets such as Ḥayim Naḥman Bialik (1873–1934) and Rachel (1890–1931). He soon returned to large forms with a String Quartet (1937), and with the first Symphony composed in Palestine (1940). In the Symphony Ben-Haim continued in the Mahlerian manner, representing and responding to the world around him. The Symphony opens with a modified quotation of the opening of Mahler's Second Symphony (Example 15.1), which represents the composer's past.

The exalted slow movement quotes a motif from the song "I Will Lift up My Eyes," which Ben-Haim had arranged a year earlier for the singer Bracha Zefira (discussed below), signifying the longing for a new reality in the East. The third movement introduces an extended instrumental quotation from *Joram* as a painful symbol of his displacement, followed by a rhythmic motif based on the Israeli *hora* dance, which sinks back into a dark military march.

None of the composers who immigrated to Palestine during this period knew one another prior to their arrival, nor did they form any unified group with an accepted leader. They confronted two opposing forces:

1. The powerful collective pressure of Zionist ideology created the **Vision of the East**, which acted on composers both from outside through reviews, and from their internal obligation to create a new Israeli style (discussed in detail below).
2. The equally powerful **Heritage of the West**, within which the composers had been trained, and which governed the repertory of performing ensembles and audiences' taste. For the immigrant composers this served as a cushion softening the trauma of resettlement.

Josef Tal (né Grünthal, 1910–2008), who emigrated in 1934 from Berlin, the center of the avant-garde in the Weimar Republic, went at first through a financially difficult period in Palestine, initially working as a photographer in Haifa and then making an unsuccessful effort as a farmer on a kibbutz. His first composition written in Palestine (1937) was an austere Passacaglia for cello solo in which he merges J. S. Bach's structural techniques with Arnold Schoenberg's atonal harmony. Likewise, the first composition of Haim (Heinz) Alexander (1915–2012) in Palestine was a Chaconne for piano (1948) based on the Baroque ostinato model and incorporating chromatic, dissonant harmonies. Ben-Haim's first composition in Palestine was the dreamy, delicate Nocturno for piano, which continues the long line of piano miniatures by Schumann, Chopin, and Debussy. The Paris-trained Verdina Shlonsky (1905–90), the only woman composer within the first generation, composed her *Five Sketches* for piano (1947) under the strong influence of Erik Satie, Darius Milhaud, and Francis Poulenc.

The quadripartite model

The attitudes of the "founders" of Israeli music may be classified into four categories. One should bear in mind that composers did change their attitudes in the course of their compositional activity and even operated in simultaneous tracks:

1. **Collective-National:** This model was created by Alexander U. Boscovich (1907–64). Born in Cluj, Transylvania, Boscovich came to Palestine for the performance of his suite *Jewish Folk Songs* (1937) and decided to stay.[9] The principal points of his ideology were that the composer should act as representative of the people (in Hebrew, *Shliach tzibur*) and avoid any personal, romantic expression; that music must express the time and place of its creation, which in the particular case of Palestine – and Israel – is the arid landscape of the country and the "dynamic" soundscape of its spoken languages – Hebrew in Sephardi accent and Arabic; that it must be based on the melodic motives of *maqāms* (the foundational modes of indigenous Middle Eastern music) and avoid tonal harmony; and that it must turn away from European Jewish music (including his own music composed in Cluj). His most representative work was *Semitic Suite* (1945), whose title stressed the local, Mediterranean nature of the composition. It was composed for piano and immediately orchestrated. Boscovich requested that the pianist play with a percussive, inexpressive touch. Example 15.2, from the opening movement, Toccata, illustrates the dominating four-note repetitive pattern within a fourth, played above a non-harmonic, organum-like drone.

Example 15.2 Alexander Boscovich, *Semitic Suite* (1945), excerpt.

Example 15.3 Marc Lavry, *Three Jewish Dances*, movement 3, "Hora" (1951), excerpt.

Still, Boscovich did not intend to compose Arabic music, and in his ideological essay he noted that an Arabic and a Jewish shepherd on adjacent hills would perform differently on their flutes. Boscovich coined the term "Mediterranean music," which related both to Eastern, Arabic music and to music of the Mediterranean basin, as opposed to German music. The concept was disseminated by critic Max Brod (1884–1968) and used – only once – by composer Menachem Avidom (Mahler Kalkstein, 1908–96) for his *Mediterranean Sinfonietta* (1951). Yet the oft-quoted term "Mediterranean Style," or, worse still, "Mediterranean School," often invoked as allegedly dominating early Israeli music, is misleading.

2. **Popular-National:** This attitude was cultivated by Marc Lavry (1903–67), who composed tuneful music that aimed at blurring the dividing line between art and popular music. He especially cultivated the *hora*, which originated in Hasidic dance in the 1920s and was marked by short, rhythmically symmetrical phrases, syncopated rhythms, and a narrow melodic range (Example 15.3).

Lavry utilized well-defined musical symbols in his folk opera *Dan hashomer* (Dan the Guard, 1945), to a libretto by Max Brod according to a play by Sh. Shalom. The opera contrasts the personal story of the love of two kibbutz members at the time of the Arab Revolt (1936–9) with the collective story of the kibbutz. *Hora* dances symbolize the young pioneers, traditional prayer modes represent the elders, and Puccini-like arias express the suffering young lovers. The foundation of the State of Israel (1948) inspired a group of works in the popular style, such as Ben-Haim's *Fanfare to Israel* (1950) and *Israel Suite* (1951), Alexander's *Six Israeli Dances* (1950), Avidom's *Mediterranean Sinfonietta* (1951), and Boscovich's *Little Suite* (1954).

3. **Individual-National:** In his introductory essay for his symphonic variations *Twelve Tribes of Israel* (1938), the composer Erich Walter Sternberg (1891–1974) rejected all outside pressures on composers to utilize models such as "Russian tunes, synagogue cantillations, or local folklore; one should rather talk in the language which emanates from oneself."[10] Sternberg's musical characterization was based on post-romantic harmony and orchestration, including a quote of the opening motive of Brahms's Symphony no. 4, and grand Mahlerian gestures that he considered befitting the representation of biblical tribes. Josef Tal insisted that his music was "Israeli" by virtue of the fact that he lived in Israel and spoke Hebrew. Quotes of motives with a strong Jewish identity provided the national elements of this attitude. For example, the second movement of Tal's early Piano Sonata (1950) applied syncretism in the way he incorporated a quotation of a simple modal folk song by his friend Yehudah Sharett, which he set as an ostinato below dissonant, atonal harmonic gestures. Tal composed seven operas on Jewish subjects, three of which were in German for German opera houses.

Still, the Individual-National attitude often led to a deliberate avoidance of national symbols. In 1957 Tal composed the dramatic scene Saul at Ein Dor. Despite the biblical verses that are the sole source of text, Tal wrote, "from the start it was decided that I would avoid any quote from traditional liturgy or any use of the conventional 'national' music and would rather compose atonal music in my own way."[11]

The most extreme representative of the Individual-National attitude was Stefan Wolpe (1902–72), the only composer of the first generation whose resettlement process failed. Wolpe escaped Germany as a persecuted communist and settled in Jerusalem in 1934. There he split his educational and musical activity into two very different worlds. As a composer he was the most extreme avant-garde in the country, employing austere modernist techniques in his strictly dodecaphonic *Four Studies on Basic Rows* (1935–6) and the *Passacaglia on an All-Interval Row* for piano (1936). In 1935 Wolpe and his circle of loyal students founded a local branch of the International Society for Contemporary Music. At the same time he realized his communist ideals through founding workers' choruses in the kibbutz movement and composing simple socialist songs, such as "Es wird die neue Welt geboren" (A New World Was Born, 1934). He felt isolated within the traditionally minded faculty of the newly founded Conservatory and he could not stand the political tension during the Arab Revolt (1936–9), and in December 1938 he emigrated for the United States.[12] His departure deprived the avant-garde group of its most dedicated representative. Ben-Haim, who came from Richard Strauss's sphere of influence, and Hanokh (Heinrich) Jacobi (1909–90), who was Hindemith's student, were opposed to dodecaphonic writing, and Sternberg, who supported Schoenberg, himself resorted to tonal writing in his large symphonic works, so that dodecaphonic writing remained in the minority in Israeli music.

4. **Cosmopolitan:** There were composers who avoided any national or Eastern connotations in their works and were completely embedded in the Heritage of the West. The cosmopolitan attitude gathered momentum after the foundation of the State of Israel, when the country finally opened to the West after many years of forced seclusion. An extreme example is Menachem Avidom's *Philharmonic Symphony* (1957),[13] which is a set of well-contrived fugues and counterpoints in neo-classical style, completely unrelated to his *Mediterranean Sinfonietta* (see above).

First encounters with Eastern music

Simultaneously with the waves of immigration from Europe there arrived large groups of religiously motivated Jewish immigrants from Yemen. The rich tradition of Yemenite music was eagerly studied by scholars, first by the pioneer ethnomusicologist Abraham Zvi Idelsohn (1882–1938), who devoted the first volume of his extensive *Thesaurus of Hebrew-Oriental Melodies* (published between 1914 and 1933) to the Yemenite tradition.[14] Yet his transcriptions into Western notation provided the immigrant composers with no more than a mere rudimentary impression of the melodies, with the crucial parameters of timbre and intonation entirely lacking. The first encounter with the actual music of the Jewish Eastern traditions came with Yemenite singer Bracha Zefira (1910?–90). Orphaned at the age of three, she was raised by foster families of different ethnic groups, whose traditional songs she fully absorbed. Later she trained at the Jerusalem Conservatory and briefly at Max Reinhardt's Theater School in Berlin. Her ambition was to penetrate the established concert audience. She first performed with improvising pianist Nahum Nardi, and from 1939 she commissioned vocal arrangements with ensembles of Western instruments from most of the immigrant composers. She first collaborated with Ben-Haim, Ödön Partos (1907–77), Lavry, Alexander, and Jacobi.[15] The combination of Zefira's unique Yemenite timbre and pure Sephardic Hebrew accent with the piano and with ensembles of members of the Palestine Orchestra created the first true East-West syncretism to become popular with the largely immigrant audiences. Ben-Haim quoted most of her songs in his symphonic and chamber works; for example, he incorporated the entire Persian song "Laila lo nim" (Sleepless Night) in the finale of his Piano Concerto (1949). Quotation was the chief device for introducing Yemenite songs into art

Example 15.4 Ödön Partos, *Visions* (1957), excerpt.

music. Whereas the melodic identity of the song was preserved, the original intonation and timbre were lost.

In 1950 the singer and choreographer Sara Levi-Tanai founded the Inbal Dance Theater, which presented Yemenite customs and traditions on stage. Yemenite composer Ovadia Tuvia (1920–2006) served as its Musical Director. The composer most involved with the Yemenite heritage was Mordechai Seter (1916–94), who quoted Yemenite songs in several of his works of the 1950s and 1960s, such as *Yemenite Suite* (1957, rev. 1966) and the oratorio *Tikkun hatzot* (Midnight Vigil, 1962). Partos quoted two of the songs he had heard from Tuvia in his *Visions* for flute and string orchestra, yet he modified the perfect fifth of the Yemenite melody into a tritone, betraying his attachment to his Hungarian heritage and the legacy of Béla Bartók and Zoltán Kodály (Example 15.4).

Composers invent the sounds of the East

Attempts at realizing the Vision of the East were made by a few composers of the first generation. Two salient examples are the Sonata for solo violin by Mordechai Seter (1954) and "Bashrav" (1953) for solo violin by Abel Ehrlich (1915–2003).[16] Seter and Ehrlich's intention was to adhere to pure melodic lines, avoiding harmonic accompaniment. Ehrlich even starts "Bashrav" with quarter tones. In the second section, nevertheless, the violin adds double-stops and chords, and its playing style is influenced by Bartók's Sonata for solo violin, which Yehudi Menuhin had performed in Tel Aviv in the early 1950s. The first movement of Seter's Sonata is based on alternations of a fast ornament and long drawn-out notes; it creates two-part dissonant combinations that are powerful and original, yet hardly Arabic.

The second generation

The second generation included composers born in the 1920s. Foremost among them were Yehezkel Braun (1922–2014), Ben-Zion Orgad (né Büschel, 1926–2006), and Zvi Avni (b. 1927). All three shared a common background: they were born in Germany and immigrated to Palestine with their families as very young children, they went through economic

Example 15.5 Yehezkel Braun, *Iturim limgilat Ruth* (1983), excerpt.

hardships and military service as youngsters, and they received their professional music education relatively late, partly with the founders, partly as autodidacts.

Yehezkel Braun was the most sincere and individual in his reaction to ideological pressure. He has stated: "I was driven to despair by two things: the very thinking about music and thinking what and how to compose, composing while thinking. It caused me pain and terrible emotional suffering. One bright day I said to myself: the hell with all that, I will write whatever I hear [in my inner ear] . . . My principle is to think in sounds, not in concepts, not in emotions, not in ideas."[17] Further on Braun describes the extremely varied soundscape that shaped his personality: songs of the Yemenite women that he heard as a child on the streets of the settlement Rehovot, gramophone records of operatic arias that his parents collected, the flute playing of the Arab shepherds that he heard as a young farmer in a kibbutz, and finally the composers he especially admired as a music student: Haydn, Bartók, and Brahms. As a prolific and spontaneous composer Braun moved from one inspiration to another, with Bartók's influence dominating his early solo concertos, inspiration from Brahms in the *Music for a Double Trio* (2001) and the *Hexagon* for string sextet (1998), and an imaginary orientalist world in the highly inspired *Iturim limgilat Ruth* (Ornaments to the Book of Ruth, 1966) (Example 15.5).

By contrast, Ben-Zion Orgad continued the collective-national attitude. He took his inspiration from the prayer modes, the cantillation formulas (*te'amim*), and the soundscape of the synagogue. An especially powerful example is his large-scale cantata *Mizmorim* (Psalms, 1968), in which five vocal soloists and two choirs present two psalms simultaneously, with clusters of orchestral sonorities in the background. In the orchestral *Movements on A* (1965), Orgad departed from archaic prayer motives, which he merged into atonal, dense Western-type sonorities. Orgad's personality was extroverted. As Superintendent of Music Education he disseminated his ideology of modern Jewish music through numerous lectures and workshops with music teachers and students.

Zvi Avni has been a prolific composer who has maintained his roots in Western atonal technique, which he merges in diverse ways with Jewish musical elements. Such is his orchestral *Meditations on a Drama* (1966), which is dominated by a powerful declamatory motive, and his moving *Se questo è un uomo* (If This Is a Man, 1998) for soprano and orchestra set to painful texts by the poet Primo Levi.

Later immigration waves

In the early 1970s the Soviet Union briefly allowed Jewish immigration to Israel. A central figure in this group of Russian Jewish émigrés was Mark Kopytman (1929–2011), who soon advanced to the position of Professor at the Academy of Music in Jerusalem and became a composer of high international standing. Kopytman commenced his cultural assimilation by composing musical adaptations of modern Hebrew poetry, especially the works of the great poet Yehudah Amichai (1924–2000), whose "October Sun" Kopytman set to music in 1974. Kopytman then turned to the exploration of the East as a deeply ingrained musical concept, by creating a heterophonic technique of his own.[18] His study of the East reached its apex in his large-scale orchestral *Memory* (1981). When the heterophonic score was nearly completed, he happened to attend a performance of the Yemenite folk singer Gila Bashari. Fascinated by her voice, he interpolated her live performance of a Yemenite traditional song at the beginning and end of the composition, and she participated in many performances of the work all over the world.

A huge immigration wave of altogether more than one million Jews from the former Soviet Union arrived in Israel beginning in 1991, over the course of about ten years. It included hundreds of well-trained musicians who effected a major change in orchestras, teaching faculties, and composition. Of special importance were composers from the Asian republics, such as two composers from Georgia, Joseph Bardanashvili (b. 1948) and Hana Ajiashvili (b. 1972). Bardanashvili has continued the Soviet tradition of composing large-scale symphonic works and retained the ethnic Georgian melos, which he merged into contemporary techniques. By contrast, the younger Ajiashvili took her advanced studies in Moscow and later trained under Pierre Boulez and Krzysztof Penderecki. Her chamber works are characterized by gentle crystalline sonorities in the high register. The Tajik composer Benyamin Yosupov (b. 1962), who studied in Moscow, has created his individual synthesis of contemporary Western compositional technique with the sonorities and melos of Muslim-Asian traditions, for example in his powerful Cello Concerto (2006) and in the rich sonorities of the *Images of the Soul* (concerto for two clarinets and orchestra, 2010).

Electro-acoustic music

Joseph Tal and Zvi Avni were the pioneers of electro-acoustic music in Israel. Tal directed a laboratory at the Hebrew University that operated from the days of the Moog synthesizer through the development of digital sound production. He also conducted extensive research into computer notation for sound generation. Avni founded a laboratory at the Academy of Music in Jerusalem. Interestingly, most of Tal's electronic works, and all of Avni's, combined live performers with electro-acoustic sounds. Examples include Tal's opera *Mezada* (1972), for live singers and electronic tape, and Avni's *Vocalise* (1964), which combines recordings of his wife, the singer Penina Avni, with electronic sounds.

The Israeli Opera

Since the collapse of Golinkin's opera in 1927, opera suffered the image and position of unloved stepchild in Israeli musical life, by contrast to symphony orchestras and chamber ensembles. The provincial Israeli Opera, founded in 1948, struggled for some three decades under financial and political difficulties until its collapse in the late 1970s. It managed to produce only a single Israeli opera, Menachem Avidom's *Alexandra the Hashmona'ite* (1956). In 1985 the New Israeli Opera (nowadays The Israeli Opera) opened, and after its first decade this company reached a high international level in its newly built opera house in Tel Aviv. The Israeli Opera created the conditions for the production of several new Israeli operas. As expected in a young state, these works turned to Israeli and Jewish historical and contemporary issues. Joseph Tal's *Joseph* (libretto by Israel Eliraz, 1995) related symbolically to the Holocaust through the personal tragedy of a German Jew at the time of World War I. Composed in dense atonal harmony and expressionistic vocal lines, it carried the traits of grand opera, for example the instruction for a full-scale ship to appear on stage in Act II.

Bardanashvili composed *A Journey to the End of Millennium* (2004) based on A. B. Yehoshua's novel about a family tragedy resulting from a religious schism in Judaism just before the year 1000, between the liberal-minded Sephardic Jews from Morocco and the conservative Ashkenazic

Jews in Germany. Composed in atonal harmony, the opera presents multiple quotations of Sephardic songs and prayer tunes. Gil Shohat (b. 1973) composed *The Child Dreams* (2010) to Hanoch Levin's symbolic play about the Holocaust, using fully tonal harmony and brilliant orchestration. The most moving Israeli opera is *Dear Son of Mine* (1999) by Haim Permont (b. 1950), to a libretto by Talma Alyagon-Rose. This chamber opera tells a traumatic story of its four characters against the background of the most painful topics of Israeli society, that is, bereavement, Jewish-Arab relations, and the absorption of immigration. It is written with a veristic approach, in chromatic harmony close to that of Alban Berg, and with Italianate vocal technique, tuneful arias, and two songs in an Arabic style.

Creative work since the 1970s

Despite the significant growth in the number of composers in Israel since the 1960s, the quadripartite model mentioned above remains effective, yet with shifting stresses and with expansions in all directions. Most young composers have engaged in advanced studies and master classes in Europe and the United States. Since the outburst of folk-like works in the early 1950s, the Popular-National attitude has declined, yet it was still maintained, especially by composer Simon Cohen (b. 1937), for example in his use of the Arabic *debka* dance form that dominates his optimistic and energetic Saxophone Concerto. The Collective-National attitude has branched off from its naïve beginnings in several directions. One of them is the historical epic, characterized by large-scale works commemorating great events in Jewish history. For example, the oratorio *Sephardic Passion* (1992) by Noam Sherrif (b. 1935) relates the momentous event of the expulsion of the Jews from Spain (1492) through a rich palette of quotations of traditional Ladino songs and from Bach's St. Matthew Passion and readings of Spanish historical documents. A contrasting and highly significant direction has been political protest. Such were most of the works by Arik Shapira (b. 1943), who has stated: "In my view revolution must be total. One must negate all historical values of the nineteenth century, to offer a replacement and to invent new values."[19] In 1982 Shapira composed *Aqeda* (The Sacrifice of Isaac). In the first movement the chorus, accompanied by brass ensemble, recites the biblical chapters about the expulsion of Hagar and Isma'el and the sacrifice of Isaac, in a single repeated austere chord that "clearly explain[s] our attitude towards the Palestinians."[20]

The ideologically committed Michael Wolpe (b. 1960) settled in Kibbutz Sde Boker in the Negev desert, which for many years represented the pioneer ideal. Wolpe founded and directs the annual Sounds of the Desert music festival, which features concerts of Israeli art and popular music side by side. He has turned to Arabic music in some of his works, such as his concerto for recorder and orchestra. In *Songs of Memory* to poems by Elisha Porat, the poet and composer joined in a powerful political statement against the war in Lebanon, as exemplified by their song about a dead soldier who returns to his home and finds he can no longer recognize it. The vocal part was intended for the fine singer Maureen Nehdar, who was born in Iran and led an ensemble of Persian music while at the same time receiving Western vocal training at the Academy of Music in Jerusalem. The Western ensemble consists of guitar, string trio, and drums that emulate Arabic music. In his orchestral *The Jackals Have Returned*, Wolpe includes a digitally treated recording of the howling of a jackal in the Jerusalem mountains. Wolpe has dedicated himself to a thorough study of early Israeli music. In several of his works he adopts Lavry's concept of blurring the dividing line between popular and art music; the Piano Trio no. 3 (1998), for example, paraphrases songs by four of Israel's most venerable composers of popular songs (Y. Admon, D. Zehavi, A. Argov, and M. Wilensky). Recently Wolpe enriched his compositional method through an exploration of sonic techniques in rock music.

The Sephardic heritage has dominated many works by Betty Olivero (b. 1954). Her parents were born in Greece, and communicated at home only in Ladino. While Betty herself did not speak fluent Ladino, her Sephardic-Mediterranean childhood culture was the most powerful element in the crystallization of her personality. Yet her musical training was completely Western: she studied piano and composition at the Music Academy in Tel Aviv and then at Yale University, followed by a prolonged stay in Italy under the guidance of Luciano Berio. Her diverse style ranges from quotations of Yemenite and Arabic songs in *Makamat* (1988), for the unique vocal quality of the singer Esti Ofri-Keinan with the accompaniment of nine instruments, to the imaginative succession of the sonorities of ten instruments in *A volo d'uccello* (1996), which belongs entirely to the Western avant-garde. The originally imaginative conjuring of the East has also changed in the 1990s into a more genuine first-hand involvement in Arabic art and popular music, especially with the establishment of a Department for Arabic Music at the Jerusalem Academy of Music and at Bar Ilan University, directed by the oud player and violinist Taiseer Elias. The effect of globalization provided a powerful incentive to adopt a more cosmopolitan attitude in Israel. Composer Menachem Zur (b. 1942) based his compositional approach on theoretical reasoning totally removed from any national consideration. He has written:

> The style and personal musical language of M. Zur is nourished by application of principles from Schenkerian analyses, principles of set-theory, by the writing of Alban Berg and the analytical articles and books of George Perle on that subject, by the music of Stravinsky, Bartók, and Berio. His harmonic language is post-tonal but with a strong drive to utilize and embed principles of traditional tonality within his own atonal style, a way to create a twelve-tone-tonality. Also, there is an attempt to unify sharply contrasted materials into a homogeneous language by finding family-resemblances of contrasted musical events that are metaphorically related as "equivalences" of one another.[21]

Zur displayed his aesthetics in his three orchestral "letters" to Schoenberg, Berg, and Stravinsky and in his large-scale, harmonically rich Violin Concerto. Zur has also been active in electro-acoustic compositions, most of them involving live performers. This global pluralism reached its peak in the 1980s. Amos Elkana (b. 1967) developed his own premeditated serial technique through which he composed his tightly cohesive works, such as his song cycle *Arabic Lessons* (1998), with poems in Hebrew, Arabic, and German. Hilat Ben-Knaz (b. 1970) has based her works on deep roots in history; witness the tight structure of her Prelude for cello solo and the dense atonal counterpoint in *Night Visions* (2012).

Two important events in the late 1990s enhanced the position of Israeli music in the country. First, the annual Israeli Music Festival was founded on the fiftieth anniversary of Israel (1998). It soon developed, especially under Musical Director Michael Wolpe, who was followed in this role by composer Boaz Ben-Moshe, into a five-day festival with orchestral, choral, and chamber music concerts taking place in Jerusalem, Tel Aviv, Haifa, and Beer Sheba.[22] In 2011 the Festival branched into a new program, Composer of the Year, dedicating each season to performing most of the orchestral works of one of the founders of Israeli music (Ben-Haim in 2011, Seter in 2012, Partos in 2013, Boscovich in 2014, and Tal in 2015). Second, three highly competent ensembles dedicated to new music were founded, Musica Nova, the 21st-Century Ensemble, and Ensemble *Meitar* (the String). These groups perform mostly Israeli music in small auditoriums, in concerts that attract young, dedicated audiences.

Notes

1 "Yishuv," literally "settlement," referred to the Jewish community in Palestine under the British mandate, 1918–48. The Jewish community enjoyed a broad margin of autonomy in internal affairs, especially in the school system.

2 Erich Kunz, "The Refugee in Flight: Kinetic Models and Forms of Displacement," *International Migration Review*, 7.2 (1973): 125–46.

3 Alice Tischler, *A Descriptive Bibliography of Art Music by Israeli Composers*, revised and expanded ed. (Sterling Heights, MI: Harmonie Press, 2011).

4 Excerpts of the opera were performed in Tel Aviv in 1924 and in Berlin in 1947. The

composer's granddaughter Ellen Weinberg in New York initiated a concert revival of most of the opera on August 20, 2012. The Mighty Five (in Russian, *moguchaya kuchka*) was a circle of Russian composers based in Saint Petersburg who formed a national school, consisting of Mily Balakirev, Alexander Borodin, César Cui, Modest Mussorgsky, and Nikolai Rimskii-Korsakov.

5 David Gurevich, Aaron Gerz, and Roberto Bachi, *The Jewish Population of Palestine: Immigration, Demographic Structure and National Growth* (Jerusalem: Jewish Agency for Palestine, 1944).

6 Irit Youngerman, *In Search of a New Identity: The First Generation of German-Born Israeli Composers*, Ph.D. thesis, Hebrew University of Jerusalem (2013).

7 Jehoash Hirshberg, *Music in the Jewish Community of Palestine, 1880–1948: A Social History* (Oxford University Press, 1995), 137.

8 The first authentic performance of *Joram* took place in Munich on November 8, 2008, initiated by Jehoash Hirshberg and his doctoral student Charlotte Vignau, and fully organized by Dr. Thea Vignau, a distinguished member of the venerable Münchner MottetenChor. Conductor Hayko Siemens led an inspired performance of the enormous score. Repeated performances took place in 2010 in Dresden and Nuremberg, and in 2012 in Tel Aviv with the Israel Philharmonic Orchestra. The Tel Aviv performance was issued by Helicon.

9 The work was later titled *The Golden Chain*.

10 Erich Walter Sternberg, "The Twelve Tribes of Israel," *Musica Hebraica*, 1–2 (1938): 27.

11 Josef Tal, *Reminiscences, Reflections, Summaries*, ed. Ada Brodsky (Jerusalem: Carmel, 1997), 176.

12 Jehoash Hirshberg, "A Modernist Composer in an Immigrant Community," in Austin

Clarkson (ed.), *On the Music of Stefan Wolpe: Essays and Recollections* (Hillsdale, NY: Pendragon Press, 2003), 75–94.

13 This work commemorated twenty years since the inauguration of the Palestine Orchestra, by then renamed The Israel Philharmonic Orchestra.

14 Abraham Zvi Idelsohn, *Hebräisch-orientalischer Melodienschatz*, vol. I, *Gesänge der jemenischen Jude* (Leipzig: Breitkopf & Härtel, 1914), later published in English and Hebrew translations. For a rich selection of studies about Idelsohn, including a comprehensive bibliography by Eliyahu Schleifer, see Israel Adler, Bathja Bayer, and Eliyahu Schleifer (eds.), *The Abraham Zvi Idelsohn Memorial Volume*, Yuval Studies of the Jewish Music Research Center 5 (Jerusalem: Magnes, 1986).

15 Bracha Zephira, *Kolot Rabim* [Many Voices] (Ramat-Gan: Masadah, 1978). In Hebrew; includes transcriptions.

16 The *bashrav* is a Turkish instrumental form.

17 Yehezkel Braun, Jehoash Hirshberg, and Rotem Luz, *Yehezkel Braun, His Life and Works* (Tel Aviv: Israeli Music Institute, 2016), ch. 5.

18 Mark Kopytman, "About Heterophony," in Yulia Kreinin (ed.), *The Music of Mark Kopytman: Echoes of Imaginary Lines* (Berlin: Kuhn, 2008), 176–232. See also Yulia Kreinin (ed.), *Mark Kopytman – Voice of Memories: Essays and Dialogues* (Tel Aviv: Israel Music Institute, 2004).

19 Arik Shapira, *Thorn among Roses* (Haifa: Oryan, 2007), 83.

20 *Ibid.*, 34.

21 Menachem Zur, program notes to September 2008 performance of his *Three Letters*.

22 Individual concerts also took place in the southern small town of Dimona and in the central Arabic city of Nazareth.

16 Cavernous impossibilities

Jewish art music after 1945

AMY LYNN WLODARSKI

For a Jew, to respond through memory and witness is to commit himself to survival as a Jew. To dedicate oneself as a Jew to survival in the age of Auschwitz is in itself a monumental act of faith.
– LIONEL RUBINOFF, "AUSCHWITZ AND THE THEOLOGY OF THE HOLOCAUST," IN PAUL D. OPSAHL AND MARC H. TANENBAUM (EDS.), *SPEAKING OF GOD TODAY: JEWS AND LUTHERANS IN CONVERSATION* (PHILADELPHIA: FORTRESS PRESS, 1974), 121–43 (122–3)

Introduction: cavernous possibilities

As others in this volume have already noted, the deceptively simple question – What is "Jewish music?" – poses crucial questions about the nature of Jewish identities, musical experiences, and investigatory methods. The problem of "Jewish music" becomes more complicated, however, when combined with other terms that also resist easy postwar classification. From the vantage point of the late twentieth century, what qualifies as "art music"? Does the term refer only to highbrow extensions of serialism, or does it also embrace popular idioms? What does one mean when speaking of music "after 1945" or, more specifically, "Jewish music after 1945"?

Central to these questions is the concept of artistic postmodernism, which Jonathan Kramer refers to as a "maddeningly imprecise musical concept."[1] The term implies some kind of relationship to modernism, the specific nature of which remains elusive. As Judy Lochhead notes, postmodern music can be characterized as either "discontinuous or continuous with the modern trajectory" and as potentially "negative or positive" in its outlook, a point nuanced by Kramer, who avers that the term can signify "a repudiation of modernism or its continuation" because it "has aspects of both a break and an extension."[2] Moreover, postmodernism resists delineation into neat categories of genre and style. As Kenneth Gloag explains:

> We cannot simply decide to be postmodern and there is no one postmodern style that merely coexists with other non-postmodern styles . . . [Rather] it is the coexistence of many different styles[,] . . . potentially endless, some of which may still reflect aspects of modernism while others may be more obviously postmodern, that becomes the identifying characteristic of postmodernism.[3]

Kramer identifies several possible characteristics of musical postmodernists, including composers who "react against modernist styles and values"; who "seek originality in . . . disunifying fragmentation, in pluralism, and in multiplicity"; and who consider music "as relevant to cultural, social, and political contexts."[4] While not intending to provide a definitive list – indeed, postmodernists would scoff at the notion – Kramer makes inroads into addressing the concept's complexity.

More generally, postmodernism surfaces as an attitude rooted in intellectual and social developments of the twentieth century. One key aspect of postmodernism is its rejection of modernist metanarratives (the "grand narratives") and embrace of the micronarrative (the "little narrative"), which becomes the "primary form of imaginative invention."[5] As Gloag emphasizes:

> In making this move there is also a resulting shift from the singular . . . to the plural. If the "little narrative" is now primary there can . . . be many such little narratives . . . [T]here are now many stories to be told, and many different voices with which to tell them. These multiple stories, and voices, now suggest a culture made up of . . . a plural and fragmented cultural, social and political landscape, with each fragmentary [micronarrative] potentially claiming its own identity and value.[6]

The pluralistic and anti-temporal nature of postmodern music problematizes traditional modes of narrative and history, which can make the assimilation of postmodernism into a cogent narrative of music history difficult. As a result, scholars working with postmodern music often adopt a case-studies approach to the repertory, allowing for micronarratives to be explored for their individual significance.

Additional historical consequences arise for postwar "Jewish art music," in that the prepositional phrase "after 1945" evokes the most catastrophic moment in modern Jewish history – the Holocaust. So devastating was that event for Jewish life and culture – arguably for humanity worldwide – that scholars throughout the disciplines have interpreted it as the "end of modern history." This *post-histoire* viewpoint has become "a *topos* of Holocaust research," one whose wide-reaching implications Jacques Derrida characterized as omnipresent in postwar discourse:[7]

> [It is] the end of history . . . the end of philosophy, the death of God, the end of religions . . . the end of the subject, the end of man, the end of the West . . . and also the end of literature, the end of painting, art as a thing of the past, the end of the past . . . and I don't know what else.[8]

German sociologist Arnold Gehlen first referred to the post-historical in 1952 and described an "epoch characterized by a state of stability and rigidity, devoid of utopian ideas, change, or development."[9] And yet, as Anton Kaes notes, there is something strikingly utopian about longing for the "end of history" – an opportunity to "create a pure moment of origin that is not contaminated by history."[10] In this regard, he sees a connection between postmodern aesthetics and the tradition of *post-histoire* utopianism: "the ease with which a postmodern artist... uses the past as 'material' that can be quoted at will is based on the belief that history and progress have reached their limit and have come to a standstill; the present is itself no more than an assemblage of quotations from the past."[11] From this standpoint, stylistic recycling has replaced modernism's emphasis on originality and innovation and the narrative of progress has been supplanted by one of free deconstructionism.

Obviously, no survey could ever capture the breadth and depth of "Jewish art music after 1945." Therefore, I present three case studies that explore the questions raised by postwar responses to the Holocaust in musical composition. The Holocaust provides one such locus for postwar musical discourse in that it has been engaged by composers with diverse relationships to their Jewishness, including religious, secular, ambivalent, and non-identifying figures. For the sake of some cohesion, this chapter focuses on the aesthetic and cultural questions raised by three composers of Jewish birth working in America whose compositional style was directly impacted by their engagement with the events of World War II. Works by Arnold Schoenberg (1874–1951), George Rochberg (1918–2005), and Steve Reich (b. 1936) serve to illustrate some of the cavernous possibilities of postwar musical expression while also raising the question of whether musical representation of the Holocaust remains a cavernous impossibility.

Arnold Schoenberg: modernism's transcendent failure

Despite the previous emphasis on postmodernism, it is important to note that modernism did not suffer a definitive closure in the latter half of the century. As David Patterson writes, all modernist composers "did not retire *en masse* after the war in deference to those involved in creating a new era."[12] In the specific case of Arnold Schoenberg, widely acknowledged as one of the progenitors of musical modernism, the composer felt compelled to respond to the Holocaust in the modernistic terms he knew best. His cantata *A Survivor from Warsaw* (1947) sets the composer's fictionalized account of a Holocaust survivor who recalls a transcendent moment of Jewish resistance – the singing of the prayer *Shema Yisroel* (Hear O Israel) in the Warsaw Ghetto – through the lens of traumatic witness. "I cannot remember everything," the narrator intones, before he attempts to reconstruct the events from the recesses of his fragmented memory. Schoenberg harkens back to his expressionist roots in the piece, which also utilizes the twelve-tone technique to structure its melodic and harmonic material.[13] Motives associated with the text – atonal trumpet fanfares; weeping gestures; shrill dissonant cries – arise from the texture, only to be submerged as the recollection passes. At the conclusion of the work, the survivor assumes a more prescient role in his recollection; his narration becomes increasingly synched to the musical soundtrack, which ultimately erupts in a dodecaphonic (or twelve-tone serialist) choral setting of the *Shema Yisroel.*

As musicologist Klára Móricz notes, Schoenberg's return to abstract musical expressionism recalled a language of anxiety from his prewar compositions:

> [Schoenberg's *Survivor*] gave concrete dramatic meaning to certain fearful gestures . . . The short, discontinuous nervous phrases, the frightening, abrupt signals . . . the sudden dynamic changes . . . are all tied to expressions of anxiety, fear, and violence in Schoenberg's earlier style.[14]

Schoenberg not only exploited these stylistic associations to characterize his narrator, but also provided corresponding textual references that helped the audiences comprehend his musical imagery. As musicologist Sabine Feisst recognizes, this was a period in which Schoenberg began to aim at the "widest possible dissemination of his music and audience appreciation, [including catering to] features of mass culture."[15] Expressionistic gestures such as those in *Survivor* would have been familiar to contemporary audiences due to their incorporation in film scores of the time, a fact that Schoenberg acknowledged with some annoyance in a letter to the critic Kurt List.[16] Moreover, *Survivor*'s twelve-tone structure and recurring motives display affinities with a more conservative, tonal presentation, suggesting that Schoenberg may have been exploring an engagement with "functional and politically engaged music, which were very topical among American composers in the 1930s and 1940s."[17]

Schoenberg's historicized return to expressionism and his conflation of abstract modernist techniques with fictional realism have caused the work to encounter both praise and condemnation. Early reviews in America and Europe praised the work's humanitarian message and cited it as evidence that modernism was relevant in the postwar landscape. Others have asserted that *Survivor* enacts the transcendent release of a specifically *Jewish* modernism from a "history that was in the process of terminating the [Jewish] moment" itself, what David Liebermann characterizes as a reclamation of modernism from the Germans.[18] But for many, *Survivor*'s overt text-music mimesis muddies Schoenberg's abstract modernist pedigree; its artistic literalism met direct challenge from the philosopher Theodor W. Adorno, who countered that Schoenberg's transcendent version of the Holocaust re-victimized the dead and trivialized their suffering.[19] More recently, Móricz has reiterated this discomfort with the work. "It is hard," she writes, "to dismiss the feeling that the *Shema* stands for an illusory triumph – for the attempt to re-create the spirit of those whose bodies perished in the Holocaust. The artistic cliché of transcendence used here has little to do with the brutal reality."[20] Ultimately, Schoenberg would defend his representational decision along ethical rather than aesthetic lines: "We should never forget [the Holocaust], even if such things have not been done in the manner in which I describe in the *Survivor*. This does not matter. The main thing is, that I saw it in my imagination."[21]

The popular success and potential failure of *A Survivor from Warsaw* sets the stage for postmodern musical responses to the Holocaust. By casting the choral *Shema Yisroel* as an act of resistance – and by setting it to a twelve-tone row – Schoenberg seemed to suggest a possible utopian transcendence for Jewish life, faith, and modernism after the war. But when tired allusions to previous style periods supplant modernist expectations for innovation, aesthetic consequences arise. Here, Schoenberg's modernism becomes regressive and reified rather than progressive and novel. Thus, by appropriating his own musical vocabulary to articulate personal ideas about Jewish faith and suffering in a post-Holocaust world, Schoenberg ultimately posed a central question for Holocaust representation: can the historicized language of modernism adequately respond to the genocide, or is a new direction necessary?

George Rochberg: postmodernism's response

For George Rochberg, there was "something profoundly moving about Schoenberg's search for faith, his struggle to regain his roots in Judaism, his deep need to raise a protective barrier against the godlessness and loss of values of his generation."[22] Rochberg had also struggled to define his own relationship to Judaism – a spiritual process he described as frustrating to Canadian-Jewish composer István Anhalt:

> Have I ever mentioned my abhorrence of the religion of Judaism, its narrow-chested, nationalistic legalism, rituals, tribal echoes – none of which I can identify with in the least? Of course, this is only part of my general distaste for *all* orthodox religions of whatever stripe. Yet I am religious[.] [M]y life is dominated by a sense of the awesomeness of whatever powers fashioned this incredible universe [and] maintains it.[23]

Throughout his life, Rochberg struggled with his identity, wondering whether "buried under layers [and] layers of secularized living" the non-religious Jew carried with him "a kind of 'genetic' suffering that comes with being born a Jew."[24] As he admitted to Anhalt, "I start[ed] reacting badly to the whole [Jewish] question, [rejected] it, because it insists on ... partness and my deepest inclinations [and] thoughts ... are toward ... wholeness, the oneness of man, of the universe, of what others call 'God' but I think of as 'world-consciousness.'"[25]

These comments derive from Rochberg's mature postmodern period, generally accepted as beginning with the Third String Quartet (1972). But in the previous decade – the compositional period in which Rochberg initiated his "postmodern turn" – the composer more openly incorporated Jewish ideas into his musical compositions and critical essays. As he admitted to Anhalt in 1969, "the urge [to reaffirm my Jewishness] is tied up with music ... [M]usic is being corrupted today, is being *lost* in the vagaries of 'false idols.' It has become *unclean*."[26] In his admonitions, Rochberg draws parallels between postwar modernism and the dangers associated with idolatry in the Second Commandment.[27] Serialism had become the Golden Calf of the musical world, assuming "the condition of a quasi-religious status among its followers and practitioners. In the process [it] becomes externalized, is abstracted away from the realities of human existence, and gives birth to an inviolate dogma or doctrine in its own right."[28] The end-result was an "uncritical and unqualified 'pursuit of truth' – without regard to the consequences for the values of human existence."[29]

During the 1960s, the aesthetical and the ethical remained closely tied for Rochberg; he polemically described science and technology in terms that recalled the apocalyptic events of World War II, suggesting a corollary between fascist ideologies and the artistic "exclusionary tactics pronounced by false prophets such as Boulez."[30] He bluntly decried modernism as a form of "aesthetic cleansing" that fosters "aesthetic ideological repression" and leads to "the narrowing of thought and gesture ... the destruction of the possibility of multiplicity ... in favor of single ideas, images, and means."[31] Against such a current, Rochberg cultivated the polystylistic technique *ars combinatoria*, a compositional method that utilizes "styles from all historical periods in the making of new music ... [in order to craft] a critical commentary on the accepted teleological approach to history and its implications in the study of music."[32] Rochberg's musical pluralism was not simply an "array of different things" but a way of "seeing new possibilities of relationships; of discovering and uncovering hidden connections and working with them structurally; of joining antipodes without boiling out their tensions."[33]

While most scholars contextualize *ars combinatoria* as an aesthetic retort to serialism, two works from the 1960s suggest that it was first developed as a means to respond to Jewish suffering in the twentieth century. The unpublished *Passions According to the Twentieth Century* (1964–7) predates Rochberg's early attempts at collage and assemblage and uses textual and musical juxtaposition to dramatize a historical narrative of Jewish suffering. With the *Passions*, Rochberg attempted to "deal with the enormity of the human tragedy that had overtaken the twentieth century, without falling into obvious clichés and pathetic sentimentalism."[34] The ambitious choral work merged two periods of Jewish persecution – Herod's slaughter and Hitler's Holocaust – in a dramatic structure that utilized musical texts ranging from the medieval period to the twentieth century.[35] Therein, Beethoven's "millions" from the Ninth Symphony encounter laments sung by the millions exterminated in the death camps; abstract jazz motifs are overcome by the banal insistence of the "Horst Wessel Lied." In his program notes, Rochberg emphasizes not the aesthetic aims of *ars combinatoria*, but its usefulness as a cultural tool of confrontation: "Since we who live in the twentieth century have inherited all of history ... [it] seem[s] right and plausible [to] use ... musical quotation ... In this cultural 'folding over' ... we cannot escape any longer the peculiar and powerful sense that all things and all times, however worthy or unworthy, belong to us. At least, we have not been able to escape their consequences, humanly and artistically."[36]

Ultimately, the *Passions* was never performed, but its dramatic concept was incorporated into Rochberg's Third Symphony (1969), which was intended to convey "the sufferings of millions upon millions of human beings at the hands of an anthropomorphized 'Twentieth Century.'"[37] Instead of vernacular citations of Jewish laments and Nazi songs, Rochberg's Third Symphony engages the Western art music tradition. A recurrent refrain from Heinrich Schütz's "Saul, was verfolgst du mich?" (Saul, Why Do You Persecute Me?, 1650) evokes the theme of Jewish persecution throughout history – from the biblical figure of David to Holocaust victims.[38] Other musical quotations suggest a spiritual meditation on mortality and human suffering, including quotations from "Durch Adams Fall" (J. S. Bach, c. 1713–14), the *Missa Solemnis* and funeral march from the Third Symphony (Beethoven, 1819–23 and 1803–4), and *The Unanswered Question* (Charles Ives, 1908, revised 1930–5).

Rochberg's assemblage explores specific sonic and structural resonances, but the intent is not purely musical. As Rochberg explains, the Third Symphony is "an offshoot of [the *Passions*] ... The texts – each of which has its associated 'music' drawn from a specific work of another composer – bear their load of awesome religious-theological meaning and unify themselves around my idea of twentieth-century man's ... struggle with his own nature."[39] Rochberg's decision to embed the *Passions'* program more abstractly into the Third Symphony suggests that the composer may have realized the limitations of his initial Holocaust project. Such concerns were already at the forefront of his mind; in his notes for the *Passions*, he explicitly demanded that no historical footage of the Holocaust be used to dramatize the production. Those images "are too raw," he explained, "too factual, too literal."[40] Ultimately, the *Passions* would prove too direct an employment of *ars combinatoria*, especially when Rochberg himself was searching for an "indirect" way to address history and, ultimately, his Jewish sense of self. As he would recognize later, "the means of human expression are insufficient and inadequate to 'name' the horrors that constitute the depths of ... [evil] human actions ... like *holocaust, ethnic cleansing* ... and *concentration camp*."[41] A more universalist tone, such as that of the Third Symphony, extended the consequences of modernism to all of humanity while constituting a "more open, pluralistic view that allows for bringing together all manner of disparate gestures and languages." Only this "veritable *inconsistency* of styles, ideas, and languages," Rochberg contended, could adequately wage war against narrow-minded zealotry, whether musical, religious, or political.[42] And yet, questions remain: are indirect methods of commentary effective, or does their lack of specificity dilute and compromise their political intent? If a diversity of voices is allowed to speak concurrently, will the audience hear the message above the din?

Steve Reich: musical documentary and secular midrash

For Steve Reich, the appeal of documentary sources grew out of a period during which the composer reengaged his Jewish heritage and incorporated myriad Jewish texts in his compositions. As Antonella Puca notes, "the rediscovery of his Jewish background in the mid-1970s oriented [Reich's compositional] approach ... in a new direction, one that aims at preserving the integrity of speech in terms both of its acoustic quality and of its semantic meaning."[43] The apex of this process was *Different Trains* (1987), a piece that featured an autobiographical program:

> The idea for the piece comes from my childhood ... [During World War II], I traveled back and forth by train frequently between New York and Los Angeles from 1939 to 1942 ... I now look back and think that, if I had been in Europe during this period, as a Jew I would have had to ride on very different trains.[44]

In *Trains*, Reich digitally sampled excerpts from taped interviews and used them to create "speech melodies," Reich's term for a type of musical transcription that attempts to replicate the distinctive rhythm, intonation, and inflection of human speech.[45] The process was distinctly linked to notions of musical ethnography and Holocaust witness, two testimonial forms that Reich equated with the concept of "musical documentary," and took its departure from Reich's admiration of Béla Bartók, who had collected folk songs in his native Hungary and incorporated their melodic and rhythmic characteristics into his art music.

Archival evidence for *Different Trains* illustrates the degree to which Reich struggled with identifying the primary subject of the work, which originally held the working title "Triple Quartet/True Story."[46] Although he contacted several Holocaust-related archives early in the process, Reich resisted the idea of writing a piece exclusively about the Holocaust. On the first page of his sketchbook, he contemplates initial actors for the piece:

Voice = ? ~~Bartok?~~ Survivor? Me?[47]

He then considers several possibilities: a four-movement work integrating autobiographical voices (Reich's own voice; Virginia, his governess; and Mr. Davis, a Pullman porter) with those of Holocaust survivors; a three-movement work exploring the different sonic possibilities of trains and air-raid sirens; and a two-movement work featuring only the voices of survivors. Initially, Reich seems wary of connecting his own personal experience to that of Holocaust survivors. In an online work journal, he remarks with some weariness that "after much thought and some depression, I have come to the conclusion that this piece will be about the HOLOCAUST. Only. World War II. All my words, those of Virginia and those of Mr. Davis seem quite trivial... The openings which [I have] worked out so far also sound trivial."[48] Three days later, Reich reverted back to his original idea and began contemplating how to create a contrapuntal fabric from his human subjects (the speech melodies) and his newly composed material.

Different Trains helped to move minimalism further from its postmodern origins as "intentionless music" that did not attempt "a calculated effect [or] paint a picture," what Philip Glass described as "non-narrative."[49] *Different Trains* possesses a narrative structure, distinct imagery, and compelling characters – all of which collaborate to present a vision of the Holocaust (and its after-impact) imagined by Reich. Even though he decided against incorporating his own voice as a speech melody, Reich functions as a speaking subject within *Different Trains*; his sequencing of the testimonial excerpts becomes a form of secondary witness to the Holocaust – a representation of his understanding of the event, its symbols, and its importance.[50] Such artistic control raises important questions about narrative and Holocaust testimony, in this case, who is the authoritative voice in *Different Trains*? If this was to be a "true story," as the original working title of the piece suggests, whose story is it and can it ever be "true"? Moreover, how does the telling of *that* story affect the integrity and primacy of the other voices that appear in *Different Trains?*

The question of authority is key with regard to Holocaust testimony, as survivors have emerged in the postwar period as a new secular authority within Jewish culture. The rise of a post-Holocaust crisis of faith – in which the presence of God as "the ultimate Author" is often rejected in light of extreme Jewish suffering – favors a more postmodern, multi-vocal approach to Judaism in which secular voices, especially those of survivors, bear significant weight in theodic and cultural debates about God, the nature of suffering, and Jewish history. Reich asserts as much in the musical documentary that followed *Different Trains*, the video-opera *The Cave* (1993/2003), in which biblical passages from Genesis are interpreted through musical *midrash*, the rabbinical practice of scriptural interpretation. Traditionally, such exegesis is the domain of Jewish religious leaders, who possess the authority to examine and reinterpret the incongruities and questions raised by the Torah in an act of "commentary [as an] authorized form of creative thought."[51] In the first act of *The Cave*, however, Reich presents midrashic texts in counterpoint with critical commentary drawn from interviews with contemporary Israelis. For example, in the scene "Who is Abraham?" the *midrash rabbah* (non-legalistic biblical exegesis) is immediately followed by an exegetical collage created by Reich from a secular cast of intellectuals – a professor of Jewish art, a social worker, an archeologist, and a political satirist. These secular voices dominate the work, and the weight that Reich gives their opinions suggests their increased interpretational authority in a post-Holocaust world.

In an interview with Jonathon Cott, Reich acknowledges that the counterpoint between the primary voices (the interviewees) and the secondary voice (the composer) constitutes a key procedural component of his secular midrash. "The speech melody of each person," he argues, "is a kind of musical portrait of that person. It's *their* melody . . . From their answers we edited out the rest of our libretto . . . The reality is that Abraham and the others only live in the words and thoughts of the living. [In] *The Cave*, they live in the words of the people we interviewed."[52] But, what ethical dimensions are raised when the musical process of secular midrash engages a historical event like the Holocaust rather than a biblical text? Reich's intervention – his *use* of the survivors' voices to perform an authoritative act of secondary witness – raises several crucial questions about Holocaust representation and artistic license in the late twentieth century. Should the voices of survivors be held as sacred voices, or can they be manipulated to tell stories that are not their own? Can anyone be an interpretive authority, and if so, what dangers arise in the free incorporation of victimized voices into art? Can an artist ever assume the voice of another without repercussions? In a postmodern era, are any historical events sacred, that is, beyond material use?

Conclusion: a cavernous impossibility

As this sampling suggests, artistic engagements of the Holocaust raise more aesthetic and ethical questions than solutions. As Alan Milchman and Alan Rosenberg contend, the debate over Holocaust representation has come to signify one of the central paradoxes of postmodern historical interpretation. They explain that postmodernism compels one to "question the traditional understanding of the relationship between 'facts,' 'representation,' and 'reality' . . . [But] if truth is discourse-institutional and context-dependent, if there is no final truth, but rather truths in the plural, are we really left with . . . anything goes?"[53] This concern figures heavily in the postwar debate over Holocaust aesthetics, which historian Alan Mintz describes as consisting of two basic positions: exceptionalist and constructivist.[54]

Exceptionalists view the Holocaust as a unique tragedy comprised of essential historical "facts" that become distorted and manipulated through the process of artistic representation. As Michael Wyschogrod bluntly declared in 1975, "any attempt to transform the Holocaust into art demeans the Holocaust and must result in poor art."[55] More recently, Berel Lang has specifically targeted postmodern relativism and its potential to negate the historical "truth" of the Holocaust. He argues that when everything becomes a matter of interpretation, it is possible for audiences to confuse figuration for historical "fact" or, even worse, to "distrust the tale as well as the teller – with no place else to turn."[56] Elsewhere he explains:

> Figuration produces stylization, which directs attention to the author and his or her creative talent. Next, figuration produces a "perspective" on the referent of the utterance, but in featuring one particular perspective it necessarily closes off others. Thus it reduces or obscures certain aspects of events.[57]

Saul Friedlander shares Lang's concerns, worrying that "the equivocation of postmodernism concerning 'reality' and 'truth' – that is, ultimately, its fundamental relativism – confronts any discourse about [the Holocaust] with considerable difficulties."[58]

As Hayden White outlines below, constructivists ask the same questions as exceptionalists:

> *Can* [the Holocaust] be responsibly emplotted in *any* of the modes, symbols, plot types, and genres our culture provides for "making sense" of such extreme events in our past? Or [does] . . . the Final Solution belong to a

special class of events, such that ... they must be viewed as manifesting only one story, as being emplottable in one way only, and as signifying only one kind of meaning? ... [Are there] set limits on the uses that can be made of [it] by writers of fiction or poetry?[59]

Unlike the exceptionalists, however, constructivists maintain that the Holocaust possesses no inscribed meaning beyond its factual core; its cultural and historical significance derive, instead, from its placement into postwar narratives, which constructivists see as the product of a dialogical relationship between event, artists, and their audiences. For White, Holocaust art is both a cultural representation of the genocide and a portrait of the artist's mode of understanding. Indeed, for constructivists the goals of representation could never be historical objectivism or literalism, notions rejected as cultural constructs themselves. Instead, artistic representations reveal contemporary relationships to the Holocaust, and their descriptive figuration becomes an undeniable marker of the relativity of Holocaust meaning within culture.

As with most debates, the "truth" lies somewhere between the poles, with postwar Holocaust representation emerging as a cavernous impossibility – resounding in its potential narratives and yet unable to approach the actual scope and horror of the genocide. As Martin Jay warns, the Holocaust "can never be made absolutely safe from either oblivion or distortion," and thus requires "an institutional framework, however imperfect, ... for critically judging our reconstructions."[60] In these three case studies, the questions posed draw attention to the aesthetic limitations and failures of each representation, illustrating that none of them solve the representational quandary. Indeed, no representational act could. But, as Berel Lang astutely notes, limits can only be defined through perceived transgressions, which themselves raise questions about aesthetic appropriateness. Recalling Adorno's infamous dictum – "to write poetry after Auschwitz is barbaric" – Lang concedes that artistic barbarism is sometimes necessary:

> A justification might be argued for the barbarism he warns against as a defense against still greater barbarism – against denial, for example, or against forgetfulness ... [I]t could be held that even certain common *mis*representations of the "Final Solution" in imaginative writing ... may nonetheless be warranted as within the limits.[61]

In closing, he observes that the limits of representation are just as culturally constructed and authored as the representations themselves. This leads him to wonder whether the limits even refer directly to the artistic product anymore, or have they become about "something else, ... a psychological or biological impulse for boundaries and taboos, perhaps ... an intrinsic incompleteness in all systematic structures."[62] Another impossible cavern to explore...

Notes

1 Jonathan D. Kramer, "The Nature and Origins of Musical Postmodernism," in Judy Lochhead and Joseph Auner (eds.), *Postmodern Music/Postmodern Thought* (New York: Routledge, 2002), 13–26 (13).

2 Judy Lochhead, Introduction to Lochhead and Auner (eds.), *Postmodern Music/Postmodern Thought*, 1–11 (5); and Kramer, "Nature and Origins," 13, 16.

3 Kenneth Gloag, *Postmodernism in Music* (Cambridge University Press, 2012), 12.

4 Kramer, "Natures and Origins," 22–3, 16.

5 Gloag, *Postmodernism in Music*, 6.

6 *Ibid.*, 5–6.

7 Anton Kaes, "Holocaust and the End of History: Postmodern Historiography in Cinema," in Saul Friedlander (ed.), *Probing the Limits of Representation: Nazism and the "Final Solution"* (Cambridge, MA: Harvard University Press, 1992), 206–22 (207).

8 Jacques Derrida, cited in *ibid.*, 206.

9 *Ibid.*, 218.

10 *Ibid.*, 222.

11 *Ibid.*, 218.

12 David Patterson, "John Cage and the New Era: An Obituary-Review," *repercussions*, 2.1 (1993): 5–30 (30).

13 See Amy Lynn Wlodarski, "'An Idea Can Never Perish': Memory, the Musical Idea, and Schoenberg's *A Survivor from Warsaw* (1947)," *Journal of Musicology*, 24.4 (Fall 2007): 581–608.

14 Klára Móricz, *Jewish Identities: Nationalism, Racism, and Utopianism in Twentieth-Century Music* (Berkeley and Los Angeles: University of California Press, 2008), 284–5.

15 Sabine Feisst, *Schoenberg's New World: The American Years* (Oxford University Press, 2011), 139.

16 Letter from Schoenberg to Kurt List, November 1, 1948, in Nuria Schoenberg Nono (ed.), *Arnold Schoenberg Self-Portrait* (Pacific Palisades: Belmont Music Publishers, 1988), 105.

17 Feisst, *Schoenberg's New World*, 139.

18 Philip V. Bohlman, *Jewish Musical Modernism, Old and New* (University of Chicago Press, 2008), 15; David Liebermann, "Schoenberg Rewrites His Will: *A Survivor from Warsaw*, Op. 46," in Charlotte M. Cross and Russell A. Berman (eds.), *Political and Religious Ideas in the Works of Arnold Schoenberg* (New York: Garland, 2000), 193–230 (212–13).

19 Theodor W. Adorno, "Commitment," in Rolf Tiedemann (ed.), *Can One Live after Auschwitz?: A Philosophical Reader* (Stanford University Press, 2003), 240–58 (252).

20 Móricz, *Jewish Identities*, 297.

21 Letter from Schoenberg to List, November 1, 1948, in Nono, *Arnold Schoenberg Self-Portrait*, 105.

22 George Rochberg, *The Aesthetics of Survival: A Composer's View of Twentieth-Century Music* (Ann Arbor: University of Michigan Press, 2004), 45.

23 Rochberg to Anhalt, February 17, 1988, in Alan Gillmor (ed.), *Eagle Minds: Selected Correspondence of Istvan Anhalt and George Rochberg* (Waterloo, ON: Wilfrid Laurier University Press, 2007), 212.

24 Rochberg to Anhalt, January 31, 1988, in Gillmor, *Eagle Minds*, 207.

25 *Ibid.*

26 Rochberg to Anhalt, July 14, 1969, in *ibid.*, 74.

27 See *ibid.*, 200–3.

28 Rochberg, *Aesthetics of Survival*, 138–9.

29 *Ibid.*, 135.

30 George Rochberg, *Five Lines, Four Spaces* (Urbana, IL: University of Illinois Press, 2009), 32.

31 *Ibid.*, 32–3.

32 Mary Berry, "Music, Postmodernism, and George Rochberg's Third String Quartet," in Lochhead and Auner (eds.), *Postmodern Music/Postmodern Thought*, 235–48 (235, 238).

33 *Ibid.*, 239.

34 Rochberg, *Five Lines*, 168.

35 Reprinted in Joan DeVee Dixon (ed.), *George Rochberg: A Bio-Bibliographic Guide to His Life and Works* (Stuyvesant, NY: Pendragon Press, 1992), 111.

36 *Ibid.*, 110–11.

37 Rochberg, *Five Lines*, 168.

38 *Ibid.*, 170.

39 Reprinted in Dixon, *Rochberg*, 159.

40 *Ibid.*, 112.

41 Rochberg, *Five Lines*, 175.

42 *Ibid.*, 167.

43 Antonella Puca, "Steve Reich and Hebrew Cantillation," *Musical Quarterly*, 81.4 (Winter 1997): 537–55 (538).

44 Steve Reich, *Writings on Music, 1965–2000*, ed. Paul Hillier (Oxford University Press, 2002), 151.

45 *Ibid.*, 152.

46 Lebensdokumente: Private Documente: Agenden, 1987, Sammlung Steve Reich, Paul Sacher Stiftung, Basel (SSR-PSS).

47 Skizzenbücher 39, SSR-PSS. Reich initially recorded himself repeating key phrases ("From New York to Los Angeles"), implying that he intended his voice to appear as a speech melody.

48 "Kronos Piece Notes," online computer file, SSR-PSS.

49 H. Wiley Hitchcock, "Minimalism in Art and Music: Origins and Aesthetics," in Richard Kostelanetz and Joseph Darby (eds.), *Classic Essays on Twentieth-Century Music* (New York: Schirmer, 1996), 303–19 (316).

50 Amy Lynn Wlodarski, "The Testimonial Aesthetics of *Different Trains*," *Journal of the American Musicological Society*, 63.1 (2010): 99–142.

51 Geoffrey H. Hartman, "Midrash as Law and Literature," *Journal of Religion*, 74.3 (July 1994): 338–55 (342).

52 "Jonathon Cott interviews Beryl Korot and Steve Reich on *The Cave*," in Reich, *Writings on Music*, 174–5.

53 Alan Milchman and Alan Rosenberg (eds.), *Postmodernism and the Holocaust* (Amsterdam: Rodopi, 1998), 1, 13, 14.

54 Alan Mintz, *Popular Culture and the Shaping of Holocaust Memory in America* (Seattle: University of Washington Press, 2001), 39–40.

55 Michael Wyschogrod, "Some Theological Reflections on the Holocaust," *Response*, 25 (Spring 1975): 65–8 (68).

56 Berel Lang, "Is it Possible to Misrepresent the Holocaust?," *History and Theory*, 34.1 (Feb. 1995): 84–9 (88).

57 Berel Lang, *Act and Idea in the Nazi Genocide* (University of Chicago Press, 1990), 43.

58 Friedlander, Introduction to Friedlander (ed.), *Probing the Limits*, 1–21 (20).

59 Hayden White, "Historical Emplotment and the Problem of Truth," in Friedlander (ed.), *Probing the Limits*, 37–53 (37–8).

60 Martin Jay, "Plots, Witnesses, Judgments" in Friedlander (ed.), *Probing the Limits*, 97–107 (107).

61 Berel Lang, "The Representation of Limits" in Friedlander (ed.), *Probing the Limits*, 300–17 (317).

62 *Ibid.*, 301.

Bibliography

Adler, Israel. "The Notated Synagogue Chants of the 12th Century of Obadiah, the Norman Proselyte." In *Contributions to a Historical Study of Jewish Music*, edited by Eric Werner, 166–99. New York: Ktav, 1976.

ed. *Hebrew Writings Concerning Music*. Munich: G. Henle, 1975.

Musical Life and Traditions of the Portuguese Jewish Community of Amsterdam in the XVIIIth Century. Yuval Monograph Series 1. Jerusalem: Magnes Press, 1974.

La pratique musicale savante dans quelques communautés juives en Europe aux XVIIe et XVIIIe siècles. Paris: Mouton & Co., 1966.

Adorno, Theodor W. "Commitment." In *Can One Live after Auschwitz?: A Philosophical Reader*, edited by Rolf Tiedemann, 240–58. Stanford University Press, 2003.

and Hanns Eisler. *Composing for the Films*. Oxford University Press, 1947.

Aharon, Merav. "Riding the Culture Train: An Ethnography of a Plan for Social Mobility Through Music." *Cultural Sociology*, 7 (2013): 447–62.

Anderson, Benedict. *Imagined Communities: Reflections on the Origin and Spread of Nationalism*. London: Verso, 1991.

Appadurai, Arjun. *Modernity at Large: Cultural Dimensions of Globalization*. Minneapolis: University of Minnesota Press, 1996.

Attwood, William G. *The Parisian Worlds of Frédéric Chopin*. New Haven: Yale University Press, 1999.

Avenary, Hanoch, Walter Pass, and Nikolaus Vielmetti. *Kantor Salomon Sulzer und seine Zeit: Eine Dokumentation*. Sigmaringen: J. Thorbecke, 1985.

Avenary, Hanoch. "Contacts between Church and Synagogue Music." In *Proceedings of the World Jewish Congress on Jewish Music, Jerusalem 1978*, edited by Judith Cohen, 89–107. Tel Aviv: Institute for the Translation of Hebrew Literature, 1982.

The Ashkenazi Tradition of Biblical Chant between 1500 and 1900: Documentation and Musical Analysis. Music Documentation and Studies Series 2. Tel Aviv University, 1978.

"Music." In *Encyclopedia Judaica*, xii:566–664, 675–8. Jerusalem: Keter; New York: Macmillan, 1971–2.

"The Concept of Mode in European Synagogue Chant." *Yuval*, 2 (1971): 11–21.

"The Cantorial Fantasia of the Eighteenth and Nineteenth Centuries: A Late Manifestation of the Musical Trope." *Yuval*, 1 (1968): 65–85.

Studies in the Hebrew, Syrian and Greek Liturgical Recitative. Tel Aviv: Israel Music Institute, 1963.

Aylward, Michael. "Early Recordings of Jewish Music in Poland." *Polin: Studies in Polish Jewry*, 16 (2003): 59–69.

Baade, Christina L. "In Response to 'Freylekhe Felker: Queer Subculture in the Klezmer Revival' by Dana Astmann." *Discourses in Music*, 5.1 (Spring 2004).

Bab, Julius. *Leben und Tod des deutschen Judentums.* Edited by Klaus Siebenhaar. Berlin: Argon, 1988.

Baker, Paula Eisenstein, and Robert S. Nelson, eds. *Leo Zeitlin: Chamber Music.* Recent Researches in Music of the 19th and Early 20th Centuries 51. Middleton, WI: A-R Editions, 2009.

Bakhur, Eliyahu. *Sefer Tuv Ta'am.* Venice, 1539.

Bartelmus, Rüdiger. *Theologische Klangrede: Musikalische Resonanzen auf biblische Texte.* Münster: LIT Verlag, 2012.

Barzel, Tamar. *New York Noise: Radical Jewish Music and the Downtown Scene.* Bloomington: Indiana University Press, 2014.

"An Interrogation of Language: 'Radical Jewish Culture' on New York City's Downtown Music Scene." *Journal of the Society for American Music,* 4.2 (2010): 215–50.

"If Not Klezmer, Then What? Jewish Music and Modalities on New York City's Downtown Music Scene." *Michigan Quarterly Review,* 42.1 (Winter 2003): 79–94.

Bayer, Bathja. "The Title of the Psalms – A Renewed Investigation of an Old Problem." *Yuval,* 4 (1982): 29–123.

"The Biblical Nebel." *Yuval,* 1 (1968): 89–131.

Beregovski, Moshe. *Jewish Instrumental Folk Music: The Collections and Writings of Moshe Beregovski.* Translated and edited by Mark Slobin, Robert Rothstein, and Michael Alpert. Syracuse University Press, 2001.

"The Altered Dorian Scale in Jewish Folk Music (1946)." In *Old Jewish Folk Music: The Collections and Writings of Moshe Beregovski,* edited and translated by Mark Slobin, 549–67. Syracuse University Press, 2000.

Berry, Mary. "Music, Postmodernism, and George Rochberg's Third String Quartet." In *Postmodern Music/Postmodern Thought,* edited by Judy Lochhead and Joseph Auner, 235–48. New York: Routledge, 2002.

Beschlüsse der ersten und zweiten israelitischen Synode, Die. Mainz: J. Gottleben'sche Buchdruckerei, 1871.

Bik, Moshe. *Klezmorim be-Orgeev/Jewish Wedding.* Edited by M. Gorali. Haifa Music Museum and Library, 1964.

Binder, Benjamin. "Kundry and the Jewish Voice: Anti-Semitism and Musical Transcendence in Wagner's Parsifal." *Current Musicology,* 87 (Spring 2009): 47–131.

Bohlman, Andrea F., and Philip V. Bohlman. *Hanns Eisler: In der Musik ist es anders.* Berlin: Hentrich & Hentrich, 2012.

"(Un)Covering Hanns Eisler's Hollywood Songbook." *Danish Yearbook of Musicology,* 35 (2007): 13–29.

Bohlman, Philip V. *Jewish Music and Modernity.* Oxford University Press, 2008.

"Wie die Popularmusik jüdisch wurde." *Transversal,* 7.1 (2006): 61–75.

Jüdische Volksmusik – Eine mitteleuropäische Geistesgeschichte. Vienna: Böhlau, 2005.

"Before Hebrew Song." In *Nationalism, Zionism and Ethnic Mobilization of the Jews in 1900 and Beyond,* edited by Michael Berkowitz, 25–59. Leiden: Brill, 2004.

"Music." In *The Oxford Handbook of Jewish Studies*, edited by Martin Goodman, Jeremy Cohen, and David Sorkin, 852–69. Oxford University Press, 2002.

and Otto Holzapfel, eds. *The Folk Songs of Ashkenaz*. Recent Researches in the Oral Traditions of Music 6. Middleton, WI: A-R Editions, 2001.

The World Centre for Jewish Music in Palestine, 1936–1940: Jewish Musical Life on the Eve of World War II. Oxford University Press, 1992.

and Mark Slobin, eds. *Music in the Ethnic Communities of Israel*. Special edition of *Asian Music*, 17.2 (1986).

Bopp, Verena. *Mailamm 1932–1941. Die Geschichte einer Vereinigung zur Förderung jüdischer Musik in den USA*. Wiesbaden: Harrassowitz, 2007.

Borchard, Beatrix. "Von Joseph Joachim zurück zu Moses Mendelssohn. Instrumentalmusik als Zukunftsreligion?" In *Musikwelten – Lebenswelten: Jüdische Identitätssuche in der deutschen Musikkultur*, edited by Beatrix Borchard and Heidy Zimmermann, 31–58. Vienna: Böhlau, 2009.

Stimme und Geige. Amalie und Joseph Joachim: Biographie und Interpretationsgeschichte. Vienna: Böhlau, 2005.

Botstein, Leon. "A Mirror to the Nineteenth Century: Reflections on Liszt." In *Liszt and His World*, edited by Christopher H. Gibbs and Dana Gooley, 517–68. Princeton University Press, 2006.

"Music, Femininity, and Jewish Identity: The Tradition and Legacy of the Salon." In *Jewish Women and Their Salons: The Power of Conversation*, edited by Emily D. Bilski and Emily Braun, 159–69. New York: Jewish Museum under the auspices of the Jewish Theological Seminary of America; New Haven: Yale University Press, 2005.

"Social History and the Politics of the Aesthetic: Jews and Music in Vienna 1870–1938." In *Vienna: Jews and the City of Music 1870–1938*, edited by Leon Botstein and Werner Hanak, 43–64. Annandale-on-Hudson, NY: Bard College, 2004.

"Whose Gustav Mahler? Reception, Interpretation, and History." In *Mahler and His World*, edited by Karen Painter, 1–54. Princeton University Press, 2002.

"The Aesthetics of Assimilation and Affirmation: Reconstructing the Career of Felix Mendelssohn." In *Mendelssohn and His World*, edited by R. Larry Todd, 5–42. Princeton University Press, 1991.

Judentum und Modernität. Essays zur Rolle der Juden in der deutschen und österreichischen Kultur, 1848 bis 1938. Vienna: Böhlau, 1991.

Boyarin, Jonathan, and Daniel Boyarin. *The Powers of Diaspora: Two Essays on the Relevance of Jewish Culture*. Minneapolis: University of Minnesota Press, 2002.

"Diaspora: Generational Ground of Jewish Identity." *Critical Inquiry*, 19.4 (1993): 693–725.

Brand, Juliane, and Christopher Hailey, eds. *Constructive Dissonance: Arnold Schoenberg and the Transformations of Twentieth-Century Culture*. Berkeley and Los Angeles: University of California Press, 1997.

Braun, Joachim. *Music in Ancient Israel/Palestine: Archaeological, Written, and Comparative Sources*. Grand Rapids, MI, and Cambridge: Wm. B. Eerdmans, 2002.

Yehezkel Braun, Jehoash Hirshberg, and Rotem Luz. *Yehezkel Braun, His Life and Works.* Tel Aviv: Israeli Music Institute, 2016.

Breivik, Magnar. "From Surabaya to Ellis Island: On Two Versions of Kurt Weill's 'Surabaya-Johnny.'" In *The Impact of Nazism on Twentieth-Century Music,* edited by Erik Levi, 77–90. Vienna: Böhlau, 2014.

Brenner, Michael. *The Renaissance of Jewish Culture in Weimar Germany.* New Haven: Yale University Press, 1996.

Brinkmann, Reinhold. "Reading a Letter." In *Driven into Paradise: The Musical Migration from Nazi Germany to the United States,* edited by Reinhold Brinkmann and Christoph Wolff, 3–20. Berkeley and Los Angeles: University of California Press.

Brubaker, Rogers. "The 'Diaspora' Diaspora." *Ethnic and Racial Studies,* 28.1 (January 2005): 1–19.

Burgh, Theodore W. *Listening to the Artifacts: Music Culture in Ancient Israel/ Palestine.* New York: T & T Clark, 2006.

Burney, Charles. *An Eighteenth-Century Musical Tour in Central Europe and the Netherlands.* Edited by Percy A. Scholes. 2 volumes. Oxford University Press, 1959.

Burstyn, Shai. "'Shirah ḥadashah-atikah': Moreshet Avraham Tzvi Idelson ve-zimrei 'shorashim.'" *Katedrah,* 128 (Tammuz 2008): 113–44.

Burwick, Frederick, and Paul Douglass, eds. *A Selection of Hebrew Melodies, Ancient and Modern, by Isaac Nathan and Lord Byron.* Tuscaloosa: University of Alabama Press, 1988.

Cahn, Steven J. "Schoenberg, the Viennese-Jewish Experience and Its Aftermath." In *The Cambridge Companion to Schoenberg,* edited by Jennifer Shaw and Joseph Auner, 191–206. Cambridge University Press, 2010.

Cairns, David. *Berlioz.* 2 volumes. Volume II, *Servitude and Greatness, 1832–1869.* London: Allen Lane, 1999.

Caplan, Hannah, and Belinda Rosenblatt, eds. *International Biographical Dictionary of Central European Émigrés 1933–1945.* 3 volumes. Munich: K. G. Sauer, 1983.

Caplan, Marvin. "The Curious Case of Bei Mir Bist Du Schön." *Congress Monthly,* 62.1 (Jan/Feb 1995): 13–16.

Chants Mystiques: Hidden Treasures of a Living Tradition. PolyGram Special Markets, 1995.

Clarkson, Austin. "What is Jewish Music?" *Contemporary Music Review,* 27.2/3 (April/June 2008): 179–92.

Clifford, James. *Routes: Travel and Translation in the Late Twentieth Century.* Cambridge, MA: Harvard University Press, 1997.

Cohen, Judah M. "Music Institutions and the Transmission of Tradition." *Ethnomusicology,* 53.2 (Spring/Summer 2009): 308–25.

  "Exploring the Postmodern Landscape of Jewish Music." In *You Should See Yourself: Jewish Identity in Postmodern American Culture,* edited by Vincent Brook, 97–118. New Brunswick, NJ: Rutgers University Press, 2006.

"Modes of Tradition? Negotiating Jewishness and Modernity in the Synagogue Music of Isadore Freed and Frederick Piket." *Jewish History and Culture*, 5.2 (Winter 2002): 25–47.

Cohen, Judith R. "'No so komo las de agora' (I'm Not Like Those Modern Girls): Judeo-Spanish Songs Meet the Twenty-First Century." *European Judaism*, 44.1 (2011): 151–64.

Cohen Mark R., ed. and trans. *The Autobiography of a Seventeenth-Century Venetian Rabbi: Leon Modena's Life of Judah.* Princeton University Press, 1988.

Cohen, Robin. *Global Diasporas: An Introduction.* 2nd edition. London and New York: Routledge, 2008 (1997).

Cohen, Yoel. *God, Jews and the Media: Religion and Israel's Media.* London and New York: Routledge, 2012.

Cohon, A. Irma. *An Introduction to Jewish Music in Eight Illustrated Lectures.* New York: National Council of Jewish Women, 1923.

Cohon, Joseph. "The Structure of the Synagogue Prayer-Chant." *Journal of the American Musicological Society*, 3.1 (Spring 1950): 17–32. Reprinted in *Journal of Synagogue Music*, 11.1 (June 1981): 58–73.

Conway, David. *Jewry in Music: Entry to the Profession from the Enlightenment to Richard Wagner.* Cambridge University Press, 2012.

Cook, Nicholas. *The Schenker Project: Culture, Race, and Music Theory in Fin-de-Siècle Vienna.* Oxford University Press, 2007.

Crawford, Dorothy Lamb. *A Windfall of Musicians: Hitler's Émigrés and Exiles in Southern California.* New Haven: Yale University Press, 2009.

Dahm, Annkatrin. *Der Topos der Juden. Studien zur Geschichte des Antisemitismus im deutschsprachigen Musikschrifttum.* Göttingen: Vandenhoeck & Ruprecht, 2007.

Davis, Ruth F., ed. *The "Oriental Music" Broadcasts 1936–1937: A Musical Ethnography of Mandatory Palestine.* Recent Researches in the Oral Traditions of Music 10. Middleton, WI: A-R Editions, 2013.

Deathridge, John. *Wagner: Beyond Good and Evil.* Berkeley and Los Angeles: University of California Press, 2008.

Dion, Lynn. "Klezmer Music in America: Revival and Beyond." *Jewish Folklore and Ethnology Newsletter*, 8.1–2 (1986): 2–8.

Dixon, Joan DeVee. *George Rochberg: A Bio-Bibliographic Guide to His Life and Works.* Stuyvesant, NY: Pendragon Press, 1992.

Doroshkin, Milton. *Yiddish in America: Social and Cultural Foundations.* Rutherford, Madison, and Teaneck, NJ: Fairleigh Dickinson University Press, 1969.

Draughon, Francesca, and Raymond Knapp. "Gustav Mahler and the Crisis of Jewish Identity." *Echo*, 3.2. www.echo.ucla.edu/Volume3-issue2/knapp_draughon/knapp_draughon1.html. Accessed February 18, 2014.

Druker, Irme. "Mikhoel-Yoysef Guzikov." *Sovetish Heymland*, 11 (November 1981): 20–81; and 12 (December 1981): 12–89.

Klezmer. Moscow: Farlag "Sovetski pisatel," 1976.

Dubin, Lois C. "The Rise and the Fall of the Italian Jewish Model in Germany: From Haskalah to Reform, 1780–1820." In *Jewish History and Jewish Memory: Essays in Honor of Yosef Hayim Yerushalmi*, edited by Elisheva Carlebach, John M. Efron, and David N. Myers, 271–95. Tauber Institute for the Study of European Jewry Series 29. Hanover, NH: University Press of New England, 1998.

Dümling, Albrecht. "The Target of Racial Purity: The 'Degenerate Music' Exhibition in Düsseldorf, 1938." In *Art, Culture, and Media under the Third Reich*, edited by Richard A. Etlin, 43–72. University of Chicago Press, 2002.

Dümling, Albrecht. "Nationalism as Racism: Nazi Policies Towards Music." In *Banned by the Nazis: Entartete Musik*." Los Angeles Philharmonic Association, 1991. Concert program.

Eddie, William Alexander. *Charles Valentin Alkan: His Life and His Music*. Aldershot, UK, and Burlington, VT: Ashgate, 2007.

Edison, Thomas A. "The Phonograph and Its Future." *North American Review*, 126 (1878): 530–6.

Ehrenreich, Eliezer. "Der erste Synagogenchor in Berlin (Aus alten Akten)." *Gemeindeblatt der jüdischen Gemeinde zu Berlin*, 19 (February 1929): 66–7.

Eisler, Hanns. *Hollywooder Liederbuch*. Leipzig: Deutscher Verlag für Musik, 2008.

Ellenson, David. "A Disputed Precedent: The Prague Organ in Nineteenth-Century Central European Legal Literature and Polemics." *Leo Baeck Institute Year Book*, 40 (1995): 251–64.

Elon, Amos. *The Pity of It All: A History of the Jews in Germany, 1743–1933*. New York: Metropolitan Books, 2002.

Engel, David. *Historians of the Jews and the Holocaust*. Stanford University Press, 2010.

Fater, Issachar. *Yidishe muzik in Poyln tsvishn beyde velt-milkhomes*. Tel-Aviv: Velt-federatsye fun poylishe yidn, 1970.

Feisst, Sabine. *Schoenberg's New World: The American Years*. Oxford University Press, 2011.

Feldman, Walter Zev. "Remembrance of Things Past: Klezmer Musicians of Galicia, 1870–1940." *Polin: Studies in Polish Jewry*, 16 (2003): 29–57.

Fifield, Christopher. *Max Bruch: His Life and Works*. 2nd edition. Woodbridge: Boydell Press, 2005.

Fischer, Jens Malte. *Gustav Mahler*. New Haven: Yale University Press, 2011.
Richard Wagners "Das Judentum in der Musik." Eine kritische Dokumentation als Beitrag zur Geschichte des Antisemitismus. Frankfurt am Main: Insel, 2000.

François-Sappey, Brigitte, ed. *Charles Valentin Alkan*. Paris: Fayard, 1991.

Freeden, Herbert. *Jüdisches Theater in Nazideutschland*. Tübingen: J. C. B. Mohr, 1964.
"A Jewish Theatre under the Swastika." *Year Book of the Leo Baeck Institute*, 1 (1956): 142–62.

Freedman, Jonathan. *Klezmer America: Jewishness, Ethnicity, Modernity*. New York: Columbia University Press, 2008.

Friedlander, Saul. Introduction to *Probing the Limits of Representation: Nazism and the "Final Solution,"* edited by Saul Friedlander, 1–21. Cambridge, MA: Harvard University Press, 1992.

Frigyesi, Judit. "Jews and Hungarians in Modern Hungarian Musical Culture." In *Modern Jews and their Musical Agendas*, edited by Ezra Mendelsohn, 40–60. Studies in Contemporary Jewry 9. Oxford University Press, 1993.

Frühauf, Tina. *Salomon Sulzer: Reformer, Cantor, Icon.* Berlin: Hentrich & Hentrich, 2012.

    The Organ and Its Music in German-Jewish Culture. Oxford University Press, 2009.

    "Jewish Liturgical Music in Vienna: A Mirror of Cultural Diversity." In *Vienna: Jews and the City of Music 1870–1938,* edited by Leon Botstein and Werner Hanak, 77–91. Annandale-on-Hudson, NY: Bard College, 2004.

Fuks, Marian. *Muzyka Ocalona: Judaica Polskie.* Warsaw: Wydawnictwa Radia i Telewizji, 1989.

Fulcher, Jane. *The Composer as Intellectual: Music and Ideology in France, 1914–1940.* Oxford University Press, 1998.

Galchinsky, Michael. "Concepts of Diaspora and Galut." In *Turning the Kaleidoscope: Perspectives on European Jewry,* edited by Sandra Lustig and Ian Leveson, 63–78. New York: Berghahn Books, 2006.

Gans, Herbert J. "The 'Yinglish' Music of Mickey Katz." *American Quarterly,* 5.3 (Autumn 1953): 213–18.

Garrett, Charles Hiroshi. "'Shooting the Keys': Musical Horseplay and High Culture." In *The Oxford Handbook of the New Cultural History of Music,* edited by Jane F. Fulcher, 245–63. Oxford University Press, 2011.

Geschlossene Vorstellung: Der Jüdische Kulturbund in Deutschland 1933–1941. Edited by Akademie der Künste. Berlin: Akademie der Künste, 1992.

Gilbert, Shirli. *Music in the Holocaust: Confronting Life in the Nazi Ghettos and Camps.* Oxford: Clarendon Press, 2005.

Gilliam, Bryan. "A Viennese Opera Composer in Hollywood: Korngold's Double Exile in America." In *Driven into Paradise: The Musical Migration from Nazi Germany to the United States,* edited by Reinhold Brinkmann and Christoph Wolff, 223–42. Berkeley and Los Angeles: University of California Press.

Gillmor, Alan, ed. *Eagle Minds: Selected Correspondence of Istvan Anhalt and George Rochberg.* Waterloo, ON: Wilfrid Laurier University Press, 2007.

Gilman, Sander L. "Are Jews Musical? Historical Notes on the Question of Jewish Musical Modernism." In *Jewish Musical Modernism, Old and New,* edited by Philip V. Bohlman, vii–xvi. University of Chicago Press, 2008.

    and Jack Zipes, eds. *Yale Companion to Jewish Writing and Thought in German Culture, 1096–1996.* New Haven: Yale University Press, 1997.

Gintsburg, Shaul M. "Iz zapisok pervogo evreia-studenta v Rossii (Lev Iosifovich Mandelshtam, 1819–1889)." *Perezhitoe,* 1 (1909): 29–31.

Gloag, Kenneth. *Postmodernism in Music.* Cambridge University Press, 2012.

Goethe, Johann Wolfgang von, and Carl Friedrich Zelter. *Briefwechsel zwischen Goethe und Zelter in den Jahren 1799 bis 1832.* Edited by Hans-Günter Ottenberg and Edith Zehm. 3 volumes. Munich: Hanser, 1991–8.

Golb, Norman. "The Music of Obadiah the Proselyte and His Conversion." *Journal of Jewish Studies,* 18.1–4 (1967): 43–63.

Goldberg, Ethan. "In the Shadow of Sulzer: The Mixed Legacy of Cantor Alois Kaiser." B.A. honors thesis. Brandeis University, 2012.

Goldberg, Geoffrey. "Jewish Liturgical Music in the Wake of Nineteenth-Century Reform." In *Sacred Sound and Social Change: Liturgical Music in Jewish and Christian Experience,* edited by Lawrence A. Hoffman and Janet R. Walton, 59–83. University of Notre Dame Press, 1992.

Goldman, Ari L. "Reviving Yiddish 'Klezmer' Music." *New York Times.* November 17, 1978.

Gradenwitz, Peter. *The Music of Israel: From the Biblical Era to Modern Times.* 2nd edition. Portland, OR: Amadeus Press, 1996.

Great Songs of the Yiddish Stage. Volume III, *Joseph Rumshinsky.* Milken Archive, 2006. Compact disc.

Grözinger, Karl E., ed. *Klesmer, Klassik, jiddisches Lied: jüdische Musikkultur in Osteuropa.* Wiesbaden: Harrassowitz, 2004.

Gruber, Ruth Ellen. *Virtually Jewish: Reinventing Jewish Culture in Europe.* Berkeley and Los Angeles: University of California Press, 2002.

Gurevich, David, Aaron Gerz, and Roberto Bachi. *The Jewish Population of Palestine: Immigration, Demographic Structure and National Growth.* Jerusalem: Jewish Agency for Palestine, 1944.

Haas, Michael. *Forbidden Music: The Jewish Composers Banned by the Nazis.* New Haven: Yale University Press, 2013.

HaCohen, Ruth. *The Music Libel Against the Jews.* New Haven: Yale University Press, 2011.

Haïk-Vantoura, Suzanne. *The Music of the Bible Revealed: The Deciphering of a Millenary Notation.* Edited by John Wheeler and translated by Dennis Weber. 2nd revised edition. Richland Hills, TX: D. and F. Scott Publishing, 1991.

Haley, Alex. *Roots.* Garden City, NY: Doubleday, 1976.

Hallman, Diana R. *Opera, Liberalism and Antisemitism in Nineteenth-Century France: The Politics of Halévy's* La Juive. Cambridge University Press, 2002.

Halter, Marilyn. "Ethnic and Racial Identity." In *A Companion to American Immigration,* edited by Reed Ueda, 161–76. Blackwell Companions to American History. New York: Wiley VCH, 2005.

Hamburger, Klara. "Understanding the Hungarian Reception History of Liszt's *Des Bohémiens et de leur musique en Hongrie* (1859/1881)." *Journal of the American Liszt Society,* 54–6 (2003–5): 75–84.

Harrán, Don. *Salamone Rossi: Jewish Musician in Late Renaissance Mantua.* Oxford University Press, 1999.

Hartman, Geoffrey H. "Midrash as Law and Literature." *Journal of Religion,* 74.3 (July 1994): 338–55.

Hasty, Katie. "Juvenile's 'Reality' Upends Ne-Yo At No. 1." *Billboard.* March 15, 2006.

Healey, John Paul. *The Solo Piano Music of Viktor Ullmann: From Prague to the Holocaust.* D.M.A. thesis. University of Cincinnati, 2001.

Hebreo: The Search for Salamone Rossi. Directed by Joseph Richlitz. Lasso Film and TV Production, 2012.

Heilbronner, Oded. "From Antisemitic Peripheries to Antisemitic Centres: The Place of Antisemitism in Modern German History." *Journal of Contemporary History,* 35.4 (October 2000): 559–76.

Heinrich Heine. *The Works of Heinrich Heine.* Translated by C. G. Leland, 12 volumes. Volume IV, *The Salon.* London: W. Heinemann, 1893.

Hentoff, Nat. "Indigenous Music." *The Nation.* January 14, 1978.

Herzl, Theodor. *Altneuland.* Berlin: Jüdischer Verlag, 1935. Originally published 1904.

Herzog, Avigdor. "Masoretic Accents." In *Encyclopedia Judaica*, xi:1098–112. 16 volumes. Jerusalem: Keter; New York: Macmillan, 1971–2.

Heskes, Irene. "Shapers of American Jewish Music: Mailamm and the Jewish Music Forum, 1931–62." *American Music*, 15.3 (Autumn 1997): 305–20.

   Passport to Jewish Music: Its History, Traditions, and Culture. Westport, CT, and London: Greenwood Publishing Group, 1994.

Hilmes, Michele. "Radio and the Imagined Community." In *The Sound Studies Reader*, edited by Jonathan Sterne, 351–62. London and New York: Routledge, 2012.

Hirsch, Lily E. *A Jewish Orchestra in Nazi Germany: Musical Politics and the Berlin Jewish Culture League.* Ann Arbor: University of Michigan Press, 2010.

Hirshberg, Jehoash. "A Modernist Composer in an Immigrant Community." In *On the Music of Stefan Wolpe: Essays and Recollections*, edited by Austin Clarkson, 75–94. Hillsdale, NY: Pendragon Press, 2003.

   Music in the Jewish Community of Palestine, 1880–1948: A Social History. Oxford University Press, 1995.

Hitchcock, H. Wiley. "Minimalism in Art and Music: Origins and Aesthetics." In *Classic Essays on Twentieth-Century Music*, edited by Richard Kostelanetz and Joseph Darby, 303–19. New York: Schirmer, 1996.

Hoberman, J. *Bridge of Light: Yiddish Film between Two Worlds.* New York: The Museum of Modern Art and Schocken Books, 1991. 2nd edition, Hanover, NH: Dartmouth College Press, 2010.

Hoffman, Lawrence. *Beyond the Text: A Holistic Approach to Liturgy.* Bloomington: Indiana University Press, 1987.

Hohenemser, Jacob. "The Jew in German Musical Thought before the Nineteenth Century." *Musica Judaica*, 3.1 (1980–1): 63–73.

Horwitz, Simi. "Cantor's Apps Bring Jewish Prayers to the iPhone Crowd." *Jewish Daily Forward.* February 15, 2013.

Hosokawa, Shuhei. "The Walkman Effect." *Popular Music*, 4 (1984): 165–80.

Howe, Irving. *World of Our Fathers: The Journey of the East European Jews to America and the Life They Found and Made.* New York: Simon and Schuster, 1976.

Hundert, Gershon, ed. *YIVO Encyclopedia of Jews in Eastern Europe.* www.yivoencyclopedia.org. Accessed February 20, 2015.

Idelsohn, Abraham Zvi. *Jewish Music: Its Historical Development.* New York: Dover, 1992. Originally published as *Jewish Music in Its Historical Development.* New York: Henry Holt, 1929.

   Hebräisch-orientalischer Melodienschatz. 10 volumes. Leipzig: Breitkopf and Härtel, 1914; Jerusalem, Berlin, and Vienna: Benjamin Harz, 1922–9; and Leipzig: Friedrich Hofmeister, 1932.

   Phonographierte Gesänge und Aussprachsproben des Hebräischen der jemenitischen, persischen und syrischen Juden. Vienna: Alfred Hölder, 1917.

Imhoff, Sarah. "The Man in Black: Matisyahu, Identity, and Authenticity." Religion and Culture Web Forum, Martin Marty Center, University of Chicago. February 2010. https://divinity.uchicago.edu/sites/default/files/imce/pdfs/webforum/022010/Matisyahupaginated.pdf. Accessed March 2, 2014.

"Industry Overview 2009." www.cmta.com/GMA_Industry_Overview_2009.pdf. Accessed February 16, 2010.

Isay, Dave, Henry Sapoznik, and Yair Reiner. *Yiddish Radio Project: Stories from the Golden Age of Yiddish Radio.* Minneapolis: HighBridge, 2002. Compact disc.

Jacobson, Israel. "Feyerliche Einweihung des Jacobs-Tempels in Seesen." *Sulamith: Eine Zeitschrift zur Beförderung der Kultur und Humanität unter den Israeliten,* 3.4 (1810): 298–303.

Janeczko, Jeff. "Negotiating Boundaries: Musical Hybridity in Tzadik's Radical Jewish Culture Series." In *The Song is Not the Same: Jews and American Popular Music,* edited by Lisa Ansell, Josh Kun, and Bruce Zuckerman, 137–68. The Jewish Role in American Life 8. West Lafayette, IN: Purdue University Press, 2011.

  "Beyond Klezmer": Redefining Jewish Music for the Twenty-First Century. Ph.D. dissertation. University of California, Los Angeles, 2009.

Jay, Martin. "Plots, Witnesses, Judgments." In *Probing the Limits of Representation: Nazism and the "Final Solution,"* edited by Saul Friedlander, 97–107. Cambridge, MA: Harvard University Press, 1992.

Jazz Singer, The. Directed by Richard Fleischer. EMI Films, 1980.

Jeffery, Peter. "Werner's The Sacred Bridge, Volume 2: A Review Essay." *Jewish Quarterly Review,* 77.4 (April 1987): 283–98.

Jewish Rock Radio. https://itunes.apple.com/us/app/jewish-rock-radio/ id393347609?mt=8. Accessed February 20, 2015.

John, Eckhard. "Music and Concentration Camps: An Approximation." *Journal of Musicological Research,* 20 (2001): 269–323.

Joselit, Jenna Weissman. *The Wonders of America: Reinventing Jewish Culture, 1880–1950.* New York: Hill and Wang, 1994.

Judaica Sound Archives. faujsa.fau.edu/jsa/home.php. Accessed February 20, 2015.

Jumpin' Night in the Garden of Eden, A. Directed by Michal Goldman. First Run Features, 1987.

Jütte, Daniel. "His Majesty's Mahler: Jews, Courts, and Culture in the Nineteenth Century." *Jahrbuch des Simon-Dubnows-Institut,* 11 (2012): 149–62.

  "Die Grenzen der Musik: Verbürgerlichung, Antisemitismus und die Musikästhetik der Moderne im Kontext der Geschichte jüdischer Interpreten (1750–1900)." In *Musikwelten – Lebenswelten: Jüdische Identitätssuche in der deutschen Musikkultur,* edited by Beatrix Borchard and Heidy Zimmermann, 227–49. Vienna: Böhlau, 2009.

  "Juden als Virtuosen: Eine Studie zur Sozialgeschichte der Musik sowie zur Wirkmächtigkeit einer Denkfigur des 19. Jahrhunderts." *Archiv für Musikwissenschaft,* 66.2 (2009): 127–54.

  "'Mendele Lohengrin' und der koschere Wagner. Unorthodoxes zur jüdischen Wagner-Rezeption," In *Integration und Ausgrenzung. Studien zur deutsch-jüdischen Literatur- und Kulturgeschichte von der Frühen Neuzeit bis zur Gegenwart,* edited by Mark H. Gelber, Jakob Hessing, and Robert Jütte, 115–29. Tübingen: Niemeyer, 2009.

Kaes, Anton. "Holocaust and the End of History: Postmodern Historiography in Cinema." In *Probing the Limits of Representation: Nazism and the "Final*

Solution," edited by Saul Friedlander, 206–22. Cambridge, MA: Harvard University Press, 1992.

Kanfer, Stefan. *A Summer World: The Attempt to Build a Jewish Eden in the Catskills, from the Days of the Ghetto to the Rise and Decline of the Borscht Belt.* New York: Farrar, Straus, and Giroux, 1989.

Kangas, William. "The Ethics and Aesthetics of (Self)Representation: Arnold Schoenberg and Jewish Identity." *Leo Baeck Institute Year Book,* 45.1 (2000): 135–70.

Kapelye. *Future & Past.* Flying Fish FF 70249, 1981, compact disc.

Karas, Joža. *Music in Terezín, 1941–1945.* New York: Pendragon, 1985.

Kater, Michael H. *Composers of the Nazi Era: Eight Portraits.* Oxford University Press, 2000.

  The Twisted Muse: Musicians and Their Music in the Third Reich. Oxford University Press, 1997.

  Different Drummers: Jazz in the Culture of Nazi Germany. Oxford University Press, 1992.

Katz, Israel J. "The 'Myth' of the Sephardic Musical Legacy from Spain." In *Proceedings of the Fifth World Congress of Jewish Studies in Jerusalem,* edited by Avigdor Shinan, 4 volumes, iv:237–43. Jerusalem: World Union of Jewish Studies, 1973.

Katz, Jacob. *The Darker Side of Genius: Richard Wagner's Anti-Semitism.* Hanover, NH: University Press of New England, 1986.

  From Prejudice to Destruction: Anti-Semitism, 1700–1933. Cambridge, MA: Harvard University Press, 1980.

Katz, Mark. *Capturing Sound: How Technology Has Changed Music,* revised edition. Berkeley and Los Angeles: University of California Press, 2010.

Katz, Ruth. "Why Music? Jews and the Commitment to Modernity." In *Deutsche Juden und die Moderne,* edited by Shulamit Volkov, 31–8. Munich: Oldenbourg, 1994.

  "Exemplification and the Limits of 'Correctness': The Implicit Methodology of Idelsohn's Thesaurus." In *The Abraham Zvi Idelsohn Memorial Volume,* edited by Israel Adler, Bathja Bayer, and Eliyahu Schleifer, 365–71. Yuval Studies of the Jewish Music Research Center 5. Jerusalem: Magnes, 1986.

Kelman, Ari Y. *Station Identification: A Cultural History of Yiddish Radio in the United States.* Berkeley and Los Angeles: University of California Press, 2009.

Kessous-Dreyfuss, Annie. "D'un 'Psaume' de Benedetto Marcello à une 'Mélodie juive' de Charles Valentin Alkan: le parcours d'un 'Air.'" *Acta Musicologica,* 77.1 (2006): 55–74.

Kheifets, Ilia. "Evreiskaia muzykalnaia idioma i kompozitsionnaia tekhnika (na primere dvukh proizvedenii M. I. Glinki i M. P. Musorgskogo)." *Vestnik evreiskogo universiteta v Moskve,* 5.23 (2001): 49–76.

Khvol'son, Daniel. *The Semitic Nations.* Cincinnati, 1872.

Kilmer, Anne Draffkorn, and Richard L. Crocker. *Sounds from Silence: Recent Discoveries in Ancient Near Eastern Music.* Bit Enki Publications, 1976, LP.

Kirshenblatt-Gimblett, Barbara. "Sounds of Sensibility." *Judaism,* 47.1 (Winter 1998): 49–78.

Introduction to Mark Zborowski and Elizabeth Herzog. *Life Is with People: The Culture of the Shtetl*, ix–xlviii. New York: Schocken Books, 1995.

Klezmatics, The. *Rhythm + Jews*. Piranha PIR 25–2. 1991, compact disc.

Klezmatics, The. *Wonder Wheel*. Jewish Music Group JMG 18033–2, 2006, compact disc.

Klezmer Conservatory Band. *Yiddishe Renaissance*. Vanguard Records 79450–2, 1981, LP.

Klezmorim, The. *East Side Wedding*. Arhoolie 3006, 1977, LP.

Klezmorim, The. *Streets of Gold*. Arhoolie 3011, 1978, LP.

Klezmorim, The. *Metropolis*. Flying Fish 70258, 1981, LP.

Kligman, Mark. "The Music of Kol Nidre." In *All These Vows: Kol Nidre*, edited by Lawrence A. Hoffman, 67–70. Woodstock, VT: Jewish Lights Publishing, 2011.

Knittel, K. M. *Seeing Mahler: Music and the Language of Antisemitism in Fin-de-Siècle Vienna*. Farnham, UK, and Burlington, VT: Ashgate, 2010.

Kopytman, Mark. "About Heterophony." In *The Music of Mark Kopytman: Echoes of Imaginary Lines*, edited by Yulia Kreinin, 176–232. Berlin: Kuhn, 2008.

Koskoff, Ellen. *Music in Lubavitcher Life*. Urbana, IL, and Chicago: University of Illinois Press, 2000.

Kramer, Jonathan D. "The Nature and Origins of Musical Postmodernism." In *Postmodern Music/Postmodern Thought*, edited by Judy Lochhead and Joseph Auner, 13–26. New York: Routledge, 2002.

Kreinin, Yulia, ed. *Mark Kopytman – Voice of Memories: Essays and Dialogues*. Tel Aviv: Israel Music Institute, 2004.

Kuhn, Ernst, Jascha Nemtsov, and Andreas Wehrmeyer, eds. *"Samuel" Goldenberg und "Schmuyle." Jüdisches und Antisemitisches in der russischen Musikkultur*. Berlin: Ernst Kuhn, 2003.

Kun, Josh. Liner notes to *The Barry Sisters: Our Way*. Stereophonic, 2008. Compact disc.

   Audiotopia: Music, Race, and America. Berkeley and Los Angeles: University of California Press, 2005.

   "The Yiddish are Coming: Mickey Katz, Antic-Semitism, and the Sound of Jewish Difference." *American Jewish History*, 87.4 (1999): 343–74.

Kunz, Erich. "The Refugee in Flight: Kinetic Models and Forms of Displacement." *International Migration Review*, 7.2 (1973): 125–46.

Kushner, David. *The Ernest Bloch Companion*. Westport, CT: Greenwood Press, 2002.

Lachmann, Robert. *Gesänge der Juden auf der Insel Djerba*. Yuval Monograph Series 7. Jerusalem: Magnes Press of the Hebrew University, 1978. Originally published 1940.

Lang, Berel. "Is it Possible to Misrepresent the Holocaust?" *History and Theory*, 34.1 (Feb. 1995): 84–9.

   "The Representation of Limits." In *Probing the Limits of Representation: Nazism and the "Final Solution,"* edited by Saul Friedlander, 300–17. Cambridge, MA: Harvard University Press, 1992.

   Act and Idea in the Nazi Genocide. University of Chicago Press, 1990.

Lebensdokumente. Sammlung Steve Reich. Paul Sacher Stiftung, Basel (SSR-PSS).

Lebrecht, Norman. *Why Mahler? How One Man and Ten Symphonies Changed Our World.* New York: Random House, 2011.

Lechleitner, Gerda, ed. *The Collection of Abraham Zvi Idelsohn (1911–1913).* Vienna: Verlag der Österreichischen Akademie der Wissenschaften, 2005.

Lederhendler, Eli. "The Diaspora Factor in Israeli Life." In *Israeli Identity in Transition*, edited by Anita Shapira, 109–36. Westport, CT: Praeger, 2004.

Levi, Erik, and Florian Scheding, eds. *Music and Displacement: Diasporas, Mobilities, and Dislocations in Europe and Beyond.* Lanham, MD: Scarecrow Press, 2010.

Levi, Erik. *Music in the Third Reich.* New York: St. Martin's Press, 1994.

Levine, Lawrence W. *Highbrow/Lowbrow: The Emergence of Cultural Hierarchy in America.* The William E. Massey Sr. Lectures in the History of American Civilization 1986. Cambridge, MA, and London: Harvard University Press, 1988.

Lewandowski, Louis. *Todah w'simrah: vierstimmige Chöre und Soli für den israelitischen Gottesdienst.* 2 volumes. Berlin, 1876–82.

Kol rinnah u't'fillah: ein und zweistimmige Gesänge für den israelitischen Gottesdienst. Berlin, 1871.

Liebermann, David. "Schoenberg Rewrites His Will: A Survivor from Warsaw, Op. 46." In *Political and Religious Ideas in the Works of Arnold Schoenberg*, edited by Charlotte M. Cross and Russell A. Berman, 193–230. New York: Garland, 2000.

Limberg, Margaret, and Hubert Rübsaat, eds. *Germans No More: Accounts of Jewish Everyday Life, 1933–1938.* Translated by Alan Nothnagle. New York: Berghahn Books, 2006.

Lochhead, Judy. Introduction to *Postmodern Music/Postmodern Thought*, edited by Judy Lochhead and Joseph Auner, 1–11. New York: Routledge, 2002.

Loeffler, James. "Hatikvah: The Colorful History of the Israeli National Anthem." *My Jewish Learning*, www.myjewishlearning.com/culture/2/Music/Israeli_Music/ Folk_Music/hatikvah.shtml?p=1. Accessed February 20, 2015.

"Hava Nagila's Long, Strange Trip: The Unlikely History of a Hasidic Melody." www.myjewishlearning.com/culture/2/Music/Israeli_Music/Folk_Music/Hava_ Nagila.shtml. Accessed February 20, 2015.

"'In Memory of Our Murdered (Jewish) Children': Hearing the Holocaust in Soviet Jewish Culture." *Slavic Review*, 73.3 (Fall 2014): 585–611.

"Do Zionists Read Music from Right to Left? Abraham Tsvi Idelsohn and the Invention of Israeli Music." *Jewish Quarterly Review*, 100.3 (Summer 2010): 385–416.

The Most Musical Nation: Jews and Culture in the Late Russian Empire. New Haven: Yale University Press, 2010.

"Richard Wagner's 'Jewish Music': Antisemitism and Aesthetics in Modern Jewish Culture." *Jewish Social Studies*, 15.2 (Winter 2009): 2–36.

"Di Rusishe Progresiv Muzikal Yunyon No. 1 fun Amerike: The First Klezmer Union in America." *Judaism*, 47.1 (Winter 1998): 29–40.

A Gilgul fun a Nigun: Jewish Musicians in New York 1881–1945. Harvard Judaica Collection Student Research Papers 3. Cambridge, MA: Harvard College Library, 1997.

Margoliouth, George, and Jacob Leveen. *Catalogue of the Hebrew and Samaritan Manuscripts in the British Museum.* London: Trustees of the British Museum, 1965.

"Matisyahu Live on the Jimmy Kimmel Show." www.dailymotion.com/video/x76v1_matisyahu-live-on-jimmy-kimmel-show_creation. Accessed March 2, 2014.

Matut, Diana. *Dichtung und Musik im frühneuzeitlichen Aschkenas.* Studies in Jewish History and Culture 29. 2 volumes. Leiden and Boston: Brill, 2011.

Mazor, Yaacov. *The Klezmer Tradition in the Land of Israel: Transcriptions and Commentaries.* Yuval Music Series 6. Jerusalem: Magnes Press, Hebrew University, 2000.

McKinnon, James W. "On the Question of Psalmody in the Ancient Synagogue." *Early Music History*, 6 (October 1986): 159–91.

Mendels, Doron, and Aryeh Edre'i. *Zweierlei Diaspora zur Spaltung der antiken jüdischen Welt.* Göttingen: Vandenhoeck & Ruprecht, 2010.

Mendelsohn, Ezra. "On the Jewish Presence in Nineteenth-Century European Musical Life." In *Modern Jews and their Musical Agendas*, edited by Ezra Mendelsohn, 3–16. Studies in Contemporary Jewry 9. Oxford University Press, 1993.

Milchman, Alan, and Alan Rosenberg, eds. *Postmodernism and the Holocaust.* Amsterdam: Rodopi, 1998.

Milewski, Barbara. "Remembering the Concentration Camps: Aleksander Kulisiewicz and His Concerts of Prisoners' Songs in the Federal Republic of Germany." In *Dislocated Memories: Jews, Music, and Postwar German Culture*, edited by Tina Frühauf and Lily E. Hirsch, 141–60. Oxford University Press, 2014.

Milken, Lowell. "About Us." www.milkenarchive.org/about/message/lowell#/about. Accessed February 20, 2015.

Mintz, Alan. *Popular Culture and the Shaping of Holocaust Memory in America.* Seattle: University of Washington Press, 2001.

Mlotek, Chana, and Mark Slobin, eds. *Yiddish Folksongs from the Ruth Rubin Archive.* Detroit: Wayne State University Press, 2007.

Molho, Michael. *Uso y costumbres de los sefardíes de Salónica.* Madrid and Barcelona: Consejo Superior de Investigaciones Científicas, 1950.

Móricz, Klára. *Jewish Identities: Nationalism, Racism, and Utopianism in Twentieth-Century Music.* Berkeley and Los Angeles: University of California Press, 2008.

Moscato, Judah. *Nefutsot Yehudah.* Venice, 1889.

Moszkowski, Alexander. *Der jüdische Witz und seine Philosophie: 399 Juwelen echt gefaßt.* Berlin: Eysler, 1922.

Mundy, Rachel. "The 'League of Jewish Composers' and American Music." *Musical Quarterly*, 96.1 (Spring 2013): 50–99.

Music and Arts in Motion, 3.3 (2011). www.musicandartsinaction.net/index.php/maia/issue/view/Vol%203%2C%20No%203. Accessed February 17, 2015.

Musique Judéo-Baroque: Rossi, Saladin, Grossi. Boston Camerata. Directed by Joel Cohen. Harmonia Mundi 191021, 2001, compact disc (orig. 1979, LP).

Nadel, Arno. "Die Renaissance der synagogalen Musik." *Jüdische Rundschau.* September 28, 1928.

"Jüdische Musik." *Der Jude*, 7 (1923): 227–36.

Nathan, Hans, ed. *Israeli Folk Music: Songs of the Early Pioneers.* Recent Researches in the Oral Traditions of Music 4. Madison, WI: A-R Editions, 1994.

Naumbourg, Samuel, ed. *Zemiroth Yisrael: chants religieux des Israélites.* Paris, 1847–64.

Negus, Keith. *Music Genres and Corporate Cultures.* New York: Routledge, 1999.

Nemtsov, Jascha. *Der Zionismus in der Musik. Jüdische Musik und nationale Idee.* Wiesbaden: Harrassowitz, 2009.

  Die Neue Jüdische Schule in der Musik. Wiesbaden: Harrassowitz, 2004.

  and Ernst Kuhn, eds. *Jüdische Musik in Sowjetrussland: Die "Jüdische Nationale Schule" der zwanziger Jahre.* Berlin: Ernst Kuhn, 2002.

Netsky, Hankus. *Klezmer: Music and Community in Twentieth-Century Jewish Philadelphia.* Philadelphia: Temple University Press, 2015.

  "Secular Jewish Musical Expression – Is Nothing Sacred?" *Journal of Synagogue Music,* 37 (Fall 2012): 173–86.

Newman, Ernest. *The Life of Richard Wagner.* 4 volumes. Volume I, *1813–1848.* Cambridge University Press, 1976.

Niekerk, Carl. *Reading Mahler: German Culture and Jewish Identity in Fin-de-Siècle Vienna.* Rochester: Camden House, 2010.

Nono, Nuria Schoenberg, ed. *Arnold Schoenberg Self-Portrait.* Pacific Palisades: Belmont Music Publishers, 1988.

Norman, Bob. "Echoes from the Shtetl: Reviving Jewish Klezmer Music." *Sing Out!,* 28.4 (July/August 1980): 2–7.

Nugent, Frank S. "The Continental Brings in a Film of 'The Dybbuk.'" January 28, 1938.

Nulman, Macy. *Concise Encyclopedia of Jewish Music.* New York: McGraw Hill, 1975.

Painter, Karen. "From Biography to Myth: The Jewish Reception of Gustav Mahler." *Jahrbuch des Simon-Dubnow-Instituts,* 11 (2012): 259–81.

  "Jewish Identity and Anti-Semitic Critique in the Austro-German Reception of Mahler, 1900–1945." In *Perspectives on Gustav Mahler,* edited by Jeremy Barham, 175–94. Aldershot, UK, and Burlington, VT: Ashgate, 2005.

  "Contested Counterpoint: 'Jewish' Appropriation and Polyphonic Liberation." *Archiv für Musikwissenschaft,* 58.3 (2001): 201–30.

Patterson, David. "John Cage and the New Era: An Obituary-Review." *repercussions,* 2.1 (1993): 5–30.

Pepys, Samuel. *The Diary of Samuel Pepys.* Edited by Robert Latham and William Matthews. 13 volumes. London: Bell and Hyman, 1974.

Perlman, Itzhak. *In the Fiddler's House.* EMI Classics 55555, 1995, compact disc.

Piatelli, Elio. *Canti liturgici ebraici de rito italiano.* Rome: Edizioni De Santis, 1967.

Poethig, Eunice. *The Victory Song Tradition of Women of Israel.* Ph.D. dissertation. Union Theological Seminary, 1985.

Pont, Graham. "Byron and Nathan: A Musical Collaboration." *The Byron Journal,* 27 (1999): 51–65.

Potter, Pamela. *Most German of the Arts: Musicology and Society from the Weimar Republic to the End of Hitler's Reich.* New Haven: Yale University Press, 1998.

Princeton University Sefer Hasidim Database. http://etc.princeton.edu/sefer_hasidim/index.php. Accessed February 17, 2015.

Pro Musica Hebraica. promusicahebraica.org. Accessed February 20, 2015.

Protokolle und Aktenstücke der zweiten Rabbinerversammlung. Frankfurt am Main: E. Ullmann, 1845.

Puca, Antonella. "Steve Reich and Hebrew Cantillation." *Musical Quarterly*, 81.4 (Winter 1997): 537–55.

Rabinovitch, Israel. *Muzik bay yidn un andere eseyen af muzikalishe temes.* Montreal: Eagle Publishing, 1940.

Rabinovitch, Simon. "Diaspora, Nation, and Messiah." In *Jews and Diaspora Nationalism: Writings on Jewish Peoplehood in Europe and the United States*, edited by Simon Rabinovitch, xv-xli. Waltham, MA: Brandeis University Press, 2012.

Rahden, Till van. "'Germans of the Jewish Stamm': Visions of Community between Nationalism and Particularism, 1850 to 1933." In *German History from the Margins*, edited by Neil Gregor, Nils Roemer, and Mark Roseman, 27–48. Bloomington: Indiana University Press, 2006.

Raz-Krakotzkin, Amnon. "Exile through Sovereignty: A Critique of the 'Negation of the Exile' in Israeli Culture." *Theory and Criticism*, 4 (Fall 1993): 23–55 (Part 1); 5 (Fall 1994): 113–32 (Part 2).

Regev, Motti, and Edwin Seroussi. *Popular Music and National Culture in Israel.* Berkeley and Los Angeles: University of California Press, 2004.

Reich, Steve. *Writings on Music, 1965–2000.* Edited by Paul Hillier. Oxford University Press, 2002.

Ricoeur, Paul. *On Translation.* Translated by Eileen Brennan. London and New York: Routledge, 2006.

Ringer, Alexander L. "Strangers in Strangers' Land: Werfel, Weill, and The Eternal Road." In *Driven into Paradise: The Musical Migration from Nazi Germany to the United States*, edited by Reinhold Brinkmann and Christoph Wolff, 243–60. Berkeley and Los Angeles: University of California Press.

Rischin, Moses. *The Promised City: New York's Jews, 1870–1914.* Cambridge, MA, and London: Harvard University Press, 1977.

Robboy, Ronald. "Reconstructing a Yiddish Theatre Score: Giacomo Minkowski and His Music to *Alexander; or, the Crown Prince of Jerusalem.*" In *Inventing the Modern Yiddish Stage: Essays in Drama, Performance, and Show Business*, edited by Joel Berkowitz and Barbara Henry, 225–50. Detroit: Wayne State University Press, 2012.

Rochberg, George. *Five Lines, Four Spaces.* Urbana, IL: University of Illinois Press, 2009.

    The Aesthetics of Survival: A Composer's View of Twentieth-Century Music. Ann Arbor: University of Michigan Press, 2004.

Romero, Elena. *Bibliografía analítica de ediciones de coplas sefardíes.* Madrid: Consejo Superior Investigaciones Científicas, 1992.

Rose, Paul Lawrence. *Wagner: Race and Revolution.* New Haven: Yale University Press, 1992.

Rosen, Jody. "G-d's Reggae Star: How Matisyahu Became a Pop Phenomenon." *Slate.* March 14, 2006. www.slate.com/articles/arts/music_box/2006/03/gds_reggae_star.html. Accessed March 2, 2014.

Rosenberg, Neil V., ed. *Transforming Tradition: Folk Music Revivals Examined.* Urbana, IL, and Chicago: University of Illinois Press, 1993.

Rosengren, Henrik. "'A Wagner for the Jews': Moses Pergament, Richard Wagner and Anti-Semitism in Swedish Cultural Life in the Interwar Period." *Scandanavian Journal of History*, 38.2 (2013): 245–61.

Roskies, David G. *The Jewish Search for a Usable Past.* Bloomington: Indiana University Press, 1999.

Rossi: HaShirim Asher Lishlomo. Pro Cantione Antiqua. Directed by Sidney Fixman. Carlton Clasics 3036600452, 1998, compact disc.

Rossi, Salamone. *Ha-shirim.* Venice: Bragadini, 1622.

Rothstein, Robert A. "Klezmer-Loshn." *Judaism*, 47.1 (Winter 1998): 23–9.

Rubin, Joel, and Joshua Horowitz. *Bessarabian Symphony: Early Jewish Instrumental Music.* Wergo SM-1606–2, 1994, compact disc.

Rubin, Joel E. "Music without Borders in the New Germany: Giora Feidman and the Klezmer-Influenced New Old Europe Sound." *Ethnomusicology Forum*, 24.2 (August 2015): 205–29.

and Michael Aylward. *Chekhov's Band: Eastern European Klezmer Music from the EMI Archives 1908–1913.* London: Renair Records, 2015. Liner notes.

"'They Danced It, We Played It': Adaptation and Revitalization in Post-1920s New York Klezmer Music." In *Studies in Jewish Civilization*, volume XIX, *I Will Sing and Make Music": Jewish Music and Musicians Throughout the Ages*, edited by Leonard J. Greenspoon, Ronald A. Simkins, and Jean Cahan, 181–213. Omaha: Creighton University Press, 2008.

The Art of the Klezmer: Improvisation and Ornamentation in the Commercial Recordings of New York Clarinettists Naftule Brandwein and Dave Tarras 1922–1929. Ph.D. thesis. City University of London, 2001.

"Rumenishe shtiklekh (Romanian pieces). Klezmer Music among the Hasidim in Contemporary Israel." *Judaism*, 47.1 (Winter 1998): 12–23.

Ruderman, David. *The World of a Renaissance Jew: The Life and Thought of Abraham ben Mordecai Farissol.* Cincinnati: Hebrew Union College Press, 1981.

Rumshinsky, Joseph. *Klangen fun mayn lebn.* New York: A. Y. Biderman, 1944.

Sadan, Dov. *Ha-menagen ha-mufla: Chai Yosef Michel Guzikov u-svivehem.* Tel Aviv: M. Newman, 1947.

Said, Edward. "The Mind of Winter: Reflections on Life in Exile." *Harper's.* September 1984.

Salamone Rossi Hebreo: Baroque Music for the Synagogue and the Royal Court. The Zamir Chorale of Boston, et al. Directed Joshua Jacobson. HaZamir HZ 910, 1997, compact disc.

Salomone Rossi Hebreo: Il terzo libro de' varie sonate, sinfonie, gagliarde, brandi e correnete. Il Ruggiero. Directed by Emanuela Marcante. Tactus TC 571801, 1997, compact disc.

Salamone Rossi: The Songs of Solomon. 2 volumes. New York Baroque. Directed by Eric Milnes. PGM 108 and 113, 1996 and 1997, compact disc.

Salmen, Walter. *"Denn die Fiedel macht das Fest": Jüdische Musikanten und Tänzer vom 13. bis 20. Jahrhundert.* Innsbruck: Edition Helbling, 1991.

Saminsky, Lazare. *Music of the Ghetto and Bible.* New York: Bloch Publishing, 1934.

Sandro, Nahma. *Vagabond Stars: A World History of Yiddish Theater.* 2nd edition. Syracuse University Press, 1996.

Sanneh, Kelefa. "Dancehall with a Different Accent." *New York Times.* March 8, 2006.

Sapoznik, Henry. *Klezmer! Jewish Music from Old World to Our World.* New York: Schirmer Books, 1999.

Schechter, Joel. "Back to the Popular Source." In *Popular Theatre: A Sourcebook,* edited by Joel Schechter, 3–11. London and New York: Routledge, 2003.

Schiller, Benjie-Ellen. "The Hymnal as an Index of Change in Reform Synagogues." In *Sacred Sound and Social Change: Liturgical Music in Jewish and Christian Experience,* edited by Lawrence A. Hoffman and Janet R. Walton, 187–212. University of Notre Dame Press, 1992.

Schiller, David. *Bloch, Schoenberg, and Bernstein: Assimilating Jewish Music.* Oxford University Press, 2003.

Schleifer, Eliyahu. "Idelsohn's Scholarly and Literary Publications: An Annotated Bibliography." In *The Abraham Zvi Idelsohn Memorial Volume,* edited by Israel Adler, Bathja Bayer, and Eliyahu Schleifer, 53–180. Yuval Studies of the Jewish Music Research Center 5. Jerusalem: Magnes, 1986.

Schoenbaum, David. "Fiddlers on the Roof: Some Thoughts on a Special Relationship." In *Liberalism, Anti-Semitism, and Democracy: Essays in Honour of Peter Pulzer,* edited by Henning Tewes and Jonathan Wright, 273–87. Oxford University Press, 2001.

Schroeder-Nauenburg, Beate. *"Der Eintritt des Jüdischen in die Welt der Kunstmusik": Die Anfänge der Neuen Jüdischen Schule: werkanalytische Studien.* Wiesbaden: Harrassowitz, 2007.

Schumann, Robert, and Clara Schumann. *The Complete Correspondence of Robert and Clara Schumann.* Edited by Eva Weissweiler and translated by Hildegard Fritsch and Ronald Crawford. 2 volumes. New York: Peter Lang, 1994.

   The Marriage Diaries of Robert and Clara Schumann. Edited by Gerd Nauhaus and translated by Peter Ostwald. London: Robson, 1994.

Schumann, Robert. *The Musical World of Robert Schumann.* Edited and translated by Henry Pleasants. London: Gollancz, 1965.

Schwarz, Boris. "Musorgsky's Interest in Judaica." In *Musorgsky, in Memoriam, 1881–1981,* edited by Malcolm Hamrick Brown, 85–94. Ann Arbor: UMI Research Press, 1982.

Schwartz, Martin. *Klezmer Music: Early Yiddish Instrumental Music, The First Recordings: 1908–1927, From the Collection of Dr. Martin Schwartz.* El Cerrito, CA: Folklyric Records, 1997. Compact disc.

Sefer Hasidim. Bologna 1538.

Sefer Hasidim. Manuscript Parma 3280H.

Seidman, Naomi. *Faithful Renderings: Jewish-Christian Difference and the Politics of Translation.* University of Chicago Press, 2006.

Seroussi, Edwin. "Music: The 'Jew' of Jewish Studies." *Jewish Studies,* 46 (2009): 3–84.

   "Sephardic fins des siècles: The Liturgical Music of Vienna's 'Türkisch-Israelitische' Community on the Threshold of Modernity." In *Jewish*

Musical Modernism, Old and New, edited by Philip V. Bohlman, 55–79. University of Chicago Press, 2008.

"'Yesod 'eḥad lahen.' Gilui ha-mizraḥ ve-'aḥdutan shel mesorot ha-musikah ha-yehudiot ve-mishnat 'Avraham 'Idelson." *Pe'amim*, 100 (2004): 125–46.

Spanish-Portuguese Synagogue Music in Nineteenth-Century Reform Sources from Hamburg: Ancient Tradition in the Dawn of Modernity. Yuval Monograph Series 11. Magnes Press of the Hebrew University of Jerusalem, 1996.

"Two Spanish-Portuguese 'Cantorial Fantasias' from Hamburg (1838)." In *Die Sefarden in Hamburg: zur Geschichte einer Minderheit*, edited by Michael Studemund-Halévy and Peter Koj, 171–84. Hamburg: Buske, 1994.

"The Turkish Makam in the Musical Culture of the Ottoman Jews: Sources and Examples." *Israel Studies in Musicology*, 5 (1990): 43–68.

Seter, Ronit. "Israelism: Nationalism, Orientalism, and the Israeli Five." *Musical Quarterly*, 97.2 (Summer 2014): 238–308.

Shandler, Jeffrey. *Jews, God, and Videotape: Religion and Media in America*. New York University Press, 2009.

Shapira, Arik. *Thorn among Roses*. Haifa: Oryan, 2007.

Shavit, Yaacov. *Athens in Jerusalem: Classical Antiquity and Hellenism in the Making of the Modern Secular Jew*. Translated by Chaya Naor and Niki Werner. London: Frank Cass, 1997.

Shelemay, Kay Kaufman. *Let Jasmine Rain Down: Song and Remembrance among Syrian Jews*. University of Chicago Press, 1998.

Shelleg, Assaf. *Jewish Contiguities and the Soundtrack of Israeli History*. Oxford University Press, 2014.

"Israeli Art Music: A Reintroduction." *Israel Studies*, 17.3 (Fall 2012): 119–49.

Shepard, Richard F. "Klezmer Music Makes Leap to Carnegie Hall." *New York Times*. February 18, 1983.

Shiloah, Amnon. *Jewish Musical Traditions*. Detroit: Wayne State University Press, 1992.

Sholem Aleichem. "Stempeniu, A Jewish Romance." In *The Shtetl: A Creative Anthology of Jewish Life in Eastern Europe*, edited and translated by Joachim Neugroschel, 287–375. New York: Perigree/G. P. Putnam's Sons, 1982. Original Yiddish edition 1888.

Shternshis, Anna. *Soviet and Kosher: Jewish Popular Culture in the Soviet Union, 1923–1939*. Indiana University Press, 2006.

Carol Silverman, "Gypsy/Klezmer Dialectics: Jewish and Romani Traces and Erasures in Contemporary European World Music," *Ethnomusicology Forum*, 24.2 (August 2015): 159–80.

Slobin, Mark. "From Vilna to Vaudeville: Minikes and *Among the Indians* (1895)." In *Popular Theatre: A Sourcebook*, edited by Joel Schechter, 202–11. London and New York: Routledge, 2003.

"The Destiny of 'Diaspora' in Ethnomusicology." In *The Cultural Study of Music: A Critical Introduction*, edited by Martin Clayton, Trevor Herbert, and Richard Middleton, 284–96. New York: Routledge, 2003.

Fiddler on the Move: Exploring the Klezmer World. Oxford University Press, 2000.

ed. Special edition of *Diaspora*, 3.3 (Winter 1994).

Yiddish Theater in America: "David's Violin" (1897) and "Shloyme Gorgl" (189-). Nineteenth-Century American Musical Theater 11. New York and London: Garland, 1994.

"The Neo-Klezmer Movement and Euro-American Revivalism." *Journal of American Folklore*, 97.383 (1982): 98–104.

Tenement Songs: The Popular Music of the Jewish Immigrants. Music in American Life. Urbana, IL, and Chicago: University of Illinois Press, 1982.

Soloveitchik, Haym. "Rupture and Reconstruction: The Transformation of Contemporary Orthodoxy." *Tradition*, 28.4 (Summer 1994): 64–130.

Sorin, Gerald. *A Time for Building: The Third Migration, 1880–1920.* Volume III of *The Jewish People in America*, edited by H. L. Feingold. 5 volumes. Baltimore and London: Johns Hopkins University Press, 1992.

Soyer, Daniel. *Jewish Immigrant Associations and American Identity in New York, 1880–1939.* Cambridge, MA, and London: Harvard University Press, 1997.

Spottswood, Richard K. *Eastern Europe.* Volume III of *Ethnic Music on Records: A Discography of Ethnic Recordings Produced in the United States, 1893 to 1942.* 7 volumes. Urbana, IL: University of Illinois Press, 1990.

Statman, Andy, and Zev Feldman. *Jewish Klezmer Music.* Shanachie 21002, 1979, LP.

Steinberg, Michael. *Judaism Musical and Unmusical.* University of Chicago Press, 2007.

Stengl, Theo, and Herbert Gerigk. *Lexikon der Juden in der Musik mit einem Titelverzeichnis jüdischer Werke.* Berlin: Berhard Hahnefeld Verlag, 1941.

Sternberg, Erich Walter. "The Twelve Tribes of Israel." *Musica Hebraica*, 1–2 (1938): 27.

Stutschewsky, Joachim. *Ha-Klezmorim: Toldotehem, orakh-hayehem, v'yezirotehem.* Jerusalem: Bialik Institute, 1959.

Sulzer, Salomon. *Schir Zion: Gesänge für den israelitischen Gottesdienst*, 2nd edition. Leipzig: M. W. Kaufmann, 1865. Originally published 1840–1.

Schir Zion: ein Zyklus religiöser Gesänge zum gottesdienstlichen Gebrauche der Israeliten. Vienna, 1840.

Swack, Jeanne. "Anti-Semitism at the Opera: The Portrayal of Jews in the Singspiels of Reinhard Keiser." *Musical Quarterly*, 84.3 (2000): 389–416.

Synagogal Music in the Baroque. The Cameran Singers. Directed by Avner Itai. The Hebrew University of Jerusalem Jewish Music Research Centre. AMTI CD 9101, 1991, compact disc.

Szpilman, Władysław. *The Pianist: The Extraordinary True Story of One Man's Survival in Warsaw, 1939–1945.* New York: Picador, 2003.

Tal, Josef. *Reminiscences, Reflections, Summaries.* Edited by Ada Brodsky. Jerusalem: Carmel, 1997.

Tarras, Dave. *Music for the Traditional Jewish Wedding.* Center for Traditional Music and Dance Ethnic Heritage Recording Series, 2008, compact disc. (Orig. *Master of the Jewish Clarinet: Music for the Traditional Jewish Wedding.* Balkan Arts Center LP 1002, 1979, LP.)

Tarshish, Allan. "The Charleston Organ Case." *American Jewish Historical Quarterly*, 54.4 (1965): 411–49.

Taruskin, Richard. *On Russian Music*. Berkeley and Los Angeles: University of California Press, 2009.

Täuschel, Annakatrin. *Anton Rubinstein als Opernkomponist*. Berlin: Ernst Kuhn, 2001.

Taylor, Timothy D. *Global Pop: World Music, World Markets*. New York: Routledge, 1997.

Tischler, Alice. *A Descriptive Bibliography of Art Music by Israeli Composers*. Revised and expanded edition. Sterling Heights, MI: Harmonie Press, 2011.

Tissard, François. *De Iudeorum ritibus compendium*. Paris, 1508.

Tzadik. www.tzadik.com. Accessed February 27, 2014.

Uhlig, Theodor. "Dramatisch." *Neue Zeitschrift für Musik*, 32.33 (April 23, 1850): 169–71.

Wagner, Richard. *Judaism in Music and Other Essays*. Translated by William Ashton Ellis. Lincoln, NE, and London: University of Nebraska Press, 1995.

    Selected Letters of Richard Wagner. Edited and translated by Stewart Spencer and Barry Millington. London: Dent, 1987.

Walden, Joshua S. *Sounding Authentic: The Rural Miniature and Musical Modernism*. Oxford University Press, 2014.

    "The 'Yidishe Paganini': Sholem Aleichem's Stempenyu, the Music of Yiddish Theatre, and the Character of the Shtetl Fiddler." *Journal of the Royal Musical Association* 139.1 (2014): 89–136.

    "'An Essential Expression of the People': Interpretations of Hasidic Song in the Composition and Performance History of Ernest Bloch's *Baal Shem*." *Journal of the American Musicological Society*, 65.3 (Fall 2012): 777–820.

    "Leaving Kazimierz: Comedy and Realism in the Yiddish Film Musical *Yidl Mitn Fidl*." *Journal of Music, Sound, and the Moving Image*, 3.2 (Autumn 2009): 159–93.

    "Music of the 'Folks-Neshome': 'Hebrew Melody' and Changing Musical Representations of Jewish Culture in the Early Twentieth Century Ashkenazi Diaspora." *Journal of Modern Jewish Studies*, 8.2 (July 2009): 151–72.

Weich-Shahak, Susana. "Social Functions of the Judeo-Spanish Romances." In *Studies in Socio-Musical Sciences*, edited by Joachim Braun and Uri Sharvit, 245–56. Ramat-Gan: Bar-Ilan University, 1998.

    "Stylistic Features of the Sephardic Coplas." In *Hispano-Jewish Civilization after 1492: Proceedings of the Misgav Yerusalayim's Fourth International Congress, 1992*, edited by Michel Abitbol, Galit Hasan-Rokem, and Yom Tov Assis, 101–24. Jerusalem: Misgav Yerushalayim, 1997.

Weiner, Marc A. *Richard Wagner and the Anti-Semitic Imagination*. Lincoln, NE: University of Nebraska Press, 1995.

Weissenberg, Samuel. "Eine jüdische Hochzeit in Südrussland." *Mitteilungen zur jüdischen Volkskunde*, 15.1 (1905): 59–74.

Weitz, Eric D. *Weimar Germany: Promise and Tragedy*. Princeton University Press, 2007.

Werner, Eric. *The Sacred Bridge: The Interdependence of Liturgy and Music in Synagogue and Church during the First Millennium*. Volume II. 2 volumes. *New York*: Ktav, 1984.

"Jewish Music." In *The New Grove Dictionary of Music and Musicians*, edited by Stanley Sadie, ix:614–34. 20 volumes. London: Macmillan, 1980.

A Voice Still Heard: The Sacred Songs of the Ashkenazic Jews. University Park, PA: Pennsylvania State University Press, 1976.

Mendelssohn: A New Image of the Composer and His Age. Translated by Dika Newlin. London: Collier-Macmillan, 1963.

The Sacred Bridge. Volume I. 2 volumes. New York: Columbia University Press, 1959.

White, Hayden. "Historical Emplotment and the Problem of Truth." In *Probing the Limits of Representation: Nazism and the "Final Solution,"* edited by Saul Friedlander, 37–53. Cambridge, MA: Harvard University Press, 1992.

Wlodarski, Amy Lynn "Musical Memories of Terezín in Transnational Perspective." In *Dislocated Memories: Jews, Music, and Postwar German Culture*, edited by Tina Frühauf and Lily E. Hirsch, 57–72. Oxford University Press, 2014.

"The Testimonial Aesthetics of *Different Trains*." *Journal of the American Musicological Society*, 63.1 (2010): 99–142.

"'An Idea Can Never Perish': Memory, the Musical Idea, and Schoenberg's *A Survivor from Warsaw* (1947)." *Journal of Musicology*, 24.4 (Fall 2007): 581–608.

Wollock, Jeffrey. "The Soviet Klezmer Orchestra." *Eastern European Jewish Affairs*, 30.1 (Summer 2000): 1–36.

"European Recordings of Jewish Instrumental Folk Music, 1911–1914." *Association for Recorded Sound Collections Journal*, 28.1 (1997): 36–55.

www.jdubrecords.org. April 19, 2003. http://web.archive.org/web/20030618040339/ http://www.jdubrecords.org/. Accessed March 4, 2013.

Wyschogrod, Michael. "Some Theological Reflections on the Holocaust." *Response*, 25 (Spring 1975): 65–8.

Yating, Tang. "Reconstructing the Vanished Musical Life of the Shanghai Jewish Diaspora: A Report." *Ethnomusicology Forum*, 13.1 (January 2004): 101–18.

Youngerman, Irit. *In Search of a New Identity: The First Generation of German-Born Israeli Composers*. Ph.D. thesis. Hebrew University of Jerusalem, 2013.

Zemtsovskii, Izalii. "Muzykalnyi idishizm: K istorii unikalnogo fenomena." In *Iz istorii evreiskoi muzyki*, edited by Leonid Gural'nik, i:119–24. St. Petersburg: Evreiskii obschchinnyi tsentr Sankt-Peterburga, 2001.

Zephira, Bracha. *Kolot Rabim*. Ramat-Gan: Masadah, 1978.

Zimmermann, Heidy. *Tora und Shira: Untersuchungen zur Musikauffassung des rabbinischen Judentums*. Bern: Peter Lang, 2000.

Zimmermann, Reiner. *Giacomo Meyerbeer: Eine Biographie nach Dokumenten*. Berlin: Parthas, 1991.

Zon, Bennett. *Representing Non-Western Music in Nineteenth-Century Britain*. University of Rochester Press, 2007.

Zylbercweig, Zalmen. *Leksikon fun yidishn teater*. 6 volumes. New York: Hebrew Actors Union of America, 1934.

Index

Cambridge Companions to Music